I0485314

Proceedings of the Twelfth International Symposium on

Human Aspects of Information Security & Assurance (HAISA 2018)

Dundee, Scotland, UK
29-31 August 2018

Editors

Nathan Clarke
Steven Furnell

Centre for Security, Communications & Network Research
University of Plymouth
United Kingdom

ISBN: 978-0-244-40254-9

Preface

It is now widely recognised that technology alone cannot provide the answer to security problems. A significant aspect of protection comes down to the attitudes, awareness, behaviour and capabilities of the people involved, and they often need support in order to get it right. Factors such as lack of awareness and understanding, combined with unreasonable demands from security technologies, can dramatically impede their ability to act securely and comply with policies. Ensuring appropriate attention to the needs of users is therefore a vital element of a successful security strategy, and they need to understand how the issues may apply to them and how to use the available technology to protect their systems.

With the above in mind, the Human Aspects of Information Security and Assurance (HAISA) symposium series specifically addresses information security issues that relate to people. It concerns the methods that inform and guide users' understanding of security, and the technologies that can benefit and support them in achieving protection.

This book presents the proceedings from the 2018 event, held in the city of Dundee, in Scotland, during August 2018. A total of 24 reviewed papers (from 37 submitted) are included, spanning a range of topics including user attitudes and awareness, management and modelling of security, and the suitability of technologies that people are expected to use. All of the papers were subject to double-blind peer review, with each being reviewed by at least two members of the international programme committee.

We would like to thank the authors for submitting their work and sharing their findings, and the international programme committee for their efforts in reviewing the submissions and ensuring the quality of the resulting event and proceedings. We would also like to thank Professor Karen Renaud and the local organising committee for making all the necessary arrangements to enable this symposium to take place. Special thanks go to Dr Paul Haskell-Dowland for his assistance in producing the proceedings. Final thanks are due to Emerald (publishers of the sponsoring journal, *Information & Computer Security*) as an ongoing supporter of the event.

Nathan Clarke and Steven Furnell
Symposium Co-Chairs, HAISA 2018

Dundee, August 2018

International Programme Committee

William Buchanan	Edinburgh Napier University	United Kingdom
Jeff Crume	IBM	United States
Adele Da Veiga	University of South Africa	South Africa
Jan Eloff	SAP	South Africa
Simone Fischer-Huebner	Karlstad University	Sweden
Stefanos Gritzalis	University of the Aegean	Greece
Paul Haskell-Dowland	Edith Cowan University	Australia
Kevin Huguenin	UNIL-HEC Lausanne	Switzerland
Murray Jennex	San Diego State University	United States
Andy Jones	University of Hertfordshire	United Kingdom
Christos Kalloniatis	University of the Aegean	Greece
Vasilios Katos	Bournemouth University	United Kingdom
Sokratis Katsikas	University of Piraeus	Greece
Costas Lambrinoudakis	University of Piraeus	Greece
Fudong Li	University of Portsmouth	United Kingdom
Shujun Li	University of Surrey	United Kingdom
Javier Lopez	University of Malaga	Spain
Haris Mouratidis	University of Brighton	United Kingdom
Malcolm Pattinson	University of Adelaide	Australia
Nathalie Rebe	University of Burgundy	France
Karen Renaud	Abertay University	United Kingdom
Nader Sohrabi Safa	University of Warwick	United Kingdom
Rossouw von Solms	Nelson Mandela University	South Africa
Kerry-Lynn Thomson	Nelson Mandela University	South Africa
Theodore Tryfonas	University of Bristol	United Kingdom
Aggeliki Tsohou	Ionian University	Greece
Ismini Vasileiou	University of Plymouth	United Kingdom
Jeremy Ward	Hewlett Packard Enterprise Security	United Kingdom
Merrill Warkentin	Mississippi State University	United States
Zihang Xiao	Palo Alto Networks	United States
Ibrahim Zincir	Yasar University	Turkey

Contents

Which Individual, Cultural, Organisational and Interventional Factors explain Phishing Resilience?

K. Parsons[1], M. Butavicius[2], M. Lillie[1], D. Calic[2], A. McCormac[2] and M. Pattinson[3]

[1] School of Psychology, University of Adelaide, South Australia
[2] Defence Science and Technology Group, Edinburgh, South Australia
[3] Business School, University of Adelaide, South Australia
e-mail: {Kathryn.Parsons; Meredith.Lillie; Malcolm.Pattinson}@adelaide.edu.au;
{Marcus.Butavicius; Dragana.Calic; Agata.McCormac}@dst.defence.gov.au

Abstract

We report on the results of an online phishing study, and the factors that predict the ability to resist phishing attacks, which is termed *phishing resilience*. It is important to understand the factors that predict phishing resilience, because they can be used to develop effective strategies to protect organisational information security. We measured a larger number of individual, cultural, organisational and interventional factors than any previous study. Findings indicate that information security awareness (ISA) is most predictive of phishing resilience, which highlights the importance of security education. Results also suggest that older participants are less susceptible to phishing attacks and individuals who are very influenced by social pressure are more susceptible. When people trusted in the infallibility of technical safeguards, such as spam filters, they had lower phishing resilience, whereas people who preferred using a more rational decision making style had higher phishing resilience. These results suggest that teaching people not only how to behave, but also to stop and think before responding to emails, may ensure that they will have the best chance of resisting phishing attacks.

Keywords

Phishing; Social Influence; Cyber Security; Information Security Awareness; Individual Differences; Phishing Resilience

1   Introduction

Phishing is a form of social engineering, in which deception and social influence are used in an effort to convince an individual to divulge personal or sensitive information. In most phishing attacks, the victim is sent an email that is disguised as a known company or organisation, requesting that they click on a link or download an attachment (Butavicius *et al.*, 2015).

Although phishing has been studied for over a decade, it remains one of the greatest threats to organisational information security (Pricewaterhouse Coopers (PWC), 2015, Telstra Corporation, 2017). In a recent report, 76% of information security professionals indicated that their organisation had experienced phishing attacks in 2017 (Wombat Security Technologies, 2018). In an effort to reduce this threat, it is important to better understand why certain people are less prone to fall for phishing attacks, which has been termed *phishing resilience*. Knowing which factors improve phishing resilience can be used to develop tailored training and education for those who are most at risk.

Previous studies have attempted to shed light on this problem, and have measured performance in phishing studies together with other individual, cultural, organisational or interventional factors (e.g., Sheng *et al.*, 2010, Welk *et al.*, 2015). However, as there are limits on the number of variables that can be measured in a single experiment, previous research has focused on a limited number of factors. For example, Sheng *et al.* (2010) limited their study to the effects of age, gender and aspects of security awareness, and Welk *et al.* (2015) focused on personality variables, including the role of trust and impulsivity and aspects of security behaviour and awareness. This means it is difficult to determine the factors that are most influential in predicting phishing resilience.

In this paper, we measure phishing resilience, and examine a larger number of individual, cultural, organisational and interventional factors than any previous study. It is only through assessing these factors together that we can understand which of the factors are most influential in predicting the ability to resist phishing attacks. This paper is organised as follows. In the next section, we provide a summary of related research, followed by an outline of our research aims. Section 3 presents our research method, and the results of our study are described in Section 4. In Section 5, we discuss the implications of our research findings and make concluding remarks.

2 Background

Previous research on people's susceptibility to phishing has revealed several potential predictors of phishing resilience. For example, previous phishing studies have consistently shown that age is important, with older participants regularly found to be less susceptible, and younger participants, particularly those between the ages of 18 and 25, found to be most susceptible to phishing attacks (Darwish *et al.*, 2012, Jagatic *et al.*, 2007, Sheng *et al.*, 2010). A number of studies have found that women are more susceptible to phishing attacks than men (e.g., Jagatic *et al.*, 2007, Sheng *et al.*, 2010), but Kumaraguru *et al.* (2007) did not find significant differences based on gender.

Previous research has demonstrated that people who are more resilient have higher information security awareness (ISA) (McCormac *et al.*, 2017). However, the relationship between resilience and phishing performance (i.e., phishing resilience) is yet to be examined. Findings have demonstrated that people who are better able to control their impulsivity are less susceptible to phishing, but these results have been inconsistent. For example, Welk *et al.* (2015) measured impulsivity using a self-report scale and found that people with lower impulsivity were less susceptible to phishing. Other studies have used the Cognitive Reflection Test (CRT) (Frederick, 2005) to measure impulsivity. While Butavicius *et al.* (2015) found that individuals who scored higher on the CRT were better at detecting phishing emails, Kumaraguru *et al.* (2007) found the opposite.

Phishing emails often include influence principles, which are tactics that can persuade people to comply with a given request. Cialdini (2009) outlined six influence principles, namely, authority, consistency, liking, reciprocity, scarcity and social proof, and all of these principles have been used within phishing emails (Akbar, 2014). For instance, in a demonstration of the liking principle, participants who were sent a phishing email that appeared to be from a friend were significantly more likely to comply with the request than those who received the email from an unknown address (Jagatic *et al.*, 2007). Evidence suggests that there are large individual differences in susceptibility to these influence principles, such that certain principles will have the opposite effect on some individuals (Kaptein *et al.*, 2012). However, these individual differences are yet to be examined in a phishing context.

Previous research has indicated that national culture is a strong predictor of phishing susceptibility, where those who are orientated towards the needs of the individual rather than the needs of society were less susceptible to phishing attacks (Butavicius *et al.*, 2017). From an organisational perspective, Calic *et al.* (2016) argued that individuals who feel particularly stressed with their job may not follow security rules, and therefore greater job stress and poorer organisational security culture might be associated with greater phishing susceptibility. Although findings have revealed that ISA is associated with both job stress (McCormac *et al.*, 2017) and organisational security culture (Parsons *et al.*, 2015), the relationship between phishing resilience and these variables is yet to be examined. In regards to interventional factors, previous findings have indicated that phishing resilience is associated with better ISA and better knowledge of phishing threats and risk (Butavicius *et al.*, 2017, Parsons *et al.*, 2017, Welk *et al.*, 2015).

In this paper, we measured phishing resilience and its relationship to a range of factors. In line with the recommendation by Karjalainen (2011), rather than using a theory-verification approach, we used an exploratory approach, and the factors of interest were chosen based on previous research findings. As such, we measured individual (e.g., demographics and impulsivity), cultural (e.g., individualism vs collectivism), organisational (e.g., job stress and organisational security culture) and interventional factors (e.g., information security awareness). The aim of this paper was to determine the factors that are most predictive of phishing resilience.

3 Method

3.1 Participants

A total of 607 participants (304 male and 303 female) completed an online experiment. All participants were recruited via Qualtrics panels and were all working Australian adults who spend at least 10% of their work time using a computer or portable electronic device. Approximately 8% of participants were between 18 and 29 years of age; 19% were between 30 to 39 years; 25% between 40 and 49 years; 27% between 50 to 59 years, and 20% were aged 60 years and older.

3.2   Study Design

An online experiment was conducted in two stages. The first stage was conducted in May 2017 and consisted of an online survey where participants were asked questions about ISA, and were also asked to complete questions relating to job stress, resilience and organisational security culture. The second stage was conducted between May and July 2017 and the same participants were invited to take part in this second online survey.

In the second stage, participants took part in a phishing study and were also asked to complete measures of national culture, cognitive ability and susceptibility to social influence. A unique ID was used to match the data of participants across the first and second stage. Ethics approval was obtained from the Human Research Ethics Subcommittee of the University of Adelaide, School of Psychology.

3.3   Measures

3.3.1   Individual factors

Participants were asked to provide their age and gender. For subsequent measures, responses were given on a five-point Likert Scale (1 = 'Strongly disagree' to 5 = 'Strongly agree') unless otherwise specified.

Participants' level of resilience was measured using the *Brief Resilience Scale*, which is a six-item measure by Smith *et al.* (2008). The Cronbach's alpha in this study was .89. Participants were also asked to complete the *Susceptibility to Persuasive Strategies* scale (Kaptein *et al.*, 2012). This scale consists of 20 items and measures how vulnerable an individual is to each of Cialdini's (2009) influence principles, namely, authority, consistency, liking, reciprocity, scarcity and social proof (Cronbach's alpha = .81).

Participants' tendency to use a systematic decision making style was measured using a sub-scale of the *Rational and Intuitive Decision Styles Scale* (Hamilton *et al.*, 2016). This *Rational Decision Making Scale* includes five items to measure rational or systematic decision making (Cronbach's alpha = .86). Participants were also asked to respond to the *Cognitive Reflection Test (CRT)*, which consists of three items, such that higher scores relate to a tendency to control impulsivity (Frederick, 2005).

3.3.2   Cultural factors

Participants' tendency to perceive themselves as independent from others or connected to others was measured using the short version of Singelis' (1994) *Self-Construal Scale* (Fernández *et al.*, 2005). The scale includes two factors to measure Independent tendencies (i.e., *Uniqueness* and *Low context*) and two factors to measure Interdependent tendencies (i.e., *Group loyalty* and *Relational interdependence*).

3.3.3   Organisational factors

Participants' level of job stress was measured using the *Job Stress Scale*, which is a five-item measure by Lambert *et al.* (2006). *Organisational Security Culture* was also measured using the six items from Parsons *et al.* (2015). The Cronbach's alpha values obtained in this study were .86 and .65, respectively.

3.3.4   Interventional factors

Participants' awareness of the information security threats associated with email use (i.e., *Email use ISA*) were measured using the *Email Use* focus area of the Human Aspects of Information Security Questionnaire (HAIS-Q) (Parsons *et al.*, 2017). This consists of nine items and the Cronbach's alpha value was .78. Participants' knowledge of the fallibility of certain information technology safeguards was measured using the *Trust in Technical Controls Scale* (Butavicius *et al.*, 2018), which includes four items and the Cronbach's alpha value was .60.

3.4 Procedure

Participants were informed that the study was assessing how people manage their emails. They were presented with image of 14 emails, from the inbox of a fictitious individual, namely, 'Alex Jones'. These included 7 genuine emails and 7 phishing emails, and both types of emails either contained one of Cialdini's (2009) six influence principles, or no principle. For each email, participants were asked to respond to the statement *"It is okay to click on the link in this email"* on a five-point scale from 'strongly disagree' to 'strongly agree'.

4   Results

To measure phishing resilience, the hit rate was calculated, which is the portion of phishing emails that were correctly managed. Phishing emails were scored as correctly managed if participants responded with 'disagree' or 'strongly disagree' to the statement *"It is okay to click on the link in this email"*. A higher score represents better performance and the mean score was .61 ($SD = .34$). A series of Pearson's correlation analyses were conducted to determine which individual, cultural, organisational and interventional factors relate to phishing resilience. These results are displayed in Appendix A.

In regards to individual factors, results suggest that older participants had significantly higher phishing resilience ($r = .21$, $p < .001$), and were therefore less susceptible to phishing. However, there were no significant differences based on gender ($r = -.07$, $p = .08$) or the level of resilience of participants ($r = .06$, $p = .12$). Results also indicated that participants who were more susceptible to Cialdini's (2009) social influence principles generally had lower phishing resilience. However, there was no relationship between phishing resilience and susceptibility to the reciprocity principle ($r = -.05$, $p = .23$). Participants who scored higher on the CRT ($r = .14$, $p < .001$) and those who preferred a rational decision making style ($r = -.22$, $p < .001$) were significantly less susceptible to phishing attacks.

In regards to cultural factors, only Group Loyalty was significant ($r = -.15$, $p < .001$), which means that people who were more orientated towards the needs of the group rather than the needs of the individual had lower phishing resilience. The organisational factor of organisational security culture was also significant, with findings indicating that individuals who reported better security culture tended to be more resilient against phishing attacks ($r = .16$, $p < .001$). There were no differences based on the level of job stress reported by participants ($r = -.04$, $p = .37$). There was a significant relationship between phishing resilience and both of the measured interventional factors, namely Email Use ISA ($r = .29$, $p < .001$) and Trust in Technical Controls Scale ($r = -.27$, $p < .001$). This means that people who had more knowledge of safe email practices or more awareness of the fallibility of technical safeguards such as spam filters had better phishing resilience.

A multiple regression analysis was conducted to evaluate which variables best predict phishing resilience (see Table 1). All Variance Inflation Factor (VIF) values were below 2, indicating that multicollinearity had not occurred. The regression model accounted for approximately 17% of the variation in phishing resilience ($R^2_{adj} = .165$, $F = 10.97$, $p < .001$). The most important predictors were, in order from highest to lowest, Email Use ISA, age, susceptibility to social proof, preference for rational decision making and trust in technical controls.

Variable	B	β standardised	t-value	p
Age	**.03**	**.11**	**2.84**	**.005***
Susceptibility Authority	-.03	-.06	-1.27	.204
Susceptibility Consistency	-.01	-.02	-.39	.696
Susceptibility Liking	.01	.01	.31	.758
Susceptibility Scarcity	.00	.00	.01	.994
Susceptibility Social Proof	**-.05**	**-.11**	**-2.22**	**.027***
Cognitive Reflection Test	.01	.04	1.00	.315
Rational Decision Making	**-.01**	**-.09**	**-2.19**	**.029***
Group Loyalty	-.03	-.06	-1.31	.192
Organisational Security Culture	.00	.03	.80	.427
Email Use ISA	**.01**	**.17**	**3.82**	**.000****
Trust in Technical Controls	**-.01**	**-.09**	**-2.10**	**.036***

* $p < .005$, ** $p < .001$

Table 1: Summary of multiple regression analysis for phishing resilience

5   Discussion

This study reports on the results of an online phishing study, and revealed that 61% of phishing emails were managed correctly. Although this result is higher than previous role-play phishing studies, in which 52% (Parsons *et al.*, 2013) and 48% (Sheng *et al.*, 2010) of phishing emails were managed correctly, from a real-world perspective, this is still a concerning finding. While a number of previous studies have investigated the factors associated with the ability to resist phishing attacks, findings have been inconsistent, and each study has focused on a limited number of factors (e.g., Kumaraguru *et al.*, 2007, Welk *et al.*, 2015). In this study, we measured a larger number of potential independent variables than any previous study.

In line with previous findings (e.g., Butavicius *et al.*, 2017, Welk *et al.*, 2015), individuals who had better awareness of what constitutes safe email behaviour and recognised the fallibility of technical safeguards had significantly higher phishing resilience. This highlights the importance of communicating information security risks and threats to employees. It is important to not only ensure they are aware of how they should behave, but also understand that protections such as spam filters are insufficient.

Our results also supported the previous finding (e.g., Jagatic *et al.*, 2007, Sheng *et al.*, 2010) that older people are less likely to fall for phishing attacks. This highlights the importance of communicating information security risks to young people. It remains to be seen if this difference is associated with more complacency and willingness to take risks in younger people, which may decrease with age, or if it represents a generational difference, which would then increase as these younger people become a larger portion of the workforce.

Our findings provide support for the influence of impulsivity in phishing performance. The preference for rational (as opposed to intuitive) decision making predicted phishing resilience. These results therefore highlight the importance of teaching people to stop and think before responding to emails. Finally, our results revealed that people who are more susceptible to the social proof principle are more susceptible to phishing. In other words, the social proof principle is based on the idea that people want to do what others are doing (Cialdini, 2009), and they may therefore have a greater need to want to follow the instructions in a phishing email.

Despite the importance of these findings, there are limitations. For example, our study did not directly measure phishing susceptibility, as participants were not required to click on links or enter personal information. Additionally, although this study measured the largest number of factors of any study and their effect on phishing resilience, the regression model accounted for 17% of variance. This means that other factors that were out of scope of the current study would account for the additional variance. This study did not examine the influence of risk-taking and did not examine the effectiveness of different types of training provided to employees. It is important to replicate this research with a larger number of participants to see if the same relationships are found. Although phishing attacks have threatened organisations for over a decade, we have yet to find a simple solution. With the growing sophistication and diversity of these attacks, it is increasingly important to conduct this research to ensure that employees and organisations have the best chance of avoiding serious security breaches.

6 References

Akbar, N. (2014). Analysing persuasion principles in phishing emails. Masters degree, University of Twente.

Butavicius, M., McCormac, A., Parsons, K., Calic, D. and Pattinson, M. (2018), Predicting information security awareness of employees: The effect of individual, cultural, organisational and interventional factors. Manuscript in preparation.

Butavicius, M., Parsons, K., Pattinson, M. and McCormac, A. (2015), "Breaching the Human Firewall: Social Engineering in Phishing and Spear-Phishing Emails", 26th Australasian Conference of Information Systems (ACIS), Adelaide.

Butavicius, M., Parsons, K., Pattinson, M., McCormac, A., Calic, D. and Lillie, M. (2017), Understanding susceptibility to phishing emails: Assessing the impact of individual differences and culture. *Proceedings of the 11th International Symposium on Human Aspects of Information Security & Assurance (HAISA 2017).* S. Furnell and Clarke, N. L. University of Plymouth pp 12-23.

Calic, D., Pattinson, M., Parsons, K., Butavicius, M. and McCormac, A. (2016), Naïve and accidental behaviours that compromise information security: What the experts think *Proceedings of the 10th International Symposium on Human Aspects of Information Security and Assurance (HAISA 2016).* S. Furnell and Clarke, N. Frankfurt, Germany pp 12-21.

Cialdini, R. B. (2009), *Influence: Science and Practice.* New York, William Morrow.

Darwish, A., El Zarka, A. and Aloul, F. (2012), "Towards understanding phishing victims' profile", International Conference on Computer Systems and Industrial Informatics (ICCSII), Sharjah, UAE, IEEE.

Fernández, I., Paez, D. and González, J. L. (2005), "Independent and interdependent self-construals and socio-cultural factors in 29 nations", *Revue Internationale de Psychologie Sociale,* Vol. 18, No. 1, pp 35-63.

Frederick, S. (2005), "Cognitive reflection and decision making", *Journal of Economic Perspectives,* Vol. 16, No. 4, pp 25-42.

Hamilton, K., Shih, S.-I. and Mohammed, S. (2016), "The development and validation of the rational and intuitive decision styles scale", *Journal of Personality Assessment,* Vol. 98, No. 5, pp 523-535.

Jagatic, T. N., Johnson, N. A., Jakobsson, M. and Menczer, F. (2007), "Social phishing", *Communications of the ACM,* Vol. 50, No. 10, pp 94-100.

Kaptein, M., de Ruyter, B., Markopoulos, P. and Aarts, E. (2012), "Adaptive persuasive systems: a study of tailored persuasive text messages to reduce snacking", *ACM Transactions on Interactive Intelligent Systems (TiiS),* Vol. 2, No. 2, pp 10.

Kaptein, M. and Eckles, D. (2012), "Heterogeneity in the effects of online persuasion", *Journal of Interactive Marketing,* Vol. 26, No. 3, pp 176-188.

Karjalainen, M. (2011). Improving Employees' Information Systems (IS) Security Behaviour: Toward a Meta-Theory of IS Security Training and a New Frameword for Understanding Employees' IS Security Behaviour. PhD, University of Oulu.

Kumaraguru, P., Rhee, Y., Sheng, S., Hasan, S., Acquisti, A., Cranor, L. F. and Hong, J. (2007), "Getting users to pay attention to anti-phishing education: evaluation of retention and transfer", Proceedings of the Anti-Phishing Working Groups 2nd Annual eCrime Researchers Summit, Pittsburgh, PA, ACM.

Lambert, E. G., Hogan, N. L., Camp, S. D. and Ventura, L. A. (2006), "The impact of work–family conflict on correctional staff: A preliminary study", *Criminology and Criminal Justice,* Vol. 6, pp 371-387.

McCormac, A., Calic, D., Butavicius, M., Parsons, K., Pattinson, M. and Lillie, M. (2017), Understanding the relationships between resilience, work stress and information security awareness. *Proceedings of the 11th International Symposium on Human Aspects of Information Security & Assurance (HAISA 2017).* S. Furnell and Clarke, N. Adelaide, Australia, University of Plymouth pp.

Parsons, K., Calic, D., Pattinson, M., Butavicius, M., McCormac, A. and Zwaans, T. (2017), "The Human Aspects of Information Security Questionnaire (HAIS-Q): Two further validation studies", *Computers & Security,* Vol. 66, pp 40-51.

Parsons, K., McCormac, A., Pattinson, M., Butavicius, M. and Jerram, C. (2013), Phishing for the Truth: A Scenario-Based Experiment of Users' Behavioural Response to Emails. *Security and Privacy Protection in Information Processing Systems - IFIP Advances in Information and Communication Technology.* L. J. Janczewski, Wolf, H. and Shenoi, S., Springer.Vol. 405, pp 366-378.

Parsons, K., Young, E., Butavicius, M., McCormac, A., Pattinson, M. and Jerram, C. (2015), "The Influence of Organisational Information Security Culture on Cybersecurity Decision Making", *Journal of Cognitive Engineering and Decision Making: Special Issue on Cybersecurity Decision Making,* Vol. 9, No. 2, pp 117-129.

Pricewaterhouse Coopers (PWC) (2015), Turnaround and transformation in cybersecurity: Key findings from The Global State of Information Security Survey 2016.

Sheng, S., Holbrook, M., Kumaraguru, P., Cranor, L. F. and Downs, J. (2010), "Who falls for phish?: a demographic analysis of phishing susceptibility and effectiveness of interventions", Proceedings of the SIGCHI Conference on Human Factors in Computing Systems, ACM.

Singelis, T. M. (1994), "The measurement of independent and interdependent self-construals", *Personality and Social Psychology Bulletin,* Vol. 20, No. 5, pp 580-591.

Smith, B. W., Dalen, J., Wiggins, K., Tooley, E., Christopher, P. and Bernard, J. (2008), "The brief resilience scale: assessing the ability to bounce back", *International Journal of Behavioral Medicine,* Vol. 15, No. 3, pp 194-200.

Telstra Corporation (2017), Telstra Cyber Security Report 2017.

Welk, A. K., Hong, K. W., Zielinska, O. A., Tembe, R., Murphy-Hill, E. and Mayhorn, C. B. (2015), "Will the "Phisher-Men" reel you in?: Assessing individual differences in a phishing detection task", *International Journal of Cyber Behavior, Psychology and Learning,* Vol. 5, No. 4, pp 1-17.

Wombat Security Technologies (2018), State of the Phish 2018. Pittsburgh, PA,.

	1	2	3	4	5	6	7	8	9	10	11	12	13
1. Phishing susceptibility	-												
2. Age	.21**	-											
3. Susceptibility Authority	-.20**	-.16**	-										
4. Susceptibility Consistency	-.11**	-.12**	.34**	-									
5. Susceptibility Liking	-.10*	-.10*	.20**	.29**	-								
6. Susceptibility Scarcity	-.20**	-.22**	.41**	.37**	.35**	-							
7. Susceptibility Social Proof	-.30**	-.22**	.42**	.29**	.38**	.44**	-						
8. Cognitive Reflection Test	.14**	.08*	-.13**	-.08*	.02	-.11**	-.13**	-					
9. Rational Decision Making	-.22**	-.12**	.21**	.23**	.24**	.38**	.29**	-.27**	-				
10. Group Loyalty	-.15**	-.08*	.30**	.32**	.29**	.29**	.38**	-.06	.13**	-			
11. Organisational Security Culture	.16**	.11**	.00	.14**	-.11**	-.13**	-.23**	.01	-.13**	.01	-		
12. Email use ISA	.29**	.18**	-.09*	.10*	.02	-.12**	-.27**	.11	-.13**	-.01	.38**	-	
13. Trust in Technical Controls	-.27**	-.11**	.21**	.13**	.02	.22**	.35**	-.26**	.30**	.12**	-.17**	-.38**	-
Mean	.61	N/A	3.17	3.56	3.48	2.96	2.74	.80	15.91	3.34	22.01	38.60	8.69
SD	.34	N/A	.66	.54	.55	.72	.73	1.00	3.51	.61	3.21	4.88	2.54

$* p < .005, ** p < .001$

Table 1: Pearson's correlation matrix and descriptive statistics for variables of interest

A Social Engineering Prevention Training Tool: Methodology and Design for Validating the SEADM

F. Mouton[1], M. J. Pepper[2] and T. Meyer[3]

[1]Defence Peace Safety & Security, [2,3]Department of Computer Science
[2]Council for Scientific and Industrial Research, [2,3]University of Cape Town,
[3]Pretoria, South Africa, [2,3]Cape Town, South Africa
e-mail: moutonf@gmail.com; mikejpepper@gmail.com; tmeyer@cs.uct.ac.za

Abstract

The information people possess is often of great value and thus, when stored electronically, is typically guarded by complicated security mechanisms. Such mechanisms are frequently upgraded in order to counteract threats that aim to obtain the information being guarded. Accordingly, the "social engineer" seeks to attack and exploit the weakest link in this information security system: the user. The general public is often not aware that they may be subjected to acts of social engineering (SE), and are hence not aware of what to look for and how to react appropriately in such situations. This leaves the unsuspecting public in a vulnerable position with very little assistance at their disposal.

The Social Engineering Prevention Training Tool (SEPTT) project of which we are part sought to address SE vulnerability by developing a tool that can be used in any scenario to determine if the user is being subjected to acts of SE, and to provide guidance as to the correct manner of response to follow in said scenario. The authors previously expanded on the original Social Engineering Attack Detection Model and produced the updated version 2, i.e. SEADMv2. A test methodology to validate the updated model is presented together with a preliminary design for the web application.

Keywords

Social engineering, attack prevention, Mitnick's attack cycle, SEADMv2, social engineering attack detection model, social engineering attack examples, social engineering attack framework.

1   Introduction

Social engineers make use of psychological ploys that compromise the user's emotional state, hence allowing an "exploit" to take place (Bezuidenhout, Mouton, & Venter, 2010; Mouton, Leenen, Malan, & Venter, 2014; Mouton, Malan, et al., 2014). This psychological manipulation can be performed using various techniques through multiple channels and mediums. However, the overall goal is the same. By exploiting psychological vulnerabilities of users, social engineers destabilise users' thinking so as to elicit responses – and hence perform information-gathering – that would not be possible had the user been in a more stable state of mind (Bezuidenhout et al., 2010; Mouton et al., 2012). This ultimately leads to the attacker achieving a predetermined objective, often unbeknownst to the victim. The success of these attacks can often be attributed to individuals not perceiving themselves as potential victims of such attacks and hence not being aware of the types of techniques used in their execution (Mouton, Leenen, & Venter, 2015). This ignorance may be due to the users' lack of knowledge of the potential gains an attacker can attain from the information they possess.

The 'art' of influencing people to divulge sensitive information is known as social engineering and the process of doing so is known as a social engineering attack. There are various definitions of social engineering and also a number of different models of social engineering attack (Mitnick and Simon, 2002; Culpepper, 2004; Thornburgh, 2004; Åhlfeldt *et al.*, 2005; Hamill, Deckro and Jr., 2005; Nohlberg, 2008; Hadnagy, 2010; Kingsley Ezechi, 2011; Lenkart, 2011; Mouton, Leenen, *et al.*, 2014). The authors considered a number of definitions of social engineering and social engineering attack taxonomies in a previous paper, *Towards an Ontological Model Defining the Social Engineering Domain*, and formulated a definition for both social engineering and social engineering attack (Mouton, Leenen, *et al.*, 2014). In addition, the authors proposed an ontological model for a social engineering attack. It is important to ensure that a standardised definition is used throughout all the work within a single domain. For the purpose of this paper, definition for social engineering used throughout this paper is as follows: "the science of using social interaction as a means to persuade an individual or an organisation to comply with a specific request from an attacker where either the social interaction, the persuasion or the request involves a computer-related entity" (Mouton, Leenen, *et al.*, 2014).

There has been a significant amount of research performed into defining the field of social engineering and furthermore social engineering prevention, there has not yet been any research into the development of a tool. As far as the authors are aware, there is currently no tool available that can be used to detect social engineering attacks and give users an indication of the action they should take in a given scenario. This naturally leaves people in a vulnerable position, with the only assistance available to them being generic 'tips' on things to look out for. The Social Engineering Prevention Training Tool (SEPTT) project of which we are part aims at addressing this gap by implementing the Social Engineering Attack Detection Model Version 2 (SEADMv2) proposed by (Mouton et al., 2015) as a web application, in order to determine whether it is effective at assisting users to successfully differentiate between harmless requests and genuine SE attacks. SEADMv2 aims to guide its users towards understanding of the appropriate action to take in given scenarios, hence reducing the probability of them falling victim to an SE attack.

2 Background

This section analyses the current frameworks available to model SE attacks, with emphasis on the framework proposed by Mitnick and Simon (2002; 2005). The differing SE attack classifications are also outlined, as they are pivotal in creating SE attack scenarios that accurately depict real-world attacks for the experiment to follow.

2.1 Mitnick's Attack Cycle

In order to combat the vulnerability of the unsuspecting public, the first step is to understand how SE attacks are structured so that each aspect of the attack can be accounted for. Mitnick's attack cycle is pivotal in this regard as it is the most widely accepted SE attack framework, since its phases are consistent across all attack types (Mitnick and Simon, 2005). The cycle breaks an SE attack down into several phases, each of which contains a predetermined goal. These phases are discussed in the following subsections, with reference to alternate models that define similar phases.

2.1.1   Information-gathering

Initially, the social engineer gathers as much information about the target as possible (Mouton, Malan, et al., 2014). This information-gathering can take many forms and aims at acquiring information and resources necessary to successfully perform an attack (Van De Merwe and Mouton, 2017). The quality of information attained plays a vital role in successfully creating a relationship with the target, a stage that is pivotal in the overall success of the attack (Mouton, Malan, et al., 2014). Techniques such as gathering Facebook pictures of the target's friends and identifying the language and tone used between the target and those friends are examples of techniques that could be used in this phase (Abraham and Chengalur-Smith, 2010). Such information would assist in masquerading as one of the target's friends in order to exploit their relationship and attain valuable information from that individual.

2.1.2   Develop rapport and trust

Once sufficient information is gathered about the target, the social engineer attempts to establish a relationship with the target as the target will be more likely to divulge the requested information to the attacker if there is an existing relationship (Mouton, Malan, et al., 2014). Developing this relationship relies on the information gathered in the previous phase, as the approach used is tailored to the information available. For example, social engineers may use insider information to masquerade as someone within an organisation; misrepresent their identity by pretending to be a specific individual; cite individuals known by the target as common connections aid in an individual's credibility; or appear to occupy an authoritative role (Mouton, Malan, et al., 2014). In doing this, the attacker hopes to establish some trust connection with the target (Gao and Kim, 2007), which will make the target more susceptible to exploitation in the next phase.

2.1.3   Exploit trust

Once a relationship has been established, the attacker attempts to exploit this trust to gain information from the target. In Mitnick's attack-cycle model, this is achieved through manipulation of the target's emotional state by preying on the seven psychological vulnerabilities noted by Gragg (2002). They are: strong affect, overloading, reciprocation, deceptive relationship, diffusion of responsibility and moral duty, authority, integrity and consistency (Mitnick and Simon, 2005; Chantler and Broadhurst, 2006; Scheeres, 2008; Workman, 2008). By exploiting these psychological vulnerabilities, the target's emotional state is altered and she or he becomes more likely to comply with the attacker's requests for information (Mouton, Malan, et al., 2014).

2.1.4   Utilise information

Lastly, Mitnick's model notes the phase in which the information gathered in the previous phase is utilised to achieve the predefined goal (Mitnick and Simon, 2005). Should insufficient information be attained, the model cycles back to phase one. Other models fail to recognise this phase and deem the social engineering attack to be successful once the required information is retrieved from the target.

2.2 Attack Classifications

SE attacks can be classified according to the manner in which the communication takes place during the exploit, and the interaction between attacker and target (Mouton, Malan, et al., 2014). By understanding the different types of attacks, one can generate attack scenarios representative of possible real-life attacks, with a broad enough coverage to account for the differing manners in which these are performed.

According to Mouton, Leenen et al. (2014), SE attacks can be divided into direct and indirect attacks. In this classification, indirect attacks are those where a third-party medium is used to facilitate the communication between attacker and target. In such attacks, communication takes place when a target accesses the third party medium without interaction from the social engineer. Mediums such as USB flash drives and pamphlets are used to exploit the target in some way (Abraham and Chengalur-Smith, 2010).

Direct attacks are those where two or more parties are involved in a direct conversation. Direct attacks are differentiated in this model on whether they are one-sided or two-sided. One-sided attacks are classified as *unidirectional communication* and two-sided as *bidirectional communication*. Bidirectional communication takes place when two or more parties partake in a conversation. . This type of communication can be likened to the communication described by Ivaturi and Janczewski (2011, 2012) and is often performed over interactive media such as email and face-to-face conversations as both parties need to be able to contribute. Unidirectional communication occurs when there is communication between attacker and target without the target being able to converse with the attacker in a back-and-forth manner. Examples of the media used for such communication are emails and one-way text messages. Diagrams depicting these different types of communication can be found in a paper by Mouton *et al.* (2014) entitled, *Towards an Ontological Model Defining the Social Engineering Domain.*

3 Social Engineering Attack Detection Model Version 2 (SEADMv2)

The SEADMv2 (Mouton et al., 2015) is a revision of the model initially proposed by Bezuidenhout et al. (2010). This revised model provides users with a state diagram that can be used to determine: firstly, if they are being subjected to acts of SE; and secondly, the appropriate action they should take. It achieves this by asking the users questions about their current scenario, the answers to which determine their transitions through the model (seen in Figure 1 below). The model eventually reaches a termination state, at which point the user is given one of two instructions: "perform the request" or "defer or refer request". The instruction to "perform the request" indicates to the user that she or he should comply with the requester's demands and perform the relevant action as it is unlikely to be an SE attack. The instruction to "defer or refer request" indicates to the user that she or he may be subjected to an SE attack and should thus *refer* the request to someone better-suited to deal with it, or *defer* the request completely – whichever would be more applicable to the user in a real-life situation.

This version 2 of the SEADM improves upon the Bezuidenhout et al. (2010) first iteration through expanding upon the states proposed, hence increasing the model's coverage and making it more user-friendly. Additionally, the 'state' component in the previous model, which required the user to evaluate his or her emotional state, has been omitted and is now dealt with by a separate psychological measure developed by Mouton et al. (2012).

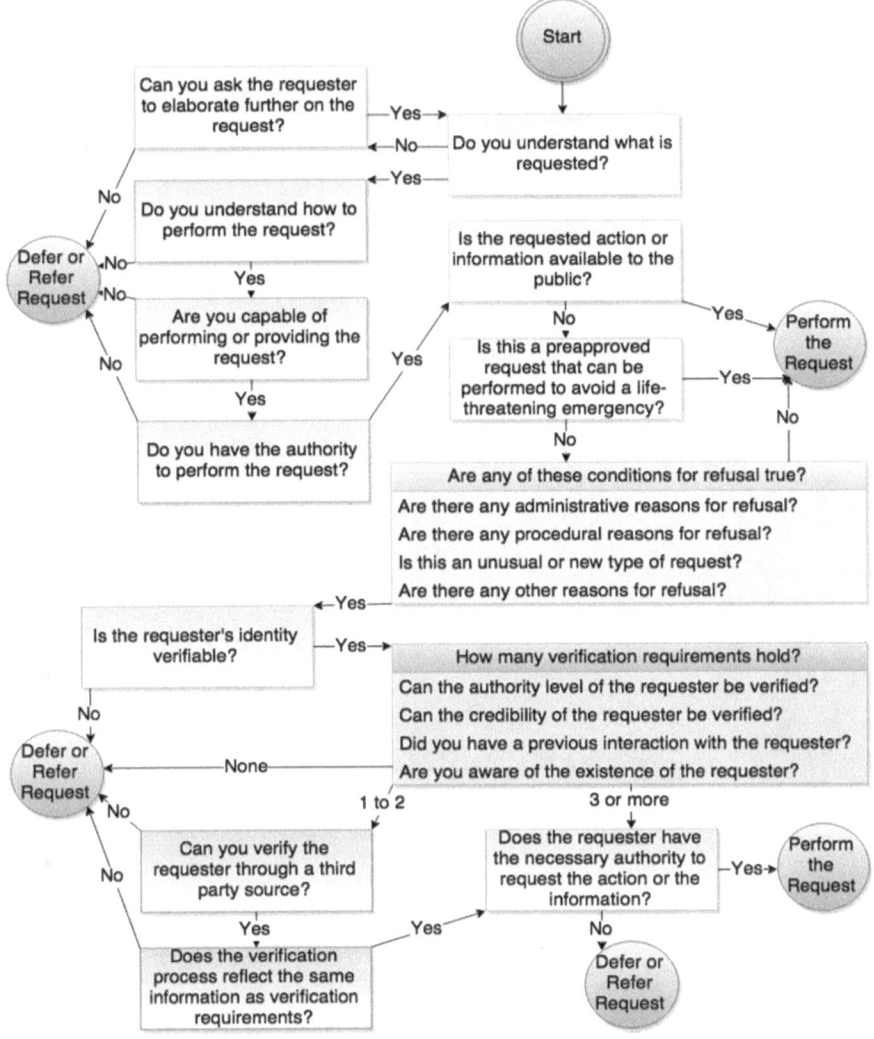

Figure 1: Social Engineering Attack Detection Model version 2 (SEADMv2)
(Mouton, Leenen and Venter, 2015)

The information on how to process each of the states is discussed in an article by Mouton, Leenen and Venter (2015) entitled, "Social Engineering Attack Detection Model: SEADMv2". The SEADMv2 has also been further developed into a finite state machine, where the colour coded areas of the SEADMv2 is further reduced to a set of states (Mouton *et al.*, 2017, 2018). This allows the model to be fully extensible and allows one to further ask more questions per state and is thus not limited to the predefined set of questions. The designed web implementation of the SEPTT caters for all the rules of the finite state machine. The finite state machine is depicted in Figure 2.

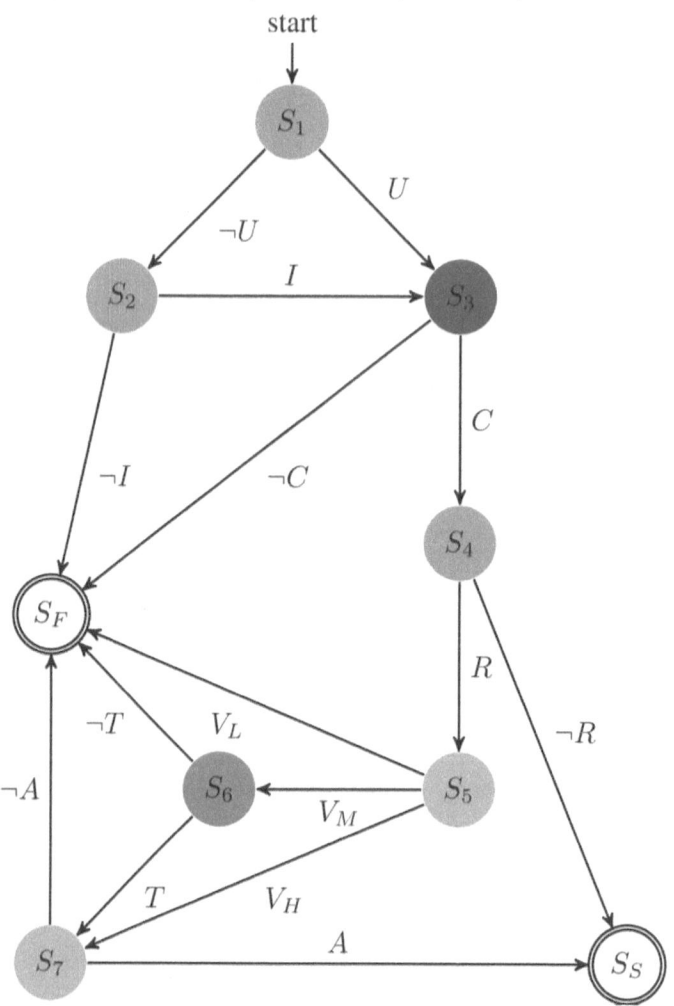

Figure 2: Finite State Machine of the SEADM (Mouton et al., 2017, 2018)

4   Methodology

A two-stage experiment is proposed with an identified 45 subjects. Subjects will be sent a link to the questionnaire and invited to participate in a two stage experiment and provided with instructions on how to go about completing the experiment. The order in which questions were asked in both stages was randomised to avoid any ordering effects on subjects' answers. The two stages of the experiment are discussed below, as well as the data transformation that was performed to transform the results to a usable format for statistical testing.

Proposed Experiment

Stage 1: The first stage will consist of the 10 potential SE attack scenarios mentioned above, each with four possible answers: two "perform the request" options and two "defer or refer the request" options. For example, in order to choose to "defer or refer the request", the subject had to choose a multiple-choice option that did not comply with the requests in the scenario, or that deferred the situation to someone better-equipped to deal with it. These answers will provide a record of how subjects respond to each scenario without assistance from the SEADMv2-model application. This will form the "without model" before-treatment data collection stage, and serve as the control results of the experiment.

Stage 2: Upon completion of stage 1, the subjects will be informed that they must now make use of the SEADMv2 web model to guide their answers to the previous 10 scenarios. To achieve this, the same 10 scenarios will be presented to the subjects in a random order. However now, for each scenario, they would have to use the information in that scenario to progress through the SEADMv2 model by answering "yes" or "no" to the questions it asked. The result of this stage of the experiment will be a record of how subjects react to each scenario when they have the guidance of the SEADMv2 model and constitutes the "With Model" after-treatment data.

Responses to the questionnaire will be limited to one per person to prevent the same person answering it multiple times and skewing the data.

5   Proposed Design and Implementation

The hypotheses that this experiment seeks to test are:

- that user interaction with the SEADMv2 web application will significantly increase the user's ability to recognise and avoid genuine SE attack requests; and
- user interaction with the SEADMv2 web application will significantly increase the user's ability to recognise and reply favourably towards harmless requests.

The efficacy of the model will be assessed through a two-stage experiment, whereby subjects will be given 10 scenarios that are possible social engineering attacks, with four possible options of how to respond to each scenario. Subjects had to choose the option that most accurately depicted how they would react in each scenario, first without the use of the SEADMv2 model (stage 1 of the experiment) and then (in stage 2) with use of the SEADMv2 model.

To perform this experiment, a web application will be created that allows users to traverse the SEADMv2. The research subjects who will use the tool have been identified, and necessary consent and ethical issues are being duly managed.

This section discusses the design considerations and techniques that will be employed to develop the application, as well as the scenarios that were created to assess the tool's efficacy. The questionnaire through which the experiment was conducted is also discussed.

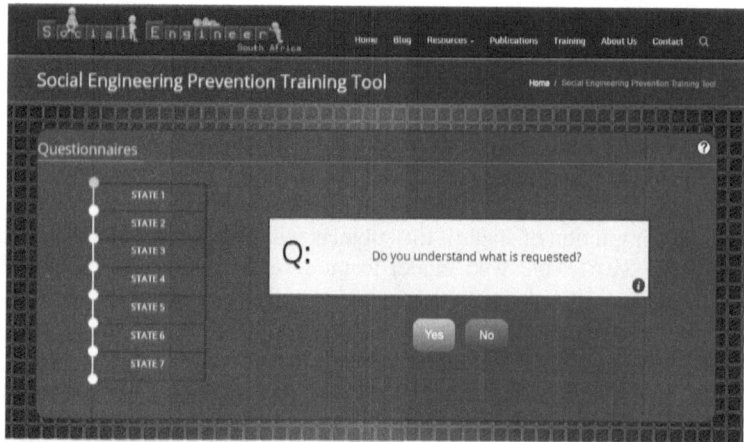

Figure 3: Social Engineering Prevention Training Tool (Web Application)

5.1 Web application

The web application (seen above in Figure 3) consists of a question box that poses a question to the user that is dependent on the user's current state within the SEADMv2 model. Each question aims to assess the user's knowledge of the current situation before the user transitions to the next state in the model. (Eventually, at the final stage, the user has decided on the correct action to take.) Below each question, there are two buttons that allow the users to answer "yes" or "no". There is a progress bar on the left side of the interface indicating to the users their current position in the model, and informational buttons that can be used to aid the users in the event that they seek clarity on some aspect of the current question. A rapid application design (RAD) approach was used to develop this web application, hence ensuring that the resulting application was developed to specification and within time constraints. The web application will be hosted on www.social-engineering.co.za and make use of a MySQL database to store the SEADMv2 model.

5.2 Social engineering scenarios

Ten believable real-life situations were drafted into scenario format. These scenarios focused on two phases of Mitnick's attack-cycle model, namely the *develop rapport and trust* phase and the *exploit trust* phase (Mitnick and Simon, 2002). The scenarios also employed request techniques used within these phases by successful SE attackers. Each request scenario terminated with four possible responses for the user to choose from: two responses that signalled compliance with the request (i.e., responses indicating that the user felt the request was not an SE attack), and two responses that did not comply with the request (i.e., two responses indicating user suspected the request was an SE attack).

The 10 scenarios comprised eight that were characteristic of genuine SE attacks, and two that were characteristic of harmless requests that could be complied with. After completing the experiment, it became clear that a more even split between genuine-attack scenarios and harmless scenarios would have been ideal, as the low number of harmless scenarios affected the credibility of those results. This lack of foresight, as discussed in the "limitations" sub-section below, arose during the planning stages of the experiment when the only consideration was that there should be harmless scenarios, with insufficient consideration of how many there should be in relation to the number of potentially harmful. This led to the less-than-ideal 8/2 split.

In order to ensure that the scenarios are diverse enough to model the different types of real-world attacks, the SE attack classifications developed by Mouton, Leenen, and Venter (2016) is to be used as templates. Of the ten scenarios that were created for the experiment, five depicted unidirectional communication, four depicted bidirectional communication, and one depicted indirect communication. To provide the reader with a sense of the content and structure of the scenarios, five of the ten are briefly outlined in the section below and includes the following types:

- two unidirectional communication scenarios;
- two bidirectional communication scenarios; and
- one indirect communication scenario.

5.2.1   Unidirectional communication scenarios

Unidirectional communication is a one-sided conversation where the social engineer communicates with the target, but the target has no means to communicate back with the social engineer (Mouton, Leenen, et al., 2014).

5.2.2   Scenario 1

Summary: While at work you receive an email from a new email address indicating that a new person (the sender) from your company's external accounting firm has started working on the time reports for this quarter and hence she needs you to send your preliminary time report through as soon as possible. The email address that the message comes from has the same domain as previous emails from the accounting firm and the signature of the email is the same as all previous emails from various other employees of the accounting firm. What action do you take?

Notable aspects of scenario: you understand how to perform the request; you are capable of performing the request and have the authority to do so; information requested is sensitive and not publicly available; this is a unique request and not pre-authorised; there are administrative reasons to not perform this request; the requester's identity, authority and credibility are verifiable; you have had no previous interaction with the requester but can verify the requester's intentions.

Possible responses to scenario:

    A.   since you do not have much work to do, you get working on your preliminary time report immediately and email it to the requester as soon as possible.

    B.   you reply to the email, asking her a few complementary questions and, based on her answers, either provide her your preliminary time report or refuse to send it to her.

    C.   you contact your superior to find out whether or not they approve of you sending your preliminary time report to the person requesting it.

    D.   you refuse to send her your preliminary time report.

Suggested (i.e., secure) action: Perform the request, i.e., choose option A or B.

5.2.3   Scenario 2

Summary: Whilst sitting in a lecture at university, your lecturer introduces a guest lecturer from an external organisation. The guest lecturer gives a bit of information about his organisation and hands out a small assignment that will count towards your final grade at the end of the year. The assignment asks for your student number as well as date of birth and last seven digits of your identification document (ID) number. The guest lecturer assures you that the information will only be used for recruitment purposes. What action do you take?

Notable aspects of scenario: You understand how to perform the request; You are capable of performing the request and have the authority to do so; Information requested is not available to the public; This is not a pre-approved request; There are administrative reasons for refusal; The requester's identity is not verifiable.

Possible responses to scenario:

    A.   you provide all the requested information.

    B.   you ask the guest lecturer a few complementary questions and based on his answers decide whether to provide the information.

    C.   you ask the guest lecturer to rather contact your lecturer directly to obtain this information.

    D.   you do not provide the information and also do not tell the guest lecturer where to get it as you deem it to be sensitive information.

Suggested (i.e., secure) action: Defer or refer request, i.e., choose option C or D.

5.2.4   Bidirectional communication scenarios

Bidirectional communication is when two or more parties take part in the conversation, in other words, a two-way conversation occurs. Each party consists of an individual, a group of individuals or an organisation (Mouton, Leenen, et al., 2014).

5.2.5   Scenario 3

Summary: You receive a message on Facebook from a person you do not know who claims he is a marketing agent for the Rocking the Daisies Festival. The message tells you about a competition to win free tickets to the festival. All that is required is that you send through a video explaining how excited you are about the festival and why you think you should win. You verify that there is in fact a competition to win tickets by going onto the Rocking the Daisies Facebook page and seeing the competition advertised as the person explained. The message states further that they would like to assist you with your entry as they receive commission for each entry they provide assistance to. To do this, they ask that you send your video to them directly, along with your full name, date of birth and Facebook login details (email and password), since an entry requires a link to your Facebook account. What action do you take?

Notable aspects of scenario: You understand how to perform the request; you are capable of performing the request and have the authority to do so; information requested is sensitive and not publicly available; this is a new type of request and not pre-authorised; there are administrative reasons for refusal; the requester's identity is not verifiable.

Possible responses to scenario:

    A. you record your video in a few days and send him your video along with all the information requested, since he only needs it to enter you into the competition.

    B. you record your video in a few days and send him your video along with all the information requested (however you are a bit wary about giving out your Facebook login details and decide to change your Facebook password 24 hours after sending it to him).

    C. you record your video in a few days, but decide to rather enter the competition yourself by going to the official festival website and entering the competition there, without sending the person who contacted you on Facebook any of your details.

    D. you decide not to enter the competition at all (since the person on Facebook was asking for your Facebook login details for the competition, you conclude that the entire competition must be fake and decide that it is best not to enter).

Suggested (i.e., secure) action: Defer or refer request, i.e., choose option C or D.

5.2.6   Scenario 4

Summary: As a university student, you are walking to the turnstile entrance of the computer lab when a person you do not know approaches you. The person looks like a student and asks you to swipe them through the turnstile using your student card as they have forgotten theirs at home. You know that swiping in other students to labs is not allowed, but you can see that the student is stressed and has an assignment to submit within the next 15 minutes. What action do you take?

Notable aspects of scenario: You understand how to perform the request; you are capable of performing the request; you do not have the authority to perform the request.

Possible responses to scenario:

A. you swipe the student in immediately, since you know how stressful it is submitting an assignment at the last minute and you know there is no time to waste.
B. even though the student is stressed and needs to get into the lab as soon as possible, you decide to ask the student a few questions and based on his/her answers make a decision on whether to swipe him/her in or not.
C. you refuse to help the student at all and tell the student he/she should not have waited until the last minute to submit the assignment and he/she should always have their student card on them while on campus.
D. you give the student directions to the access control offices where the student can prove his/her identity and hopefully get access to a computer lab within 15 minutes to submit the assignment.

Suggested (i.e., secure) action: Defer or refer request, i.e., choose option C or D.

5.2.7   Indirect communication scenario

Indirect communication occurs when a third-party medium is used as a form of transporting the communication. Typical third-party media include physical media such as flash drives or pamphlets or virtual media such as web pages. There is no direction interaction between the target and the social engineer (Mouton, Leenen, et al., 2014).

5.2.8   Scenario 5

Summary: Whilst walking on campus you see a flash drive lying on the ground. It has no identifiable traits on the outside that can be used to identify the owner. You have lost flash drives before and are aware of how much work could be lost that may be saved on the flash drive and feel sorry for whoever may have lost it. What action do you take?

Notable aspects of scenario: You understand how to perform the action; you are capable of performing the action; you do not have the authority to interfere with someone else's property.

Possible responses to scenario:

A. you first scan the flash drive for viruses and if it is found to be virus-free, start examining all folders and opening all files stored on the flash drive to hopefully identify the owner.
B. you decide to install a virtual machine on your computer and use that virtual machine to examine all folders and open all files on the flash drive in an attempt to identify the owner.
C. you give the flash drive to a friend and ask him/her to try identify the owner by examining the files on his/her computer.
D. leave the flash drive where it is, without plugging it into any computer or opening any of the files.

Suggested (i.e., secure) action: Defer or refer request, i.e., choose option C or D.

5.2.9   Response retrieval

To perform the experiment, a Google Forms questionnaire will be used. This questionnaire will present people with the various SE attack scenarios. They are able to select the multiple choice option they feel most accurately depicts how they would react to each scenario. This form of data capture was chosen for its efficiency and ease of use as a link to the questionnaire could be sent out to subjects, with instructions on how to participate in the experiment. Another benefit of this form of data capture is that the results are already in an electronic format, hence reducing the number of errors made during data capture. Furthermore, the results of a Google Forms questionnaire can be exported as .csv file, allowing for easy interpretation of the data using a Python script.

6   Conclusions and Future Work

In conclusion, there is a clear need to develop a tool that can be used in any scenario to determine if the user is being subjected to acts of SE, and to provide guidance as to the correct manner of response to follow in said scenario. The authors have determined that a web implementation of the SEADMv2 model is an effective modus to train individuals in reducing the number of errors made by subjects on various types of scenarios. As such, a methodology and subsequent design of such a web tool is being developed. It is expected to have a significant effect in decreasing the number of errors made on scenarios that employed indirect and bidirectional communication. By executing the envisaged experiment the model efficacy is expected to be validated and also sized. Alongside this web tool, the team has also published work on a mobile implementation of the same model. The results from that research indicates also indicates that a web tool will aid in the prevention of social engineering attacks (Mouton, Teixeira and Meyer, 2017). Future work can also be performed to increase the efficacy of the model in the areas where it was proven to be ineffective by altering the states in the model that deal with aspects unique to scenarios of those types.

7 References

Abraham, S. and Chengalur-Smith, I. (2010) 'An overview of social engineering malware: Trends, tactics, and implications', *Technology in Society*, 32(3), pp. 183–196. doi: http://dx.doi.org/10.1016/j.techsoc.2010.07.001.

Åhlfeldt, R.-M. *et al.* (2005) 'Security Issues in Health Care Process Integration? a Research-in-Progress Report.', in *EMOI-INTEROP*, pp. 1–4.

Bezuidenhout, M., Mouton, F. and Venter, H. S. (2010) 'Social engineering attack detection model: SEADM', in *Information Security for South Africa*. Johannesburg, South Africa, pp. 1–8. doi: 10.1109/ISSA.2010.5588500.

Chantler, A. N. and Broadhurst, R. (2006) *Social engineering and crime prevention in cyberspace.* Queensland University of Technology. Available at: http://eprints.qut.edu.au/7526/1/7526.pdf.

Culpepper, A. M. (2004) *Effectiveness of using red teams to identify maritime security vulnerabilities to terrorist attack.* Naval Postgraduate School.

Gao, W. and Kim, J. (2007) 'Robbing the cradle is like taking candy from a baby', in *Proceedings of the Annual Conference of the Security Policy Institute (GCSPI)*. Amsterdam, Netherlands, pp. 23–37.

Gragg, D. (2002) *A Multi-Level Defense Against Social Engineering.* Available at: http://taupe.free.fr/book/psycho/social engineering/Social Engineering - Sans Institute - Multi Level Defense Against Social Engineering.pdf.

Hadnagy, C. (2010) 'Social Engineering: Past, Present and Future'. (social-engineer.org podcast). Available at: http://www.social-engineer.org/episode-010-social-engineering-past-present-and-future/.

Hamill, J. T., Deckro, R. F. and Jr., J. M. K. (2005) 'Evaluating information assurance strategies', *Decision Support Systems*, 39(3), pp. 463–484. doi: http://dx.doi.org/10.1016/j.dss.2003.11.004.

Ivaturi, K. and Janczewski, L. (2011) 'A Taxonomy for Social Engineering attacks', in Grant, G. (ed.) *International Conference on Information Resources Management*, pp. 1–12.

Ivaturi, K. and Janczewski, L. (2012) 'A Typology Of Social Engineering Attacks? An Information Science Perspective', in *PACIS 2012 Proceedings*.

Kingsley Ezechi, A. (2011) *Detecting and combating Malware.* University of Debrecen. Available at: http://hdl.handle.net/2437/105305.

Lenkart, J. J. (2011) *The vulnerability of social networking media and the insider threat new eyes for bad guys.* Naval Postgraduate School. Available at: http://calhoun.nps.edu/public/handle/10945/5562.

Van De Merwe, J. and Mouton, F. (2017) 'Mapping the Anatomy of Social Engineering Attacks to the Systems Engineering Life Cycle', in Furnell, S. and Clarke, N. (eds) *Proceedings of the Eleventh International Symposium on Human Aspects of Information Security & Assurance*. Adelaide, Australia, pp. 24–40.

Mitnick, K. D. and Simon, W. L. (2002) *The art of deception: controlling the human element of security*. Edited by W. Publishing. Indianapolis: Wiley Publishing.

Mitnick, K. D. and Simon, W. L. (2005) *The art of intrusion: the real stories behind the exploits of hackers, intruders and deceivers.* Edited by W. Publishing. Indianapolis: Wiley Publishing.

Mouton, F., Malan, M. M., *et al.* (2014) 'Social engineering attack framework', in *Information Security for South Africa*. Johannesburg, South Africa, pp. 1–9. doi: 10.1109/ISSA.2014.6950510.

Mouton, F., Leenen, L., *et al.* (2014) 'Towards an Ontological Model Defining the Social Engineering Domain', in Kimppa, K. et al. (eds) *ICT and Society*. Springer Berlin Heidelberg (IFIP Advances in Information and Communication Technology), pp. 266–279. doi: 10.1007/978-3-662-44208-1_22.

Mouton, F. *et al.* (2017) 'Underlying finite state machine for the social engineering attack detection model', in *2017 Information Security for South Africa (ISSA)*. Johannesburg, South Africa, pp. 98–105. doi: 10.1109/ISSA.2017.8251781.

Mouton, F. *et al.* (2018) 'Finite state machine for the social engineering attack detection model: SEADM', *SAIEE ARJ*, 109(2), pp. 133–147. Available at: http://www.scielo.org.za/scielo.php?script=sci_arttext&pid=S1991-16962018000200004.

Mouton, F., Leenen, L. and Venter, H. S. (2015) 'Social Engineering Attack Detection Model: SEADMv2', in *International Conference on Cyberworlds (CW)*. Visby, Sweden, pp. 216–223. doi: 10.1109/CW.2015.52.

Mouton, F., Leenen, L. and Venter, H. S. (2016) 'Social engineering attack examples, templates and scenarios', *Computers & Security*, 59, pp. 186–209. doi: http://dx.doi.org/10.1016/j.cose.2016.03.004.

Mouton, F., Malan, M. M. and Venter, H. S. (2012) 'Development of cognitive functioning psychological measures for the SEADM', in *Human Aspects of Information Security & Assurance*. Crete, Greece, pp. 40–51.

Mouton, F., Teixeira, M. and Meyer, T. (2017) 'Benchmarking a Mobile Implementation of the Social Engineering Prevention Training Tool', in *Information Security for South Africa*. Johannesburg, South Africa, pp. 106–116. doi: 10.1109/ISSA.2017.8251782.

Nohlberg, M. (2008) *Securing Information Assets: Understanding, Measuring and Protecting against Social Engineering Attacks*. Stockholm University.

Scheeres, J. W. (2008) *Establishing the human firewall: reducing an individual's vulnerability to social engineering attacks*. DTIC Document.

Thornburgh, T. (2004) 'Social engineering: the "Dark Art"', in *Proceedings of the 1st annual conference on Information security curriculum development*. New York, NY, USA: ACM (InfoSecCD '04), pp. 133–135. doi: 10.1145/1059524.1059554.

Workman, M. (2008) 'A test of interventions for security threats from social engineering', *Information Management & Computer Security*. Emerald Group Publishing Limited, 16(5), pp. 463–483.

Motivating Users to Consider Recommendations on Password Management Strategies

P. Mayer[1,2], A. Kunz[1] and M. Volkamer[1,2]

SECUSO – Security, Usability, Society
[1]Technische Universität Darmstadt
[2]Karlsruher Institut für Technologie

Abstract

It has been proposed to offer users better recommendations on password management strategies. While we support this proposal, we worried whether people would consider and read such recommendations. To that end, we designed a total of nine different messages intended to motivate users to read recommendations on password management strategies and evaluated them in comparison to a control message. To maximise the effectiveness of our messages, we base them on well-established message types and on behavioural factors which have repeatedly been shown to influence human behaviour in the information security context. The most astonishing result for us was that the baseline condition performed as good as the motivational conditions.

Keywords

Motivation, Message Types, Password Management

1   Introduction

Many, usually very stringent, rules regarding secure password usage exist: we should always compose our password as seemingly random strings, change them frequently, never reuse them for multiple purposes, never write them down, never share them with others and the list goes on. The fact is that people face a severe overload (Adams and Sasse, 1999). They can simply not cope with all their passwords. As a result, many users (in particular when not using password managers) decrease the number and/or rigour of the rules they apply (Stobert, 2014). Indeed, often not all rules need to be applied in all contexts in order to render passwords reasonably secure. For more than a decade, security experts have recommended writing down passwords as long as they can be stored securely (Schneier, 2005; Kotadia, 2005). Likewise, password expiration policies have increasingly come under fire (Adams and Sasse, 1999; Chiasson and van Oorschot, 2015; CESG, 2016; Grassi et al., 2017). Some contexts even demand violation of some rules, e.g. when sharing a wifi password with friends or in a family.

Password managers can immensely help decrease a user's mental load associated with passwords, but most users - in particular most lay users - do not use password managers (Hoonakker et al., 2009; Stobert, 2014) and they make false assumptions about the context the password is used for when deciding to decrease the number and/or rigour of the rules they apply (Stobert, 2014). Thus, according to Stobert and Biddle (2015), what is missing are clear recommendations for password management strategies which include considerations regarding the context (e.g. when applying such coping strategies is viable and when it poses security risks) and the use of password managers. While we concur with this finding, we were afraid that people would not be likely to read such recommendations for the following reasons: (1) because of the abundance of contradicting advice on password security not aligned with current research (Murray et al., 2017), (2) as Beautement et al. (2008) note, users and organisation only have a limited capacity to read and follow new recommendations, and (3) because research has shown that users often do not pay attention to security recommendations or instructions - even when they are right in front of them (Chiasson et al., 2006) and in particular when the material is too involved (Herley, 2009). Also, learning to assess contexts could include a steep learning curve, making motivation essential for an effective learning process (Schiefele, 2009). Thus, we considered it necessary to first motivate people to consider the recommendations.

In this paper, we focus on the motivational step. Our main goal is to develop and evaluate motivating messages regarding their effectiveness. We conducted an online study with nine different motivational messages. Interestingly, and also surprisingly when considering earlier research results (Beautement et al., 2008), our results show that most participants stated a high intention to read our recommendations on password management strategies. Furthermore, our findings support earlier findings that different message types are equally effective (Olembo et al., 2014) and that different behavioural factors are equally effective (private communication with one of the authors of Kajzer et al., 2014).

2 Message Composition

We focus on textual messages to facilitate reuse of our messages in practice: such messages can be easily included in all kinds of information materials (e.g. flyers, newsletters, computer-based trainings, narrated for videos, etc.).

To maximise the effectiveness of our messages, we draw from well-established *message types* described in the literature and *reliable behavioural factors* which have repeatedly been shown to influence human behaviour in the information security context.

2.1 Message Types

Message types represent the general tone of the message. Multiple message types have been proposed and evaluated in different information security contexts (Boss et al., 2015; Siponen, 2014). According to Olembo et al. (2014), only the following message types are relevant in the context of motivational texts:

- *Risk:* Behaviour change is based on communicating risks as well as threats and effective coping strategies.

- *Norm:* Behaviour change is based on communicating how others behave and what social norms exist.

- *Analogy:* Behaviour change is based on exploiting the direct personal experience of the person and drawing parallels between new ideas and existing knowledge.

Due to the lack of empirical evidence regarding the performance of these message types in the area of recommendations on password management strategies, we decided to include all three message types in our study.

2.2 Reliable Behavioural Factors

Additionally, in order to maximise the effect, we phrased our messages so that they would address behavioural factors which have been shown to be reliable predictors of human behaviour in the information security context. Various behavioural theories and corresponding factors have been studied in the information security context. According to Lebek et al. (2014) and Mayer et al. (2017), presenting the results of systematic literature reviews regarding behavioural theories in the information security context, the relevant theories are in particular: Theory of Planned Behaviour, Protection Motivation Theory, General Deterrence Theory, and Technology Acceptance Model. Mayer et al. identify in (Mayer et al., 2017) those factors reliably exhibiting significant results across multiple studies in the information security context. They term the factors fulfilling these criteria *reliable factors*. These reliable behavioural factors are:

- *Perceived Severity of Threats:* magnitude of possible negative consequences, part of Protection Motivation Theory.

- *Response Efficacy:* perceived efficacy of a specific coping action with respect to countering a threat, part of Protection Motivation Theory.

- *Self-efficacy:* the perception of an individual about her/his own ability to successfully perform a specific action, part of Protection Motivation Theory and Theory of Planned Behaviour.

- *Response Cost:* all costs associated with performing a specific coping action, part of Protection Motivation Theory.

- *Attitude:* the feelings of an individual regarding a certain behaviour, part of Theory of Planned Behaviour.

- *Subjective Norms:* any behavioural expectations an individual perceives to be set by her/his environment, part of Theory of Planned Behaviour.

- *Controllability:* an individual's perception of environmental aspects influencing her/his ability to perform a certain behaviour, part of the Perceived Behavioural Control aspect of the Theory of Planned Behaviour.

- *Perceived Certainty of Sanctions:* the likelihood, that an illicit act is followed by sanctions (i.e. punishment), part of General Deterrence Theory.

- *Perceived Severity of Sanctions:* the magnitude of sanctions put on an individual following illicit behaviour of that individual, part of General Deterrence Theory.

- *Perceived Usefulness:* the subjective perceptions regarding increases in productivity stemming from showing a specific behaviour, part of Technology Acceptance Model.

- *Perceived Ease of Use:* an individual's subjective perception of whether using a specific system is free of effort, part of Technology Acceptance Model.

Note that *Subjective Norms* is not considered a factor in the following, since it was already considered as a message type (cf. section 2.1). In addition, two more reliable behavioural factors were excluded from our messages: controllability and attitude. Controllability was excluded since it refers to external aspects (e.g. a website's password policy) which are difficult to control. Attitude was excluded since it refers to an individual's personal feelings. These, by definition, need to be highly personalised to feel appropriate, which is not possible when formulating generic messages as in this work. Each message was designed to address each of the remaining eight behavioural factors.

2.3   Composition of Final Messages

Based on the pre-considerations outlined in the last two sections, we designed for each message type three messages varying the intensity of the phrasing regarding the reliable behavioural factors and one control message (i.e. ten messages in total). The treatment messages were all composed of three parts: (1) an introduction, (2) the motivational part, and (3) a closing sentence leading over to the recommendations. The introduction and the closing part were the same for all the messages, the motivational part was phrased according to the message type (risk, norm, analogy) and the intensity (low, medium, high). The control message was composed only of the introduction and the closing sentence; it did not contain a motivational part. All messages were worded to be used in the context of small and medium-size enterprises (SME). Due to space constraints we can only present two exemplary messages in the following: the control message and one treatment message (risk, low phrasing intensity). The messages are translated to English from their original wording in German.

2.3.1   Control message:

Passwords can fall into wrong hands in a variety of different ways. If we choose weak passwords, they might be guessed easily. If we don't pay attention, we can be observed when entering our passwords. When we write them down, they can be easily stolen.

To prevent such security incidents, plenty of different guidelines exist for securing our passwords: passwords have to be difficult to guess (i.e. as long as possible, and chosen at random), contain numbers and additional characters, contain no information about the user (e.g. date of birth of partner or children), only be used for one purpose (e.g. a user account for PCs, for log-ins on websites, one password for one particular program, etc.), they must not be written down or given away to others and they have to be entered only unobserved. Following all of these rules at all times is difficult. However, a password often doesn't need to fulfil all these rules to be reasonably secure.

The best part of it: Everything you need to know about choosing reasonably secure passwords and remembering them in your everyday life will be explained in the following!

2.3.2   Risk message, low phrasing intensity:

Passwords can fall into wrong hands in a variety of different ways. If we choose weak passwords, they might be guessed easily. If we don't pay attention, we can be observed when entering our passwords. When we write them down, they can be easily stolen.

To prevent such security incidents, plenty of different guidelines exist for securing our passwords: passwords have to be difficult to guess (i.e. as long as possible, and chosen at random), contain numbers and additional characters, contain no information about the user (e.g. date of birth of partner or children), only be used for one purpose (e.g. a user account for PCs, for log-ins on websites, one password for one particular program, etc.), they must not be written down or given away to others and they have to be entered only unobserved. Following all of these rules at all times is difficult. However, a password often doesn't need to fulfil all these rules to be reasonably secure.

The best part of it: It is easy to assess, which rules have to be followed in which situations. Anyone can learn it, even you! This knowledge is useful, because passwords, which are not reasonably secure, are an underestimated risk for competitive medium-sized organisations. Therefore, don't risk anything! Never be misled to choose passwords, which are not reasonably secure. Everybody, who endangers the organisation, has to expect appropriate consequences. Instead, do your part: Choose reasonably secure passwords to protect the organisation effectively.

Everything you need to know about choosing reasonably secure passwords and remembering them in your everyday life will be explained in the following!

3   Methodology for Empirical Evaluation

To evaluate the effectiveness of our messages, we conducted an online user study. Thereby, we were seeking to answer the following research questions:

RQ_1: Which of the message types (risk, norm, analogy) is most effective regarding motivating potential recipients to read through the recommendations?

RQ₂: Which of the intensity levels of each message type is most effective regarding motivating potential recipients to read through the recommendations?

The study design was developed iteratively in a rigorous process including feedback from experts in the fields of psychology and information security. The final methodology comprises the following four parts:

1. **Brief introduction:** Participants saw a short briefing, explaining the general topic of the study. We did give the participants a scenario of being employed in a SME and having come across the messages in an organisational context. This scenario served to equalise the context in which our messages were interpreted across participants.

2. **Displaying the message:** Then, each participant was randomly assigned to one condition (corresponding to either one of the nine treatment messages or the control message) and the respective message for that condition was shown. Note that, as outlined in section 2.3, our messages included a closing sentence leading over to the recommendations which is necessary for using them in practice. However, the study design did not include any recommendations in order to decrease bias and overhead.

3. **Questions about behavioural intention:** Thereafter, the participant had to indicate her/his intention to read the recommendations on a 5-point Likert scale. The respective item was taken from (Siponen and Vance, 2010) and adopted for our context: *"I intend to read the recommendations on how I can choose reasonably secure passwords for all of my accounts"*.

4. **Demographics:** In the end, the participants had to answer three demographic questions, pertaining to the size of the organisation they work for in their everyday jobs, their profession and their age.

The study was performed using the clickworker crowdsourcing service (an equivalent of the Amazon MTurk service for the German market). The actual survey was realised on a university hosted Limesurey instance. All participants received a compensation of 1.50€ for completing the survey. The methodology of this study conforms to all requirements of our university's ethics commission.

4   Results and Discussion

4.1   Participant Demographics

In total, we collected valid data-sets from 302 participants, where around 30 data-sets could be collected for each of the ten messages. 41.6% of the participants work in small or medium-sized organisations (<500 employees), 20.1% work in large organisations (>=500 employees). The remaining 38.3% chose to not disclose the size of the organisation they work for or are unemployed. Only 15.8% of the participants work in the IT or IT-security sector. Participants were 18 to 64 years old, the median age being 35 years.

4.2 Effectiveness of the Messages

The overall intention to read the recommendations was high with a mean of 4.13 in the 5-point scale answers. Figure 1 depicts the behavioural intention scores of the ten messages. A closer inspection of our two experimental factors (message type and intensity) with a two-way ATS test (Erceg-Hurn and Mirosevich, 2008) yielded non-significant results on the $\alpha = 0.05$ level for both main effects and the interaction. Consequently, no follow-up tests were conducted.

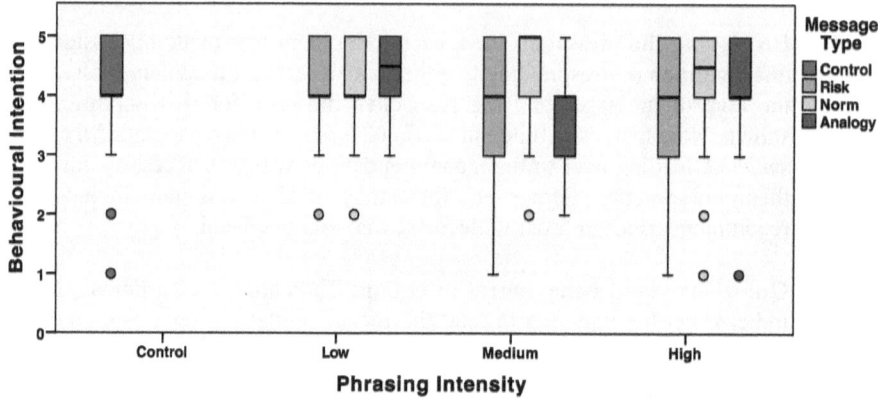

Figure 1: The behavioural intention along the two experimental factors (message type and phrasing intensity)

4.3 Discussion

Our results give further evidence supporting the findings that the different message types are equally effective (Olembo et al., 2014) and that different behavioural factors are equally effective (private communication with one of the authors of Kajzer et al., 2014). The non-significant results of the motivational messages compared to the control group came as a surprise to us. Literature reports significant effects on the behavioural intention for both, the message type (Olembo et al., 2014) and the behavioural factors used in the phrasing of the messages (Mayer et al., 2016). Our results indicate that, although the messages were designed very carefully based on research results, these prior findings cannot be transferred to our scenario of motivating users to read recommendations on password management strategies. We believe that the explanation of these findings lies in the high scores we observed in all conditions, even in the baseline condition (control). A staggering 23 out of 28 participants in the control group stated to either agree or strongly agree in relation to intending to read the recommendations. Therefore, we assume that users are very motivated to read recommendations on how to manage passwords effectively. However, we argue that our results are not only relevant for researchers of password security. They seem to indicate that it is of the essence to assess the baseline individually for each context and evaluate whether motivational messages are relevant in that specific context. Our results show that in the context of recommendations on password security this does not seem to be the case: the baseline already indicates a high motivation. Yet, in other contexts motivational messages have had success in promoting secure behaviour (e.g. Olembo et al., 2014). Thus, the decision whether motivational messages should be used needs to be investigated for each context individually.

4.4 Limitations

A limitation of our study is that we did not measure actual behaviour, but only behavioural intention. Additionally, we must acknowledge that the scenario we gave the participants restricts our findings to the organisational context. Last but not least, our control message was composed of the introduction and the last sentence which were the same for all treatment messages. While we believe the possibility to be low, a minimal message only stating the existence of recommendations would have allowed us to judge whether the introduction and the last sentence are actually responsible for the motivational effect we observed in all conditions.

5 Conclusion

In this paper, we presented the results of an online user study evaluating the effectiveness of nine different motivational messages. The messages were constructed based on findings in the literature. Interestingly, and also surprisingly when considering earlier research results like (Beautement et al., 2008), our results show that most participants stated a high intention to read our recommendations on password management strategies. Also, our results indicate that (a) different message types are equally effective and (b) that different behavioural factors are equally effective.

6 Acknowledgement

This work has been developed within the project 'KMU AWARE' which is funded by the German Federal Ministry for Economic Affairs and Energy under grant no. BMWi-VIA5-090168623-01-1/2015. The authors assume responsibility for the content. This work was further supported by the German Federal Ministry of Education and Research in the Competence Center for Applied Security Technology (KASTEL).

7 References

Adams, A. and Sasse, M. A. (1999), „Users are not the enemy.", *Communications of the ACM*, Vol. 42, No. 12, pp. 40-46.

Beautement, A., Sasse, M. A., and Wonham, M. (2009), "The compliance budget: managing security behaviour in organisations," *Proceedings of the 2008 workshop on New security paradigms*, pp. 47–58.

Boss, S. R., Galletta, D. F., Lowry, P. B., Moody, G. D. and Polak, P. (2015), What do users have to fear? "Using fear appeals to engender threats and fear that motivate protective security behaviors.", *MIS Quarterly*, Vol. 39, No. 4, pp. 837–864.

Chiasson, S. and Van Oorschot, P. C. (2015), "Quantifying the security advantage of password expiration policies.", *Designs, Codes and Cryptography*, Vol. 77, No. 2-3, pp. 401-408.

Chiasson, S., van Oorschot, P. C. and Biddle, R. (2006), "A Usability Study and Critique of Two Password Managers." *USENIX Security Symposium*, pp. 1-16.

Communications-Electronics Security Group (2016), "Password Guidance: Simplifying Your Approach." Technical report.

Erceg-Hurn, D. M. and Mirosevich, V. M. (2008), "Modern robust statistical methods: an easy way to maximize the accuracy and power of your research." *American Psychologist*, Vol. 63, No. 7, pp. 591-601.

Herley, C. (2009), "So long, and no thanks for the externalities: the rational rejection of security advice by users." *Proceedings of the 2009 workshop on New security paradigms workshop*, pp. 133-144.

Hoonakker, P., Bornoe, N. and Carayon, P. (2009), "Password authentication from a human factors perspective: Results of a survey among end-users." *Proceedings of the Human Factors and Ergonomics Society Annual Meeting*, Vol. 53, No. 6, pp. 459-463.

Kajzer, M., D'Arcy, J., Crowell, C. R., Striegel, A. and Van Bruggen, D. (2014), "An exploratory investigation of message-person congruence in information security awareness campaigns." *Computers & security*, Vol. 43, pp. 64-76.

Kotadia, M. (2005), "Microsoft security guru: Jot down your passwords". https://www.cnet.com/news/microsoft-security-guru-jot-down-your-passwords/ [visited: 09.08.2016]

Lebek, B., Uffen, J., Neumann, M., Hohler, B. and H. Breitner, M. (2014), "Information security awareness and behavior: a theory-based literature review", *Management Research Review*, Vol. 37, No. 12, pp. 1049-1092.

Mayer, P., Kunz, A. and Volkamer, M. (2017), "Reliable Behavioural Factors in the Information Security Context." *Proceedings of the 12th International Conference on Availability, Reliability and Security*, No. 9.

Murray, H. and Malone, D. (2017), "Evaluating password advice," *Irish Signals and Systems Conference*.

Grassi, P.A. et al., 2017. Digital Identity Guidelines: Authentication and Lifecycle Management, National Institute of Standards and Technology.

Olembo, M. M., Renaud, K., Bartsch, S. and Volkamer, M. (2014), "Voter, what message will motivate you to verify your vote." *Workshop on Usable Security*.

Schiefele, U. (2009), "Interest and Learning From Text." *Scientific Studies of Reading*, Vol. 3, No. 3, pp. 257–279.

Schneier, B. (2005), "Write Down Your Password", https://www.schneier.com/blog/archives/2005/06/write_down_your.html [visited: 09.08.2016]

Siponen, M., Adam Mahmood, M. and Pahnila, S. (2014), "Employees' adherence to information security policies: An exploratory field study." *Information & management*, Vol. 51, No. 2, pp. 217–224.

Siponen, M., & Vance, A. (2010), "Neutralization: new insights into the problem of employee information systems security policy violations." *MIS quarterly*, pp. 487-502.

Stobert, E. (2014), "The agony of passwords: can we learn from user coping strategies?." *CHI'14 Extended Abstracts on Human Factors in Computing Systems*, pp. 975-980.

Stobert, E. and Biddle, R. (2015), "Expert password management." *International Conference on Passwords*, pp. 3-20.

The Quest to Replace Passwords Revisited – Rating Authentication Schemes

V. Zimmermann[1], N. Gerber[2], M. Kleboth[1], A. von Preuschen[1], K. Schmidt[1] and P. Mayer[2]

[1]FAI - Work and Engineering Psychology - Technische Universität Darmstadt
[2]SECUSO - Security, Usability, and Society, Karlsruhe Institute for Technology
e-mail: zimmermann@psychologie.tu-darmstadt.de

Abstract

Six years ago Bonneau et al. (2012) proposed a framework to comparatively evaluate authentication schemes. They applied their framework to 35 different authentication schemes to identify alternatives to the ubiquitous text password. However, in their work no sole authentication scheme proved to be suitable for every application scenario, hence the quest to replace passwords has not yet been solved. This paper revisits the rating process and describes the application of an extended version of the original framework to an additional 40 authentication schemes identified in a literature review. All schemes were rated in terms of 25 objective features assigned to the three main criteria usability, deployability, and security. The rating process and results are presented along with a discussion of the benefits and pitfalls of the rating process. Our goal thereby is not to claim victory over text passwords, but to help decision makers in identifying suitable authentication schemes for their specific application scenario. The results were also made publicly available in an authentication choice support system named ACCESS to foster the further extension of the knowledge base and future development of the rating process.

Keywords

Authentication Scheme, Password, Rating, ACCESS

1. Introduction

Authentication has long become an integral part of daily life. Every single authentication process provides access to private data like emails, account data, personal documents, or photos. A loss thereof to an unauthorized third party can thus have a huge impact on private life or businesses. The password as an authentication scheme still is ubiquitous. Although it is often used for various reasons such as low technical requirements or habit, the security of the scheme very much depends on the end user. With every new user account and every new password cognitive load is increasing so that usability is often preferred over security by users: For example, users often choose the same password across accounts, keep an insecurely stored written record or choose unsecure dictionary passwords (e.g., Adams *et al.* 1997, Johnson and Grawemeyer, 2011, Wash *et al.*, 2016).

To mitigate the issues associated with text passwords, many alternative schemes have been developed including biometric or token-based schemes. Bonneau *et al.* (2012) compared these to the text password across a variety of features and, surprisingly, found that replacing the password was not as easy as imagined. None of the analyzed schemes received high scores in all of the three evaluated categories usability, deployability, and security. Still, the comparison has proven to be very helpful in identifying authentication schemes best-suited for a certain purpose or certain requirements in research and practice alike. Thus, the initial work by Bonneau *et al.* (2012) serves as a basis for the evaluation of further authentication schemes. To realize an even more objective evaluation with an increased differentiation between authentication schemes additional sub features have been formulated by Mayer *et al.* (2016). The sub features were formulated as partially exclusive axioms to clearly allocate a scheme to a certain class of features.

Application of the evaluation framework by Bonneau *et al.* (2012) and the refinement of Mayer *et al.* (2016) facilitates an objective comparison between authentication schemes and allows for the selection of schemes fulfilling specific application requirements. However, while their results demonstrate the suitability of the rating for researchers and practitioners, the coverage of authentication schemes by their work is still very limited. Mayer *et al.* (2016) applied their finer-grained ratings only to the original data set from Bonneau *et al.* (2012) and an additional ten schemes. Compared to these 45 schemes, a far greater number of schemes have been proposed in the literature and decision-makers in research and practice would greatly benefit from an update and extension of the data set to choose suitable authentication schemes from. In order to advance the diversity of authentication scheme in the rated pool, this paper describes the process and results of a rating of 40 additional authentication schemes identified in the literature. The core contributions of this work are three-fold:

1. The pool of authentication schemes rated using the same methodology is significantly extended from 45 to 85. Thereby, not only the number, but also the diversity in the pool of available schemes is increased. This extension offers decision makers a greater selection when choosing appropriate authentication schemes for their specific application scenarios.

2. The ratings are integrated into the free, online authentication choice support system ACCESS (Renaud et al., 2014; SECUSO, 2016) so that practitioners and researchers can easily benefit from our results.

3. The advantages and pitfalls of the rating process are discussed to support others in the future rating of authentication schemes and to provide a starting point for solving ambiguous results within the community.

The remainder of the paper is structured as follows. Section 2 describes the methodology of the rating process. Section 3 presents exemplarily the rating results. Due to space constraints, the complete rating results are made available within ACCESS (c.f. contribution 2). In section 4, use cases as well as advantages and limitations of the rating process are discussed. Finally, section 5 concludes the paper.

2. Method

One of the primary goals of this research was to supplement and update the original rating of authentication schemes by Bonneau *et al.* (2012). Further, the aim was to increase the level of detail and thereby the usefulness of the rating for researchers and practitioners. To that end, a literature search via Google Scholar was conducted which revealed a total of 164 relevant publications dealing with authentication schemes. All publications addressed or evaluated the user interaction with or perception of the authentication schemes. Papers only describing technical aspects or algorithms were not considered. From the analysis 40 authentication schemes which were not already included in the rating by Bonneau *et al.* (2012) could be extracted. Even though all schemes were extracted from research papers, a significant number of these schemes are actually used in practice, e.g., Challenge Questions, Face Recognition, Passphrases, and Google's Android Pattern Unlock.

Our second step was to rate the schemes according to the 63 sub features specified by Mayer *et al.* (2016) and shown in Appendix B. These were derived from the original 25 features of authentication schemes as defined by Bonneau *et al.* (2012). The sub features are extensions of the original features and provide a more detailed way to evaluate authentication schemes. For example, the feature "Accessible" is split into the three sub features "Accessible with Read/Write-Impairments", "Accessible with Visual Impairments" and "Accessible with Physical Impairments". They are also partially exclusive in that a scheme can only fulfil one of the sub features but not two at the same time. This allows for the allocation of schemes to distinctive classes. An example for this is the feature "Proprietary" with the sub features "Proprietary" or "Non-Proprietary".

The rating process was structured as follows: similar to Bonneau *et al.* (2012) three of the authors each rated a subset of the 40 identified authentication schemes in terms of every sub feature. Any arising questions or problems were discussed within the research group including an additional three independent researchers. Whenever possible, the rating was based on the description of the scheme or other data provided by the authors in the original publication. Where the original publication was not available or sufficient, e.g. where the scheme was only described in a review paper, additional literature describing the scheme was considered. In case a publication did not provide any specifics regarding a criterion, e.g., because the scheme was presented only on a conceptual level, the rating was logically derived from the description of the scheme. For example, even though some descriptions of biometric schemes did not actually state the number of secrets to remember to rate the feature "Memorywise-Effortless" the information was logically derived from the conceptual approach which is based on detecting biometric features that users carry with them naturally and do not have to remember. All ratings were conducted for using the authentication scheme with a PC or laptop.

In general, the ratings of authentication schemes widely used in various forms and without an identifiable "original" publication such as the fingerprint scheme or different password schemes were based on the *concept* of the scheme, rather than the specifics of a *certain implementation*. The idea behind this approach was that a scheme should not be excluded by a decision-maker beforehand due to a low rating based on a single implementation. A researcher or practitioner deciding to use such a scheme could easily adapt certain aspects of an implementation according to his or her context of use. An example is setting a limit to the number of login attempts allowed before temporarily blocking an account, which affects the rating of the feature "Resilient-to-Throttled-Guessing". To preserve internal consistency, all new schemes were also compared to the ones that had already been rated by Bonneau *et al.* (2012) and Mayer *et al.* (2016) thus giving similar authentication schemes identical ratings. Examples include the already rated "Iris Scan" that shares features with the newly added "Retina Scan".

3. Results

Due to space constraints, the rating results will be presented exemplarily for three authentication schemes and two usability, deployability and security features each. The three exemplary schemes are Retina Scan, Google's Android Pattern Unlock and the scheme Déjà Vu as proposed Dhamija and Perrig (2000). The complete rating results can be accessed online and via ACCESS (see Appendix A).

Retina Scan is a biometric authentication scheme that identifies the user by his/her unique patterns on the retina blood vessels (Figure 1a). The patterns are detected optically by casting an unperceived beam of low-energy infrared light into the user's eye and measuring the absorption levels of light. In general, an appropriate scanner is required to perform the authentication. The Retina Scan is different from the Iris Scan where near infrared images of the iris are used for authentication. Similar to the Finger Print the Retina Scan is a general concept with a variety of implementations.

Android Pattern Unlock is a recall-based graphical authentication scheme mainly used on mobile phones. To authenticate the user draws a memorized path visiting up to nine dots on a 3x3 grid. Each dot can only be visited once (Figure 1b).

Déjà Vu is a recognition-based graphical scheme. The user memorizes a portfolio of pictures, which are algorithmically generated from random seeds (see Figure 1c). During authentication the user is provided with a challenge set that contains some of the images from his/her portfolio as well as a number of distractors. The user's task is to identify the previously chosen images from the challenge set. In contrast to the more general concept of retina scans, Déja Vu is described as a specific authentication scheme with an original publication and implementation details.

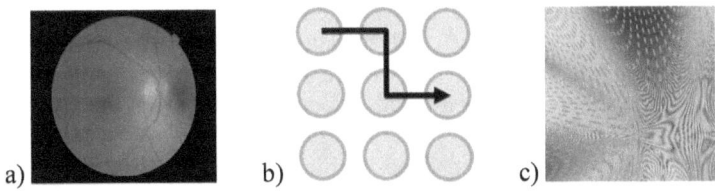

a)   b)   c)

Figure 1: a) Retinal blood vessels used for Retina Scans, b) Android Pattern Unlock, c) Random art "Déjà Vu" picture from www.random-art.org

Usability. In the usability category Bonneau's feature "Memorywise-effortless" is split into the three exclusive sub features: "No-Secret-to-Remember", "One-Secret-to-Remember" and "More-than-One-Secret-to-Remember". As Retina Scans solely rely on measurable characteristics of the user, they are assigned the feature "No-Secret-to-Remember". "One-Secret-to-Remember" is mainly provided by systems like single sign-on services that require only a single secret to gain access to multiple different systems. This is not the case for Déjà Vu and Android Pattern Unlock, which require the user to create a new, individual secret for each verifier and consequently were rated "More-than-one-Secret-to-Remember". Moreover, according to the original publication the scheme Déjà Vu requires the user to be able to recognize multiple pictures per login.

The schemes Déjà Vu and Android Pattern lock were rated "easy-recovery-from-loss" as forgotten or stolen secrets could easily be replaced by new ones without having to overcome unreasonable burdens, e.g. by sending a recovery link via email. In contrast, Retina Scan was rated as "no-easy-recovery-from-loss" as a compromised account or a physical inability to further use the scheme results in having to replace the scheme with an alternative one.

Deployability. In terms of deployability the feature "Negligible-Cost-per-User" is considered. For retinal scans the standard cameras in laptops and smartphones are not feasible as measuring instruments. Thus, the user or service provider has to purchase additional scanning devices which results in high acquisition costs. Accordingly, Retina Scans were rated to have "Non-Negligible-cost-per-User". The scheme Déja Vu can be used with any standard PC and browser so that no additional devices have to be acquired. And even though Déjà Vu requires the verifier to store multiple seed values for the generated pictures in a secure manner, the resulting costs were considered to be negligible which resulted in the "Negligible-Cost-per-User" rating. From a technical perspective Android Pattern Unlock also requires negligible-cost-per-user for implementation. It can theoretically be used with any mobile phone, PCs with a touch screen and standard PCs using a mouse to draw the path in the grid. Still, the scheme has been developed and patented by Google (Google Inc., 2011). As we were not able to quantify potential license fees, e.g., for commercial purposes, we assumed "negligible-cost-per-user" but marked with a "?".

Another deployability feature is the maturity of the schemes. Google's Android Pattern Unlock is well studied in the literature and widely used in large number of Android mobile phones. Similarly, Retina Scans have been studied in academia and are used in practice, e.g., by government agencies, for medical purposes and ATM identity verification. Both schemes were thus granted all three sub features "adopted-in-academics", "adopted-repeatedly" and "adopted-beyond-academics". Déjà Vu has been proposed in the literature, but we are not aware of an application outside academia. The schemes was thus granted "adopted-in-academics" only.

Security. A scheme is considered "Non-Resilient-to-Phishing" if a potential attacker only needs to feign the identity of the verifier to obtain authentication credentials from users. More sophisticated methods of phishing, for example schemes that require the attacker to pose as a user and as a verifier are not considered in the definition by Mayer *et al.* (2016). As the Retina Scan and Android Pattern Unlock only involve a static characteristic, namely the unique patterns on the retina blood vessels and the string resulting from the path on the grid respectively, and an attacker only needs to pose as a verifier we rated the method as "Non-Resilient-to-Phishing". In contrast the Déjà Vu scheme is rated "Resilient-to-Phishing", as the attacker first needs to pose as the user to obtain the user specific challenge, which he or she then needs to present when posing as verifier. Additionally, it is not possible to obtain the entire user portfolio within one trial, since only a subset of chosen pictures is presented in each challenge set.

As the schemes Déjà Vu and Android Pattern Unlock require an active user input, they cannot be executed without the user's consent and are thus granted the feature "requiring-explicit-consent". The scheme Retina Scan requires a certain scanning device and an exact positioning of the user. It is thus unlikely that the authentication takes place without the user noticing. The scheme was therefore rated "requiring-explicit-consent" as well. Still, it is possible to track certain other biometrics, e.g., capturing the face with a camera or the keystroke dynamics while typing, without the user taking notice which would result in the rating "non-requiring-explicit-consent".

4. Discussion

The following section presents examples for the application of the rating by researchers and practitioners and discusses benefits and limitations of the rating process in its current form. Further, an outlook on the application of the rating within ACCESS (Mayer, *et al.* 2016) is provided.

4.1. Application of the Rating by Researchers

The results of the rating process can be useful for authentication research as they allow researchers to quickly identify appropriate authentication schemes for study purposes or software applications developed within a research project. It further allows a thorough comparison of newly developed authentication schemes with a variety of existing approaches on the three categories usability, deployability and security. One practical example for the use of the rating is a project on user-friendly authentication and encryption within the Centre for Research in Security and Privacy (CRISP). Within the project certain limitations for the choice of the authentication scheme exist, e.g., it should be cost-free for the user, deployable in web browsers, and users should not need to carry additional items for authentication. Further, even though it is impossible to determine an absolute security value, the authentication scheme (and thus the encrypted communication) should be resistant to a variety of attacks and relatively secure compared to other authentication schemes. First, the rating process described here allowed for excluding authentication schemes that did not meet the criteria set in the project and rank others in terms of the remaining objective security, usability and deployability features. Second, the rating was used to identify the best performing schemes out of five different categories, such as knowledge-based and biometric schemes. The resulting schemes were analysed in terms of user perceptions in a laboratory study revealing three schemes preferred by the participants. These three schemes will now be evaluated against each other, e.g., within mock-ups, to identify the most suitable one for this use case.

4.2. Application of the Rating by Practitioners

Practitioners may use the results of the rating for similar purposes as researchers, e.g. for study purposes or for comparing own with existing approaches. Apart from that, the rating may support practitioners in identifying an appropriate authentication scheme for their service, web application, or product. It provides an overview over a range of existing schemes and, similar to the research example described above, allows excluding schemes that do not meet the requirements given by the product or the target user group.

4.3. Benefits and Limitations of the Rating Process

As described above, the rating process provides a number of benefits for researchers and practitioners alike: support in the choice of an existing authentication scheme for one's own application or study, a comparison of new schemes with existing ones, and requirement- as well as context-based ratings of authentication schemes. Still, the rating process in its current form and the results described here suffer from several shortcomings that should be acknowledged and addressed in the future:

First, the rating process was based on the literature available to us. Some schemes, e.g., "Marbles" (von Zezschwitz *et al.,* 2013) which is an authentication scheme originally designed for smart phones with the aim to avoid smudge attacks were only described in a few papers or on a conceptual level. In particular, some details and technical information necessary for the rating were not available, so that the rating had to be based on similar schemes and/or logically derived from the conceptual approach. For the future the rating would thus benefit from being checked for correctness by the developers of the rated authentication schemes that are experts for their work. Other schemes, however, were described in many papers and in many different forms or implementations. One example is keystroke dynamics, where various implementations and service providers exist. In this case, the broader concept of authentication using keystroke dynamics independent from a single implementation was rated. In cases where this was not possible, we searched for review papers or a "common" way of implementation. Still, for future work it might be beneficial to rate and name different implementations separately and include the reference to the developers of that implementation.

Second, the rating was conducted at one point in time and with certain search terms and thus does not claim to cover an exhaustive list of existing authentication schemes. Besides, it is possible that schemes have been developed and improved further or that schemes are not available any more. To provide a valuable and actual resource for researchers and practitioners it would therefore be beneficial if the database would be regularly checked and updated by members of the community.

One way to allow for the checking of the rating scores by the developers of authentication schemes and the regular updating of the database by the community is provided by ACCESS, the authentication choice system that is presented in more detail in section 4.4.

4.4. Outlook

The rating process described in this paper was purposefully based on the criteria used within ACCESS of which a first version has already been presented in Renaud *et al.* (2014) and implemented by Mayer *et al.* (2016). A second version has now been released (Mayer *et al*, 2018). ACCESS supports authentication researchers and practitioners in providing information on the included authentication schemes (information module) and showing the five most suitable schemes given the weighting or exclusion of certain sub features according to the usage scenario (decision support module). The third feature, the discussion module, allows for updating and extending the knowledge base with additional authentication schemes.

For researchers and practitioners alike, the major benefit of ACCESS is that it presents the results of the rating process described above in a comprehensive and easily manageable form. All schemes are briefly described so that also practitioners not familiar with the schemes are provided with basic information. The decision support module allows for an easy individualization of the decision process for an authentication scheme. For example, developers of an online web service might assign high priority to browser-compatibility and likely aim to exclude costly schemes. They could easily arrange these features according to their preference in a drag and drop menu and be provided with a list of the best performing schemes given their individual use case.

To be consistent with the ACCESS knowledge base, the aforementioned ratings were used to generate equivalence classes for all authentication schemes similar to Mayer *et al.* (2016). The final step has been the transfer of the rating results presented here to the ACCESS database, thereby increasing the number of included authentication schemes from 45 to 85. With the provision of our results within ACCESS we hope to allow a large number of researchers and practitioners to benefit from our work. Further, we hope to thereby encourage other members of the community to add further schemes to the platform and participate in discussing and solving potential ambiguities in the rating process.

5. Conclusion

This paper describes the rating process of 40 authentication schemes in terms of the three categories usability, security and deployability based on the framework introduced by Bonneau *et al.* (2012) and refined by Mayer *et al.* (2016). The rating offers researchers as well as practitioners an aid in the choice of appropriate authentication schemes for their specific application scenarios and allows comparisons with newly developed schemes. To make the results easily available for the community, the rating results have been included into the knowledge base of ACCESSv2 (SECUSO, 2016), an authentication choice support system that allows the requirement-based rating of the authentication schemes. ACCESS also enables regular updating and correction of the data by the community and the developers of authentication schemes. Finally, the advantages and pitfalls of the rating process were discussed to support others in the future rating of authentication schemes and to provide a starting point for solving ambiguous results within the community.

6. Acknowledgement

The research reported in this paper was supported by the German Federal Ministry of Education and Research (BMBF) and by the Hessian Ministry of Science and the Arts within CRISP (www.crisp-da.de/). This work was further supported by the German Federal Ministry of Education and Research in the Competence Center for Applied Security Technology (KASTEL).

7. References

Adams, A., Sasse, M. A., and Lunt, P. (1997), "Making passwords secure and usable.", in *People and Computers XII*, pp1-19, Springer, London.

Bonneau, J., Herley, C., van Oorschot, P.C. and Stajano, F. (2012), "The Quest to Replace Passwords: A Framework for Comparative Evaluation of Web Authentication Schemes", in *Proceedings of the IEEE Symposium on Security and Privacy 2012*, pp553-567, IEEE.

Dhamija, R. and Perrig, A. (2000, August), "Deja Vu-A User Study: Using Images for Authentication", in *Proceedings of the 9th USENIX Security Symposium*, Usenix.

Google Inc. (2011). *US Patent No. 20110283241*, Touch Gesture Actions From A Device's Lock Screen. Washington, D.C.: US Patent & Trademark Office.

Grawemeyer, B. and Johnson, H. (2011), "Using and managing multiple passwords: A week to a view. ", *Interact. Comput. 23*, pp256–267, doi: 10.1016/j.intcom.2011.03.007.

Mayer, P., Neumann, S., Storck, D. and Volkamer, M. (2016), "Supporting Decision Makers in Choosing Suitable Authentication Schemes", in *Proceedings of the Tenth International Symposium on Human Aspects of Information Security & Assurance (HAISA 2016)*, pp67-77.

Mayer, P., Stumpf, P., Weber, T., Volkamer, M. (2018), ACCESSv2: A Collaborative Authentication Research and Decision Support Platform, Who Are You?! Adventures in Authentication.

Renaud, K., Volkamer, M. and Maguire, J. (2014, June), "ACCESS: Describing and Contrasting", in *International Conference on Human Aspects of Information Security, Privacy, and Trust*, pp183-194, Springer, Cham.

Von Zezschwitz, E., Koslow, A., De Luca, A. and Hussmann, H. (2013, March), "Making graphic-based authentication secure against smudge attacks", in *Proceedings of the 2013 international conference on Intelligent user interfaces*, pp277-286, ACM.

Wash, R., Rader, E., Berman, R. and Wellmer, Z. (2016, June), "Understanding password choices: How frequently entered passwords are re-used across websites", in *Symposium on Usable Privacy and Security (SOUPS)*, pp175-188, Usenix.

Appendix A: Online-Appendix

The complete results and a description of the rated authentication schemes and rating features can be accessed with the following link: http://www.arbing.psychologie.tu-darmstadt.de/home/forschung_4/forschungsergebnisse_fai.de.jsp

The rating results are further integrated in ACCESS: https://access.secuso.org/

Appendix B: Rating Features

Figure 2: Categories, features (Bonneau *et al.*, 2012) and sub features (Mayer *et al.*, 2016) applied in the rating process.

An Authentic Self:
Big Data and Passive Digital Footprints

L. Y. Williams[1] and D. M. Pennington[2]

[1]Faculty, MSIT, MSCM, School of Business and Information Technology, Purdue Global University
[2]Department of Computer and Information Sciences, The University of Strathclyde, United Kingdom
email: lwilliams4@purdueglobal.edu; diane.pennington@strath.ac.uk

Abstract

The ability to allow users to create online communities of interest and to share a variety of personal information, collectively referred to as social media, is gradually being built into an expanding range of applications. Some of these applications, such as computer operating systems, were not originally intended to collect information from the user. Thus, users may not be aware that their digital information is being collected. Devices such as smart televisions, smart cars, and even smart grids, are now collecting massive quantities of user data without the user's knowledge. Users of social media, and the internet in general, leave fragments of their activities and intentions behind them across an increasing range of technologies. These fragments collectively and passively create a hidden identity built up from metadata of which the user is mostly unaware. Given that the user builds this hidden identity during the normal course of their day, without editing elements that the user may not wish to share with others, might the passive digital footprint more accurately reveal the individual's genuine or authentic self than the individual realises? We propose that an aggregated, passively collected digital portrait of a user's unconscious but connected activities may reveal a more genuine view of that person's self than would be deduced from sources over which the user has conscious control. This more accurate and potentially revealing portrait of the individual requires a review of how privacy has been classically defined in both legal as well as ethical constructs.

Keywords

Passive digital footprint, data analytics, privacy, identity, Internet of Things, linkage attack, Big Data

1   The ubiquitous collection of personal data

Akamai (2016), a global leader in content delivery systems, estimates that as of the first quarter in 2016 there were well over a billion internet users. Internet users now have access to an unprecedented range of media content as well as tapping into connected services that allow them to monitor and control devices attached to the Internet of Things [IoT]. As IoT devices are used to deliver and manage these services, the devices themselves are collecting usage data. Many IoT systems are not immediately recognizable as a connected device and are often deployed as an embedded or mobile application connected to the internet using a variety of wireless technologies, such as radio-frequency identification [RFID] and Bluetooth.

Users of technology now feed a constant stream of personal data to dozens of applications and devices, either consciously by using social media and communal gaming or unconsciously through their interaction with their vehicles, smart televisions, household equipment, and cyberphysical systems [CPS] deployed in their community. Sadeghi et. al. (2015) note that "smart products do not only collect data during their production but also when they are deployed and used by customers", with the data being stored either by the vendor or on the device itself.

Although exacerbated by the relatively recent explosion of IoT deployment, the privacy concerns surrounding ubiquitous data collection are not new. In 2007, a pair of researchers at The University of Texas at Austin revealed the vulnerability of private data, even data collected in a supposedly anonymous fashion. Greengard (2008, pg. 17) states that this research "proved that it was possible to identify individuals among a half-million participants by using public reviews published in the Internet Movie Database (IMDb) to identify movie ratings within Netflix's data. In fact, eight ratings along with dates were enough to provide 99% accuracy, according to the researchers". Note that this research was done 11 years ago; the technology has advanced considerably since that time.

The aggregation technique used by the University of Texas researchers is known as a linkage attack. A linkage attack combines individually non-sensitive or anonymized data with data from other records until a highly accurate aggregated profile of the user is assembled.

Lawfully deployed data analytics present no less of a threat to an individual's privacy. Over the past couple of decades, several attempts have been made to protect an individual's personal data from data mining exposure. In the United States, this type of safeguard usually falls within the scope of various governmental security standards or regulations such as HIPAA (2017), which protects the privacy of Americans' personally identifying health information. Unfortunately, these types of standards do not exist in many business contexts.

Many internet users are unaware of how exposed their personal data may be. Most users now realize that they should protect personal data residing on their computers with anti-malware software and should also be leery of unsolicited email. At the same time, internet users have been slow to realize that every time they use an internet-connected device of any type, either consciously or unconsciously, a trail of artefacts recording that activity is left behind. Digital artifacts can include obvious, consciously created information, such as email, instant messaging, and social media posts. More insidious is unconsciously created data which includes web search histories, cell phone or Global Positioning System [GPS] locations, even metadata gleaned from commonly used office applications.

Location tracking can reveal more about an individual's activities and relationships than simply where the person is located at any given point. As the Me and My Shadow website (2017) comments:

Location data can also be used to map out your relationships with others. If you and another person, or other people, are in the same place at specific times of the day, it's possible to infer what relationships you have with these people - if, for example, they are co-workers, lovers, roommates, or family members.

Or, to take another example, if you are a government employee and are in the same cafe as a specific journalist, you could be flagged as a leaker.

Location data is collected by a myriad of devices and sensors. Mobile phones log location information and can easily serve as a GPS device. Mobile location services use the GPS chip in the phone which then communicates with standard GPS satellites. This type of tracking leaves a range of artefacts that are accessible to anyone or anything, such as phone apps, that have access to the device. Mobile devices that are capable of connecting to Wi-Fi collect additional location artefacts and keep logs of all the locations where the device connected to Wi-Fi, giving an even more detailed picture of where the device has been.

2 Examples of unconsciously provided personal data

During an average internet session, a user may be asked several times by an array of entities to provide personal data for a variety of reasons. Perhaps a user is asked to provide a valid name and address to a website to make a purchase, or the user may have to provide an e-mail address to another website to subscribe to a newsletter. These are examples of providing information consciously, but a rapidly increasing percentage of personal data is now collected unconsciously.

A growing number of online entities that were originally designed as social media platforms are evolving into large scale data analytics sites. In this trend, the social media serves as a front end for users while the genuine purpose of the site is to gather personal information both consciously and unconsciously. Drachen et. al. (2012) note that free-to-play [F2P] games provided by Facebook and Google Play aid their ability to analyse player behaviours. This analysis in turn increases potential monetization by understanding player interaction with the games. Ahmad and Srivastava (2014) state that the immersive nature of online gaming environments encourages players to engage with the game, revealing a range of behaviours, such as cooperation or deceit. Given the exposure of player characteristics, these gaming environments provide unprecedented opportunities for studying human behaviour in a granular fashion.

Chen et. al. (2015) provide an overview of an even more widespread and invasive vector of unconsciously provided personal information. The Internet of Things integrates classically networked industrial objects with a massive number of personal objects such as household video cameras and smart televisions. While clustering behavioural patterns can provide general insight into object usage, using the public internet as a transmission conduit makes identifying individual users of objects relatively trivial.

Another major source of unconsciously provided personal information resides in mobile devices such as smartphones and tablets. Most cell phones manufactured within the last four or five years allow the handset to switch between "Wi-Fi" (IEEE 802.11 standard) and cellular radio signals. While 1st and 2nd generation cellular signal is relatively impervious to useful interception, 3rd generation signal is somewhat more vulnerable. Given that 3rd generation signal [3G] enhances the ability to transmit data as well as voice, the potential for extracting unconsciously provided personal information from both signal as well as device storage becomes obvious. Goda et. al. (2015) outline the various types of information available on a mobile device and the methods for data extraction from both signal transmission and the handset. Among the types of information that can reside in a smartphone, Casey (2011) describes:

> Although compact, these handheld devices can contain personal information including call history, text messages, e-mails, digital photographs, videos, calendar items, memos, address books, passwords, and credit card numbers. These devices can be used to communicate, exchange photographs, connect to social networks, blog, take notes, record and consume video and audio, sketch, access the Internet, and much more. As the technology develops, higher data transmission rates are allowing individuals to transfer more data (e.g., digital video), and the computing power in these devices enables us to use them in much the same way as we used laptop systems over the past decade. Because these devices fit in a pocket or bag, they are often carried wherever a person goes and can be used to determine a person's whereabouts at a particular time.

Insel (2017) comments on other human characteristics that may be derived from mobile device use. The author notes that the manner in which a device is used, including typing and scrolling patterns, can be used to deduce a range of behavioural aspects. Keyboard interaction with a mobile device can reveal the subject's reaction time, attention span, and memory reliability. This data can then be used to deduce the user's behavioural tendencies, cognition, and even mood at the time of use.

3   Integrating data analytics with digital forensics

Digital forensics, data analytics, and linkage attacks share many of the same techniques for aggregating data to form a profile of a user, varying mostly by intent of use. Digital forensics is an extension of traditional evidence gathering and is associated with the investigation of data found on a variety of devices and networks. Data analytics is not necessarily concerned with identification of an individual or that person's activities but is rather a means of deriving patterns and relationships from large data sets i.e. Big Data. Linkage attacks can be defined as the "de-anonymization" of data provided by or about an individual, derived by analysing data relationships contained in two or more unrelated databases. Merener (2012, pg. 378) comments that anonymization typically removes "the variables that uniquely associate records to the corresponding individuals, such as name, email address, social security number". The author then notes that this step is insufficient to prevent algorithmic linkage of other variables in the data that can still serve as a type of digital fingerprint.

Shen et. al. (2014) discuss a more targeted type of linkage attack, a "User Identity Linkage Attack", which can link an individual's information across a range of online social networks. When data analytics and/or linkage attack methods are combined with digital forensics, the raw data derived by use of forensic techniques can then be analysed with a high degree of accuracy regarding the identity and activities of the individual under analysis. In addition, because a major goal of digital forensics is to provide nonrepudiation of evidence, the resulting profile gained by combining these tools is unlikely to have been modified by the individual, which lends a greater degree of veracity to the profile.

Digital forensics adhere to the legal rules of evidence as practiced in the location where the forensics operation takes place. Traditionally, digital forensics has been used to collect data that a suspect may have stored on physical media, such as a hard drive. Where digital forensics begin to raise concerns regarding an individual's passive digital footprint is when it is combined with sensor data provided by IoT devices. Caviglione et. al. (2017) note that common types of IoT implementations create an intersection between the digital world and the physical world through the use of sensors. The authors state:

> For example, IoT nodes can provide evidence of when a person was present in a room by investigating in-door presence sensor values. Obviously, such investigations are linked to further privacy issues, especially as sensors might be influenced not only by a single user but by an undefined set of influencers: several individuals could trigger a presence sensor in a room each day, not just the potential criminal.

This blurring of personal data as it exists in the digital world with its physical counterpart allows the investigator to assemble an extremely accurate portrait of a suspect. If this portrait were placed in the hands of a corporate or governmental entity, the privacy implications are disturbing.

4 Does unconsciously provided personal information reveal the "authentic self"?

Users of social media consciously craft an online identity and may compile a set of differing identities based on what the user perceives as different audiences. Matic's (2011, pg. 20) research indicates that "users constantly assess their online environment and based on their assessment they construct their own Internet playground where they choose roles they find suitable". So, what would unconsciously provided personal information reveal about an individual? Linking and analysing relationships between an individual's differing self-constructed identities would provide insights into that individual's consciously provided self-perception. If unconsciously provided personal information is added to that analysis, as is commonly done in digital forensics, the elements of intent, motivation, and exposure of deception come into play.

5 Discussion

Williams and Neal (2012) point out the similarities in technique between data mining and linkage attacks, stating that both types of information gathering and analysis pose a similar risk of personal data exposure. When digital forensics techniques are added, the combination of consciously and unconsciously generated data makes identifying an individual and that individual's activities, behaviours, and motivation relatively straightforward.

Analysis of a job candidate's social media information has become an accepted practice for human resource departments in the United States. Data analytics is also increasingly used by educational institutions to guide students toward courses and subjects where they may have a greater chance of academic success, based on their individual characteristics as revealed by the data. As Johnson (2014) notes, there are inherent ethical dilemmas in this type of "technosocial" system, which can include reducing an individual's autonomy over their own aggregated profile. Pistilli et. al. (2014) go further to state that acting on insights gained from data analytics presents the possibility of social engineering, which may or may not be advantageous or helpful to the individual whose data is analysed.

The use of continually refined data analytics, combined with the possible inclusion of digital forensics to add unconsciously provided data to the digital profile, provides a path to discovering more about an individual than would be uncovered through consciously provided information. Indeed, the combined data would likely provide deeper insight into an individual's characteristics, motivations, and actions than personal introspection might reveal. This ability to track a person's actions across a broad range of devices is unparalleled in history. The unguarded nature of much of this data provides an unprecedented opportunity to observe an individual's behaviour in a deeper manner than has ever been possible before.

Fairfield and Shtein (2014, pg. 39) state "[t]he nature of big data technology fundamentally challenges traditional methods of framing ethical principles". The traditional ethical and legal definitions of privacy are no longer sufficient for dealing with the overwhelming quantity and detail of personal data being generated by individuals both consciously and unconsciously. The changing nature of Big Data and the resulting analytically derived information will require legislators and businesses to develop more flexible and sophisticated ethical constructs to deal with the sheer quantity of personal data available, as well as the minefield of revelation embedded within that data.

6 References

Ahmad, M.A., & Srivastava, J. Behavioral data mining and network analysis in massive online games. *Proceedings of the 7th ACM International Conference on Web Search and Data Mining*, 673-674, 2014. doi:10.1145/2556195.2556196

Akamai's State of the Internet Report Q1 2016. (2016). Retrieved from https://www.akamai.com/uk/en/multimedia/documents/state-of-the-internet/akamai-state-of-the-internet-report-q1-2016.pdf

Casey, I. *Digital evidence and computer crime: Forensic science, computers and the Internet.* 2011. Waltham, MA: Academic Press.

Caviglione, L., Wendzel, S. and Mazurczyk, W. (2017). The Future of Digital Forensics: Challenges and the Road Ahead. IEEE Security & Privacy, 15(6), pp.12-17.

Chen, F., Deng, P., Wan, J., Zhang, D., Vasilakos, A.V., & Rong, X. Data mining for the Internet of Things: Literature review and challenges. *International Journal of Distributed Sensor Networks - Special Issue on Big Data and Knowledge Extraction for Cyber-Physical Systems,* 2015. doi:10.1155/2015/431047

Drachen, A., Sifa, R., Bauckhage, C., & Thurau, C. Guns, swords and data: Clustering of player behavior in computer games in the wild. *2012 IEEE Conference on Computational Intelligence and Games (CIG).* doi:10.1109/cig.2012.6374152

Fairfield, J. & Shtein, H. (2014) Big Data, Big Problems: Emerging Issues in the Ethics of Data Science and Journalism, *Journal of Mass Media Ethics,* 29:1, 38-51.

Greengard, S. Privacy matters. *Communications of the ACM 2008, 51*(9), 17-18. doi:10.1145/1378727.1378734

Goda, B.S., Bair, J.W., & Costarella, C.E.. Cell Phone Forensics. *Proceedings of the 16th Annual Conference on Information Technology Education - SIGITE '15, 2015.* doi:10.1145/2808006.2808022

Health Information Privacy. Retrieved from http://www.hhs.gov/hipaa

Insel, T. R., 2017. Digital Phenotyping: Technology for a New Science of Behavior. *Journal of the American Medical Association,* 318:13, 1215 - 1216.

Johnson, J.A., 2014. The Ethics of Big Data in Higher Education. *International Review of Information Ethics,* 7, pp.3–10.

Matic, I., 2011. The Social Construction of Mediated Experience and Self Identity in Social Networking. *The International Journal of Interdisciplinary Social Sciences,* 5, 13 - 21.

Me and My Shadow. 2017. Location tracking. [ONLINE] Available at: https://myshadow.org/location-tracking. [Accessed 9 May 2018].

Merener, M.M. Theoretical Results on De-Anonymization via Linkage Attacks. *Transactions on Data Privacy,* 377-402, 2012. Retrieved November 2, 2017, from http://www.tdp.cat/issues11/tdp.a074a11.pdf

Pistilli, M.D., Willis, J.E., Campbell, J.P. (2014) Analytics Through an Institutional Lens: Definition, Theory, Design, and Impact. In: Larusson J., White B. (eds) Learning Analytics. Springer, New York, NY

Sadeghi, A.R., Wachsmann, C., & Waidner, M. *Security and privacy challenges in industrial internet of things.* Paper presented at the Proceedings of the 52nd Annual Design Automation Conference, San Francisco, California 2015.

Shen, Y., Wang, F. and Jin, H. (2014). Defending against User Identity Linkage Attack across Multiple Online Social Networks. In: *WWW'14 Companion*. Seoul, Korea: ACM, pp.375, 376.

Williams, L. and Neal, D. (2012). The digital aggregated self: A literature review. In: The International Conference on Cyber-enabled Distributed Computing and Knowledge Discovery 2012. Sanya, China: IEEE, pp.170 - 177.

Are Attributes on Social Media Platforms Usable for Assisting in the Automatic Detection of Identity Deception?

E. van der Walt and J.H.P. Eloff

Department of Computer Science, University of Pretoria, South Africa
e-mail: estee.vanderwalt@gmail.com, eloff@cs.up.ac.za

Abstract

Social Media Platforms (SMPs) allow any person to easily communicate with their friends or the general public at large. People can now be targeted at great scale, most often for malicious purposes. The mere fact that more people are using SMPs exposes more people to various forms of cyber threats such as cyber-bullying. The problem is that many of these cyber-attacks involve some form of identity deception, where the attackers lie about who they are. The solution proposed in this paper is to work towards developing a model for Identity Deception Detection (IDD) on SMPs by identifying and using metadata that is freely available on SMPs. This metadata includes attributes that describes a user account on an SMP. The aim is to use only these attributes, as opposed to the contents of a communication, for determining if people are lying about their identities. By discarding contents, an identity deception detection model can be developed with lower overhead. A prototype is discussed that runs an experiment using the metadata (attributes) that defines the identity of a user on an SMP. The results show promise for further research in developing solutions for assisting with the automatic detection of identity deception.

Keywords

Cyber-security, identity deception, fake identities, social media, big data, Twitter

1   Introduction

Today, it is said that over 4 billion people, or more than half of the world's population have access to the Internet and that more than 3.1 billion interact with other people on social media platforms (SMPs) (Chaffey, 2018). This phenomenal growth in the number of online identities resulted in new social interaction abilities on SMPs, being added on a daily basis, with the intention to benefit society at large. Some examples of these benefits include the tracking of natural disasters (Chun et al., 2014) and the prediction of public crowd gatherings (ben Khalifa et al., 2016). However, this growth in the number of online identities not only brought social benefits but also facilitates activities that are deceitful and potentially harmful to societies. Consider for example the online activities in February 2018 where 13 Russians were charged by the United States Justice Department for subverting the 2016 political campaign (Apuzzo and LaFraniere, 2018). They created social media accounts as if they were American citizens with the assumed intention to create discord in the democracy system through the content they posted. In these types of deceitful activities attackers lie about their online identities by providing false information for account attributes on SMPs.

Within the cyber-security world, these types of activities are commonly known as impersonation or identity deception (Donath, 1999). The growth in the number of online identities on SMPs and the resulting voluminous of the data has made it very difficult, if not impossible, to know who to trust on SMPs (Ribeiro et al., 2016). Furthermore, humans are gullible and do not, for example, have the ability to discern the truth from lies (Sandy et al., 2017). SMPs on the other hand allow malicious humans, to deceive (Cook et al., 2014).

The cyber-threat of malicious individuals together with the intrinsic vulnerability of SMPs increase the risk for humans to be exposed to identity deception. Most of the countermeasures available today for minimizing this risk can either be classified as of legal or technological nature. The Children's Internet Protection Act (CIPA) (Kierkegaard, 2008) is a good example of a legal instrument but unfortunately does not address the illegal or harmful use of fake identities. Besides legal instruments, various technologies have been proposed to assist in the protection of humans against identity deception on SMPs, for example, plugins (Rashidi and Fung, 2016), APIs (Muller and Thiesing, 2011), and software systems (Egele et al., 2013). These technologies differ in who they protect from, what deception they can detect, and the various methods used to detect identity deception.

This paper focuses on the technological aspect of countering the act of identity deception. For this paper in particular, an attempt is made to determine attributes of accounts on SMPs that have the potential to assist in the automatic detection of identity deception. The contributions of the research results reported on in this paper are summarized as follows:

- To identify the attributes freely available on SMPs that can play a role in detecting identity deception through a literature review.
- To implement and execute an experiment based on supervised machine learning for assisting the automatic detection of identity deception.

Section 2 of this paper identifies existing identity related attributes found on SMPs. The section furthermore discusses how these attributes have been applied in related work on identity deception detection. This discussion leads into a definition for the requirements, such as to use content from humans only, expected of a prototype aiming to assist in the automatic detection of identity deception on SMPs by humans in section 3. Section 4 proposes a high-level design for the prototype. Sections 5 and 6 explicate and discuss the experimental results following the prototype's implementation.

2   Background and related work

Many examples of cyber threats that have materialised in real-life incidents can be found on SMPs, such as a woman who was falsely lured through Facebook to be killed (de Villiers, 2017). In these cases, the attackers lied by changing various of their social media account attributes that defines their identities to hide who they are. SMP data are mostly known for the content added by its users. Past research used the content itself to detect non-humans accounts, also known as bots (Dickerson et al., 2014)

(Rashidi and Fung, 2016). A challenge was held by DARPA in 2016 to detect bots on Twitter specifically (Subrahmanian et al., 2016). The overall conclusion was that a large set of initial bots can be detected through rules based on heuristics, behaviours, linguistics, and inconsistencies. Noteworthy from the DARPA challenge was that not only the content was used to detect these bots. Besides posting content, SMP users are required to open an account with the SMP before they can start posting content (Facebook, 2017). During this registration process they are requested to give information like their name (Facebook, 2017), location (Twitter, 2018), and even birth date in some cases (LinkedIn, 2017). This data is also generally referred to as metadata or attributes (Sloan et al., 2015). These attributes not only identify the user but also serves to distinguish them from another user. Take Twitter for example. In Twitter, the name of the user and the location are examples of attributes describing the user. It is noticeable that the same attributes are found across the different SMPs. This indicates that a proposal towards detecting identity deception could somehow also apply to other SMPs.

Past related work proposed various identity attributes, and also combined some identity attributes to engineer new features, to detect identity deception. Feature engineering is the process of using domain knowledge to construct new pieces of information (Domingos, 2012). In this case, the attributes available in SMPs are used to create new information about the identity of a user. Lee et al. (Lee et al., 2010), Ribeiro et al. (Ribeiro et al., 2018), and Thomas et al. (Thomas et al., 2013) used linguistic features extracted from various SMPs to detect identity deception. Examples of such linguistic features are: the collection of specific words (Ribeiro et al., 2018), repetitions of content (Lee et al., 2010), and sharing the same naming structure, for example "JohnSmith" being very similar to "JohnSmit2" (Thomas et al., 2013). Non-verbal attributes like the date the account was opened (Tsikerdekis, 2017), the type of SMP (Thomas et al., 2013), and profile update time (Gurajala et al., 2016) were useful where the information provided for an account is scarce. Network features, like accounts in the same domain (Thomas et al., 2013), friends (Gurajala et al., 2016), and followers (Gurajala et al., 2016) were used to detect deception. Lastly, identity attributes like gender (Hancock and Toma, 2009), location (Alowibdi et al., 2015), profile image (Hancock and Toma, 2009), age (Tuna et al., 2016), profession (Tuna et al., 2016), name (Peddinti et al., 2017), and email (Xiao et al., 2015) were proposed indicators towards detecting identity deception. Many of the attributes used to detect identity deception, required additional processing to extract knowledge about the identity of a person. For example, the content had to be parsed for specific words to determine sentiment (Ribeiro et al., 2018) and each profile image was manually labelled to determine of that person was an adult or not (Tuna et al., 2016). This additional work required, adds overhead to a model proposing to assist in the automated detection of human identity deception on SMPs.

Cresci et al. (Cresci et al., 2015) and Varol et al. (Varol et al., 2017) used a combination of attributes and features in their research with the aim of reducing the overhead required to develop an identity deception detection model. They showed that the identity and non-verbal attributes were not only easy to mine, but also just as accurate at detecting identity deception for bots, compared to using network, linguistics, or other content related features. Even though Cresci et al. (Cresci et al., 2015) and Varol et. al (Varol et al., 2017) focussed on detecting deceptive non-human accounts on SMPs, these same SMP attributes apply to humans. For this reason, the authors propose to use the identity and non-verbal attributes on SMPs in an experiment to not only assist in the automated detection of human identity deception, but also to understand which attributes are more indicative of such deceptiveness. The following common attributes, amongst others, were identified in SMPs, like Facebook (Facebook, 2017) and Twitter (Twitter, 2018), through each platform's API reference: the name of the user, their profile image, their location, status description, and the date they created their SMP account.

Cresci et al. (Cresci et al., 2015) furthermore proposed machine learning algorithms like decision tree, random forest, support vector machines (SVMs), adaptive boosting, k-nearest neighbours and logistic regression for their research experiments. Gupta et al. (Gupta et al., 2013) in turn suggested Naïve Bayes and decision trees to detect bots successfully. Xiao et al. (Xiao et al., 2015) proposed logistic regression, random forests, and SVMs to detect deceptive accounts. The related work, although focussed on detecting bots, not only had success in detecting deceptive identities on SMPs, but also used the attributes freely available on SMPs. For these reasons, this paper will use supervised machine learning as a method to develop a model that can assist to detect identity deception by humans on SMPs.

3 Establishing the requirements

The following requirements for the research presented in this paper have been accumulated through related work:

- Use a dataset that consists of a large volume of heterogeneous data, created at high velocity. SMPs, being a big data platform, are a good source of such data (Van der Walt and Eloff, 2015).
- Use only attributes freely available on an SMP (Twitter, 2018) (Facebook, 2017) (LinkedIn, 2017).
- Ignore non-human accounts in the SMP data (Cresci et al., 2015).
- Ignore content posted by users on an SMP (Varol et al., 2017).
- The attributes used for the model, should describe the identity of the person (Meligy et al., 2017).
- Develop a supervised machine learning model (Cresci et al., 2015)
- The data should contain both examples of deceptive and trustworthy people. Supervised machine learning requires a labelled dataset (Kuhn et al., 2016).
- Compare the results from various machine learning models (Varol et al., 2017).
- Automate the detection due to SMPs' big data nature (Chaffey, 2018).

The next section provides a high-level design for the prototype.

4   High-level design of a prototype for the automated assistance of identity deception detection on SMPs

To describe the components of the prototype, the Unified Modelling Language (UML) is employed. UML is a visual modelling language for systems (O'Regan, 2017). It helps to define a prototype during the design phase instead of during development. This approach not only describes the prototype at the beginning of development, but also minimizes the risk of the prototype not complying with the requirements and only finding this out at the end of the development. For this prototype, the authors propose three components:

- Prepare – For the prototype, freely available SMP attributes are available. The attributes should describe the identity of the user and not include any content they posted. The data should also contain examples of both deceptive and trustworthy accounts. To adhere to these requirements, this component retrieves the data from Twitter as an example of an SMP, cleans the data from any non-human accounts, labels the data for supervised machine learning, and finally prepares the data for supervised machine learning.
- Discover – Supervised machine learning is required to build and evaluate models assisting in the detection of human identity deception on SMPs. This component allows for experimentation by using the prepared data to train various supervised machine learning algorithms using different parameters, such as resampling (Domingos, 2012), and hyperparameters (Dickerson et al., 2014).
- Detect – Due to the nature of the data, more specifically its volume and heterogeneity, the process if identity deception detection should be automated. This component allows for unassisted identity deception detection and uses the most accurate machine learning model discovered during experimentation.

For this research, the proposed prototype was built using infrastructure provided by the Future SOC Lab in Potsdam, Germany (FSOC, 2018). The Twitter data was mined using Apache Flume (Apache, 2018) and stored in a SAP HANA (SAP, 2017) in-memory database consisting of 2TB of RAM and 8TB of storage. Machine learning models were built using the Caret package in R (Kuhn et al., 2016). The prototype components, their functions, and how each component addresses the requirements expected of a prototype assisting in the automated detection of human identity deception on SMPs are illustrated in Figure 1. The next section shows some results delivered by the running prototype.

5   Experimental results

Identity attributes from Twitter accounts were mined, using a Java API (Yamamoto, 2018) together with Apache Flume (Apache, 2018) during 2016. Apache Flume was able to import volumes of data whilst ignoring non-English-speaking accounts, before sending the data to SAP HANA for further processing. 224 796 Twitter accounts and 606 million tweets were finally stored in SAP HANA. 53 091 of the Twitter accounts were discarded at this point, using rules from the research of Cresci et al. (Cresci et al., 2015). These discarded accounts were found to belong to non-human or bot accounts. The tweets were ignored as the prototype requires only those attributes describing the identity of the person. An additional 15 000 deceptive human accounts were manually fabricated and injected into the corpus to create a labelled corpus of deceptive and non-deceptive accounts. These injected examples of deceptive accounts each had one or more identity attributes not representative of the truth. For example, the profile image would be of someone else or the location would be a place different from their indicated GPS location. The attributes in the final prepared dataset only contained those attributes describing the identities of both trustworthy and deceptive humans.

The experiment executed with the prototype, used the aforementioned prepared identity data. The results from this experiment, using supervised machine learning and 10-fold cross validation (Peddinti et al., 2017) (Fire et al., 2014), is shown in Table 1. Given PR-AUC, which measures the Precision-Recall performance of a machine learning model (Davis and Goodrich, 2006), it is shown that at best, the Adaboost and nnet (neural net) algorithms detected identity deception by humans with a score of 0.317 and 0.306 (1 being the best, 0 being the worst) respectively.

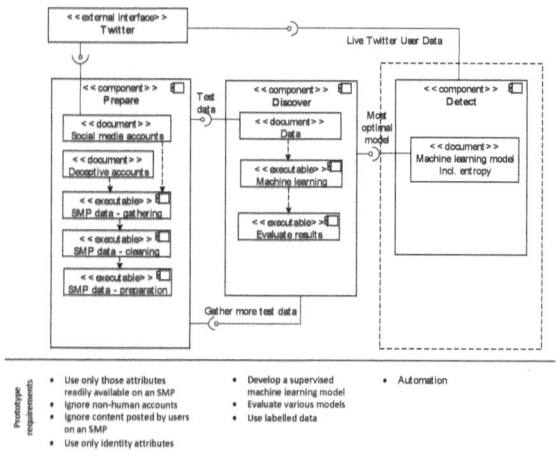

Figure 1: UML component diagram of the proposed prototype

Algorithm	Accuracy	Kappa	F1-score	ROC-AUC	PR-AUC
random forest	0.800	0.236	0.331	0.755	0.280
Adaboost	0.788	0.186	0.287	0.702	0.317
nnet	0.730	0.170	0.282	0.734	0.306

Table 1: Results from the experiment

6   Discussion of results

For this paper, the Accuracy, Kappa, F1 score, and AUC (Area Under the Curve) was considered to assist in the evaluation of the models. The F1 score and AUC metrics are often used in research detecting spam and bot accounts to determine the effectiveness of the machine learning models (Ferrara et al., 2016) (Fire et al., 2014) (Xiao et al., 2015). Although 10-fold cross validation was used to train the models, it is known that the F1 score and ROC-AUC (Receiver Operator Characteristics Curve) suffers (Menardi and Torelli, 2014) (Jeni et al., 2013) in skewed distributions. More recently the PR-AUC (Precision-Recall Curve) has been recommended as an alternative to ROC-AUC (Saito and Rehmsmeier, 2017) (Davis and Goadrich, 2006). Based on all the information provided, the PR-AUC was regarded as the final metric to evaluate the machine learning models with. The results were still suboptimal as the AUC for a random predictor equals 0.50 (Powers, 2011).

The following recommendations are proposed to address the weak model performance results and to improve the prototype:

- Experiment with additional features to increase the accuracy of the prototype. For example, by combining SMP attributes like whether the gender on the profile image matches the gender of the SMP user, further lies can potentially be identified. These attributes should still be freely available on SMPs.
- Improve the completeness of attributes on SMPs as many identity attributes were found to be incomplete i.e. not completed by the users at the time of creating the user account. If some of these attributes, like location and profile image were made compulsory by the SMP provider, identity deception detection accuracy could potentially increase.
- Additional validation could be performed by SMPs upon user registration to ensure the veracity of SMP attributes. By, for example, getting someone else to validate that the profile image is representative of that user, could prevent potential identity deception.

7   Conclusion and future work

This paper showed how, besides the content, many attributes exist on SMPs that could be indicative of human identity deception. A prototype was proposed, showing how metadata (attributes) freely available on SMPs can be used to train supervised machine learning models. It is also shown by means of the experimental results provided in this paper how these supervised machine learning models can be a step in the right direction for assisting with the automatic detection of humans lying about their identities on SMPs. Furthermore, the results also uncovered the influence of a skewed labelled dataset and the difficulty in using only the meta-data (attributes) describing the identity of a human on SMPs. It was found that many of the identity attributes were incomplete and it was therefore difficult to create an accurate model to assist in the automated detection of identity deception by humans on SMPs. Future work will focus on increasing the accuracy of the machine learning models. One way of achieving this will be to introduce engineered features, additional to the attributes, such as "age-determined-from-profile-image".

8 References

Alowibdi, J. S., Buy, U. A., Philip, S. Y., Ghani, S. & Mokbel, M. 2015. Deception detection in Twitter. *Social Network Analysis and Mining,* 5, 1-16.

Apache. 2018. Flume. Available: https://flume.apache.org/ [Accessed 16 May 2018].

Apuzzo, M. & Lafraniere, S. 2018. 13 Russians Indicted as Mueller Reveals Effort to Aid Trump Campaign. *The New York Times,* 16 Feb 2018.

Ben Khalifa, M., Redondo, R. P. D., Vilas, A. F. & Rodríguez, S. S. 2016. Identifying urban crowds using geo-located Social media data: a Twitter experiment in New York City. *Journal of Intelligent Information Systems,* 1-22.

Chaffey, D. 2018. *Global social media research summary* [Online]. Smart Insights. Available: https://www.smartinsights.com/social-media-marketing/social-media-strategy/new-global-social-media-research/ [Accessed 23 Jun 2018].

Chun, Y., Hwang, H. S. & Kim, C. S. 2014. Development of a Disaster Information Extraction System based on Social Network Services. *nternational Journal of Multimedia and Ubiquitous Engineering.*

Cook, D. M., Waugh, B., Abdipanah, M., Hashemi, O. & Abdul Rahman, S. 2014. Twitter Deception and Influence: Issues of Identity, Slacktivism, and Puppetry. *Journal of Information Warfare,* 13, 58-71.

Cresci, S., Di Pietro, R., Petrocchi, M., Spognardi, A. & Tesconi, M. 2015. Fame for sale: efficient detection of fake Twitter followers. *Decision Support Systems,* 80, 56-71.

Davis, J. & Goadrich, M. The relationship between Precision-Recall and ROC curves. Proceedings of the 23rd international conference on Machine learning, 2006. ACM, 233-240.

De Villiers, J. 2017. Suspects use fake Facebook profile to lure women, rape and kill them. *News24* [Online]. Available: https://www.news24.com/SouthAfrica/News/suspects-use-fake-facebook-profile-to-lure-women-rape-and-kill-them-20171104 [Accessed 4 Nov 2017].

Dickerson, J. P., Kagan, V. & Subrahmanian, V. Using sentiment to detect bots on Twitter: Are humans more opinionated than bots? Advances in Social Networks Analysis and Mining (ASONAM), 2014 IEEE/ACM International Conference on, 2014. IEEE, 620-627.

Domingos, P. 2012. A few useful things to know about machine learning. *Communications of the ACM,* 55, 78-87.

Donath, J. S. 1999. Identity and deception in the virtual community. *Communities in cyberspace,* 1996, 29-59.

Egele, M., Stringhini, G., Kruegel, C. & Vigna, G. Compa: Detecting compromised accounts on social networks. NDSS, 2013.

Facebook. 2017. The Facebook Graph API. Available: https://developers.facebook.com/docs/graph-api/overview [Accessed 8 Jan 2018].

Ferrara, E., Wang, W.-Q., Varol, O., Flammini, A. & Galstyan, A. Predicting online extremism, content adopters, and interaction reciprocity. International Conference on Social Informatics, 2016. Springer, 22-39.

Fire, M., Kagan, D., Elyashar, A. & Elovici, Y. 2014. Friend or foe? Fake profile identification in online social networks. *Social Network Analysis and Mining,* 4, 1-23.

Fsoc. 2018. The HPI Future SOC lab. Available: https://hpi.de/en/research/future-soc-lab.html [Accessed 8 June 2018].

Gupta, A., Lamba, H., Kumaraguru, P. & Joshi, A. Faking sandy: characterizing and identifying fake images on twitter during hurricane sandy. Proceedings of the 22nd international conference on World Wide Web, 2013. ACM, 729-736.

Gurajala, S., White, J. S., Hudson, B., Voter, B. R. & Matthews, J. N. 2016. Profile characteristics of fake Twitter accounts. *Big Data & Society,* 3, 2053951716674236.

Hancock, J. T. & Toma, C. L. 2009. Putting your best face forward: The accuracy of online dating photographs. *Journal of Communication,* 59, 367-386.

Jeni, L. A., Cohn, J. F. & De La Torre, F. Facing imbalanced data--Recommendations for the use of performance metrics. Affective Computing and Intelligent Interaction (ACII), 2013 Humaine Association Conference on, 2013. IEEE, 245-251.

Kierkegaard, S. 2008. Cybering, online grooming and ageplay. *Computer Law & Security Review,* 24, 41-55.

Kuhn , M., Weston, S., Williams, A., Keefer, C., Engelhardt, A., Cooper, T., Mayer, Z. & Al., E. 2016. caret: Classification and regression training. R package version 6.0-73.

Lee, K., Caverlee, J. & Webb, S. The social honeypot project: protecting online communities from spammers. Proceedings of the 19th international conference on World wide web, 2010. ACM, 1139-1140.

Linkedin. 2017. LinkedIn Developers. Available: https://developer.linkedin.com/ [8 Jan 2018].

Meligy, A. M., Ibrahim, H. M. & Torky, M. F. 2017. Identity Verification Mechanism for Detecting Fake Profiles in Online Social Networks.

Menardi, G. & Torelli, N. 2014. Training and assessing classification rules with imbalanced data. *Data Mining and Knowledge Discovery,* 1-31.

Muller, F. & Thiesing, F. Social networking APIs for companies—An example of using the Facebook API for companies. Computational Aspects of Social Networks (CASoN), 2011 International Conference on, 2011. IEEE, 120-123.

O'regan, G. 2017. Unified Modelling Language. *Concise Guide to Software Engineering.* Springer.

Peddinti, S. T., Ross, K. W. & Cappos, J. 2017. Mining Anonymity: Identifying Sensitive Accounts on Twitter. *International AAAI Conference on Web and Social Media.* Montreal, Canada.

Powers, D. M. 2011. Evaluation: from precision, recall and F-measure to ROC, informedness, markedness and correlation.

Rashidi, B. & Fung, C. BotTracer: Bot user detection using clustering method in RecDroid. Network Operations and Management Symposium (NOMS), 2016 IEEE/IFIP, 2016. IEEE, 1239-1244.

Ribeiro, M. H., Calais, P. H., Santos, Y. A., Almeida, V. A. & Meira Jr, W. Characterizing and Detecting Hateful Users on Twitter. Twelfth International AAAI Conference on Web and Social Media, 2018 Palo Alto, California, USA. AAAI Press, 676-679.

Ribeiro, M. T., Singh, S. & Guestrin, C. Why should i trust you?: Explaining the predictions of any classifier. Proceedings of the 22nd ACM SIGKDD International Conference on Knowledge Discovery and Data Mining, 2016. ACM, 1135-1144.

Saito, T. & Rehmsmeier, M. 2017. Precrec: fast and accurate precision–recall and ROC curve calculations in R. *Bioinformatics,* 33, 145-147.

Sandy, C., Rusconi, P. & Li, S. 2017. Can Humans Detect the Authenticity of Social Media Accounts? *3rd IEEE International Conference on Cybernetics (CYBCONF).* Exeter, UK.

Sap. 2017. SAP HANA. Enterprise Edition. Available: https://www.sap.com/uk/developer/topics/sap-hana.html [Accessed 10 June 2018].

Sloan, L., Morgan, J., Burnap, P. & Williams, M. 2015. Who tweets? Deriving the demographic characteristics of age, occupation and social class from Twitter user meta-data. *PloS one,* 10, e0115545.

Subrahmanian, V., Azaria, A., Durst, S., Kagan, V., Galstyan, A., Lerman, K., Zhu, L., Ferrara, E., Flammini, A. & Menczer, F. 2016. The darpa twitter bot challenge. *IEEE Computer Magazine,* 49, 38-46.

Thomas, K., Mccoy, D., Grier, C., Kolcz, A. & Paxson, V. Trafficking Fraudulent Accounts: The Role of the Underground Market in Twitter Spam and Abuse. USENIX Security, 2013. Citeseer, 195-210.

Tsikerdekis, M. 2017. Identity Deception Prevention Using Common Contribution Network Data. *IEEE Transactions on Information Forensics and Security,* 12, 188-199.

Tuna, T., Akbas, E., Aksoy, A., Canbaz, M. A., Karabiyik, U., Gonen, B. & Aygun, R. 2016. User characterization for online social networks. *Social Network Analysis and Mining,* 6, 104.

Twitter. 2018. Twitter API. Available: https://dev.twitter.com/overview/api [Accessed 8 Jan 2018].

Van Der Walt, E. & Eloff, J. H. P. 2015. Protecting minors on social media platforms - A Big Data Science experiment *HPI Cloud Symposium "Operating the Cloud".*

Varol, O., Ferrara, E., Davis, C. A., Menczer, F. & Flammini, A. Online human-bot interactions: Detection, estimation, and characterization. Eleventh International AAAI Conference on Web and Social Media, 2017 Montreal, Canada. 280-289.

Xiao, C., Freeman, D. M. & Hwa, T. Detecting clusters of fake accounts in online social networks. Proceedings of the 8th ACM Workshop on Artificial Intelligence and Security, 2015. ACM, 91-101.

Yamamoto, Y. 2018. Twitter4J. Available: http://twitter4j.org/en/ [Accessed 16 May 2018].

Adapting Cyber-Security Training to Your Employees

M. Pattinson[1], M. Butavicius[2], B. Ciccarello[1], M. Lillie[1],
K. Parsons[2], D. Calic[2] and A. McCormac[2]

[1]Adelaide Business School, University of Adelaide, South Australia
[2]Defence Science and Technology Group, Edinburgh, South Australia
e-mail: {malcolm.pattinson, beau.ciccarello, meredith.lillie}@adelaide.edu.au;
{marcus.butavicius, kathryn.parsons, dragana.calic,
agata.mccormac}@dst.defence.gov.au

Abstract

The aim of this paper is twofold. First, it introduces the concept of a framework of controls that relates to the human aspects of cyber security, which is adaptable to different types of organisations and different types of employees. A review of the literature confirmed that Adaptive Control Frameworks (ACFs) for cyber security exist, but only in terms of hardware and software controls. The second aim of this paper is to empirically test the effectiveness of one of these adaptive controls, namely, the type of training provided. A total of 1048 working Australian adults completed the Human Aspects of Information Security Questionnaire (HAIS-Q). This included questions relating to the types of cyber-security training they had received and how often it was provided, and a set of questions called the Cyber-security Learning Styles Inventory to identify their preferred learning styles for training. The frequency of training did not directly predict Information Security Awareness (ISA) levels. However, the extent to which the training received was matched with an individual's learning preferences was positively associated with ISA levels. This finding supports the hypothesis that if training interventions are adapted to the learning styles of individuals, their level of ISA will improve and therefore their non-malicious behaviour, whilst using a digital device to do their work, will be safer. The practical implications of this finding, as well as suggestions for further research on the ACF, are also discussed.

Keywords

Information Security (InfoSec), Human Aspects of Cyber Security (HACS), Human Aspects of Information Security Questionnaire (HAIS-Q), Adaptive Control Framework (ACF), Information Security Awareness (ISA), Learning Styles, Training.

1. Introduction

It is increasingly acknowledged that the most effective means of mitigating information security (InfoSec) risks within an organisation is to address the behaviour of employees who use digital devices to do their work (Proofpoint 2018). This implies that human vulnerabilities should be addressed in parallel with, but not instead of, implementing hardware and software controls (Furnell, S 2008).

1.1. Aim of this Paper

The aim of this paper is twofold. First, it is to introduce the concept of a framework of controls relating to the human aspects of cyber security. A review of the major International Standards shows that control frameworks exist and are recommended for non-human aspects of cyber security. For example, the Australian Standard (AS_ISO/IEC_27002 2015) provides adaptive controls for hardware and software. However, such standards do not cover controls such as education, training and awareness sessions. Consequently, there is a need to develop an ACF for these types of controls. The second aim of this paper is to validate an aspect of an ACF relating to human behaviour, in an online study. Specifically, this involves an empirical demonstration of how training controls can be adapted to an organisation's needs by providing training that matches with the preferred learning styles of employees who use digital devices to do their job.

The next section provides a review of the literature relating to ACFs, individual learning styles and ISA. This is followed by an explanation of the methods used to collect and analyse the survey data. The findings and results are then presented, limitations are acknowledged and conclusions are stated.

2. Literature Review

For the purposes of this paper, a cyber-security ACF is defined as a set of identified controls, or countermeasures together with instructions on how to implement them, such that they will prevent, deter, detect, and enable recovery from cyber-security breaches. These controls include policies, procedures, software and hardware. This will ensure that the confidentiality, integrity and availability (CIA) of digital information is maintained at an acceptable level. The framework is 'adaptive' because the controls are tailored to suit the organisation and its employees.

For the purposes of this paper, the term 'information security', that is InfoSec, refers to the preservation of the CIA of all forms of information, namely, written, printed, digital, transmitted and internet-based. On the other hand, 'cyber security' is a subset of 'information security' and refers to "protecting the CIA of digital-information assets against threats and attacks that use the internet in some manner;" (von Solms, B & von Solms, R 2018, p. 6).

2.1   Adaptive Control Framework (ACF)

ACFs are not a new concept. For example, in the field of electrical and electronic engineering, Tayebi, A and Chien, C-J (2007) proposed "a unified framework for adaptive iterative learning control design for uncertain nonlinear systems" (p. 1907). Furthermore, in the field of urban planning and development, Liu, HX *et al.* (2007) presented an ACF for traffic management systems for the betterment of emergency evacuations when natural disasters occur. In the field of InfoSec, the National Institute of Standards and Technology document (NIST 2017) describes its framework as "adaptive to provide a flexible and risk-based implementation that can be used with a broad array of cybersecurity risk management processes" (p. 6). They insist that this framework should be adapted by organisations to suit the organisation's policies and procedures.

Generally, the current information security auditing frameworks, guidelines and standards are still heavily focused on the technical components (AS_ISO/IEC_27002 2015; ISACA 2012; NIST 2017). Although these guidelines and standards recognise the importance of user awareness and training, they do not provide detailed instructions or implementable strategies, but at least they acknowledge that this area is often overlooked (Cichonski, P *et al.* 2012). Similarly, ISACA's COBIT5 (ISACA 2012) also recognises the human element, but does not include human factors as an auditable component of an IT audit. The human aspects (i.e., culture, ethics and behaviour) are considered to be the worst governed and managed areas with regard to InfoSec (ISACA 2012).

In summary, there is scant evidence of any existing literature on frameworks that include controls that are adaptable to human factors within the context of digital InfoSec. However, research by Abawajy, J (2014) showed that the most effective ISA delivery method was one that was preferred by users, although a combination of delivery methods proved to be more effective than any single method.

The next section, examines how cyber-security training can be adapted to the preferred learning styles of an employee and how this impacts on their ISA.

2.2 Learning Styles

Organisations deliver InfoSec training and awareness programs to their employees in a wide range of formats, including (but not limited to) videos, interactive modules and tests, infographics, posters, podcasts, newsletters, phishing simulations and seminars. Each of the different formats has the potential to either correspond or conflict with an employee's learning preferences. For example, a visual learner prefers to learn using predominantly visual formats. Felder, RM (1996) defines an individual's learning style as "characteristic strengths and preferences in the ways they take in and process information" (p. 1).

Researchers have developed reliable tools for measuring individual differences in learning preferences (Leite, WL *et al.* 2010). The existence of individual differences in learning preferences suggests that training may be most effective when the training mode is consistent with an individual's learning style. In the literature this is referred to as the 'meshing hypothesis', that is, an individual will experience a better learning outcome when taught in a manner that matches their learning preferences.

The meshing hypothesis and its application in education settings has received criticism from several authors due to inconclusive evidence (Kirschner, PA 2017; Newton, PM & Miah, M 2017; Pashler, H *et al.* 2008). However, several studies in the field of information systems have demonstrated the benefit of meshing learning styles and training (Recker, J *et al.* 2014). Cegielski, CG *et al.* (2011) examined learning styles and object-oriented computer programming and found that performance increases when the instructional strategies closely matched the student's preferred learning styles.

Several models and assessment tools have been developed within the learning style preference literature. Examples include the Felder, RM and Soloman, BA (2000) Index of Learning Styles Questionnaire (FSLSM), the Kolb Learning Styles Inventory (Kolb, AY 2005) and the VARK Learning Styles Inventory (Fleming, ND 2001). The VARK Learning Styles Inventory is widely used because it is brief, freely available, easy to administer and has clear practical implications for modifying the format of training to match the preferences of different learners. The simplicity of the VARK Learning Styles Inventory also means it can be easily adapted to suit a specific research purpose. Therefore, we chose to adapt the VARK model for this current study which relates to cyber-security training. The VARK model uses 16 items to assess an individual's learning preferences across four different perceptual modalities: visual (V), aural (A), read/write (R), and kinaesthetic (K). Individuals can have a single learning preference for one of the four modalities, or a preference for multiple modalities, including all four.

2.3   Information Security Awareness (ISA)

In this study, the effectiveness of a training intervention was determined by an ISA score. ISA is defined as an individual's knowledge of, and attitude towards, safe, risk-averse behaviour when using a digital device such as a workstation computer at work, a home laptop, a mobile phone or a tablet device. In other words, 'Am I doing anything that may put at risk the confidentiality, the integrity or the availability of digital data'? This data may belong to the individual, the organisation they work for, or another individual or organisation. This current research uses Parsons, K *et al.* (2014) definition of ISA. This definition is made up of the following three components:

a) What a person 'knows' about behaving in a safe manner (Knowledge);

b) How a person 'feels' about behaving in a safe manner (Attitude) and

c) What a person actually 'does' when using a digital device (Behaviour).

Parsons, K *et al.* (2017) have demonstrated that an individual's ISA, as measured by the Human Aspects of Information Security Questionnaire (HAIS-Q) (McCormac, A, Zwaans, T, *et al.* 2017), is a valid indication of how well the individual behaves when using a digital device.

3   Method

Using the Qualtrics survey platform, a population of Australian adults was invited to take part in an online study. These participants were required to be over the age of 18, currently employed, and working in Australia. The survey contained questions on demographics and ISA. To measure ISA, we used the HAIS-Q (Parsons et al., 2014; 2017) and in our study this achieved an acceptable Cronbach's alpha score of .96

overall (for further details see McCormac, A, Calic, D, *et al.* (2017). The survey also contained questions on the types of InfoSec training the participants had received and their preferred learning styles in the context of cyber security. To achieve this, the VARK Learning Styles Inventory (Fleming, ND 2001), which was originally designed to investigate general learning preferences across a range of activities, was modified and adapted to a cyber-security context. The instructions were modified to read:

> 'Choose the answers that best describe your preference when *learning about using computers for work*. For each statement, please select *more than one* if a single answer does not match your preference.'

Also, six of the original sixteen items from the VARK instrument (Fleming, ND 2001) were modified to relate to learning about computers at work (see Table 1 below). Participants responded by selecting one or more response options. Note that in Table 2 below the type of learning style is indicated by the letters V, A, R and K, but participants did not see this information when completing the survey. This new set of questions represents the Cyber-security Learning Styles Inventory.

Item	Response Options
You are participating in training that includes a test you are required to pass. You would learn most from:	Seeing examples. (V)
	Listening to the presenter. (A)
	Reading written instructions. (R)
	Watching a demonstration. (K)
Remember a time when you learned how to do something new on a computer. You learned best by:	Watching a demonstration. (K)
	Listening to somebody explaining it and asking questions. (A)
	Looking at visual cues, e.g., diagrams or charts. (V)
	Reading written explanations, e.g., a manual or blog. (R)
You want to learn a new computer program. You would:	Read the written instructions that came with the program. (R)
	Talk with people who know about the program. (A)
	Learn how to use it through trial and error. (K)
	Follow the diagrams in the instructions. (V)
I like websites that have:	Things I can click on or interact with. (K)
	Interesting design and visual features. (V)
	Interesting written descriptions, lists or explanations. (R)
	Audio channels where I can hear podcasts, radio programs or interviews. (A)
Do you prefer a presenter or instructor who uses:	Demonstrations or practical sessions. (K)
	Question and answer sessions or guest discussions. (A)
	Handouts, books, or readings. (R)
	Diagrams, charts or graphs. (V)
You have completed a test at the end of a training course, and would like to receive feedback. You would like to receive feedback by:	Having your results displayed visually, e.g., on graphs or diagrams. (V)
	Using examples from what you have done. (K)
	Having someone talk you through it. (A)
	Using a written description of your results. (R)

Table 1: Cyber-security Learning Styles Inventory

Participants were also asked two questions about the nature of cyber-security training they had received at work. The first question related to the frequency of such training (see Training Frequency in Table 2 below), with 7 forced-choice options. Only 3.5% of the participants selected the final response option of 'Other (Please specify)' and an analysis of the associated open-text responses did not reveal any consistent themes. Therefore, these responses were excluded from analysis. The second question, about the cyber-security training that participants had received, related to the mode of training (see Training Type in Table 2 below). The response options were modelled on the VARK instrument (Fleming, ND 2001), but adapted to InfoSec education and training, and participants responded on a five point Likert scale (where '1' = 'Strongly disagree' and '5' = 'Strongly agree').

Item description	Item	Response Options
Training Frequency	How frequently does your place of work provide information security education, training or awareness programs?	Never
		Every two years
		Annually
		Twice a year
		Every three months
		At least once a month
		Other (please specify)
Training Type	Please indicate whether the following statements apply to the security education, training and awareness programs that you have received in your place of work	They include speaking and listening (e.g., discussions, seminars). (A)
		They include reading or writing (e.g., handouts, note-taking). (R)
		They include visual depiction of information (e.g., diagrams, graphs, charts). (V)
		They include experience and practice, either simulated or real (e.g., real-life examples, demonstrations, guest lecturers). (K)

Table 2: Training Items

4   Results

After filtering and quality checks, 1,048 responses (from participants that were over the age of 18, currently employed, and working in Australia) were analysed. Of these, 51% were females and participants were evenly distributed across age categories, with 11.8% of them aged between 18 and 29, 23.8% aged between 30 and 39, 21.4% aged between 40 and 49, 23.4% aged between 50 and 59 and 19.3% aged 60 and over.

The six items of the Cyber-security Learning Styles Inventory were summed to create Visual, Aural, Read/Write and Kinaesthetic subtotals for each participant with a range of 0 to 6. These were then recoded such that sub-totals of more than 4 were designated as 'Preferred' and the remaining were coded as 'Not preferred'. Scores on the Training Type question were recoded such that where participants indicated that they 'Agree' or 'Strongly agree' on the Likert scale they were classified as 'Received' whilst all other responses (i.e., 'Disagree', 'Strongly disagree' and 'Neither agree nor disagree') were classified as 'Not received'.

Overall analysis of training modes indicated a disparity between the modes of training that people preferred, compared to the mode of training they had received. Preliminary analysis of the responses to 'Training Modes Received' showed that, across the sample, the training modes were evenly split across the four learning-style categories (see Table 3 below). However, an examination of the 'Preferred Learning Styles' showed a different pattern of results, with a higher percentage of respondents indicating that kinaesthetic training would be their preferred method for learning about using computers for work.

	Visual	Aural	Read/write	Kinaesthetic
Training Modes Received	55.7%	57.8%	55.7%	57.9%
Preferred Learning Styles	24.4%	28.6%	35.1%	45.5%

Table 3: Overall comparison between training modes received and preferred learning styles.

To more closely examine the relationship between preferred and received modes of training, the data was examined at an individual level. A new variable, 'Training Match', was calculated to indicate whether the learning style preference matched with the training mode received or not. A score of one indicated that the participant received training in a least one style that was consistent with their learning preferences. All other participants received a score of zero. In addition, participants who responded inconsistently to the questions by indicating that they received no cyber-security training for the 'Training Frequency' question but indicated that they had received certain types of cyber-security training in the 'Training Type' question were classified as a Non-match (i.e., 0). Overall, 39.6% ($N = 415$) of the sample were classified as having received matched training.

An examination of the Pearson correlation coefficient between the variables (see Table 4 below), showed that Age, Gender and Training Match all correlated significantly with ISA. In addition, Age correlated significantly with Gender whilst Training Frequency was also positively and significantly correlated with Training Match.

In order to tease apart the relative contribution of these variables in predicting ISA, a three-stage hierarchical multiple linear regression (refer Table 5 below) was conducted. In the multiple regression, there were no signs of multi-collinearity with Variance Inflation Factors (VIF) for all independent variables less than 2. In addition, there was no evidence of outliers with Cook's distances being less than 1 for these variables. In the first stage of the regression, Age and Gender were entered to control for the effects of these demographic variables as demonstrated in previous research (McCormac, A, Zwaans, T, *et al.* 2017). In the second stage, Training Frequency was entered to examine the role of increased training opportunities. In the third and final stage, Training Match was entered to examine whether matching training mode to learning style for cyber-security training improved ISA over and above the effects of demographic variables and increased training frequency.

Variable	Mean	SD	VIF	1	2	3	4
1. Age Range	N/A	N/A	1.04				
2. Gender	N/A	N/A	1.03	-.18**			
3. Training Frequency	2.5	1.6	1.65	-.06	-.02		
4. Training Match	.4	.5	1.65	-.02	-.01	.63**	
ISA	257.2	32.1	-	.27**	.08*	.06	.12**

(* = correlation significant at the .05 level, ** = correlation significant at the .01 level, two-tailed).

Table 4: Descriptive statistics and correlations

At Stage 1, both Age and Gender were significant and together explained 8% of the variance in ISA ($F(2,1008) = 46.63, p < .001$). In Stage 2, adding Training Frequency improved the fit of the model, and the Training Frequency variable was significant. However the overall fit increased by less than half a percent ($F(3,1007) = 33.55, p <.001$). In Stage 3, the additional Training Match variable was significant, however, its inclusion caused Training Frequency to be removed from the final model ($F(4,1006) = 27.74, p < .001$). In other words, while Training Frequency appeared to be associated with improved ISA in the second model, much of its contribution was negated once the more predictive variable of Training Match, with which it covaries, was included in the final model. Overall, this final model explained approximately 10% of the variance in the data with the strongest predictor being Age followed by Gender and then Training Match.

5   Discussion of Results

The frequency of training did not appear to directly predict ISA. However, the extent to which the training received actually matched (i.e. meshed with) an individual's learning preferences was positively associated with ISA. Increased frequency of training may be important only in so much as it may provide greater opportunity for the training messages to be presented in a variety of formats. This, in turn, would increase the likelihood that an employee's preferred learning style was 'covered'. Ultimately, it was the matching of the training mode with the employee's preferred learning style (for cyber-security training) that was positively associated with their ISA score. This finding supports the ACF hypothesis; namely, that training interventions should be adapted to the needs of the individuals for higher ISA scores and therefore more risk-averse InfoSec behaviours.

Our results also validated previous research that showed that older employees and females tended to have better ISA (McCormac, A, Zwaans, T, *et al.* 2017). In fact, Age and Gender were stronger predictors of ISA than the variables associated with training. However, changing the age and gender profile of an organisation's employees is not ethical or practical. In contrast, modes of training may be easily measured and this information can be used to address training needs to directly improve ISA.

Variable	Model 1			Model 2			Model 3		
	B (SE)	**β** standardised	**t**	**B** (SE)	**β** standardised	**t**	**B** (SE)	**β** standardised	**t**
Age Range	6.95 (.75)	.28	9.26**	7.07 (.75)	.29	9.43**	7.04 (.75)	.29	9.42**
Gender	8.46 (1.96)	.13	4.32**	8.61 (1.95)	.13	4.40**	8.59 (1.95)	.13	4.41**
Training Frequency				1.63 (.62)	.08	2.62*	.10 (.79)	.01	.12
Training Match							7.81 (2.53)	.12	3.08**
Adj R^2	.08			.09			.10		
Δ Adj R^2	.08			.05			.01		
F	46.63			33.55			27.75		

(* = correlation significant at the .05 level, ** = correlation significant at the .01 level, two-tailed).

Table 5: Summary of hierarchical, three-stage, multiple linear regression analysis of variables predicting ISA

6   Limitations and Future Directions

In the real world, it may be impractical to survey the training mode needs of all staff and then tailor the training to each individual preference. However, it may still be beneficial to understand learning preferences within certain organisational teams or groups. Rather than surveying all the employees, this approach would involve surveying only a sample of people in different work areas using the Cyber-security Learning Styles Inventory. This learning style profile could then be used to tailor training packages for these work areas (rather than individuals). However, it is a question for further research as to how much ISA can be improved by tailoring training at a group level. Further research should also investigate how individual tailoring of other aspects of the ACF (e.g., cyber-security awareness messaging such as intranet posts and posters) may improve ISA.

7   Conclusions

This paper reported on a research project that established the need for a framework of human controls that could be adapted to the different types of employees within an organisation. This paper also reported on the results of an online survey that collected and analysed data relating to one of these adaptive controls, namely, the cyber-security training that employees had received, and its impact on their naïve and accidental InfoSec behaviour when using a digital device for work.

The concept of an ACF is referred to by International Standards (AS_ISO/IEC_27002 2015; ISO_3100 2018; NIST 2017) and by training organisations Proofpoint (2018) and MediaPro (2017) as an important approach to mitigating cyber-security risks. Despite this need, this study found that current standards and guidelines are devoid of any such mechanism when it comes to educating, training and communicating with employees. More specifically, a review of the standards mentioned above revealed no published guidance on human-based controls. This led to the hypothesis that if cyber-security training is adapted (i.e. meshed) to the needs of an individual, the naïve and accidental behaviour of this individual should be safer. Hence, this paper presented a case study which supports this hypothesis by showing that an individual's level of ISA is increased if the training is meshed with an individual's preferred learning style.

There is a developing body of academic literature focusing on the human aspects of cyber security, such as user vulnerability to phishing attacks (Furnell, S 2007), ISA (Parsons, K *et al.* 2014) and InfoSec culture (Da Veiga, A & Eloff, J 2010). The ACF conceptualised and tested in this paper seeks to formalise this research into practical guidelines that can be implemented in any organisation to evaluate and improve their InfoSec posture.

In line with this goal, our research suggests that an organisation could improve ISA by simply increasing the amount of training it provides. However, this is an inefficient and costly strategy. Rather than just increasing the amount of training, an organisation can save time and money by ensuring that the training is provided in formats relevant, or matched, to its employees. This is consistent with the ACF such that the human-based control known as 'training' is most effective when it is adapted to the needs of the employees and that this, in turn, should improve an organisation's level of security of its digital information assets.

8   References

Abawajy, J 2014, 'User preference of cyber security awareness delivery methods', *Behaviour & Information Technology*, vol. 33, no. 3, pp. 237-248.

AS_ISO/IEC_27002 2015, *Information Technology - Security Techniques - Code of practice for Information security management*, (27002:2015), Standards Australia.

Cegielski, CG, Hazen, BT & Rainer, RK 2011, 'Teach them how they learn: Learning styles and information systems education', *Journal of Information Systems Education*, vol. 22, no. 2, pp. 135-146.

Cichonski, P, Millar, T, Grance, T & Scarfone, K 2012, 'Special Publication 800-61 Revision 2', *Computer Security Incident Handling Guide.*

Da Veiga, A & Eloff, J 2010, 'A framework and assessment instrument for information security culture', *Computers & Security*, vol. 29, no. 2, pp. 196-207.

Felder, RM 1996, 'Matters of style', *ASEE prism*, vol. 6, no. 4, pp. 18-23.

Felder, RM & Soloman, BA 2000, 'Learning styles and strategies', *At URL: http://www. engr. ncsu. edu/learningstyles/ilsweb. html.*

Fleming, ND 2001, *Teaching and learning styles: VARK strategies*, IGI Global.

Furnell, S 2007, 'Phishing: can we spot the signs?', *Computer Fraud & Security*, vol. 2007, no. 3, pp. 10-15.

Furnell, S 2008, 'Securing the Human Factor', in H Lacohée, P Cofta, A Phippen & S Furnell (eds), *Understanding Public Perceptions: Trust and Engagement in ICT Mediated Services*, International Engineering Consortium.

ISACA 2012, *COBIT5: A Business Framework for the Governance and Management of Enterprise IT*, ISACA, USA.

ISO_3100 2018, *Risk management - Guidelines*, International Standards Organization.

Kirschner, PA 2017, 'Stop propagating the learning styles myth', *Computers & Education*, vol. 106, pp. 166-171.

Kolb, AY 2005, 'The Kolb learning style inventory–version 3.1 2005 technical specifications', *Boston, MA: Hay Resource Direct*, vol. 200, p. 72.

Leite, WL, Svinicki, M & Shi, Y 2010, 'Attempted validation of the scores of the VARK: Learning styles inventory with multitrait–multimethod confirmatory factor analysis models', *Educational and Psychological Measurement*, vol. 70, no. 2, pp. 323-339.

Liu, HX, Ban, JX, Ma, W & Mirchandani, PB 2007, 'Model reference adaptive control framework for real-time traffic management under emergency evacuation', *Journal of urban planning and development*, vol. 133, no. 1, pp. 43-50.

McCormac, A, Calic, D, Butavicius, M, Parsons, K, Pattinson, M & Lillie, M 2017, 'Understanding the Relationships between Resilience, Work Stress and Information Security Awareness', in S Furnell & N Clarke (eds), *Proceedings of the 11th International Symposium on Human Aspects of Information Security & Assurance (HAISA 2017)*, Adelaide, South Australia, pp. 80 - 90.

McCormac, A, Zwaans, T, Parsons, K, Calic, D, Butavicius, M & Pattinson, M 2017, 'Individual differences and information security awareness', *Computers in Human Behavior*, vol. 69, pp. 151-156.

MediaPro 2017, *Best practices guide for comprehensive employee awareness programs*, viewed 12 June 2018, <https:www.mediapro.com/blog/white-paper-best-practices-guide-comprehensive-employee-awareness-programs/>.

Newton, PM & Miah, M 2017, 'Evidence-Based Higher Education–Is the Learning Styles 'Myth' Important?', *Frontiers in psychology*, vol. 8, p. 444.

NIST 2017, *Framework for improving critical infrastructure cybersecurity*, National Institute of Standards and Technology.

Parsons, K, Calic, D, Pattinson, M, Butavicius, M, McCormac, A & Zwaans, T 2017, 'The human aspects of information security questionnaire (HAIS-Q): two further validation studies', *Computers & Security*, vol. 66, pp. 40-51.

Parsons, K, McCormac, A, Butavicius, M, Pattinson, M & Jerram, C 2014, 'Determining Employee Awareness Using the Human Aspects of Information Security Questionnaire (HAIS-Q)', *Computers & Security*, vol. 42, pp. 165-176.

Pashler, H, McDaniel, M, Rohrer, D & Bjork, R 2008, 'Learning styles: Concepts and evidence', *Psychological science in the public interest*, vol. 9, no. 3, pp. 105-119.

Proofpoint 2018, *The Human Factor - people-centred threats define the landscape*, USA, viewed 7 June 2018, <www.proofpoint.com/>.

Recker, J, Reijers, HA & van de Wouw, SG 2014, 'Process model comprehension: the effects of cognitive abilities, learning style, and strategy', *Communications of the Association for Information Systems*, vol. 34, no. 9, pp. 199-222.

Tayebi, A & Chien, C-J 2007, 'A unified adaptive iterative learning control framework for uncertain nonlinear systems', *IEEE Transactions on Automatic Control*, vol. 52, no. 10, pp. 1907-1913.

von Solms, B & von Solms, R 2018, 'Cybersecurity and information security–what goes where?', *Information & Computer Security*, vol. 26, no. 1, pp. 2-9.

Acknowledgements. This project is supported by the Defence Science & Technology Group (DSTG)

Cybersecurity Awareness and Education:
A Necessary Parameter for Smart Communities

N. Gcaza

CSIR, Meiring Naude Road Brummeria, Pretoria, South Africa
e-mail: ngcaza@csir.co.za

Abstract

Information and communication technologies (ICTs) are responsible for the transformation of societies, nations and the world at large. ICTs are considered to improve the quality of life for citizens as they bring about easiness and usefulness to perform day-to-day tasks. Most significantly, ICTs have paved way to 'smart' communities whereby citizens integrate various forms of technologies in the different contexts of life. It is known however, that ICTs introduce numerous cybersecurity risks. The problem this paper addresses is that cybersecurity awareness and education in smart communities is not given the precedence it warrants. The paper therefore argues that a community cannot be deemed as 'smart' if it is not 'cyber smart'. As such, the purpose of this paper is to evaluate and highlight the cybersecurity challenges that are prevalent in smart communities.

Keywords

Smart community, ICTs, Cybersecurity awareness and education

1   Introduction

Information and communication technologies (ICTs) remain a constant transformation agent in the everyday life of society in the entire globe. From a global point of view, ICT is seen as a key driver of economic change and innovation. Nationally, ICTs are deemed as a 'catalyst for national integration' (Syed Abdul Kadir, Husin and Nadarajah, 2014). Socially, ICTs are considered to improve the quality of life for citizens in several aspects including how people communicate, play, learn, work, commute, and access health services.

Due to the benefits of ICT, governments nationwide have long committed to employing ICT as a strategy towards human development (Morawczynski, 2007). A study by Kozma and Vota (2014) shows that increased availability and access to ICT improves the quality of life in communities in developing countries. ICTs can facilitate such improvements because they bring about easiness and usefulness to perform day-to-day tasks and access to information (Morawczynski, 2007). Additionally, ICTs improve quality of life by introducing a virtual reality (cyberspace) that eliminates the barriers of time, space, and distance (Rusten and Skerratt, 2007).

ICTs have also paved way to 'smart' living, whereby citizens benefit largely from the innovative ways of doing things (Yan and Shi, 2013). The 'smart' element of living is attributed to the usage of ICTs in the different contexts of life (Lindskog, 2004). ICTs are core to smart living to an extent that one can boldly assert that there can be no smart living without the pervasive integration of ICTs. Smart living is embraced in cities that strive to be more efficient, sustainable and equitable. Inherently such cities are labelled 'smart cities'.

Albino, Berardi, and Dangelico (2015) consider quality of life for citizens as the ultimate aim of a smart city. It is a consent amongst many scholars that "all the smart city initiatives in the end aim to raise quality of life for citizens and other urban stakeholders" (Shapiro, 2006; Batty *et al.*, 2012; Ballas, 2013). Apart from ICTs, the geographic area upon which the city is based, the governing structures and the citizens are the fabric of smart cities (Dameri, 2013). The citizens of a smart city inherently form a smart community. A smart community should ideally comprise of citizens who are self-decisive, independent and aware citizens (Giffinger, 2007). To achieve this, 'smart' initiatives are afforded primarily to transform ordinary communities to smart communities through integration of ICTs, amongst other things.

Adversely, it is known that ICTs introduce numerous security risks (i.e. cybersecurity) to its users. However, that cybersecurity awareness and education in smart communities is not given the precedence it warrants. Thus, the purpose of this paper is to analyse the cybersecurity challenges that are prevalent in smart communities. A systematic literature review will be employed as the research method to fulfil this purpose. The paper contends for a smart community that is cyber smart. The sections to follow provide the research an analysis of smart communities. Thereafter, a review of cybersecurity in smart community is provided. Finally, a discussion and concluding remarks can be found.

2 Smart Communities

The inception of the smart communities can be dated back to 1993 in Silicon Valley, California (Lindskog, 2004). This city was among the first to focus on how a community could integrate information technologies towards being 'smart'. Nowadays, the concept of smart communities is used in several contexts. However, a widely accepted definition of a smart community does not exist as yet. This section will explore the concept of smart communities, the elements that make up the community as well as the technologies used in a smart community.

2.1 The smart community concept

There are many ideas presented by scholars and domain experts in attempting to define the concept of smart communities. These definitions all have one thing in common – the **use of ICTs**. Some of these definitions are as follows:

- Lindskog (2004) describes a smart community as "a geographical area ranging in size from neighbourhood to a multi-county region whose residents, organizations, and governing institutions are using **information technology** to transform their region in significant ways. Co-operation among government, industry, educators, and the citizenry, instead of individual groups acting in isolation, is preferred. The technological enhancements undertaken as part of this effort should result in fundamental, rather than incremental, changes."

- "The concept of a smart community refers to the use of **information and communication technologies** by local governments and cities to better interact with their citizens, taking advantage of all available data to solve important problems" (Mellouli, Luna-Reyes and Zhang, 2014).

- "A smart community should be defined as a community ranging from a neighbourhood to a nation-wide community of common or shared interest, whose members, organizations and governing institutions are working in partnership to use **information and communication technologies** to transform their circumstances in significant ways" (Albino, Berardi and Dangelico, 2015)

- "A smart community is a community with a vision of the future that involves the application of **information and communication technologies** in a new and innovative way to empower its residents, institutions and regions as a whole. As such, they make the most of the opportunities that new applications afford and broadband-based services can deliver – such as better health care delivery, better education and training, and new business opportunities" (Razak, Malik and Saeed, 2013).

The common component between all the studied definitions can be clearly discerned as the usage of information technologies as means to an end. In addition to the various definitions, there are numerous concepts that are used interchangeably with the term smart community. These include 'community informatics', 'intelligent communities', and 'digital communities' (Albert, 2009). Keenan and Trotter (1990) suggest that community informatics refers to the use of **ICTs** by communities in order to achieve social, economical, political and cultural goals. According to Albert (2009), virtual communities are formed by like-minded people, sharing common interest and are physically separated but virtually united by means of the **Internet**. Intelligent communities are those that view **communication bandwidth** as a necessity for the economic growth and the development of the society. A digital community extends from the intelligent community by combining **communication bandwidth** and innovative services to improve governments, businesses and the lives of the residents of the community (Albert, 2009). Similarly, these synonymous terms reinforce the use of ICTs as the key element of a smart community. Additional elements are discussed in detail in the following subsection.

2.2 The smart community elements

Oksman and Raunio (2018) argue towards smart community elements and suggest the following – smart people, smart governance, smart mobility, and smart living. Firstly, the element of smart people considers participation in public life, the level of education, creativity and flexibility. The level of education factor suggests that "smart people need to be properly educated and trained to operate in the smart city"

(Phahlamohlaka *et al.*, 2014). Creativity and flexibility relate to the resourcefulness of the community to leverage from the technological advancements of the city.

Secondly, in terms of smart governance, ICT enables citizens engagement, making the community part of the decision making process. Additionally, smart governance aids in addressing democratic issues such as power and inequality in a city (Hollands, 2008). The smart governance component is mostly directed towards promoting intra-city cooperation and community development. Smart governance makes provision for transparent governance by involving citizens' engagement (Castelnovo, Misuraca and Savoldelli, 2016). Essentially, smart governance is related to the manner in which citizens communicate with local government.

Thirdly, smart mobility speaks to local access to sustainable, innovative and safe transportation systems. It emphasizes on convenience, safety and appropriate speed of the transportation systems. Finally, the smart living facet of smart communities focuses on the standard of living for all members of the community i.e. quality of life. The World Health Organization (WHO) defines quality of life as "individuals' perception of their position in life in the context of the culture and value systems" (Whoqol Group, 1995). Quality of life is the general well-being of individuals and societies. In the context of smart communities ITU suggests that quality of life relates to lifestyle in aspects of medical care, welfare, physical safety and education (ITU-T Focus Group on Smart Sustainable Cities, 2014). All the delineated elements are given the smart label because they leverage on the benefits provided by ICTs.

2.3 ICTs in smart community

To this end, it can be clearly perceived that there is a shared assumption on what makes a community smart. The 'smartness' of a community is related to the usage ICTs to achieve the fundamental goals of the community. Moreover, the adaptability of ICTs to be employed in ways that empower and engage the community in political debate contributes to smartness of the community (Hollands, 2008). ICTs that are typically employed in a smart community include *1) Network Connectivity, 2) Smart Mobile Applications, 3)   Sensor Network, 4) Internet of Things (IoTs), 5) Cloud Computing and 6) Big Data Analysis Solutions* (Ezz El-Din, Madhvaraj and Manjaiah, 2016).

Network connectivity enables the community to access available services. In most cases, the community uses these services through smart mobile applications. These services integrate various sensors to continually collect data about the users. Sensors are configured on interconnected devices referred to as Internet of Things (IoTs) that users employ to connect and access services. The data collected from these sensors is commonly stored in the Cloud in order to benefit from convenience of Cloud Computing. Also, the data collected by these technologies is voluminous and is gathered in an exceptionally rapid rate thus the need for Big Data Analysis Solutions.

At the heart of these technologies is the data that is processed and shared by one technology to the other. Smart community technologies process personally identifiable information (PII) and household level data about citizens (Kitchin, 2016). On one hand, this information can be put to good use by service providers to address service delivery, to enhance the quality of life and to create economic development. On the other hand, the information can be misused by malicious actors thus there is need for cybersecurity efforts. Accordingly, the following section discusses cybersecurity in smart communities.

3 Cybersecurity in smart communities

It is long established that the integration of ICTs in any context introduces the challenge of cybersecurity. As such, cybersecurity is also a challenge in the smart community context. It reported that smart communities are "leading the way towards the adoption of Internet of Things (IoT) technologies that will connect widespread sensors through the cloud to harvest relevant data and automate decision-making processes. Smart cities bring great promise, however there is also risk introduced through this new connectivity and intelligence" (Kaspersky, 2015). Primarily, the adoption of IoTs increases the ways in which an attacker can infiltrate a network i.e. the attack surface (Aldairi and Tawalbeh, 2017). An attack surface is defined as "the total sum of the vulnerabilities in a given computing device or network that are accessible to a hacker" (Rouse, 2014).

A study by Juniper (2018) revealed that IoT botnets could pose an "unmanageable" cybersecurity risk. Botnets are collections of compromised computers which are remotely controlled by an originator with an intention to distribute malicious activities such as distributed denial-of-service (DDoS) attacks, spam and phishing attacks. IoT devices in a smart community can be deployed in Botnet if security requirements are ignored (Wendzel *et al.*, 2014). Kitchin (2016) identifies data privacy and data security as the key challenges that require special attention in smart communities. These challenges are discussed in detail in the following subsections.

3.1 Data privacy

In many nations, privacy is extended to citizens as a basic human right to control one's personal information from public scrutiny and unwanted intrusions (Van Der Bank, 2012). Different forms of privacy are outlined as (Martinez-Balleste, Perez-Martinez and Solanas, 2013): *1) Identity privacy* - relating to personal and confidential data. *2) Bodily privacy* - involving the integrity of the physical person. *3) Territorial privacy* - concerning personal space, objects and property. *4) Locational and movement privacy* – focusing on tracking of one's spatial behaviour. *5) Communications privacy* – concerned with the surveillance of conversations and correspondence. *Transactions privacy* – relating to monitoring of queries/searches, purchases, and other exchanges.

The use of technologies in smart communities exposes the citizens to a wide range of breaches that threaten all the listed forms of privacy (Kitchin, 2016). Smart mobile applications were identified as some of the technologies used in smart communities. These applications are known to raise privacy concerns particularly because they request permissions to device functions to gain access to user information stored in the device (Zang *et al.*, 2015). This information includes, but not limited to, images, contact details, location information, device information, personal calendars and passwords (Kitchin, 2016).

An additional concern is that the data collected by the smart mobile application can be shared with third parties without the awareness or consent of the user (Kitchin, 2016). Kitchin (2016) adds, the sensors in smart mobile devices collect data that can be analysed and used to infer the health behaviour, social affiliations, sexual orientation as well as lifestyle of users. Essentially, the data collected from these technologies is shared, re-purposed and used in unpredictable ways that smart citizens need to be aware of in effort to maintain their privacy.

3.2 Data security

When using ICT devices, the security of information generated, stored, processed and shared is always a concern. It was mentioned that IoTs are prevalent technologies in smart communities. These devices include smartphones, smart locks, smart televisions web cameras, to name but a few. These interconnected devices actively participate in processing and exchanging digital information gathered from various sensors (Khoo, 2011). These devices have a number of attack surfaces that open information to a myriad of vulnerabilities (Weber, 2010; Sicari *et al.*, 2015). It is suggested that the security challenges of IoT devices can potentially outweigh the perceived benefits of employing such devices if left unattended (Moganedi and Mtsweni, 2017).

Securing information denotes maintaining the data confidentiality, integrity and availability. According to Moganedi and Mtsweni (2017), when considering security in IoTs, focus needs to be given to data collection, data storage and data communication. Firstly, in terms of data collection, IoT devices collect different types of information that is inclusive of personal information which needs to be secured. A single vulnerability in one of the interconnected IoT devices gives a malicious actor an opportunity to manipulate the information thus compromising data integrity. Secondly, the data collected by the IoT device is often stored in the Cloud which introduces another layer of security concerns. Lastly, information communicated in IoT devices is not encrypted due to the lack of sophisticated process capabilities in devices, thus information is transmitted insecurely opening a gap for breach of confidentiality.

3.3 Cybersecurity awareness and education

Cybersecurity awareness and education is deemed as a plausible countermeasure and mitigation against cyberattacks to non-technical users such as community members. A study by Wombat Security suggests that cybersecurity awareness is effective for changing behaviour and can reduce the risk of a security breach by up to 70% (Heller, 2015). Moreover, cybersecurity awareness and education is critical in the quest of fostering a positive culture of cybersecurity. Undoubtedly, cybersecurity awareness and education has positive impact in minimizing the exposure of home users to cyber-attacks.

The increased attack surface, due to pervasive interconnectedness in ICTs, is a challenge that citizens of a smart community need to be aware of, thus cybersecurity awareness and education should be acknowledged and pursued as a key parameter in smart communities. This notion is affirmed by findings from a study by Lévy-

Bencheton and Barra (2015) which states that cybersecurity awareness and education is a lacking necessity in smart communities. Smart citizens include home users that need to be made aware of the related security challenges since smart technologies allow malicious actors into their home network.

According to Milley (2017), a hacker can access home networks to obtain sensitive information such as banking records. Also, malicious actors can spy on users by hacking into a users' webcam (Jones and Gagneja, 2017). This can potentially place all members of a household at risk. Even worse, smart mobile applications such as digital applications have a complete digital history of users, meaning that if the security is neglected this information can end up in the wrong hands with harmful results to the user (Milley, 2017).

Home users are known to be ill-informed of cybersecurity challenges and thus fall victim to cyberattacks that could have been avoided with minimal security implementations (Thomson, von Solms and Louw, 2006). Awareness and education can provide Internet users with the ability to recognise and circumvent the risks that are apparent online (Kritzinger and Padayachee, 2013).

While the working class may be getting some form of cybersecurity awareness and education from industry, home users and the society at large rely on nationally driven cybersecurity awareness and education campaigns (Christensen, 2003). As such, cybersecurity awareness and education has long been recognised as a national priority in many nations. It cannot be disputed that in the modern day, cybersecurity awareness and education is a key requirement in any community that uses ICTs, it is even more critical as a countermeasure to the increased attack surface present in a smart community.

4   Discussion

It can be gathered from the reviewed literature on smart communities that the 'smartness' of a community is inherent to the innovative integration of ICTs in the day-to-day life of citizens. It is also established that these ICTs introduce a vast array of security challenges that necessitate cybersecurity efforts, specifically awareness and education. The higher interdependency on ICTs for daily operations, the broader the attack surface. Apart from known benefits of ICTs, smart living affords malicious actors the numerous opportunities to infiltrate the network of homes users. Thus cybersecurity awareness and education is a necessity in the context of smart communities.

Accordingly, the previous section highlighted the importance of awareness and education in addressing cybersecurity challenges. Conversely, from smart community literature reviewed there is no mention of cybersecurity awareness and education, which suggests that it is not identified as one of the elements that contribute to the 'smartness' of a community. Instead, the emphasis is innovative integration of ICTs in the day-to-day life of citizens, however without cybersecurity awareness and education, these ICTs cannot be used in a secure manner. This paper argues that insecure usage of ICTs cannot be deemed 'smart'. Thus it is a recommendation that the characterisation of a smart community be re-evaluated to include cybersecurity aware citizenry.

It is imperative to note that these cybersecurity challenges are not unique to smart communities as they affect everyone who uses ICTs. Instead, due to the rapidly increasing attack surface there is a unique urgency to highlight these challenges in the context of smart communities in order to influence the architects and citizens of these communities to accept cybersecurity as a necessary consideration.

Accepting cybersecurity awareness and education as a parameter for smart communities fundamentally means ensuring that each smart city invests in awareness education campaigns for its citizens. Additionally, all role-players in the development of smart cities should be afforded cybersecurity measures in all the dimensions of smart cities. Finally, it is recommended that the level of cybersecurity should be included as one of the indicators of the 'smartness' of a city and respective community.

5   Conclusion

ICTs continuously improve how the world operates on a daily basis. It has paved way to smart communities for the sole purpose of improving the quality of life for citizen. The 'smart' label is granted on the basis of using ICTs effectively. These benefits of ICT usage are accompanied by numerous cybersecurity risks that call for cybersecurity awareness and education efforts. This study identified a lack of emphasis on cybersecurity awareness and education in smart community context and thus contended towards smart citizens that are cyber smart.

6   References

Albert, S. (2009) "Networked Communities: Strategies for Digital Collaboration: Strategies for Digital Collaboration", IGI Global, United Kingdom, ISBN: 978-1-59904-771-3

Albino, V., Berardi, U. and Dangelico, R. M. (2015) "Smart cities: Definitions, dimensions, performance, and initiatives", *Journal of Urban Technology*, 22(1), pp. 3–21.

Aldairi, A. and Tawalbeh, L. (2017) "Cyber Security Attacks on Smart Cities and Associated Mobile Technologies", *Procedia Computer Science*. Elsevier B.V., 109(2016), pp. 1086–1091.

Ballas, D. (2013) "What makes a "happy city"?", *Cities*, 32(2013), pp. 39–50.

Van Der Bank, C. M. (2012) "The Right To Privacy – South African and Comparative Perspectives", *European Journal of Business and Social Sciences*, 1(6), pp. 77–86.

Batty, M. et al. (2012) "Smart cities of the future", *European Physical Journal: Special Topics*, 214(1), pp. 481–518.

Castelnovo, W., Misuraca, G. and Savoldelli, A. (2016) "Smart Cities Governance: The Need for a Holistic Approach to Assessing Urban Participatory Policy Making", *Social Science Computer Review*, 34(6), pp. 724–739.

Christensen, J. (2003) "Solving the Cyber Security Problem : The Role of the Department of Homeland Security". Washington, D.C.

Dameri, R. P. (2013) "Searching for Smart City definition: a comprehensive proposal*"*, *International Journal of Computers & Technology*, 11(5), pp. 2544–2551.

Ezz El-Din, H., Madhvaraj, M. and Manjaiah, D. (2016) "Cyber Security in Smart Cities", *CSI Communications*, 40(3), pp. 34–36.

Giffinger, R. (2007) "Smart cities - Ranking of European medium-sized cities", http://www.smart-cities.eu/download/smart_cities_final_report.pdf, (Accessed: 10 June 2018)

Heller, M. (2015) "Cybersecurity awareness can reduce infection risk up to 70%", News, January, https://www.wombatsecurity.com/news/cybersecurity-awareness-can-reduce-infection-risk-70 (Accesses: 20 July 2018).

Hollands, R. G. (2008) "Will the real smart city please stand up?", *City*, 12(3), pp. 303–320.

ITU-T Focus Group on Smart Sustainable Cities (2014) "Smart sustainable cities: An analysis of definitions", https://www.itu.int/en/ITU-T/focusgroups/ssc/Documents/.../TR-Definitions.docx (Accessed: 10 June 2018)

Jones, A. S. and Gagneja, K. (2017) "Preventing Covert Webcam Hacking in the Civilian and Governmental Sectors", *Proceedings - 2016 International Conference on Computational Science and Computational Intelligence*, CSCI 2016, pp. 993–998.

Kaspersky (2015) "Securing Smart Cities Issues Guidelines for Smart City Technology Adoption, Seuring Smart Cities", https://www.kaspersky.com/about/press-releases/2015_securing-smart-cities-issues-guidelines-for-smart-city-technology-adoption (Accessed: 10 June 2018).

Keenan, T. P. and Mitchell Trotter, D. (1990) "The changing role of community networks in providing citizen access to the Internet", *Internet Research*, 9(2), pp. 100–108.

Khoo, B. (2011) "RFID As an enabler of the internet of things: Issues of security and privacy", *in Proceedings - 2011 IEEE International Conferences on Internet of Things and Cyber, Physical and Social Computing*, iThings/CPSCom 2011, pp. 709–712.

Kitchin, R. (2016) "Getting smarter about smart cities: Improving data privacy and data security", *Department of the Taoiseach on behalf of the Government Data Forum*.

Kozma, R. B. and Vota, W. S. (2014) "ICT in developing countries: Policies, implementation, and impact". New York: Springer. ISBN: 978-1-4614-3184-8

Kritzinger, E. and Padayachee, K. (2013) "Engendering an e-safety awareness culture within the South African context", *in AFRICON. IEEE*, pp. 839 – 843.

Lévy-Bencheton, C. and Darra, E. (2015) "Cyber security for Smart Cities: An architecture model for public transport".

Lindskog, H. (2004) "Smart communities initiatives", *Proceedings of the 3rd ISOneWorld Conference*, p. 16.

Martinez-Balleste, A., Perez-Martinez, P. and Solanas, A. (2013) "The pursuit of citizens' privacy: A privacy-aware smart city is possible", *IEEE Communications Magazine*, 51(6), pp. 136–141.

Mellouli, S., Luna-Reyes, L. F. and Zhang, J. (2014) "Smart government, citizen participation and open data", *Information Polity*, 19(1–2), pp. 1–4.

Milley, P. (2017) Privacy and the Internet of Things, Securing the Home IoT Network.

Moganedi, S. and Mtsweni, J. (2017) "Beyond the convenience of the internet of things: Security and privacy concerns", *in 2017 IST-Africa Week Conference (IST-Africa)*, pp. 1–10.

Morawczynski, O. (2007) "Unraveling the impact of investments in ICT, education and health on development: an analysis of archival data of five West African countries using regression splines", *The Electronic Journal of Information Systems in Developing Countries*, 29(1), pp. 1–15.

Oksman, V. and Raunio, M. (2018) "Citizen -centric Smart City Planning for Africa: A Qualitative Case Study of Early Stage Co-creation of a Namibian Smart Community", *in The Twelfth International Conference on Digital Society and eGovernments*, pp. 30–35.

Phahlamohlaka, J. et al. (2014) "Towards a Smart Community Centre: SEIDET Digital Village", *IFIP Advances in Information and Communication Technology*, 431(2009), pp. 107–121.

Razak, N. A., Malik, J. A. and Saeed, M. (2013) "A Development of Smart Village Implementation Plan for Agriculture: A Pioneer Project in Malaysia", *in Computing & Informatics, 4Th International Conference*, Malaysia, pp. 495–502.

Rouse, M. (2014) "Network Security", https://whatis.techtarget.com/definition/attack-surface (Accessed: 22 July 2018).

Rusten, G. and Skerratt, S. (2007) "Information and communication technologies in rural society". Routledge. ISBN: 9781134220823

Shapiro, J. (2006) "Smart cities: quality of life, productivity, and the growth effects of human capital", *The review of economics and statistics*, 88 (May)(2), pp. 324–335.

Sicari, S. et al. (2015) "Security, privacy and trust in Internet of things: The road ahead", *Computer Networks*, 76(January), pp. 146–164.

Sorrell, S. (2018) "Internet of Things for Security Providers: Opportunities, Strategies & Market Leaders 2016-2021", https://www.juniperresearch.com/researchstore/iot-m2m/internet-of-things-for-security-providers/opportunities-strategies-forecasts-(1) (Accessed: 20 July 2018).

Syed Abdul Kadir, S. L., Husin, S. and Nadarajah, D. (2014) "The Impact of ICT on Quality of Life", *in Advances in Business-Related Research Conference*. Milan, p. 13. http://eprints.um.edu.my/13400/ (Accessed: 20 July 2018).

Thomson, K.-L., von Solms, R. and Louw, L. (2006) "Cultivating an organizational information security culture", *Computer Fraud & Security*, 2006(10), pp. 7–11.

Weber, R. H. (2010) "Internet of Things - New security and privacy challenges", *Computer Law and Security Review*. 26(1), pp. 23–30.

Wendzel, S. et al. (2014) "Envisioning smart building botnets", *in Lecture Notes in Informatics (LNI), Proceedings - Series of the Gesellschaft fur Informatik (GI),* pp. 319–329.

Whoqol Group (1995) "The World Health Organization Quality of Life assessment (WHOQOL): position paper from the World Health Organization.", *Social science & medicine,* 41(10), pp. 1403–1409.

Yan, M. and Shi, H. (2013) "Smart Living Using Bluetooth-Based Android Smartphone", *International Journal of Wireless & Mobile Networks,* 5(1), pp. 65–72.

Zang, J. et al. (2015) "Who Knows What about Me? A Survey of Behind the Scenes Personal Data Sharing to Third Parties by Mobile Apps", *Technology Science.* https://techscience.org/a/2015103001/download.pdf (Accessed: 10 June 2018).

Social Networking: A Tool for Effective Cybersecurity Education in Cyber-Driven Financial Transactions

R. Maharaj and R. von Solms

Nelson Mandela University, Port Elizabeth, South Africa
e-mail: s212254189@mandela.ac.za, rossouw.vonsolms@mandela.ac.za

Abstract

Cyberspace technology and cyber-driven services are core in today's modern world. This means that cyber services can be found in many facets of societies and many of the world's industries. This is also true for banking and users of cyber-driven financial transactions. Cybersecurity education is becoming imperative for users to be able to protect themselves better against a wide variety of threats. This is especially true for banking users, who due to the financial nature, are affected by a growing number of cyber-related threats. This paper presents an educational approach using social networking to assist in educating modern users of cyber-driven financial transactions.

Keywords

E-banking, Education, Cybersecurity Education, Social Networking, Cyber-driven financial transactions.

1   Introduction

In modern times, the rise of information technology (IT) can be seen in many facets of industry. IT innovations and developments shape the way end-users interact with traditional industries. These information technologies and their "partner" cyberspace have become intertwined in end-users' lives. Cyberspace and IT can both be seen as critical aspects of end-users' day to day lives. Although cyberspace has brought about numerous benefits, it has also introduced aspects of danger and risks in end-users' modern way of living. As end-users become more and more reliant on cyberspace, the chances of them becoming potential victims of cybercrime increases unless they are made aware and vigilant of the dangers surrounding their cyber activities. Examples of these possible dangers include e-mail hacking, phishing attacks and social engineering attacks. It is essential that end-users are made aware of these potential dangers and how to protect themselves more effectively. This is particularly important for end-users involved in cyber-driven financial transactions. Due to the financial nature of these cyber-driven financial transactions, users of these cyber services are often faced with more threats. According to the Financial Fraud Action UK (Five et al., 2017), financial fraud losses across payment cards, remote banking and cheques totalled £366.4 million between January and June 2017. During that period compromised personal and financial data was seen as a key driver of the financial losses (Five et al., 2017). Criminals utilized attacks similar to the above mentioned. Thus, it is critically important that end-users, specifically when conducting cyber-driven financial transactions, are made aware of the dangers and risks associated with negligent behaviour when doing so.

This paper attempts to address the lack of education surrounding end-user cyber-driven financial transactions by introducing an alternative education approach utilizing two prominent social networking platforms, Facebook and YouTube. This paper will focus on the introduction of this educational approach as part of a joint research project undertaken with the South African Banking Risk Information Centre (SABRIC).

2   Background

The aim of this section is to provide a sound base and motivation for cybersecurity education, awareness and training to individuals exposed to sensitive personal and organizational cyber, especially users of cyber-driven financial transaction.

2.1   Cybersecurity Education, Awareness and Training

Cybersecurity is comprised of various elements, varying from technical to operational and behavioural security. There is no single solution to address it and therefore a multifaceted approach needs to be taken. Cybersecurity education, awareness and training provide end-users with the ability to recognize related threats where acceptable and act on them appropriately. Traditionally cybersecurity education, awareness and training programs have been targeted at organizations. However, in modern times cyberspace is at a simple "*click*" or "*tap*" away for everyone and thus cybersecurity education should be part and parcel of the lives of all end-users. This includes banking users involved in cyber-driven financial transactions, where end-users are particularly vulnerable.

2.2   Banking and Cyberspace – The shift in responsibility

Banking is one of the oldest industries in the world. As with many long-standing industries, banking has evolved over time, embracing new technologies and markets. This is also true for cyberspace, as many financial institutions and the way they transact are heavily dependent on cyberspace and IT (Horn, 2010). As financial institutions introduced more cyber-related services, it allowed users to take a more active role in their personal financial management. As seen with the introduction of the ATM and in more recent times mobile and internet banking. This shift, puts more responsibility in the hands of users, as they now become a potential point of weakness in the banking process. This statement is echoed in research where end-users are often considered weak links in the information security process (Al Awawdeh & Tubaishat, 2014; Aloul, 2012; Frauenstein & Von Solms, 2014). Thus, as mentioned in the previous section, modern banking users involved in cyber-driven financial transactions are very dependent and will benefit from appropriate education, awareness and training. As this will enable them to conduct personal banking in a more secure and safe manner, giving users peace of mind.

2.3 Cyber-Driven Financial Transaction Education

Cyber- driven financial transactions can be regarded as any transaction that occurs involving cyberspace. Examples of cyber-driven financial transactions include ATM usage, online purchases and credit card usage. As such, it can be seen that the majority of transactions that occur in modern banking can be regarded as cyber-driven financial transactions. As stated in the Ombudsman's Annual Report for Banking Services South Africa (2016), a large number of users are negatively affected by cyber-crime. Human error or, as mentioned previously, negligence is a large contributor, in financial loss experienced by users during cyber-driven financial transactions. Human error can be as a result of inexperience, improper training, the making of incorrect assumptions and other circumstances (Whittman & Mattord, 2013). Therefore, it can be argued that there is a need for proper education, awareness and training among users of cyber-driven financial transactions. Education and training are literally 'placed' between users and the cyberspace or systems utilized (Whitman & Mattord, 2012). It is through proper education, awareness and training that it is possible to foster a cyber-culture of secure cyber usage towards conducting safe cyber-driven financial transactions. It is thus clear that users may be self-responsible for malicious cyber-driven financial incidents due to their lack of related education, awareness and training or ignorance on the subject matter. Further, that education plays an important role in cyber-driven financial transactions to ensure that users are knowledgeable about utilizing cyber services in a secure manner. Through proper education, that increases their awareness, it reduces their inherent negligence and ignorance and therefore assists in mitigating the related risks associated with cyber-driven financial transactions.

Financial institutions, offering these cyber-driven financial services, do offer some educational material and services to educate their clients and therefore helping to mitigate the associated risks. Even though the educational content is correct, the content may be challenging to locate and also, the material is not necessarily presented in a manner that appeals to the average user. The following section will discuss an alternative educational approach that aims to educate users of cyber-driven financial transactions allowing them to conduct these cyber services safely and securely.

3   Instrument Implementation

It is clear from the foregoing sections that users of cyber-driven financial transactions are extremely vulnerable. This is due to the increased threats they face and the lack of appealing education surrounding the subject matter. This section will provide insight into how an alternative educational approach was created in partnership with the South African Banking Risk Information Center (SABRIC).

3.1   Research Approach

This research resides in the problem-solving domain and follows a mixed methods approach. The research approach followed is that of an experiment, utilizing an instrument within the social media domain to gather data. The instrument in this context is the cybersecurity education tool utilizing a social media quiz and video combination created in order to raise awareness and educate users of cyber-driven financial transactions.

The structure of the following sections and subsections will firstly provide the context and environment in which the instrument will be implemented; secondly to describe the instrument and its content, thirdly to describe the research agent and finally to describe the instrument's implementation.

3.2   Context of Implementation

Cyber usage and cybersecurity is a topic often addressed in the South African banking industry. The majority of security-related efforts resides in the technical space. However, technical security safeguards are only as secure as the users involved in the process at hand. As stated in literature, hardware and software security mechanisms are widely used to strengthen information systems (IS) against attacks, however, these systems are still vulnerable because of user's undesirable behaviour (Öğütçü, Testik, & Chouseinoglou, 2016). As cyber services and technology has integrated into the daily lives of many people, including those involved in cyber-driven financial transactions, it has become critical to ensure that users are educated about threats and dangers related to their cyber services. The context in which this study occurs is at a national level, using social networking platforms as an educational tool. A fun social networking quiz (to raise awareness) and a related informative video (to educate) therefore had to be created. This two-fold approach and the use of social networking form the basis of the instrument. The design of the instrument was carefully considered and is discussed in the next subsection.

3.3   The Instrument (Social Networking Game Quiz and Video)

The instrument is targeted at the majority of South African banking clients - the majority of which make use of cyber-driven financial services. Therefore, considerations in the design of the instrument include; audience-appropriate content, delivery mechanism, ease of use and understanding. Existing educational instruments used by South African banks were considered as a basis for the instrument. However, the current state of awareness and education is lacking and unappealing. During an initial discussion with the South African Banking Risk Information Center (SABRIC), a two-fold approach, a combination game-type quiz and an accompanying video, was decided upon. This approach served as the basis for the instrument for two major reasons. Firstly, social networking, particularly Facebook and YouTube are growing rapidly in South Africa and allow for a far wider audience to be reached. Secondly, a social networking game and video approach lower the audience preconceived notions about typical education, which can be seen as dull and unappealing. This makes the instrument more mass marketable. The design and content will be discussed in the following subsections.

3.3.1   Design

This subsection will address the reasons why a social networking game quiz and video combination was chosen as the most suitable instrument to raise awareness and educate users of cyber-driven financial services. The focus of this section will, therefore, be the design of the instrument.

Firstly, the instrument's approach must cater to a wide audience. Due to SABRIC's involvement, the instrument had to be designed to reach a national audience. This was achieved by making use of social networking (Facebook and YouTube) as the platform for which the instrument would be hosted. Facebook, as of the fourth quarter of 2017, has 2.2 billion active users, with a significant amount being South African (Statista, 2017). This allowed the instrument to be reached by many users of cyber-driven financial transactions, accomplishing the goal of being able to reach a wide audience. Secondly, the design of the instrument had to be "fun" and interactive. This allowed, as previously mentioned to lower the preconceived notions of traditional learning. This was achieved by using a high score type quiz format. The quiz served as an awareness-raising tool. Using a quiz format allowed for the instrument to be interactive and have that "fun" factor. This interactive approach appeals to many social networking users as quizzes are typically popular with some quizzes seeing an average of 60 000 user engagements (Boland, 2017).   Thirdly, the instrument had to allow for users to be educated in an alternative manner. This was done by a short, suitable video. Once the user completed the quiz (raising awareness) they were then prompted with a video on the subject matter. Video was used due to its ease of use and lack of effort required by the user to educate themselves. Videos produced were short as this enables a user to keep focus throughout the duration of the video, enabling them to better concentrate.

An element of educational reinforcement is also incorporated in the instrument. This is done by introducing a message after a user selects an answer. The message relates to the question, after a participant, answers the quiz questions the message is displayed. This enables the user to learn (reinforcing), alongside the "fun" quiz.

In order for the user to benefit, the content of the quiz and video is very important to ensure focused and relevant learning takes place. The content found in both the video and quiz are obviously of particular importance.

3.3.2   Content

Five quizzes with five related videos were created. Topics were chosen following close liaison with SABRIC regarding what affects the typical cyber-driven financial transaction user most. Examples of topics include online shopping, malware, card fraud, cyber hygiene and mobile banking. Online shopping will be used as an example in this paper.

The questions asked in the quizzes were topic related and pertaining to safe and secure online shopping. Table 1 represents the online shopping quiz questions and answers.

Question: Which of the following contribute to unsafe online shopping?	
Answer A:	Saving of payment information in web browsers
Answer B:	Using a well-known online merchant
Answer C:	Making use of 3-D secure payment
Answer D:	Looking for the closed padlock symbol
Correct Answer Text: Right answer! Never save payment information in your web browser as it may be used if someone gets a hold of your device.	Incorrect Answer Text: Wrong answer! Some sites (as well as all browsers) offer to "remember" your payment information (e.g. password) for your convenience upon subsequent purchases. Never accept to have your "financial information" stored on any website/web browser.

Table 1: Online Shopping Sample Question

As in the above table, quiz questions were structured as multiple-choice questions with four possible answers. The video that relates to the quiz is roughly 1 minute and 30 seconds long. As mentioned previously, the videos were kept short in order to hold the user's attention. The online shopping video comprises of the following five pointers for safe and secure online shopping. These five pointers are;

1. Look out for the padlock followed by HTTPS next to the URL when transacting online – the 'S' indicates that you are connected to a secure and encrypted website.
2. When registering on a secure site, choose a strong password and do not save your login details on any computer or mobile device. Never re-use the same password on multiple domains.
3. Avoid sharing your personal information, online merchants don't need your ID number or date of birth to process your order, but cybercriminals can use this to steal your identity.
4. Check your bank balance after making any online shopping payments. Report any fraudulent transactions to your bank as soon as possible.
5. For added online shopping verification, register your bank card with 3D Secure.

The message behind this video is to educate the users to perform online shopping in a safer and more secure manner. The video itself is an animated production, with a 'look and feel' that should appeal to users.

As discussed, this study focuses on five topics, namely; online shopping, malware, card fraud, cyber hygiene and mobile banking. However, the topic of online shopping will be discussed as an example in this paper. The instrument was designed to meet the following goals. Firstly, the instrument had to reach a wide audience. Secondly, it had to be "fun" and interactive. This was done through the creation of a social media game quiz and related video. all quizzes comprise of five, close-ended questions and are linked to the video. After a user selects an answer, regardless if it is a correct or incorrect answer, an educational message is displayed. This, as previously mentioned, adds an element of educational reinforcement.

The effectiveness of this instrument as a cybersecurity educational tool will be determined by the research agent, to be discussed in the next section.

3.4   Research Agent

The research agent consists of two parts. The initial part of the research agent constitutes the quiz. The quiz, alongside raising user awareness, has been used to capture statistical data about the level of awareness and knowledge that users of cyber-driven financial transactions possess. The quiz questions are close-ended, multiple-choice questions which relate to the most prominent threat situations users face concerning cyber-driven financial transactions. This allows for some approximation of users' awareness levels and knowledge to be rated per quiz. The primary data gathered from the quiz includes; correct and incorrect answers, while additional data captured and calculated includes; average score, number of participants, participant country, participant device, gender and average elapsed time. The ratio of correct and incorrect answers gives some indication of the users' level of awareness and knowledge on the specific topic. Incorrect answers indicate that users might lack awareness and knowledge to conduct these cyber services in a safe and secure manner.

The second part of the research agent consists of a single question asked at the end of each video. The question asked, attempts to determine if the user feels more positive and assured of the level of knowledge on the subject matter acquired. Users are only asked this question, once they complete both the quiz and the video.

Both parts of the research agent, therefore, form part of the instrument and is applied in the context of this study. The combination of both parts of research agent, indicates the level of awareness and education before and after the instrument has been used. All five quizzes and related videos follow the research agent outlined in this section. The instrument's implementation will be presented in the following section.

3.5 Implementation (Experiment)

The research agent was distributed through social media channels in the form of the final instrument. The distribution took place primarily through a Facebook campaign which took place in partnership with SABRIC. This allowed for a wider audience to be reached, as SABRIC is an authority in the local banking environment. The initial campaign began on the 27th of March 2018. SABRIC released a media statement alongside a sponsored Facebook campaign. The sponsorship consisted of promoting the associated videos themselves through paid adverts on YouTube and promoting the quizzes via sponsored adverts on Facebook directly. This sponsorship allowed for a greater target audience to be reached. While the campaign was being run, the quizzes were also shared from other sources. These sources included, the researcher's own Facebook and any participants that opted to share the quizzes themselves. At present the social media campaign is still ongoing, as such participants are still taking part in quizzes and viewing the educational videos.

The following section will discuss the results of the research agent with the focus being on the topic: online shopping.

4   Analysis and Results

As mentioned previously, there are five quizzes with five related videos. Quizzes are based on topics most prevalent to users of cyber-driven financial transactions, according to SABRIC. This section will discuss the results of a single quiz, namely; online shopping, as the social media campaign is still ongoing and part of a larger research project.

At present, the online shopping quiz has 420 participants of which 86% fully completed the quiz. This results in a total of about 389 participants. 57% of participants were female and 43% were male. A small number of participants accessed the quiz via a mobile device (37%) while the majority of participants accessed it via their desktop machine (63%). Due to social media being accessed worldwide, participants were not only from South Africa. At present 92.2% of participants are South African, while 1.8% are United States citizens, 2.4% are United Kingdom citizens, 3% are Icelandic citizens and 0.6% are from other countries.

Within the quiz, six questions relating to online shopping were asked. These questions were asked before mention was made to the associated educational video. Only once a participant has completed the initial quiz, they can view the associated video. Once the video was watched, a follow-up question was asked, in order to assess if the participant felt he/she learned something from the quiz and related video. The overall results show that participants, regardless of their score, felt as though they had learned something and that they could conduct their cyber-driven financial transactions in a more safe and secure manner. The table below shows the results for the online shopping quiz.

Question Number	Correctly Answered (%)	Incorrectly Answered (%)
1	89.0	11.0
2	51.4	48.6
3	94.4	5.6
4	79.6	20.4
5	61.9	38.1
6	75.4	24.6

Table 2. Online Shopping Participant scores

As seen in the above table, participants scored well in the quiz. Due to the videos being promoted separately from the Facebook quizzes, the online shopping video was viewed at present 38 141 times. One hundred percent of the users that answered the poll, responded positively to the question whether the video was indeed useful and added value. It can be seen from the number of views recorded that users preferred to go directly to the video rather than following the quiz-video route. This might be interpreted that a large number of users are already aware they lack proper knowledge to deal with the cyber threats they face. Irrespective of the standalone YouTube video views, results show that a combination of both the quiz and video can be a successful educational combination. In general, this study confirms that participants gained relevant knowledge and confidence on how to conduct online shopping safely and securely in cyberspace, through a social networking educational approach.

5   Conclusion

Cyber-based services are found in many businesses and industries today. This is particularly true in the banking sector, where users make use of ATMs, internet and mobile banking. These users of cyber-driven financial transactions pose a great risk to themselves, through negligent or ignorant behaviour. Therefore, relevant cybersecurity education and awareness is a must for these users. Social media and social networking can indeed be used as an educational tool towards effective cybersecurity education, under the following conditions: firstly, the material can be accessed with ease, secondly, the material is appealing to users and thirdly, that the material is not too data and time-consuming.

This study has shown that if implemented correctly and made appealing, users can be made more aware and educated through the means of social media. Allowing them to conduct their cyber-driven financial transactions in a more safe and secure manner. It is therefore concluded that, social networking and social media in general and specifically in the format used in this study, can be a possible option for the education of users of cyber-driven financial transactions. However, further research should be done to improve the process.

6 Future Work

The results shown in this paper is part of a larger ongoing study. The next stage will be to complete the social media campaign and verify all quiz results to show statistical significance. This will allow for the educational approach of utilizing social networking for cybersecurity education to be verified.

7 Acknowledgements.

The South African Banking Risk Information Center (SABRIC) is acknowledged for their contribution towards this research project.

8 References

Al Awawdeh, S., & Tubaishat, A. (2014). An information security awareness program to address common security concerns in IT unit. *ITNG 2014 - Proceedings of the 11th International Conference on Information Technology: New Generations*, 273–278. https://doi.org/10.1109/ITNG.2014.67

Aloul, F. a. (2012). The Need for Effective Information Security Awareness. *Journal of Advances in Information Technology*, 3(3), 176–183. https://doi.org/10.4304/jait.3.3.176-183

Boland, G. (2017). What to know about quizzes on social in 2017 - NewsWhip. Retrieved March 2, 2018, from http://www.newswhip.com/2017/04/know-quiz-content-2017/

Five, T., Campaign, S. F., Office, H., Taskforce, J. F., Fraud, F., Uk, A., & Five, T. (2017). 2017 half year fraud update : Fraud : January to June 2017, (September).

Frauenstein, E. D., & Von Solms, R. (2014). Combatting phishing: A holistic human approach. *2014 Information Security for South Africa - Proceedings of the ISSA 2014 Conference*. https://doi.org/10.1109/ISSA.2014.6950508

Horn, S. (2010). *Cyberville: Clicks, Culture, and the Creation of an Online Town*. Grand Central Publishing. Retrieved from https://books.google.co.za/books?id=7VGZCwAAQBAJ

Öğütçü, G., Testik, Ö. M., & Chouseinoglou, O. (2016). Analysis of personal information security behavior and awareness. *Computers & Security*, 56, 83–93. https://doi.org/10.1016/j.cose.2015.10.002

Ombudsman Annual Report for Banking Services. (2016). Ombudsman Annual Report 2016 for Banking Services.

Statista. (2017). Worldwide 2017 | Statista. Retrieved March 2, 2018, from https://www.statista.com/statistics/264810/number-of-monthly-active-facebook-users-worldwide/

Whitman, M. E., & Mattord, H. J. (2012). *Principles of information security. Course Technology*. https://doi.org/10.1016/B978-0-12-381972-7.00002-6

Whittman, M. E., & Mattord, H. J. (2013). Management of Information Security Fourth Edition, 545. https://doi.org/2013945552

A Systematic Review of Information Security Knowledge-Sharing Research

S. Al-Ahmari[1], K. Renaud[2] and I. Omoronyia[1]

[1]School of Computing Science, University of Glasgow, Glasgow, United Kingdom
[2]School of Design and Informatics, Abertay University, Dundee, United Kingdom
e-mail: s.alahmari.1@research.gla.ac.uk; k.renaud@abertay.ac.uk;
Inah.Omoronyia@glasgow.ac.uk

Abstract

It is crucial for knowledge to be shared in the information security domain. In effect, sharing ensures that knowledge and skills are propagated through the organisation. Here, we report on a systematic literature review we carried out to gain insight into the literature related to information security knowledge sharing within organisations. The literature highlights the importance of security knowledge sharing in terms of enhancing organisational security awareness, and identifies gaps that can be addressed by researchers in the area.

Keywords

Sharing, Knowledge, Information, Security, Employees

1   Introduction

Employees play a crucial role in enhancing information security (Ahmed *et al.*, 2014). Their understanding of risk can have a positive influence on the improvement of information security behaviours (Becerra-Fernandez, 2014). Yet an essential pre-requisite for secure behaviour is that people know what it is they have to do and how to do it; in other words, they possess the required *knowledge* and *skills* (know-how). While awareness drives and training are undeniably valuable and essential, the most powerful way to ensure that all employees gain the requisite knowledge and know-how is to encourage and facilitate knowledge sharing across the organisation (Mermoud *et al.*, 2018).

Knowledge sharing, of all types, improves the organisation as a whole. It facilitates trust between employees (Dang-Pham *et al.*, 2017; Dang-Pham & Nkhoma, 2017; Politis, 2003). Of particular interest in this paper is *information security* knowledge sharing. Knowledge sharing improves information security awareness, which is important when it comes to preventing security breaches (Dixon, 2000). Organisations should therefore facilitate and engender knowledge sharing. The aim is to make the knowledge accessible to all of those who need it and ultimately to improve information security across the organisation.

We now review the core concept of 'knowledge', and discuss the kinds of knowledge that could be shared in the information security context. We then report on the systematic literature review we carried out in order to gain insight into the research carried out into knowledge sharing in the information security context (Section 3). Section 4 presents our findings, Section 5 reflects, and Section 6 concludes.

2 Knowledge & Information Security

Knowledge is gained when meaning is added to information. People can gain knowledge from their environment (Feledi *et al.*, 2013) or from personal experience (Feledi & Fenz, 2012). In the information security context, people can gain knowledge from training drives, but are more likely to gain the knowledge they need from other employees in the workplace.

Knowledge can be either tacit or explicit (Dang-Pham *et al.*, 2017). The former refers to *skills* that cannot easily be recorded or expressed, which makes it difficult to share and retain (Fenz & Ekelhart, 2009). It is important for employees to transfer tacit security-related knowledge to other employees – to externalise it (Flores *et al.*, 2014). Explicit knowledge can be expressed in numbers and words (Gal-Or & Ghose, 2005) and can be recorded. Knowledge delivers the most value when it is linked to other relevant and pertinent knowledge, thereby conveying new knowledge, a process called 'combination' (Flores *et al.*, 2014).

2.1 Information Security Knowledge

Bartnes *et al.* (2016) define information security as a set of strategic management processes, policies and tools necessary for preventing, detecting, documenting and countering threats that subject non-digital and digital information systems to risks that cause damage such as loss of information and information theft. Flores et al. (2014) define knowledge sharing as the explicit or tacit transfer of values, experience, expert insight and contextual information from one person to another which helps that person to incorporate and evaluate new information and experience. Stanton et al. (2005) suggest a two-dimensional model of end-user security behaviours. The first is expertise and the second intention. We focus on benevolent intentions. In this category, people without knowledge make naïve mistakes, but knowledge leads to awareness and security assurance. Parsons et al. (2014) conclude that human errors attributable to lack of security awareness and knowledge are the principal sources of information security breaches. Using HAIS-Questionnaires and incorporating a sample of 500 employees, the authors gauged employees' awareness levels and came to the conclusion that employees with poorer security awareness subjected their organisation to security breach risks (Parsons et al., 2014). As a recommendation, the authors identified a holistic approach to employee training that emphasises knowledge and attitude as the way forward towards counteracting this problem. However, Zhang (2018) argues that knowledge expires in this field, and needs to be renewed. Moreover, Junger *et al.* (2017) show that warnings, by themselves, do not necessarily make that much of a difference to susceptibility to social-engineering attacks. Gcaza and von Solms (2017) argue that cultivating a cyber security culture, which implies that knowledge sharing has become *de rigueur*, is the best approach for addressing human factors in information security.

2.2 Information Security Knowledge Sharing

Kim and Kim (2017) show that social pressure influences compliance intention, and that compliant behaviour is influenced by knowledge. Knowledge sharing is crucial in the information security arena.

Safa and von Solms (2016) explored the process of information security knowledge sharing in organisations. They discovered that "earning a reputation and gaining promotion" and "external motivations" had a positive influence on knowledge sharing. Mermoud *et al.* (2018) report that people would share knowledge if they expected to get something valuable in return; reciprocity was deemed to be important. They suggest that organisations incentivise rather than mandate sharing.

Safa *et al.* (2016) aimed to deliver an insight into the phenomenon of information security knowledge sharing. They combined Motivation Theory and the Theory of Planned Behaviour to deliver a knowledge sharing module (Dixon, 2000). They discovered that trust was a barrier to knowledge sharing (Dixon, 2000). Dang-Pham *et al.* (2017) aimed to find out why people provided information security advice to others. They discovered that the primary barriers to sharing security knowledge were behaviour and trust. Rocha Flores *et al.* (2014) examined the impact of cultural factors on security knowledge sharing. The results show that national and cultural factors are worth considering when it comes to the nature of sharing. They concluded that the most critical barrier to sharing security knowledge was cultural. Feledi *et al.* (2013) examined the efficiency of cooperation between participants during the process of knowledge sharing. They identified the primary barrier to sharing security knowledge to be a lack of motivation on the part of employees.

2.3 Summary

The previous discussion identifies the importance of the organisation's incentive processes in encouraging knowledge sharing in the information security context. Moreover, the role of trust was highlighted, which suggests that an organisation that suffers from a lack of trust might well experience more security incidents because employees do not share knowledge. When we consider the fact that hackers extensively and actively share knowledge (Zhang *et al.*, 2015), we have to pay attention to fostering and encouraging sharing within organisations.

We will now report on the outcome of the literature review to see whether these same factors emerge.

3 Methodology

We followed Pickering and Byrne's (Gao *et al.*, 2015) systematic quantitative literature review methodology as follows:

- **Choose Databases**: Science Direct, Scopus, Web of Science and Google Scholar.

- **Choose Keywords:** for the searches were 'information security', 'Sharing knowledge',' Behaviour of the end-users.
- **Choose Time Range**: published between 2000 and 2017.
- **Inclusion Criteria**: Studies related to information security knowledge sharing for employees in the workplace. Studies on knowledge sharing security between firms, knowledge sharing security networks for end-users outside of the organisations, and knowledge sharing in technology security were excluded.

Database	Papers Found	Papers Rejected	Papers Analyzed
Web of Science	191	185	6
Scopus	25	16	9
Science Direct	54	42	12
Google Scholar	46	27	19

Table 1: Systematic Literature Review

4   Results

The literature review delivers insight into extant research, which will be reviewed in this section.

4.1   Factors affecting Security Knowledge Sharing

Several studies addressed the advantages of knowledge sharing in the organisation, especially in the security awareness domain. Hawryszkiewycz and Binsawad (2016) described barriers impeding knowledge sharing. They identified more than 160 barriers and identified the most significant barriers as: Lack of a motivation, Lack of trust, Lack of incentive and reward systems, Lack of organizational culture, Lack of leadership, Lack of technical support, Insufficient technology infrastructure. Table 2 and Figure 1. Display the factors confirmed by the studies. The starred items are the most significant.

Factors	Tested and Evaluated
Trust*	Hassan *et al.* (2013), Hassan *et al.* (2014), Dixon (2000), Hawryszkiewycz and Binsawad (2016), Herzog *et al.* (2007), Ibragimova *et al.* (2012), Im and Baskerville (2005), Johnson *et al.* (2001), Junger *et al.* (2017).
Attitude	Dixon (2000), Gcaza and von Solms (2017), Hassan *et al.* (2014), Herzog *et al.* (2007), Ibragimova *et al.* (2012), Kim and Lee (2006).
Culture*	Hassan et al. (2013), Herzog *et al.* (2007), Johnson *et al.* (2001), Kim and Kim (2017).
Motivation*	Dixon (2000), Hassan et al. (2013), Ibragimova *et al.* (2012), Johnson *et al.* (2001), Liu *et al.* (2011), Mermoud *et al.* (2018).
IT application	Hassan et al. (2013), Johnson *et al.* (2001), Liu *et al.* (2011), Nonaka (1994).
Organisational Leaders	Hassan et al. (2013), Johnson *et al.* (2001), Liu *et al.* (2011).

Table 2: Factors Influencing Knowledge Sharing

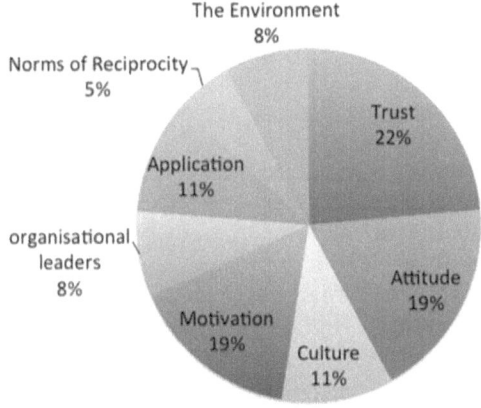

Figure 1: Factors Impacting Knowledge Sharing in the Reviewed Papers

4.2 Theory

Different theories have been proposed to explain knowledge sharing in information security. However, the *theory of planned behaviour* has proved to be the most influential. The theory revolves around the idea that an individual's attitude is a predictor of their intentions and behaviour.

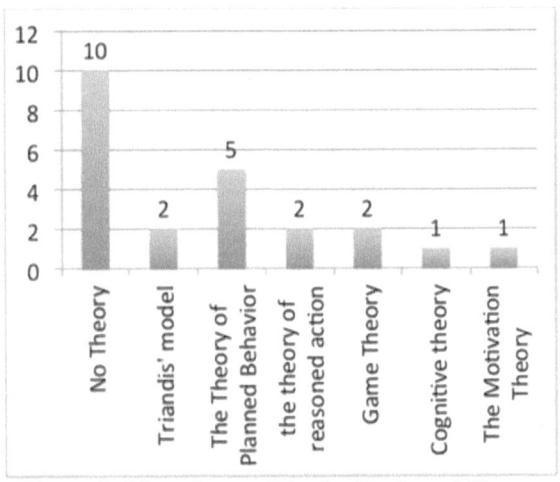

Figure 2: Theories used in the Reviewed Papers

4.3 Geographic Scope

Different investigations into knowledge sharing in information security have been conducted in various parts of the world. The Asian continent, with 41%, coverage, has experienced the highest number of studies. Europe comes in second with 27%, of studies. The North American region comes in third with 18% coverage; both Australia and Africa benefited the least from studies related to knowledge sharing in information security. Australia gained a 9% coverage while the African continent only had 5% coverage.

4.4   Methodologies

In the methodology section, it was noted that survey and literature review conceptual models were the most common techniques for examining knowledge sharing in information security. The survey technique involved questioning participants and getting to hear about their views on the topic. Some surveys were structured with others being unstructured. Participants would choose either self- or group-administered questionnaires. The literature review conceptual model entailed investigating existing theoretical studies into knowledge sharing in information security.

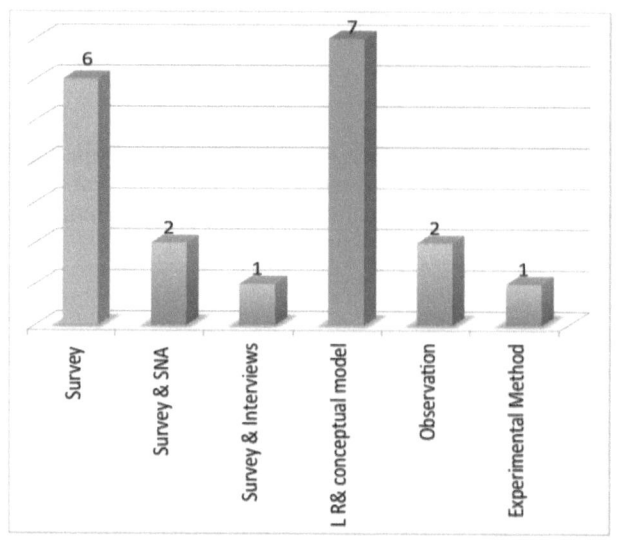

Figure 3: Deployed Methodologies used in the Reviewed Papers

5   Discussion

Knowledge sharing has a proven positive influence on security awareness among employees. We wanted to confirm the importance of security knowledge sharing and show how its influence on employees in the workplace led to enhancing resilience to cyber attacks.

The current study identified advantages of knowledge sharing in an organisational setting, especially in terms of individual security awareness. Hawryszkiewycz and Binsawad (2016) described the impact of barriers deterring knowledge sharing. The results of our study indicate that trust, motivation and culture are powerful barriers to knowledge sharing. Most of the studies did not propose effective solutions to mitigate these barriers.

Another important finding was that the studies we reviewed used only a handful of different theories. In discussing its significance to knowledge sharing, the theory proved to be more comprehensive in providing logical reasoning. Ideally, it could be argued that an employee's cognitive state would influence them in deciding on whether to participate in knowledge sharing, or not. This result may be explained by the fact that the researchers focused on the theories related to the individual, such as the Theory of Planned Behaviour. The researchers neglected theories that address barriers, such as Trust Theory.

Additionally, what is surprising is that the Asian continent, with 41% coverage, has experienced the highest number of studies investigating how knowledge sharing is achieved in the corporate sector. A possible explanation for this might be that the Asian continent has high levels of security risk which causes more consideration of security and attempts to enhance employee awareness.

The most interesting finding was that, in the methodology section, survey and literature reviews dominated the literature. The survey method does not deliver in-depth analyses of human behaviours. Surprisingly, only one study was found that used interviews or focus groups to understand the barriers affecting security knowledge sharing. This is surprising since observation, surveys and interviews are the most powerful techniques for delivering comprehensive insights that would allow for the best understanding of knowledge sharing in natural environments. Such methods have the advantage of allowing more transparency in noting down real-time data based on direct or indirect interaction between the researcher and the participants.

Safa *et al.* (2016) set out to investigate an effective model that can reduce the negative impact of the human factor in information security. In the end, the outcomes of the analysis reveal that information security knowledge sharing, experience, and collaboration have a positive impact on employees' will to comply with information security guidelines.

6   Conclusion

In conclusion, the present study was designed to gauge the impact of security knowledge sharing, the relationship between knowledge sharing and information security, and barriers to security knowledge sharing. We confirmed that security knowledge sharing increases employee awareness, mitigates risks, improves decision-making, and improves efficiency in the workplace (Parsons *et al.*, 2010; Persadha *et al.*, 2016). However, many factors affect security knowledge sharing such as trust, motivation, and attitude. Researchers should investigate how a more effective sharing mechanism can be formulated, specifically to address those factors and thereby achieve improved knowledge sharing across organisations. Based on the recent study reported by Mermoud *et al.* (2018), the role of incentivisation should also be explored.

7   References

Ahmed, G., Ragsdell, G. and Olphert, W. (2014) "Knowledge sharing and information security: a paradox?" *European Conference on Knowledge Management*, Vol. 3, pp. 1083.

Becerra-Fernandez, I. (2014), *Knowledge Management: Challenges, Solutions and Technologies*. New Jersey: Pearson, Prentice Hall.

Dang-Pham, D., Pittayachawan, S. and Bruno, V. (2017) "Why do employees share information security advice? Exploring the contributing factors and structural patterns of security advice sharing in the workplace." *Computers in Human Behavior*, Vol. 67, pp. 196-206.

Dang-Pham, D. and Nkhoma, M. (2017) "Effects of team collaboration on sharing information security advice: Insights from network analysis." *Information Resources Management Journal (IRMJ)*, Vol. 30, No. 3, pp. 58-72.

Dixon, N. M. (2000) *Common knowledge: How companies thrive by sharing what they know*. Harvard Business School Press.

Feledi, D., Fenz, S. and Lechner, L. (2013) "Toward web-based information security knowledge sharing." *Information Security Technical Report*, Vol. 17, No. 4, pp. 199-209.

Feledi, D. and Fenz, S. (2012) "Challenges of web-based information security knowledge sharing." In *Seventh International Conference on Availability, Reliability and Security (ARES)*, pp. 514-521.

Fenz, S. and Ekelhart, A. (2009) "Formalizing information security knowledge." In *Proceedings of the 4th International Symposium on Information, Computer, and Communications Security*, pp. 183-194. ACM.

Flores, W. R., Antonsen, E. and Ekstedt, M. (2014) "Information security knowledge sharing in organizations: Investigating the effect of behavioral information security governance and national culture." *Computers & Security*, Vol. 43, pp. 90-110.

Gal-Or, E. and Ghose, A. (2005) "The economic incentives for sharing security information." *Information Systems Research*, Vol. 16, No. 2, pp. 186-208.

Gao, X., Zhong, W. and Mei, S. (2015) "Security investment and information sharing under an alternative security breach probability function," *Information Systems Frontiers*, Vol. 17, No. 2, pp. 423-438.

Gcaza, N., and von Solms, R. (2017) "Cybersecurity culture: An ill-defined problem." In *IFIP World Conference on Information Security Education* pp. 98-109.

Hassan, N. H., Ismail, Z. and Maarop, N. (2013) "A conceptual model for knowledge sharing towards information security culture in healthcare organization." In *International Conference on Research and Innovation in Information Systems (ICRIIS)*, pp. 516-520.

Hassan, N. H., Ismail, Z. and Maarop, N. (2014) "Understanding Relationship Between Security Culture and Knowledge Management." In *Knowledge Management in Organizations* (Lecture Notes in Business Information Processing), pp. 397-402.

Hawryszkiewycz, I. and Binsawad, M. H. (2016) "Classifying knowledge-sharing barriers by organisational structure in order to find ways to remove these barriers." In *Eighth International Conference on Knowledge and Systems Engineering (KSE)*, pp. 73-78.

Herzog, A., Shahmehri, N. and Duma. C. (2007) "An ontology of information security." *International Journal of Information Security and Privacy (IJISP)*, Vol. 1, No. 4, pp. 1-23.

Ibragimova, B., Ryan, S. D., Windsor, J. C. and Prybutok, V. R. (2012) "Understanding the antecedents of knowledge sharing: An organizational justice perspective." *Informing Science: The International Journal of an Emerging Transdiscipline*, Vol. 15.

Im, G. P. and Baskerville, R. L. (2005) "A longitudinal study of information system threat categories: The enduring problem of human error." *SIGMIS Database*, Vol. 36, No. 4, pp. 68-79.

Johnson, G., Scholes, K. and Whittington, R. (2001) *"Exploring Corporate Strategy: Text & Cases,"* Pearson Education, 200B.

Junger, M., Montoya, L. and Overink, F-J. (2017) "Priming and warnings are not effective to prevent social engineering attacks." *Computers in Human Behavior,* Vol. 66, pp. 75-87.

Kim, S. and Lee, H. (2006) "The impact of organizational context and information technology on employee knowledge-sharing capabilities." *Public Administration Review,* Vol. 66, No. 3, pp. 370-385.

Kim, S. S. and Kim, Y. J. (2017) "The effect of compliance knowledge and compliance support systems on information security compliance behavior." *Journal of Knowledge Management*, Vol. 21, No. 4, pp. 986-1010.

Liu, D., Ji, Y. and Mookerjee, V. (2011) "Knowledge sharing and investment decisions in information security," *Decision Support Systems,* Vol. 52, No. 1, pp. 95-107.

Mermoud, A., Keupp, M., Huguenin, K., Palmié, M. and David, D. P. (2018) "Incentives for human agents to share security information: A model and an empirical test." In *17th Workshop on the Economics of Information Security (WEIS)*, pp. 1-22.

Nonaka, I. (1994) "A dynamic theory of organizational knowledge creation," *Organization Science,* Vol. 5, No. 1, pp. 14-37.

Nonaka, I. and Takeuchi, H. (1995) *The knowledge-creating company: How Japanese companies create the dynamics of innovation.* Oxford University Press.

Parsons, K., McCormac, A., Butavicius, M. and Ferguson, L. (2010) Human factors and information security: individual, culture and security environment. (No. DSTO-TR-2484). *Defence Science And Technology Organisation Edinburgh (Australia) Command Control Communications And Intelligence Div.*

Persadha, P. D., Waskita, A., Fadhila, M., Kamal, A. and Yazid, S. (2016) "How inter-organizational knowledge sharing drives national cyber security awareness: A case study in Indonesia." In *18th International Conference on Advanced Communication Technology (ICACT)*, pp. 550-555: IEEE.

Pickering, C. Grignon, J., Steven, R., Guitart, D. and Byrne, J. (2015) "Publishing not perishing: How research students transition from novice to knowledgeable using systematic quantitative literature reviews." *Studies in Higher Education,* Vol. 40, No. 10, pp. 1756-1769.

Polanyi, M. (2009) *The Tacit Dimension.* University of Chicago Press.

Politis, J.D. (2003) "The connection between trust and knowledge management: What are its implications for team performance?" *Journal of Knowledge Management*, Vol. 7, No. 5, pp. 55-66.

Rocha Flores, W., Antonsen, E. and Ekstedt, M. (2014) "Information security knowledge sharing in organizations: Investigating the effect of behavioral information security governance and national culture." *Computers & Security*, Vol. 43, pp. 90-110.

Safa, N. S. and von Solms, R. (2016) "An information security knowledge sharing model in organizations." *Computers in Human Behavior*, Vol. 57, pp. 442-451.

Safa, N. S.,von Solms, R. and Furnell, S. (2016) "Information Security policy Compliance Model in Organizations." *Computers & Security*, Vol. 56, pp. 70-82.

Said, A. R., Abdullah, H., Uli, J. and Mohamed, Z. A. (2014) "Relationship between organizational characteristics and information security knowledge management implementation," *Procedia-Social and Behavioral Sciences*, Vol. 123, pp. 433-443.

Sarkheyli, A. (2016). "Relationship between Knowledge Sharing Security and Organizational Context in the Public and Private Organizations," *AMCIS2016. Information Systems Security and Privacy (SIGSEC)*, pp. 8.

Schrage, M. (1990) *Shared minds: The new technologies of collaboration* (Ed.) New York, NY: Random House.

Stanton, J. M.. Stam, K. R., Mastrangelo, P. and Jolton, J. (2005) "Analysis of end user security behaviors." *Computers & Security*, Vol. 24, No. 2, pp.124-133.

Tamjidyamcholo, A., Baba, M. S. B., Tamjid, H. and Gholipour, R. (2013) "Information security: Professional perceptions of knowledge-sharing intention under self-efficacy, trust, reciprocity, and shared-language." *Computers & Education*, Vol, 68, pp. 223-232.

Tamjidyamcholo, A., Baba, M. S. B., Shuib, N. L. M. and Rohani, V. A. (2014) "Evaluation model for knowledge sharing in information security professional virtual community." *Computers & Security*, Vol. 43, pp. 19-34.

Wright, L. (2017) "Rethinking people, risk, and security." In *People, Risk, and Security* (pp. 7-24), Springer.

Zhang, T. (2018) "Knowledge expiration in security awareness training." *Annual ADFSL Conference on Digital Forensics, Security and Law*. Vol. 2.

Zhang, X., Tsang, A., Yue, W. T. and Chau, M. (2015) "The classification of hackers by knowledge exchange behaviors." *Information Systems Frontiers*, Vol. 17, No. 6, pp. 1239–1251.

Designing an Anti-Cyberbullying
Programme in Thailand

R. Herkanaidu[1], S.M. Furnell[1,2,3], M. Papadaki[1] and T. Khuchinda[4]

[1]Centre for Security, Communications and Network Research, University of
Plymouth, UK
[2]Security Research Institute, Edith Cowan University, Perth, Western Australia
[3]Centre for Research in Information and Cyber Security, Nelson Mandela University,
Port Elizabeth, South Africa
[4]Independent Researcher, Thailand
e-mail: {ram.herkanaidu, steven.furnell, maria.papadaki}@plymouth.ac.uk
tharabun@gmail.com

Abstract

A high number of young people in Thailand spend several hours a day online and mainly from
their smartphone. Not all of their online experiences are positive and many are victims of
cyberbullying. However this and other online safety issues are not discussed in schools or
generally in Thai society. There are no national or local programmes that address the issues and
it is not on the curriculum in schools. Therefore, to initiate such a programme workshops were
carried out to find out what kind of activities would engage Thai students. Altogether 83 students
from three schools participated in the four workshops conducted. Each session was evaluated
afterwards and suggestions for improvements were implemented in the next one. The most
successful activities were the showing of a Thai video on cyberbullying, the listing of their
online activities and the Buddhist teaching of sati (mindfulness). However, it was clear that there
is a passive acceptance of cyberbullying. It was found most would not talk about it to parents or
teachers and only sometimes with friends. Therefore, the workshops were a good introduction
to the topic of cyberbullying and demonstrate a need for more of these kinds of online safety
awareness raising initiatives.

Keywords

Awareness, Education, Children, Online Safety

1   Introduction

In Thailand, as in other less developed countries there is a lack of online safety
awareness research and education. Livingstone, Byrne and Bulger (2015) noted that,
"in many countries … and especially in the global south, there is too little research to
gain a sufficient understanding of children's practices and contexts of Internet use" (p.
9). Without it we cannot design relevant and effective education materials. Very little
research (at the time of writing) has been conducted in Thailand; therefore a survey
(Young People Online) was carried out with 206 students from 2 local schools in the
North East of the country. This was undertaken in November and December 2016
(Herkanaidu, Furnell & Papadaki, 2017) and showed that Thai students were big
consumers of the Internet. This is backed up by the Internet World Stats website (2018)

which states that out of a population of 69 million, 57 million (82%) were connected to the Internet and 46 million (66%) were on Facebook.

The survey showed that Thai students are exposed to a great deal of content and interactions that may potentially be harmful. Figure 1 below shows an infographic created to promote the findings of the survey and gives a breakdown of the most significant ones which includes that 71% of students had been upset by something online, 60% had been cyberbullied and 44% admitted they acted as the bully.

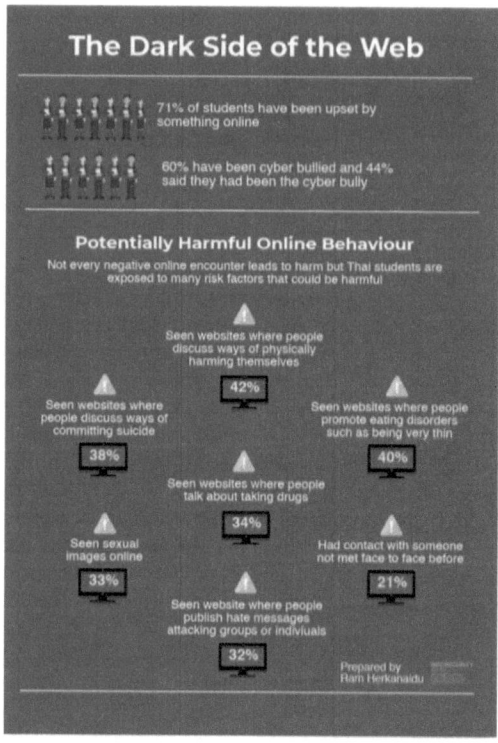

Figure 1: The Dark Side of the Web in Thailand (Herkanaidu, 2017)

This result is not unexpected. The Wisdom Society for Public Opinion Research of Thailand in 2009 found that online intimidation was 43% amongst 12 to 24 year olds (Sittichai &Smith 2013, pg. 37). The nobullying.com website describes the prevalence of bullying in Thailand, "as a normal experience children go through at schools to toughen up" (2015).

In the next section, the model that informed the research will be described as well as the pedagogic approach taken when designing the anti-cyberbullying programme. Section 3 details the design of the workshops followed by the results from the Thai classrooms. Section 4 gives an overall assessment and sets out plans for future work.

2 Methodology

2.1 Model

The Young People Online model (Figure 2a) developed by the principal researcher is a simplified version of the Global Kids Online model (Figure 2b). The latter project has the benefit of several years' worth of data that has informed their now fairly sophisticated model.

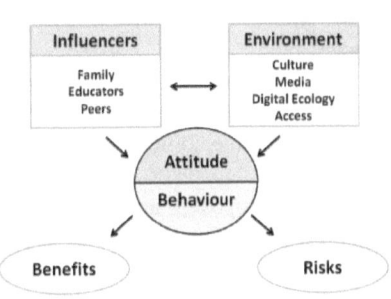

| **Figure 2a: Young People Online Model (Herkanaidu, 2017)** | **Figure 2b: EU Kids Online Model (Livingstone et al. 2015)** |

It is hoped that the young people online project will develop in a similar fashion. In the current model the attitude and behaviour of young people are determined by people who influence them, their family, teachers and other young people. The social and economic fabric of the country plays a part, cultural expectations and the ease of getting online. For instance, the survey found that 94% of girls and 85% of boys owned a smartphone (Herkanaidu, Furnell & Papadaki, 2017). This is in part due to Thailand's digital ecology where there is 70% smartphone penetration and an average user consume around 7GB of data monthly, (Leesa-Nguansuk, 2018). This is possible because mobile data coverage is extensive and inexpensive and cheap smartphones are plentiful even in rural areas where the survey was conducted.

2.2 Action Research

Action Research was thought to be the most appropriate method in determining the educational activities that would resonate with Thai students. Souto-Manning (2012) calls this "a systematic and sustained study of some aspect of teaching and learning". There are five phases and the circular nature of the process (Figure 3) means that it is ongoing and you should "identify additional questions raised by the data and plan for additional improvements, revisions, and next steps" (Ferrance, 2000, p. 13).

Figure 3: Action Research Cycle (Ferrance, 2000)

The first three phases will be used to outline our proposed anti-cyberbullying programme. The last two; action based on data and reflection will be in the next sections.

2.3 Identification of Problem Area

Online safety is not on the curriculum in Thailand. Schools have ad hoc policies around the use of smartphones and the Internet i.e. some allow students to use smartphones while others strictly prohibit it during lessons. While most schools have computers and are connected to the Internet many do not have skilled and experienced computer teachers that can deliver online safety lessons.

2.4 Collection and Organisation of Data

The Young People Online survey (Herkanaidu, Furnell & Papadaki, 2017) was an in-depth survey that looked at the online behaviour of Thai students; how they accessed the Internet, what apps and services they use, the online risks they were exposed to and the mediation from educators and parents/guardians. This was followed up in December 2017 with 13 interviews (from one of the schools in the survey) to give context to some of the findings. In the survey, "48% of parents/guardians and 64% of teachers had suggested ways to use the Internet safely. At school, over half, 53% said that teachers had made rules about what you can do on the Internet" (Herkanaidu et al. 2017). However, when asked during the interviews the actual advice was very basic. Common replies were' "don't spend too much time," "don't share bad news or bad videos," "don't chat with some boys don't use spend too much time on playing game," and "don't go to bad websites." In particular, the advice from teachers was not part of an instructive lesson they were just given informally in conversation.

2.5 Interpretation of Data

The survey and interviews indicate that young people are high users of online services especially Facebook and Facebook Messenger (Herkanaidu et al. 2017) and they do so primarily using smartphones. They are also engaging in behaviour that could be potentially harmful. Figure 1 above notes some of these such as; 21% had met with someone that they only previously knew online, 42% had seen websites where people discussed ways of physically harming themselves and 38% had seen websites where people discussed ways of committing suicide.

In the follow-up interviews when asked what they do when they encounter such sites they usually say they just ignore and if on Facebook just scroll past it. As one interviewee (via a translator) puts it, "just ignore and pass." When asked if they talked about it with parents or teachers most said they did not and when asked why not they were reticent in their replies. Talking to one teacher this reticence is because of the students' fear of the reaction of their parents. They do not want to be blamed for seeing or accessing content that has upset them. For example, one student when she was 12 had been sent a naked photo on Facebook by a foreigner. She blocked them but when asked if they told their parents she said she "don't dare to tell to her father."

There is a lack of awareness of the issues facing young people online as well as a lack of communication between them and their parents/guardians and teachers. Any programme will need to take both of these factors into account.

3   Online Safety Workshop

Originally the workshop was titled, 'Anti-cyberbullying Workshop.' However the word bully has no direct translation into Thai and it was thought that it would be best to not jump straight into the subject matter. Therefore it was given a more generic title, 'Online Safety Workshop.'

The first workshop was divided into 5 distinct activities, as outlined below.

Activity 1: Write 5 things you do online. The objective is to get students to think about all the different ways they consume online services.

Activity 2: In groups discuss and write down 5 good things and 5 bad things about being online. They are not told what constitutes a 'good thing' as opposed to a 'bad thing.' They would then present their findings in front of the class.

Activity 3: What is cyberbullying? This question is posed on the board and the class as one group are asked (with help from the teachers) what it is. This is tricky as there is no direct translation of 'bully' into Thai. In Sittichai and Smith (2013) they outline the various phrases with their associated meanings

> *"Nisai mai dee means bad habit, generally bad behavior; klang (klaēng) refers to more verbal behaviors, and tum raai (thamrāi) to more physical behaviors. Two other terms current nowadays are rang kae (rangkaē) which also means physical aggression and raow which means general aggression"* (pp 34-35).

This activity is meant to generate discussion of aspects of bullying and how it relates to online behaviour.

Activity 4: Reporting / Mediation. This is another class discussion on what a person should do if they are being cyberbullied and what advice should parents/guardians and educators advise.

Activity 5: Sati (mindfulness). Thailand is an overwhelmingly Buddhist nation so it was thought that maybe employing some Buddhist teaching within the context of the workshop would be an effective way to communicate with students. This is especially so as fellow author and workshop facilitator Dr Tharabun Khuchinda is an ex Buddhist monk. Grossman and Van Dam (2011) defines Sati as

> "*a practice or process... ranging from mindfulness of bodily sensations to awareness of more expansive mental content and processes, such as emotion and altered view of self. It connotes several features: (1) deliberate, open-hearted awareness of moment-to-moment perceptible experience; (2) a process held and sustained by such qualities as kindness, tolerance, patience and courage (as underpinnings of a stance of nonjudgmentalness and acceptance); (3) a practice of nondiscursive, non-analytic investigation of ongoing experience; (4) an awareness markedly different from everyday modes of attention*" (p 221)

This activity is meant to bring the workshop to a positive conclusion and give students a means to becoming more resilient from upsetting online interactions.

3.1 Workshop 1 & 2

These workshops were delivered to 21 M2 (13 year olds) and 28 M3 (14 year olds) students at the first of the three schools taking part in our study in Roi Et Province North Eastern part of Thailand, May 2018. The lessons were conducted in English by Ram Herkanaidu (non Thai-speaker) and translated by Dr Tharabun Khuchinda (Native Thai speaker). Each 1-hour workshop progressed in a similar fashion.

For the first activity the students were given around five minutes to write down what they did online. They were then asked in turn to name one item on their list. The catch was that they could not repeat what someone else had said already. Their answers were written on the board in Thai and in English. M2 students came up with 19 activities and M3 16 activities. The most popular were; searching for information, using Facebook, Youtube, Messenger, LINE and playing various games.

For activity 2 they were asked to organise themselves into groups of 4 or 5. They were then given 10 minutes to come up with five good and five bad things about being online. Some groups were more active than others and some students allowed others to do all the work. When they presented (In Thai) it was insisted upon that all had to speak at least once.

After the presentations the word 'Cyberbullying' was written on the board. In both workshops no one had heard of the term. They were given a few definitions (as above) and asked for more possible definitions and examples. The most common one was the sending and receiving of bad chat messages. When asked what they do if they received a bad message some said they would send a bad message back, others would block that person. When asked if they would talk to a parent or teacher all said no. They would either talk to a friend or just ignore it.

For the last activity, learning how to practice sati, they were introduced to its principles and its method demonstrated. They were told that they should never reply back or take rash actions when angry. By using sati it could be a way to calm themselves down. The last part was to get them to close their eyes and to practice the sati breathing technique.

3.1.1   Reflection on Workshops 1 & 2

These 2 workshops which were held back to back followed a similar pattern. Most students were engaged though this in part is due to the novelty of the lesson. The facilitators only had assistance from a school teacher at the start of the first workshop. It would have been very helpful if their usual teacher were present for the whole lesson. As there was a native English speaker it would maybe had made sense to do the workshop as an English lesson too.

For activity 1 to make it more interactive rather than shouting out answers students should come up to the board and write the answers. In activity 2 the students self organised themselves into groups. This process took quite a long time while students were negotiating with each other. In the first workshop one girl was left on her own until a group was found for her. From a time management point of view another way should be found to make up groups. Some students did not seem interested and let others do the thinking and writing. The presentations were fairly poor, most elicited only one or two words before passing the paper (with the list of good and bad things about being online) to another group member.

Activities 3 and 4 effectively became one. No one had heard the term cyberbullying and when they were asked for possible definitions and examples they were not forthcoming. It is possible they did not understand what was expected of them. Maybe giving them more information at the start of the activity would have helped. When asked how they cope with aspects of cyberbullying like, for example, if someone wrote something bad about them some said they would retaliate in kind and others said they would just ignore it. They do not speak to parents or teachers and only sometimes their friends. A few boys joked about calling the police.

Introducing them to sati in activity 5 was supposed to give them one way to cope with cyberbullying. M3 took this a little more seriously than the younger M2 students, asking more questions about what it was and how to do it properly. Both sets were fairly noisy throughout though.

3.2 Workshop 3

This was carried out with 16 M3 students at our second school in Roi Et. It was agreed with the director to make it into an English lesson and for the English teacher to assist us. For activity 1 they needed to list their online activities in English. The students then in turn had to write on the board, again in English. This turned out to be quite a fun exercise with the students helping each other with the spelling of the words.

For activity 2 students were already arranged in groups of 4. With the help of the 2 Thai/English speakers they would write in Thai and English and then present their respective lists in English. Activity 3 was now the combined 'what is cyberbullying?' and what to do if you have been cyberbullied. More information and examples were given at the start so they could better understand the concept. Their replies on how they react if cyberbullied was the same as the first 2 workshops. They would either react in kind or try to ignore it and they would not report it to parents or teachers. For activity 4, the practice of sati, again more information was given at the beginning to explain what it was and how it could help.

3.2.1 Reflection on Workshop 3

Turning the workshop into an English lesson was mostly positive. In activity 1 the students were more engaged and seemed to like the challenge of having to write in English. Activity 2 turned out very hard work for Tharabun. The school's English teacher disappeared for some time. The facilitators suspect that it is because her English is not very good. In Thai culture losing face (i.e. losing respect) is to be avoided. Teachers are supposed to have the answers, in this case translating Thai into English for the students. Instead Tharabun had to do this for all the groups and so extra time was allowed for the activity.

Front loading more information at the start of the cyberbullying and sati sections seemed to work better than the first two workshops. For the latter especially the students were very attentive and followed instructions on how to practice sati well.

3.3 Workshop 4

At our third school the workshop was with 18 M3 students. The only innovation from the previous workshops was the introduction of a short Thai video on cyberbulling, https://www.youtube.com/watch?v=9AMvJJgJMOs (Figure 4).

Figure 4: Thai Cyberbullying Video

(https://www.youtube.com/watch?v=9AMvJJgJMOs, 2018)

3.3.1   Reflection on Workshop 4

There was excellent cooperation from the young English teacher who as well as good English skills had very good classroom management in maintaining order and motivating the students. In activity 1 everyone wanted to write on the board realising that it is easier to be one of the first rather than one of the last (i.e. because you cannot repeat the same item). Activity 2 was similar to the other workshops in that only one or two individuals in each group were active. Presentations too were not very good; students were nervous giving one-word answers, looking at each other or on the floor. It may be a good idea to include presentation skills training as part of the programme especially as it can be a way to build confidence and self esteem.

During the playing of the video the students were very attentive. It was the best that the facilitators could find on the subject matter in Thai. Most videos have gory endings with self harm and worse. This one too (see Figure 4 above) had a hanging scene but it is over fairly quickly. When the English teacher was asked if it was appropriate for her students she thought it was very good and informative. The students were asked if they thought cyberbullying was a common feature of their lives. Quite a few agreed that it happens a lot. When asked if they reported it, just like in the other workshops, they said they would not tell teachers or parents just friends.

4   Review and Discussion

These workshops demonstrated that there is a need for online safety and cyberbulling awareness in Thailand. Of the 3 schools in this study two did have rules about the use of phones. At one, students had to hand in the phones and collect during lunchtime and after school. The other had a no phone in class rule though some were seen being used. The third school left it to individual teachers. None of the schools had a policy on cyberbullying or a reporting mechanism for students. Actually no teacher or student from the three schools had even heard the term, cyberbullying. In creating a programme thought will have to be given on how to involve teachers and parents as there is lack of general awareness of online safety issues and how to deal with them.

The action research approach whereby reflecting after each workshop to evaluate its effectiveness proved to be a good way in determining the kind of activities Thai students responded well to. It was found that for activity 1 getting the students to write by themselves on the board was a much more fun way than to just reply verbally. As there was a native English speaker turning the lesson into an English class was mostly positive as well. This is as long as you have the school's own teacher motivated to help deliver the content as was the case in the last workshop.

Activity 2 proved problematic throughout all four workshops. Some students were disengaged and left it to other to write the list of good things and bad things about being online. The presentations too were poor both in Thai and in English. Over the course of the workshops there were 19 groups that completed this activity. Table 1 gives a list of the top answers for both good and bad that had 3 or more mentions.

Good	Mentions	Bad	Mentions
Find information	13	Porn	12
LINE /Messenger chat	9	Being cheated/deceived	8
Online Shopping	9	Addicted to Phone	7
Watch News	6	Hack Facebook Account	4
Online translation	4	Hacking	4
Listen to music	4	Bad to Eyes	3
Facebook	4	Pay Money	3
Learning	3		

Table 1. Activity 2: Roi Et Workshops

The facilitators were very careful not to tell them what constituted a good or bad thing. In this way we get an unbiased insight into what they think of as good or bad. By collecting such information it can inform the content on future workshops. It's interesting to note that in the bad column there was not one mention of online harassment or other activity directly related to cyberbullying.

In the first two workshops the facilitators tried to get students to come up with their own terms of what constitutes cyberbullying. As mentioned above there is no direct translation of this word into Thai. This proved not to be so successful. In the third workshop they were given the different definitions and then asked for examples. However, it was not until the fourth workshop when the Thai cyberbullying video was shown that they truly engaged with this part. In all the workshops when asked how they deal with cyberbullying all said they would not talk to parents or teachers and only sometimes with friends. This aspect will need to be addressed in future workshop. Material should be created for schools including best practice guides on policies and rules. Teacher and parent guides on online safety and cyberbullying awareness would prove useful too.

It should be noted that in Thai society problems and conflicts are often ignored and not discussed. The commonly used phrase, 'mai pen rai' is often said in these situations. Young (2013) notes that this "can be translated as 'never mind,' 'don't worry about it,' 'forget it,' or 'don't bother. Yet it also implies the assumption that since problems and adversary will eventually become better, worrying about them will achieve nothing" (p 5). In other words, Thai's in general do not discuss problems directly with each other and actively try to avoid any kind of conflict. Any programme will need to treat this issue in an intelligent and culturally sensitive way.

The last activity introduced the Buddhist teaching of sati or mindfulness. In the first two workshops the students were quite noisy and were not that attentive. The latter two workshops were more successful possibly because there was more explanation about it and what it is supposed to achieve. Finding and adding other Thai aspects to complement the existing activities would be beneficial as the students will relate to it more easily.

5   Conclusion and Future Work

These workshops proved to be a useful first step into creating an anti-cyberbullying programme possibly as part of a wider online safety programme. It was found that cyber bullying was very common yet awareness of the issues it raised was very low. Furthermore, as a reflection of Thai society problems are rarely talked about. Students agreed that cyber bullying was a regular occurrence but they would not talk to parents or teachers about it. Any programme will need to address this fundamental issue.

The most successful activities were, the cyberbulling video and discussion and the principles of sati. The least successful was activity 2 where they had to work in groups to come up with 5 good and 5 bad things about the Internet. To develop the programme further we need to explore other kinds of activities such as the use of art, games and role playing. By testing out different approaches and activities we will have a better idea of which ones will be most effective in the Thai setting. In conjunction with creating activities for students, it will be necessary to create material for schools, teachers and parents.

6   Acknowledgements

The authors would like to thank Roi Et Rajabhat University for their cooperation in facilitating this research and also to the directors, teachers and students of the 3 schools; Demonstration School of Roi Et Rajabhat University, Boontaweewattanawittaya School and Anuban Khorkaew School. We would like to thank the International Thai Foundation for their administrative support which allows us to carry out this research work in Thailand.

7   References

Ferrance, E. (2000) Action research. Themes in education. Retrieved from https://www.brown.edu/academics/education-alliance/sites/brown.edu.academics.education-alliance/files/publications/act_research.pdf

Grossman, P., & Van Dam, N.T. (2011) Mindfulness, by any other name...: trials and tribulations of sati in western psychology and science, Contemporary Buddhism, 12:01, 219-239, DOI: 10.1080/14639947.2011.564841

Herkanaidu, R., Furnell, S.M., & Papadaki, M. (2017, April). Online Risk Awareness and Exposure of Young People in Thailand. Presented at the 16th Annual Security Conference 2017, Information Institute Conferences, Las Vegas, NV, April 18-20, 2017

Leesa-Nguansuk, S. (2018) Mobile Sales to Shrink. Retrieved from Retrieved from Bangkok Post website: https://www.bangkokpost.com/business/telecom/1412947/mobile-sales-to-shrink.

Livingstone, S., Byrne, J., & Bulger, M. (2015, April). Researching children's rights globally in the digital age. Report of a seminar held on 12-14 February 2015. LSE, London. Retrieved from http://www.lse.ac.uk/media@lse/research/Research-Projects/Researching-Childrens-Rights/pdf/Researching-childrens-rights-globally-in-the-digital-age-260515-withphotos.pdf

NoBullying.com. (2015, December 22). Bullying in Thailand. Retrieved from NoBullying.com website https://nobullying.com/bullying-in-thailand/

Sittichai, R., & Smith, P.K. (2013). Bullying and cyberbulling in Thailand: A Review. International Journal of Cyber Society and Education, 6(1), 31-44. doi: 10.7903/ijcse.1032

Souto-Manning, M., (2012) Teacher as Researcher: Teacher Action Research in Teacher Education, Childhood Education, 88:1, 54-56, DOI:10.1080/00094056.2012.643726

Young, D. (2013)Perspectives on cheating at a Thai University. Young Language Testing in Asia 2013, 3:6

An Educational Intervention
Towards Safe Smartphone Usage

W.J. Van Rensburg, K.L. Thomson and L. Futcher

Nelson Mandela University, Port Elizabeth, South Africa
e-mail: s213461846@mandela.ac.za, kerry-lynn.thomson@mandela.ac.za,
lynn.futcher@mandela.ac.za

Abstract

With the increased popularity of smartphones in modern society, smartphone users often neglect to consider security practices in the use of their devices. This paper explores whether an Educational Intervention could improve students' security knowledge with regard to the usage of their smartphones. With the use of a Pre-Test questionnaire, a customised Educational Intervention was constructed to address gaps in students' security knowledge and reported usage. With the use of a blended learning approach and a Road Trip analogy, the Educational Intervention was constructed and delivered to students through their university's Learning Management System. The results of the study show that the customised Educational Intervention was successful in addressing the identified gaps in students' security knowledge.

Keywords

Educational Intervention, Smartphone Education, Security Knowledge, Safe Smartphone Usage

1   Introduction

There has been a significant increase in the popularity of smartphones since their inception, and it was estimated that the number of global smartphone users will reach 2.5 billion users by the end of 2018 (Statista, 2018). The use of smartphones has seen a major increase due to the vast variety of productivity tools, entertainment, functions and features they offer to their users. These functions and features are provided through mobile applications (Awad & Krishnan, 2006). Smartphone users are aware of the benefits these applications provide them, however, they are generally not aware of the risks that smartphones and their associated applications pose to their privacy and personal information (Allam et al., 2014).

The purpose of this paper is to demonstrate that a customised Educational Intervention, utilising a blended learning approach, can improve students' security knowledge with regards to their smartphone usage. This research focused on the reported behaviour of students regarding their smartphones usage. A Pre-Test, in the form of a questionnaire, was conducted to determine students' general smartphone usage, security knowledge, and concern towards their personal information. The purpose of the Pre-Test was to identify gaps in students' security knowledge in order to develop a customised Educational Intervention for the particular audience. After students completed the Educational Intervention they were presented with a Post-Test questionnaire to determine whether the Educational Intervention did in fact improve their security knowledge and perception towards secure smartphone usage. Figure 1 shows the research process followed to conduct the study.

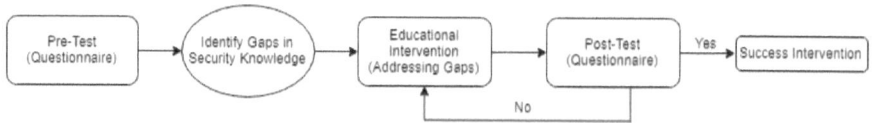

Figure 1: Research Process Diagram

The participants for the study were Information Technology (IT) students from a higher education institution in South Africa. The sample was selected based on convenience as the researcher had access to the students whose curriculum included smartphone behaviour as part of their IT Skills course. The same sample of students was used throughout the study.

The structure of the paper is as follows: Section 2 provides background on smartphone usage and common threats related to smartphone users, while Section 3 presents the results from the Pre-Test that was used to identify gaps in the students' security knowledge. Section 4 presents the design of the Educational Intervention. This is followed by Section 5 which highlights the results and findings from both the Pre-Test and the Post-Test conducted after exposure to the Educational Intervention. Section 6 contains the discussion related to the results from the study, and Section 7 concludes the paper.

2   Background

Smartphones have become an integral part of modern society. Smartphones have changed how users conduct themselves in their day to day lives and in online environments. The use of smartphones amongst users has brought new ways of productivity and connectivity in their personal lives. Prominent areas where smartphones have had an impact include business, education, health, and social life (Sarwan & Soomro, 2013). Mobile applications are third party software programs providing smartphones with unique functionality that can be downloaded and accessed directly from a smartphone (Mylonas et al., 2011).

With regards to the process of downloading mobile applications, users often neglect to review what a specific application will request from them in return for its functionality. When users download applications they are generally more focused on the features of the application rather than on the security the application provides (Zhang et al., 2017). Esmaeili (2014) identified that the confidence users might have in the perceived security controls in place of official marketplaces (for example, Google Play Store) has led to users neglecting to take security into consideration when selecting an application to download. This is of great concern with regards to information security when users use smartphones.

Smartphone users often become the target of cyberattacks due to their lack of security considerations (Dawson et al., 2015). Smartphones can be seen as a vault of private information which attackers often try and exploit by uploading malicious applications to various application marketplaces. In this context, the number of cybercrimes committed through malicious mobile applications has also seen an increase (Felt et al, 2011). RSA Quarterly Fraud Report stated that in Q1 of 2018 they discovered over 8,000 rogue mobile applications and since 2015 there has been a 680% increase in mobile app fraud (RSA, 2018). Sensitive information that can be found on smartphones include contact details, communication records, location information, e-mails and banking details (Jeon et al., 2011). As a result of this, a great amount of personal information is available on smartphones. This makes the protection of such information a critical issue that needs to be addressed. Information security relating to smartphones can be described as the knowledge, attitude, and behaviour that users apply in protecting their personal information (Allam et al, 2014), and creating awareness could be used as a means of reducing security risk (Kruger & Kearney, 2006). Allam et al (2014) also state that increasing awareness influences behaviour, which could ultimately reduce risk by focussing on smartphone users and not just on the smartphone as a device.

Adopting appropriate security controls alone is not enough to protect information assets on smartphones. This is because the behaviour of the smartphone user plays a critical role in the security of information in the use of smartphones (Esmaeili, 2014). Information security is seen as a means of reducing security risk across numerous threat areas. Educational interventions are often used to address a lack of awareness that users might have in a specific risk area.

Identifying the gaps in security knowledge that smartphone users might have could assist in the creation of an appropriate Educational Intervention. With the use of such an Educational Intervention, gaps in security knowledge could be addressed which ultimately could lead to a change in the behaviour of smartphone users. The next section discusses the Pre-Test used to identify where students might lack adequate knowledge to protect themselves against risks introduced through the use of smartphones.

3   Pre-Test to identify gaps in smartphone users' behaviour and knowledge

A Pre-Test consisting of a questionnaire was used to identify concepts surrounding smartphone adoption, usage, knowledge and privacy concerns smartphone users might have whilst using their smartphones. The questionnaire was set up in four sections, each addressing one of these criteria. The use of the questionnaire assisted the researcher in identifying gaps in the students' security knowledge on which the customised Educational Intervention could be structured. With the results of the questionnaire the following gaps in students' smartphone security knowledge were identified:

1. Knowledge of where applications should be downloaded (for example, official marketplaces, third-Party marketplaces or developer website).
2. The importance of updating applications, updating operating systems, and uninstalling applications that are no longer in use.
3. Awareness of threats to smartphones.
4. Awareness of the risk that applications might pose to users' privacy and personal information.
5. Physical access controls and the encryption of information stored on smartphones.
6. What to consider in the application listing when selecting an application to download.

These gaps identified were addressed in the Educational Intervention. The following section discusses the design of the Educational Intervention, and Section 5 provides a discussion comparing the results of the Pre-Test and Post-Test.

4 Educational Intervention

Based on the results from the Pre-Test, it was apparent that a need for an Educational Intervention existed. Smartphone users need to have an adequate understanding as to why it is important to approach the use of their smartphones in a secure manner. The Educational Intervention was created using a blended learning approach. Blended learning is an approach using online and face-to-face instruction activities (Boelens et al., 2015) to provide a more flexible approach of delivering educational content to students in higher educational institutions. With the use of a blended learning approach, students could work through the educational material provided to them as frequently as required and from wherever they wanted to access it.

Based on the gaps identified during the Pre-Test, the researcher designed PowerPoint slides to assist in the reflection on the results from the Pre-Test. The results were presented to the students in a theory lecture, where a discussion on the various gaps in knowledge took place. Here students were introduced to various topics identified as gaps in their personal security knowledge relating to their smartphone usage. The reflection was used to assist in the initial creation of awareness amongst the students about certain risk areas related to their smartphones. Reflection learning is seen as an active and awareness related process that can occur anytime and anywhere. Reflection assists students in re-evaluating and learning from decisions and choices they made, how they made them and what they should do in the future (The University of Sheffield, n.d.). In this reflection lecture, students were presented with the results of their study and were made aware of the areas in which they show a lack of security awareness relating to their smartphone usage.

After the reflection lesson, the students were informed that they would be given a week to work through the educational material made available to them on their Moodle Site and that they would be tested again a week later. The Moodle site is an example of a Learning Management System (LMS) where students can find their course material. With the use of an LMS, students were able to access the educational content from remote locations and work through the material outside of a typical class environment.

The Educational Intervention was designed using questionnaire software called QuestionPro. This software allowed the researcher to develop a custom lesson plan where, based on the answers given in the Educational Intervention, relevant educational material would be presented to the students. As a whole, all gaps in knowledge were addressed, but if incorrect answers were given, additional material was provided to increase their knowledge. The educational material was presented through various media that included videos and slides.

The researcher's approach to designing the Educational Intervention was by using the analogy that '*Downloading smartphone applications is like taking a road trip*'. With this analogy, the researcher developed the educational content around numerous aspects that should be considered when setting off on a road trip. With the use of analogies, concepts that are similar can be used to build a conceptual bridge to connect what is known to what is new. Analogies can be used to form an understanding of complex concepts and allow students to construct their own knowledge surrounding topics addressed (Glynn, 2004).

Each step in taking a road trip was used to assist in the development of the Educational Intervention. Tables 1 to 7 address each stage of taking a road trip, how it relates to the analogy, and what content was covered in the Educational Intervention to address the gaps in knowledge identified.

Road Trip Analogy	Gap in Knowledge Addressed
You should know how you are getting to your destination (what route are you taking).	You should know where you are going to download your application from (reputable application marketplace).

Table 1: Plan Your Destination

The Educational Intervention addressed this topic by delivering relevant information on why it is important to download applications from an official application marketplace. The information was presented with the use of slides explaining that the safest route to take when downloading applications is by going through official marketplaces, as applications on these marketplaces are screened for malicious software.

Road Trip Analogy	Gap in Knowledge Addressed
Before leaving on your road trip you need to ensure that your vehicle is well maintained and ready to go on the road.	Performing regular maintenance on your smartphone strengthens the device against any threats it might encounter.

Table 2: Perform Maintenance

The Educational Intervention addressed this topic by delivering relevant information on how smartphone users can do maintenance on their devices to strengthen it. The topics that were covered during the Intervention were 1) why it is important to update applications when new updates are released; 2) why keeping the Operating System of the smartphone up to date is important; and 3) why it is important to uninstall applications that are no longer being used.

Road Trip Analogy	Gap in Knowledge Addressed
Know about the threats to your vehicle and ensure you have protection when threats occur (vehicle insurance).	Know the threats that smartphones might encounter and how to mitigate these threats (security software).

Table 3: Be Aware of Threats

The Educational Intervention made use of videos that discussed the various threats to smartphones and how users can mitigate these threats. The videos, accompanied by slides, discussed the various threats and what smartphone users can do to mitigate them, as well as what solutions or preventative measures they can deploy to prevent threats from happening. Topics included, for example, why it is important to turn off Wi-Fi when it is not in use.

Road Trip Analogy	Gap in Knowledge Addressed
Whilst you are on your road trip you may discover obstacles along your way e.g. a section of road that is closed due to road works (taking a detour).	Setting out to download a new application and discovering that the application you are about to download is requesting too much information.

Table 4: Potential Obstacles

The Educational Intervention addressed this topic by discussing that when downloading an application and discovering that the potential application might request access to unnecessary information, or is not going to provide the required features, it is recommended that you start looking at some alternative applications.

Road Trip Analogy	Gap in Knowledge Addressed
The valuable property you are taking with you will be packed in your vehicle's trunk that can be locked to ensure no one has access to it	Valuable information stored on smartphones also needs to be protected by ensuring that physical access controls are in place and information stored on smartphones is encrypted

Table 5: Protecting Valuables

The Educational Intervention addressed this gap in knowledge by displaying solutions that users can employ to encrypt personal information stored on their device so that only they can access their information. The material included the importance of having screen lock protection on one's smartphones to ensure no unauthorised user can access resources and information on their smartphones.

Road Trip Analogy	Gap in Knowledge Addressed
When going on your road trip you will stop to visit various places on route (e.g. fuel stops, food stops).	When you set out to download applications you need to stop and view certain features in the application listing before making your selection

Table 6: Taking the Journey

The Educational Intervention highlights eight 'stops' users should consider before installing an application. The eight stops can be found in the listing of the application and can give users a good overall indication of the application. The Educational Intervention discussed each of the eight stops in detail. The eight stops included were App Rating, App Review, Number of Downloads, Privacy Policy, Detailed Information, Last Update Released, Permissions Requested and Developer.

Road Trip Analogy	Gap in Knowledge Addressed
Planning your journey from start to end and knowing what to expect and how to mitigate any threats along your way will ensure your safe arrival at your destination.	Taking a pro-active approach in the use of your smartphone. Knowing what to expect and being able to mitigate against any threats along the way

Table 7: Arriving at your destination

The final topic covered in the Educational Intervention gave an overall discussion on the previously mentioned topics that users should know to ensure that they can be confident in the secure usage of their smartphones. This provided users with a checklist that they could go through to ensure their smartphone is ready for its road trip. This checklist included:

- Ensure that your smartphone Operating System and mobile applications are frequently updated.
- Only download mobile applications from official application marketplaces (e.g. Google Play Store).
- Verify the permissions requested by the developer, and reputability of the mobile application developer.
- Avoid unknown and unsecured Wi-Fi networks.
- Ensure that your device is protected from unauthorised access.
- Install good security software onto your smartphone.

Once students completed the Educational Intervention they were given a Post-Test. The next section compares the results from the Pre-Test to the results of the Post-Test. This was done in order to determine whether the Educational Intervention assisted in addressing the gaps in students' smartphone security knowledge and their reported behaviour.

5 Discussion of Pre-Test and Post-Test results

The majority of students (98%) that completed the Post-Test were smartphone owners. The smartphone operating systems amongst students ranged from Android, iOS, Blackberry to Windows. The majority of students (88%) own smartphones running Google's Android operating system. These students use their smartphones for various tasks including downloading of applications. The researcher asked the students where they download their applications from as downloading applications from sources other than official marketplaces could result in malicious software being installed on smartphones. The Educational Intervention addressed this topic and why it is important to download applications from official marketplaces. The results from the Post-Test showed a 10% decrease in students reported behaviour when downloading applications from third-party marketplaces after completing the Intervention.

Students primarily use smartphones to connect to their social media sites. The most popular social media platforms amongst students were WhatsApp (97.3%), YouTube (92.1%), Facebook (81.5%) and Instagram (68.4%). Although the students primarily use smartphones for social media, they also use several different applications on their smartphones. The researcher wanted to determine whether students uninstall applications they are no longer using. From the results of the Post-Test the percentage of students that always uninstall unused applications went from 60% to 70% after the Educational Intervention. The reasons students say they uninstall applications were (1) to free up space, (2) replacing it with a better application, and (3) for security reasons. A positive result with regards to the security knowledge of students is that the percentage of students that uninstall applications for security reasons increased from 25.4% to 44.5%.

In the Pre-Test, students stated that they base their decision to install applications on the (1) application rating, the (2) application reviews, (3) popularity, (4) ease of use, (5) look of the application, and, lastly, on the (6) permissions requested by the application. It can be seen that security features were not seriously considered during the Pre-Test. After the Educational Intervention, the results changed and although students stated they select applications based on the (1) application reviews and (2) application ratings, they also stated (3) permissions requested has a greater influence on their decision when selecting an application. Therefore, the security feature of Permissions Requested was of greater importance to the students in the Post-Test.

Topics covering smartphone security in the Educational Intervention focussing on Encryption, Updating Applications, Screen Lock protection, and the use of public Wi-Fi networks also improved after the Intervention. Table 8 below shows the improvement in students' knowledge regarding what features they relate to smartphone security.

Topic	Pre-Test	Post-Test
Encryption	76%	81%
Updating Applications	41%	66%
Screen-Lock Protection	66%	76%
Use of Wi-Fi network	39%	61%

Table 8: What Students Relate to Smartphone Security

The Pre-Test identified what threats, related to smartphones, students are currently aware of. This assisted in educating students about threats that they currently are not aware of. In the Educational Intervention, less emphasis was placed on a topic such as Viruses as the majority of students (92.8%) were already aware of it. Threats such as Malware, Ransomware, Rootkits, and Trojans were identified as threats that fewer students were aware of. The Intervention addressed these threats by giving relevant information about each specific threat and how to mitigate against these threats. The results in Table 9 show the increase in awareness of threats after the Educational Intervention.

Topic	Pre-Test	Post-Test
Malware	61.9%	83.2%
Ransomware	31.9%	59.4%
Rootkits	16.6%	33.5%
Trojans	61.4%	76.1%

Table 9: Student Awareness Relating to Smartphone Threats

After the Intervention students' awareness of what security software is essential to have on their smartphones also increased. Students considered the use of appropriate security software such as anti-virus software, anti-spyware software, encryption software, firewall software, and lock-screen protection essential prior to the intervention, but only had anti-virus and lock-screen protection installed on their smartphone. After the Educational Intervention, the percentage of students that use the various security software increased. Although anti-virus software and lock-screen protection were the most used security software amongst students, there was a reported increase in the use of other security software. Table 10 shows the increase in the reported adoption amongst various security software.

Security Software	Pre-Test	Post-Test
Anti-Virus	63.8%	72.3%
Anti-Spyware	16.1%	22.6%
Encryption Software	27.6%	44.5%
Firewalls software	27.1%	34.8%
Lock Screen Protection	73.8%	78.7%

Table 10: Smartphone Security Software Adoption

The level of awareness amongst students with regards to the risk applications pose to their privacy and personal information also increased. The results identified that students' awareness relating to risk increased from 86.6% to 90.3% after the Educational Intervention. Users indicated that they are more aware of risk that downloading applications from third-party marketplaces pose to their privacy. They also showed a positive improvement on the need to use encryption when storing information on their smartphones. Many students in the Pre-Test did not care for reviewing permissions requested, but after the Intervention, 60.6% of students answered that it should be reviewed.

The reported concern that students indicated they had with regards to personal information stored on their devices, and the loss thereof, in the Post-Test increased after acquiring the knowledge through the Intervention. In the Pre-Test, 77% of students stated that they were extremely concerned about their personal information. However, the percentage in the Post-Test increased to 81.3%. When users are conscious of threats they might encounter they could begin to behave in a manner that reduces the possibility of the risk.

The use of the blended learning approach accompanied with the Road Trip analogy assisted in the positive results in the study. The reflection lesson prior to the Educational Intervention assisted in creating initial awareness amongst the students and allowed them to be able to identify gaps they were unaware of. The Educational Intervention, utilising of an adaptive-like questionnaire, was used to address the gaps in knowledge students had in a specific area with the intention that, with an increase in knowledge, there will be an increase in awareness, which could result in a change of users' behaviour. From the results of the study, it can be argued that the use of the Educational Intervention had a positive impact on students' security knowledge and reported smartphone usage.

6   Conclusion

Through the use of an Educational Intervention it was discovered that smartphone users' knowledge could be improved and that universities should ensure that they use interventions to address the gaps in security knowledge smartphone users might have. Although there are many Educational Interventions available, what makes this intervention different is the fact that it is customised to the audience based on the results of their Pre-Test and the way they answered it.

Future research could investigate whether a broader implementation of this Educational Intervention could have the same results with a different age group of smartphone users. A similar study could be conducted with the addition of further topics such as jail-breaking or rooting of smartphones that might have been excluded with this sample of smartphone users.

7 Acknowledgements

The financial assistance of the National Research Foundation (NRF) towards this research is hereby acknowledged. Opinions expressed, and conclusions arrived at, are those of the authors, and cannot necessarily be attributed to the NRF.

8 References

Allam, S., Flowerday, S. V., Flowerday, E. (2014) Smartphone information security awareness: A victim of operational pressures. Computers and Security, 42. https://doi.org/10.1016/j.cose.2014.01.005

Awad, N., & Krishnan, M. (2006). The Personalization Privacy Paradox: An Empirical Evaluation of Information Transparency and the Willingness to Be Profiled Online for Personalization. MIS Quarterly, 30(1), 13-28. doi:10.2307/25148715

Boelens, R., Van Laer, S., De Wever, B., & Elen, J. (1998). BLENDED AND ONLINE LEARNING IN ADULT EDUCATION AND TRAINING. The Women's Review of Books, 15(5), 27. https://doi.org/10.2307/4022859

Dawson, M., Wright, J., & Omar, M. (2015). Mobile Devices: The Case for Cyber Security Hardened Systems. Mobile Computing and Wireless Networks: Concepts, Methodologies, Tools, and Applications, (January), 1103–1123. https://doi.org/10.4018/978-1-4666-8751-6.ch047

Esmaeili, M. (2014). Assessment of Users' Information Security Behavior in Smartphone Networks. ProQuest Dissertations and Theses, 146. https://doi.org/10.13140/RG.2.1.3456.7129

Felt, A., Finifter, M., Chin, E., Hanna, S., Wagner, D. (2011) A survey of mobile malware in the wild. In: Proc. of the 1st ACM workshop on security and privacy in smartphones and mobile devices (SPSM '11). ACM; p. 3-14.

Glynn, S.M. 2004. Connect concepts with questions and analogies. In Cases in middle and secondary science education, eds. T.R. Koballa and D.J. Tippins, 136–142. Upper Saddle River, NJ: Pearson Education.

Jeon, W., Kim, J., Lee, Y., & Won, D. (2011). A practical analysis of smartphone security. Lecture Notes in Computer Science (Including Subseries Lecture Notes in Artificial Intelligence and Lecture Notes in Bioinformatics), 6771 LNCS (PART 1), 311–320. https://doi.org/10.1007/978-3-642-21793-7_35

Kruger, H., Kearney, W. (2006) A prototype for assessing information security awareness. Comput Secur 2006; 25(1):289-96.

Mylonas, A., Dritsas, S., Tsoumas, B., & Gritzalis, D. (2011). Smartphone security evaluation - The malware attack case. SECRYPT 2011 - Proceedings of the International Conference on Security and Cryptography, (July), 25–36. Retrieved from http://www.scopus.com/inward/record.url?eid=2-s2.0-80052493767&partnerID=tZOtx3y1

RSA. (2018) Current State of Cybercrime. Retrieved 23 July 2018 from https://www.rsa.com/content/dam/premium/en/report/rsa-fraud-report-q1-2018.pdf

Sarwan, M., & Soomro, T. R. (2013). The impact of smartphone's on Society. Proceedings of the Annual Hawaii International Conference on System Sciences, 98(2), 1734–1742. https://doi.org/10.1109/HICSS.2013.623

Statista, "Smartphone users worldwide 2014-2020" [Online]. Available: https://www.statista.com/statistics/330695/number-of-smartphone-users-worldwide/. [Accessed: 15-Apr-2018].

The University of Sheffield. (n.d.). Reflective Learning for Students. Retrieved June 11, 2018, from https://www.sheffield.ac.uk/lets/toolkit/learning/reflective

Zhang, X. J., Li, Z., & Deng, H. (2017). Information security behaviors of smartphone users in China: an empirical analysis. The Electronic Library, 35(6), 1177–1190. https://doi.org/10.1108/EL-09-2016-0183

Privacy Practices, Preferences, and Compunctions: WhatsApp Users in India

J. Dev, S. Das and L Jean Camp

Indiana University Bloomington
e-mail: jdev@iu.edu, sancdas@iu.edu, ljcamp@indiana.edu

Abstract

WhatsApp messaging platform incorporates features that pose privacy challenges, including Last Seen, Live Location, and personal profile information. The largest population of mobile messaging applications users in India use WhatsApp. Yet research on Indian perspectives towards privacy and security in social networking platforms is sparse. We queried privacy attitudes and behaviours of 213 Indian participants, using both open and closed-ended questions. The majority of participants reported that they actively use the privacy controls on multiple data types, especially in group communications. Note that, in India, groups are common not just is social settings but also in schools and workplaces. A comparison with the results of a prior study of Saudi Arabian participants shows significant overlap in access control, with more Saudis expressing concerns about being contacted by strangers. We consider our findings and propose recommendations like including more refined access control and specific culturally sensitive privacy defaults.

Keywords

WhatsApp, Social and Cultural effects, Social Media, Usable Privacy and Security, Accessibility.

1   Introduction

WhatsApp blurs the gap between social networking and traditional messaging services, allowing communication among multiple users by simplifying group communication and broadcasting messages. Consequently, it has privacy settings in place for its various features. For example, WhatsApp allows privacy control by restricting information access from 'Everyone' to 'My Contacts' for individual users. WhatsApp was designed in the US and owned by Facebook, yet India is home to the largest number of active users of WhatsApp in South-east Asia, counting over 200 million active users as of February 2017 (Singh 2017).   Our goal is a culturally grounded understanding of privacy perceptions, including those of recently added features, in the under-studied population of Indian nationals.   User studies have identified privacy concerns, and a similar study which focused on the Saudi users found that Saudi women had particular concerns about stranger contact (Rashidi *et al.* 2016).

WhatsApp already has controls including security notifications, end-to-end encryption and two-step authentication PIN for enhanced privacy (WhatsApp Security, 2018). Yet privacy depends on settings and user practices. (De Luca *et al.* 2016) and this affects the user's usage decisions for a Mobile Instant Messaging (MIM) platform. Our results identify concerns, some of them more relevant to specific demographics, and we offer recommend privacy preserving practices in the platform. The goal of this paper is a more nuanced understanding of the privacy concerns for different cultural groups on a global platform. These recommendations are also immediately actionable implementations for WhatsApp designers to support the privacy requirements for diverse users.

2   Related Work

Our research was grounded in a similar study investigating the Saudi Arabian users of WhatsApp (Rashidi et al. 2016). Saudi Arabia has the highest percentage of population using WhatsApp globally, at 78% compared to India at 28% (Statistica 2018). While adoption rate is higher in Saudi Arabia, WhatsApp is the dominant messaging application in India (Singh 2017). Thus, we can provide a comparison between the nation with the highest density of adoption, and the nation with the most adopters (see in Section 4).

A core motivation of our work is that privacy studies in social networking has primarily focused on 'Western, Educated, Industrialized, Rich and Democratic'(WEIRD) societies and the social networking applications used by these populations, which is culturally distinct from Asian populations (Risk 1998). For instance, privacy risk perception of American and German participants was found to be higher than their Chinese counterparts (Risk 1998). One of the factors is the presence of stricter privacy laws (Rights 1974; Bennett et al. 2018; Cornock 2018). In general, WEIRD populations are not necessarily representative of other populations in terms of behavioural research (Henrich, Heine & Norenzayan 2010), and this has been reified in research on mobile phone sharing practices in Bangladesh (Ahmed, Haque, Chen & Dell 2017). More recent research showed that nation of origin in the Indian subcontinent is a significant factor specially for mobile privacy (Sambasivan 2018). Further, WEIRD citizens are not the largest user base of WhatsApp (Statistica 2018). Prior research has showed that privacy concerns of internet users varies across different cultural and political settings as well as between people with different levels expertise (van Schaik, Jansen, Onibokun, Camp & Kusev 2018).

An early study of social media privacy attitudes and behaviour in India used a survey of 407 participants to evaluate privacy and security attitudes (Kumaraguru & Cranor 2005). The design was grounded in similar surveys that included only American participants Indian participants were found to have higher levels of trust in information disclosure in the public and private sectors, which sharply contrasted with privacy attitude of participants in the United States. In India, posting of students' grades along with their full names on physical, publicly visible departmental noticeboards is common and even those published on websites have low security (Scientific American Blog Network, 2017). The differences between countries and the lower level of privacy concern in India were further reified by cross cultural research on privacy by Wang et al. (Wang, Norice & Cranor 2011). However, research in risk perceptions on various other social media platforms (including Friendster, MySpace, and Facebook) has reported weak correlations between user's privacy choices and their online behaviour (Risk, 1998; Acquisti & Gross 2006). Privacy preferences, measured using a standard Likert scale, were found to be significant but to have the least impact on behaviour (Garg & Camp 2013). In contrast, King, Lampinen and Smolen report privacy attitudes to be a consequence of previous events rather than overall risk perception (King, Lampinen & Smolen 2011).

Supporting this result, Lewis, Kaufman and Christakis argue that privacy behaviours are a result of 'social influence' and 'personal incentive' (Lewis, Kaufman & Christakis 2008) such as peer attitudes and cultural biases. Patil and Kobsa have similarly argued against risk perception being a primary determinant of privacy (Patil & Kobsa 2004; Kobsa, Patil & Meyer 2012). If privacy attitudes are primarily a function of cultural attitudes, then examination of privacy in different cultures is needed to provide a more comprehensive support for different populations of customers.

Privacy concerns vary based on data type as well as data content. For example, perception and valuation of location sharing as a privacy risk vary across contexts and between individuals, and nations (Consolvo *et al.* 2005; Cvrcek, Kumpost, Matyas & Danezis 2006). Consistently studies of WEIRD populations across a range of demographics have found that data recipient and data type is a stronger factor in privacy concerns, not the generic preferences of the sender (Patil & Lai 2005; Lorenzen-Huber, Boutain, Camp, Shankar &Connelly 2011). These results motivated our inclusion of demographic and student status as questions in our study design, as described below in Section 3. WhatsApp accounts are connected to mobile numbers of individual users which itself is potentially privacy-sensitive data type, given that these numbers in India are further linked with important identifiable data including name but often extending to voter identification and financial credentials (Jain, Jain & Kumaraguru 2013).

In summary, previous research work indicates that the specific data shared by WhatsApp may have privacy concerns and further that these concerns may be different in India than in WEIRD populations. Both related work and marketplace realities argue for the importance of citizens of India as participants in research in the specific case of WhatsApp.

3   Method

Our inquiry was grounded in survey questions that have previously been asked in studies of privacy and social media extended to address the specific case of WhatsApp in India. We investigate how participants perceive and manage privacy. Our study population comprised of people who explicitly self-identify as Indian and use WhatsApp. Our core research questions are the following:

RQ1: What privacy concerns do Indians express about MIM platforms?

RQ2: How do features and demographics affect privacy preferences in MIM platforms?

RQ3: How new features impact the acceptability of MIM platforms?

RQ4: How are one-sided connections perceived by the MIM users?

The survey purposefully echoes the one used in a study of privacy concerns conducted with WhatsApp users in the Saudi Arabian population (Rashidi *et al.* 2016). The current version of WhatsApp has integrated a few of the recommendations suggested by the Saudi participants, particularly more granular access control (Rashidi et al. 2016). We evaluated whether these recommendations were applicable in the culturally different Indian population by inquiring about familiarity and use. In addition to new privacy controls, we also explored the extent to how new features, specifically Live Location, have been received and whether these have resulted in new privacy concerns.

There was a total of 83 questions, including the study information sheet, two pre-screening questions, two attention verification questions, and questions relevant to WhatsApp usage. Fifteen additional questions focus on demographics and general technology use. The demographic questions included standard questions as used in privacy for WEIRD populations: age, income, education, and employment status. The WhatsApp questions were divided into four basic mobile phone specific questions, four general questions regarding WhatsApp including news of Facebook acquiring WhatsApp, five WhatsApp usage frequency information related questions, and 26 questions about individual features. The features that we asked about were Auto-Download, Chat Backup, Read Receipts, Live Location and Status. In addition, there were 23 questions regarding user privacy concerns, privacy settings, and general WhatsApp settings questions. The remaining three questions asked about how much the participants liked or disliked certain features. The survey was distributed through snowball sampling to Indian WhatsApp users living both in India and abroad. We received a total of 454 self-reported answers from participants who use mobile messaging, of which 213 were WhatsApp users from India. Sixty-four percent were male, with more than half having at least a bachelor 's degree. Single people were also significantly over-represented at 76%. Participants were equally divided into students and non-students; meaning students were significantly over-represented.

4   Results and Analysis

The analysis presented in this work combines complementary qualitative results and quantitative analysis. The qualitative results allow individuals to express their concerns in their own words. The quantitative analysis enables explicit comparisons which can be used to reject specific hypotheses and compare aggregate results. As determined by previous surveys, WhatsApp is indeed widely used, with 74.65% participants reporting usage at least once a day. Unsurprisingly, the primary reason for adopting WhatsApp is because it is used by friends and family. Community perception was another reason; WhatsApp has millions of downloads with high ratings, good reviews, and a strong positive reputation. This is unsurprising, as popularity as a driving force for selecting apps has been repeatedly reported in empirical analyses of app selection (e.g., Chia, Yamamoto & Asokan 2012). Ease of use, overall functionality, and low cost were also popular reasons for use reported by our participants.

We asked about general sensitivity of features and use of settings. In terms of *feature sensitivity*, participants described their use and expressed concern about specific features and the data shared by those features. One repeated theme was that content is being harvested from messages: 'My major concern is privacy and usage of personal chats to target advertisements to the people'. Another participant mentioned: '... things I have written (about) on WhatsApp such as clothing, shoes, travel holidays, appear next day on my Facebook ads feed'. Participants had a sense of privacy breach even though WhatsApp offers end-to-end message encryption. Feature specific usage statistics and privacy concerns are as follows.

We inquired about specific features in addition to general concern. The use of Chat *Backup*, which arguably lessons privacy, and *Blocking*, which increases it, were both reported by a super-majority of users. Arguably, the 75.12% who use *Chat Backup* feature, which indicates that they value the ability to retrieve data if lost. This echoes previous qualitative work on two-factor authentication tokens that illustrated denial of access to data is a greater concern than privacy and security (Das, Dingman & Camp 2018). *Blocking* prevents others from contacting them individually and was used 73.24% of participants. The major reasons for doing this were reported as previously disturbing inter-actions (26.83%), unfamiliarity (19.82%), an end to previous relationships (either romantic or friendship) (15.24%), and personal conflict (13.41%). Lack of reciprocity in information disclosure (refusal to show profile components like profile photo and status) was a factor for some (12.50%) of the participants. Some simply stated their refusal to contact (12.20%) specific people without additional details. Fifty-three (24.88%) participants reported that they did not block anyone.

Muting is the most widely used, with 88.73% participants reports its use in different groups. Only one participant was unaware of this feature. *Muting* is more socially complex than *Blocking*, as discussed in the analysis section.

A similar supermajority majority of participants have switched off *Auto Download* (72.77%). This could indicate concerns about privacy, intrusion upon personal space, security, cost of mobile data, or concerns about media storage. Of the participants who report that they disabled *Auto Download*, for 73.55% reported that the dominant reason was to avoid receiving media from group chats. Others were unwilling to download media from specific people or groups.

Location is consistently identified as a privacy issue across cultures. Yet 73.24% of our participants report having shared their location over WhatsApp, only 25.82% never shared their location, while nineteen people (0.94%) were unaware that the feature existed. Additionally, WhatsApp has added a new feature called *Live Location* which allows users to share their live location (precision within 100 meters) for either 15 minutes, one hour or eight hours. Nearly half (46.51%) of the participants report that they do not need to hide their *Live Location*. Most respondents report not changing any privacy settings when the *Live Location* feature was introduced (80.73%), even though it requires that the users change their phone location settings from *Only while using the app* to *Always*. This is quite different than the location settings from the Saudi Arabian population.

As with previous work, our participants were especially concerned about their privacy in groups and suggested being able to "leave (a) group without alerting others". This is confirmed by the overwhelming number of participants who use the Mute feature (88.73%) to mute group conversations, but do not leave the group. WhatsApp creates a group notification whenever a user who leaves a group. Participants also indicated restricting Auto-download. 73.74% respondents also said that they "block (individuals) who try to contact them beyond groups, shown in Figure 2(right). Participants in the survey indicated that they want to be asked before being added to a group (72.30%) or at least otherwise asked before being added to specific groups (13.15%). This was quite similar to Saudi participants.

WhatsApp users have reported varying profile feature settings across communication recipients. Profile information includes *Profile Photo, About, Read Receipts, Last Seen* and *Status*. *About* is a feature that allows users to add a 140-character description of themselves. *Read Receipts* allow others who have a user's phone number to know if they have viewed their messages, in the form of checkmarks. A single check mark means that the message is sent, a double check mark means that the message is delivered, and double blue check mark on a message means that the message has been viewed by the receiver. *Status* allows users to add pictures, videos, texts about. Most of our participants report no concern about sharing information and using features for those in their contact list. A counter example was those people not willing to share *Last Seen* with anybody. We see a greater comfort of sharing details and willingness to share *Profile Photo* and *About*.

Concern about use of features was correlated. *Asking before addition* to a group is positively correlated with *blocking, disabling auto-download, muting and turning off last seen*. Thus, there is a consistency in individual privacy among users in both one-on-one and group communication. People who express the belief that some features invade their privacy choose to *hide status, profile photo, last seen* and *social relationships*. In addition, such concern is correlated with the refusal to use read receipts, as can be seen in Figure 1.

From the correlation matrix between privacy concern of users and features they use, as shown in Figure 1, we observe that people who are highly concerned about being contacted by strangers over WhatsApp are highly correlated (0.28) with people who use blocking feature and with people who are frequently contacted by strangers.

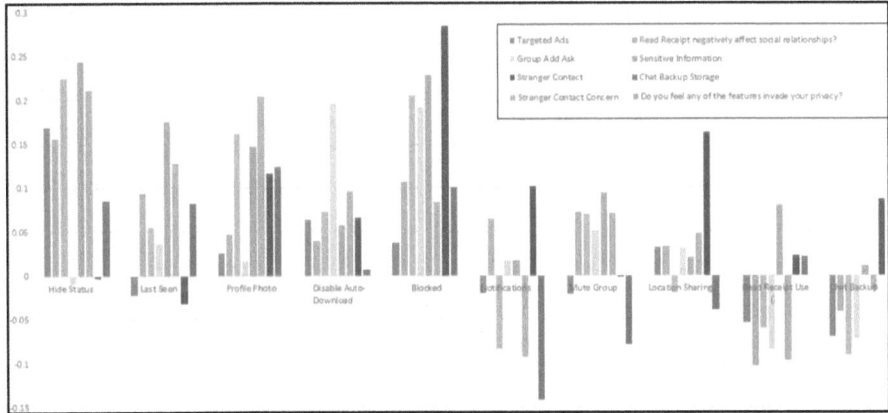

Figure 1: Privacy Concern vs Feature Correlation

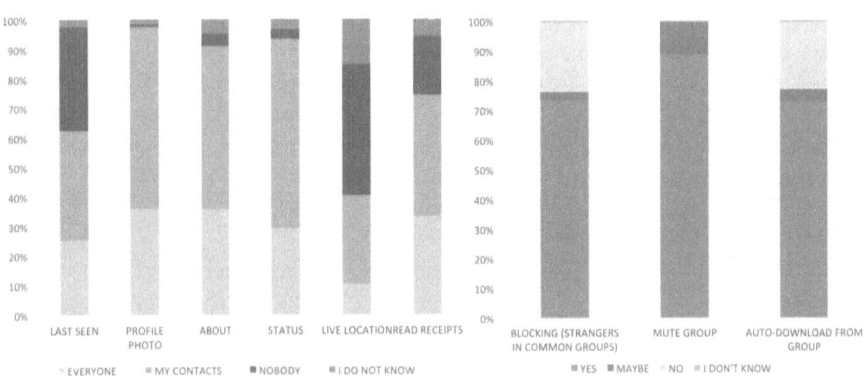

Figure 2 : Audience and Group Settings across WhatsApp (left – What are your audience settings for each of the following features; right – Do you use the Blocking/Mute/Auto-Download feature?)

5   Recommendations

Essentially our recommendations are to improve access control and to communicate risks more clearly. WhatsApp can be more privacy-preserving by allowing users to create specific trusted groups among contacts to view status and other sensitive information, while blocking it for others. In particular, groups are problematic.

Enhance Group Controls: Over 13% of participants have specific groups that they do not want to participate in. We recommend settings that allow users to be invited to a group, instead of being directly added, and giving the control to them of choosing whether to be a part of the group. Additionally, when a user is in a group with the individual who was blocked by them, the blocked can still view your messages and information, including Live Location, which requires correct implementation of exception lists. WhatsApp already incorporates exception lists to selectively choose participants who receive a user's status updates. However, it does not yet have exception lists within groups for individuals. Another feature that was specifically suggested would be the ability to leave a group without alerting others. Given proliferation of targeted and sometimes hostile political discourse on social networking platforms across the world, including WhatsApp in India, there is an argument for importance and urgency.

Bundle Settings: As observed earlier, privacy concerns about certain features are strongly linked with one another. For example, people who believe that certain features invade their privacy, hide their profile photo, status and location. Making bundles of actions to enable privacy can create a situation where WhatsApp more seamlessly address privacy concerns, particularly for users who share sensitive information. The current bundle does not seem to address expressed wishes.

Communicate privacy more clearly through reminders: Multiple participants expressed concerns about privacy preservation of the content of their messages in WhatsApp. The heuristic for the design of anonymous systems *"Say why, not how"* applies here (Norcie, Blythe, Caine & Camp 2014). End-to-end encryption in WhatsApp is a significant security benefit, but awareness among those who have adopted the technology was surprisingly low. To address the preferences of such participants, WhatsApp could provide an occasional, concise risk audit that would be technically meaningful to the user.

Integrate cultural differences and data sensitivity: The analysis of perceptions and concerns of Indians who use WhatsApp found high levels of similarities with WEIRD populations on the decision variables (trust in community, ratings, and reputation) for the selection of an application. Previous work which identified data type and data recipient as dominate factors in privacy concern in WEIRD populations (Risk 1998) were also present in these results for Indian users. However, a greater concern was reflected when users were part of a community, especially in groups, which is also reflected in the reluctance of participants to share certain data types with certain audience as shown in Figure 2 (left).

WhatsApp is used in occupational and education environments more widely in India than in the western nations. *Read receipts* carry a different connotation when there are significant power differentials between the people demanding a receipt and the person providing it. *Modifiable read receipts* were a thus, a repeated request, for plausible deniability of having read a message. Also, participants were inclined to be more socially conscious as they suggested *chat deletion without the receiver's knowledge* in groups. This message recall feature has already been implemented in updated versions of WhatsApp as of February 2018. Participants also recommended periodic deletion of chats, which has been reflected in the fact that majority of users switched off auto-download, especially for group chats.

We acknowledge there are limitations to this study. We focused on Indian WhatsApp users. Since our primary motive was to understand the privacy concerns of active users, our participants do not include participants who do not use WhatsApp. People with greater privacy concerns might disproportionately opt out or discontinue use of WhatsApp, which was out of scope for this study. Additionally, snowball sampling was the initial method for participant recruitment, which to a certain extent, influences inter-relation between participants.

6   Conclusion

It is simple to argue that WhatsApp should not reveal too much information without proper knowledge and consent of the users; to understand the privacy preserving limit, actually doing so a major challenge. This paper is a contribution to a greater understanding of the balance between user experience and, system acceptability in support of that goal. Our study indicates when it comes to an MIM application like WhatsApp, Indians express high levels of privacy concern regarding the features they use. The results in this work are another indicator that location is privacy sensitive, and when possible, people do not want this shared to 'Everyone'.

One of the participants' expressed a clearer and evocative illustration of access control as social negotiation than any the authors can provide. This argument was for reciprocal access control, with an objection to an inability to automate their responses to others: "*I don't want a new feature in particular.... but want to improve the Last Seen feature. When you turn off the Last Seen feature, no one can see (it) and .... but there are people who turn on their Last Seen when they like to stalk other people's Last Seen, which shouldn't happen. .... I would like to improvise it too; once you select to hide your Last Seen, you cannot unhide your Last Seen for 15 days at least.*" It is thus apparent that Indian users would welcome feature improvements that considers cultural differences and integrates enhanced privacy settings in a platform like WhatsApp, which they widely use.

We did not include a recommendation for reflexive access control over time, because this is not a straight-forward technical implementation. As there are cultural sensitivities for currently implemented access control, reflexive access control in social networks where individuals have repeated interactions would no doubt multiply these. This is a rich domain for possible future work as we seek to understand how to empower individuals to obtain the information control they prefer on WhatsApp. Also, we observed that WhatsApp use varies differently across gender and has substantively different privacy concerns. We would like to make a quantitative elaboration on privacy attitude and demographic correlation in our future work.

7 Acknowledgement

This research was supported in part by the National Science Foundation under CNS 1565375, Cisco Research Support, and the Comcast Innovation Fund. Any opinions, findings, and conclusions or recommendations expressed in this material are those of the author(s) and do not necessarily reflect the views of the the US Government, the National Science Foundation, Cisco, Comcast, nor Indiana University. We would also like to acknowledge the assistance of Joshua Streiff and Olivia Kenny who provided valuable feedback on the draft of this paper.

8 References

Acquisti, A. and Gross, R., 2006, June. Imagined communities: Awareness, information sharing, and privacy on the Facebook. In International workshop on privacy enhancing technologies (pp. 36-58). Springer, Berlin, Heidelberg.

Ahmed, S.I., Haque, M.R., Chen, J. and Dell, N., 2017. Digital Privacy Challenges with Shared Mobile Phone Use in Bangladesh. Proceedings of the ACM on Human-Computer Interaction, 1(CSCW), p.17.

Chia, P.H., Yamamoto, Y. and Asokan, N., 2012, April. Is this app safe?: a large scale study on application permissions and risk signals. In Proceedings of the 21st international conference on World Wide Web (pp. 311-320). ACM.

Consolvo, S., Smith, I.E., Matthews, T., LaMarca, A., Tabert, J. and Powledge, P., 2005, April. Location disclosure to social relations: why, when, & what people want to share. In Proceedings of the SIGCHI conference on Human factors in computing systems (pp. 81-90). ACM.

Cornell Student Scrapes Indian Exam Results, Exposes the System's Flaws - Scientific American Blog Network, 2017, https://blogs.scientificamerican.com/guest-blog/cornell-student-scrapes-indian-exam-results-exposes-the-systems-flaws/, (Accessed on 06/14/2018).

Cvrcek, D., Kumpost, M., Matyas, V. and Danezis, G., 2006, October. A study on the value of location privacy. In Proceedings of the 5th ACM workshop on Privacy in electronic society (pp. 109-118). ACM.

Das, S., Dingman, A. and Camp, L.J., 2017, Why Johnny Doesn't Use Two Factor A Two-Phase Usability Study of the FIDO U2F Security Key. In Pre-proceedings of Financial Cryptography and Data Security 2018.

De Luca, A., Das, S., Ortlieb, M., Ion, I. and Laurie, B., 2016, June. Expert and non-expert attitudes towards (secure) instant messaging. In Symposium on Usable Privacy and Security (SOUPS).

Garg, V. and Camp, L., 2013. Ex ante vs. ex post: Economically efficient sanctioning regimes for online risks. SSRN Electronic Journal.

Henrich, J., Heine, S.J. and Norenzayan, A., 2010. Most people are not WEIRD. Nature, 466(7302), p.29.

Jain, P., Jain, P. and Kumaraguru, P., 2013, October. Call me maybe: Understanding nature and risks of sharing mobile numbers on online social networks. In Proceedings of the first ACM conference on Online social networks (pp. 101-106). ACM.

King, J., Lampinen, A. and Smolen, A., 2011, July. Privacy: Is there an app for that?. In Proceedings of the Seventh Symposium on Usable Privacy and Security (p. 12). ACM.

Kobsa, A., Patil, S. and Meyer, B., 2012. Privacy in instant messaging: An impression management model. Behaviour & Information Technology, 31(4), pp.355-370.

Kumaraguru, P. and Cranor, L.F., 2005. Privacy indexes: a survey of Westin's studies. (CMU-ISRI-5-138), Technical report, Institute for Software Research International, Carnegie Mellon University , Pittsburgh, PA

Lewis, K., Kaufman, J. and Christakis, N., 2008. The taste for privacy: An analysis of college student privacy settings in an online social network. Journal of Computer-Mediated Communication, 14(1), pp.79-100.

Lorenzen-Huber, L., Boutain, M., Camp, L.J., Shankar, K. and Connelly, K.H., 2011. Privacy, technology, and aging: a proposed framework. Ageing International, 36(2), pp.232-252.

Norcie, G., Blythe, J., Caine, K. and Camp, L.J., 2014, February. Why Johnny can't blow the whistle: identifying and reducing usability issues in anonymity systems. In Proceedings 2014 Workshop on Usable Security. https://doi. org/10.14722/usec.

Patil, S. and Kobsa, A., 2004, September. Instant messaging and privacy. In Proceedings of HCI (Vol. 4, pp. 85-88).

Patil, S. and Lai, J., 2005, April. Who gets to know what when: configuring privacy permissions in an awareness application. In Proceedings of the SIGCHI conference on Human factors in computing systems (pp. 101-110). ACM.

Rashidi, Y., Vaniea, K. and Camp, L.J., 2016. Understanding Saudis' privacy concerns when using WhatsApp. In Proceedings of the Workshop on Usable Security (USEC'16).

Rights, F.E., 1974. Privacy Act of 1974, 20 U. SC § 1232g.

Risk, T.P., 1998. Cross-cultural differences in risk perception. Management Science, 44(9), p.1205.

Singh, M., 2017, 'Whatsapp hits 200 million active users in India', http://mashable.com/2017/02/24/whatsapp-india-200-million-active-users/Dka5Ao6c5sqW, (Accessed on 05/10/2018)

Statistica, 2018, 'Share of population in selected countries who are active whatsapp users as of 3rd quarter 2017', https://www.statista.com/statistics/291540/mobile-internet-user-whatsapp/, (Accessed on 05/10/2018)

Ur, B. and Wang, Y., 2013, May. A cross-cultural framework for protecting user privacy in online social media. In Proceedings of the 22nd International Conference on World Wide Web (pp. 755-762). ACM.

van Schaik, P., Jansen, J., Onibokun, J., Camp, J. and Kusev, P., 2018. Security and privacy in online social networking: Risk perceptions and precautionary behaviour. Computers in Human Behavior, 78, pp.283-297.

Wang, Y., Norice, G. and Cranor, L.F., 2011, June. Who is concerned about what? A study of American, Chinese and Indian users' privacy concerns on social network sites. In International Conference on Trust and Trustworthy Computing (pp. 146-153). Springer, Berlin, Heidelberg.

WhatsApp Security, 2018, https://www.whatsapp.com/security/. (Accessed on 04/18/2018).

Sambasivan, N., Checkley, G., Batool, A., Ahmed, N., Nemer, D., Sanely, L., Matthews, T., Consolvo, S., and Churchill, E., 2018 August. In Symposium on Usable Privacy and Security (SOUPS).

POINTER: A GDPR-Compliant Framework for Human Pentesting (for SMEs)

J. Archibald and K. Renaud

School of Design & Informatics, Abertay University, Dundee, Scotland
e-mail: {j.archibald,k.renaud}@abertay.ac.uk

Abstract

Penetration tests have become a valuable tool in any organisation's arsenal, in terms of detecting vulnerabilities in their technical defences. Many organisations now also "penetration test" their employees, assessing their resilience and ability to repel human-targeted attacks. There are two problems with current frameworks: (1) few of these have been developed with SMEs in mind, and (2) many deploy spear phishing, thereby invading employee privacy, which could be illegal under the new European General Data Protection Regulation (GDPR) legislation. We therefore propose the **PoinTER** (**P**repare **TE**st **R**emediate) Human Pentesting Framework. We subjected this framework to expert review and present it to open a discourse on the issue of formulating a GDPR- compliant Privacy-Respecting Employee Pentest for SMEs.

Keywords

Penetration testing; Privacy Preservation; SME; GDPR

1   Introduction

Companies often employ security companies to test their systems' security: to detect vulnerabilities. This procedure is referred to as *"carrying out a penetration test"* (pentest), which aims to reveal vulnerabilities in the company's defences. The idea is that these can be addressed before malicious actors potentially find and exploit them. SMEs are in an unenviable position of being increasingly targeted by cyber criminals, and not having the financial resources to defend themselves as well as large companies can (Saleem *et al.*, 2017; Wlasuk, 2012). It has been estimated that as many as 60% of small businesses who experience an attack go out of business so this matter needs urgent attention.

Even if an SME *can* afford to have a penetration test carried out, there are two problems. The first is the nature of the penetration tests themselves, which are often technically-focused (Yeo, 2013; Tiller, 2004; Bacudio *et al.*, 2011). The second is that the pentest frameworks are generally constructed with larger companies in mind, especially when it comes to remediation, which is often unrealistic given SMEs' limited resources (Berger & Jones, 2016).

2   Human-Centred Penetration Testing

Most penetration tests, by focusing on technical vulnerabilities (Staiwan *et al.*, 2017; Tang, 2014; Xynos *et al.*, 2010), neglect the human's role in the security loop. To ensure that a full range of vulnerabilities are detected, a penetration tester should also test human resilience to attack. This is especially important because recent reports reveal that three quarters of organisations, across the board, experienced a phishing attack in 2017. (GOV.UK, 2018). Few tests are specifically tailored to the SME context (Berger & Jones, 2016) and technical penetration tests cannot reliably identify human vulnerabilities.

Some researchers have proposed methodologies for human-focused pentesting, but many of these target employees with spear phishing attacks. This is problematical because the effective spear phish relies on the pen tester uncovering personal details and figuring out how to exploit their new knowledge of the employee's personal interests and concerns. This could be considered an unacceptable violation of their privacy, especially in the light of the new General Data Protection Regulation (GDPR) legislation (https://gdpr-info.eu/) (Kenner, 2017).

While hackers undeniably deploy spear phishing as an attack vector (TREND Micro, 2012), and many are specifically targeting SMEs (Pickard-Whitehead, 2017), it does not seem appropriate for the "good guys" to appropriate techniques used by the "bad guys". Pen testers aim to practice their skills ethically and defensively, as suggested by their title. In this respect, they are fundamentally different from the usual cyber attacker: their ethical perspectives are diametrically opposed. Hence, we need to consider developing a *privacy-respecting GDPR-compliant* human pentest framework to inform the pentesting industry at large.

We set out to develop this framework, which can be used by pentesters when probing and revealing the SME employee vulnerabilities. Before we discuss the framework, we first address the ethics of spear phishing, when carried out by pentesters.

3   Human Pen Testing: Privacy & GDPR

Social engineering attacks target employees, both digitally and otherwise. Social engineers use email, SMS, phone, removable media and in-person interaction to manipulate individuals to carry out actions the social engineer wants them to perform.

When carrying out a spear phishing attack, a hacker will research an employee's personal interests on social networking websites. The knowledge is used to construct an enticing phishing message redirecting the employee to a reputable looking website. Scattergun phishing attacks, on the other hand, send out generic messages to a wide range of targets and do not attempt to match messages to people's specific interests. Both of these can be used by pentesters, with the former having a much greater chance of success (Team Graphus, 2017).

When a pentester tests for resilience to spear phishing, he/she is essentially authorised to utilise the online footprint of key privileged employees in an organisation. A profile is constructed to tailor emails that are likely to engender trust via familiarity. If the targeted employee clicks on the embedded link, a number of different strategies can be deployed. Kumaraguru *et al*. (2009) suggests forwarding the person directly to a page that explains how to resist these kinds of attacks. They call this the "teachable moment". This approach has been adopted by some companies[1]. Others require the deceived employee to engage in an online training course[2] or report the employee to their line manager.

There is evidence that employees are angered by these kinds of approaches, considering them to breach the trust that ought to exist between employer and employee[3]. More importantly, it probably violates the new GDPR regulations, even if the personal information it uses is publicly available. The British Heart Foundation and RSPCA were fined recently for using publicly available information to target wealthy donors: they were using the information for a purpose the information's owner had not approved it for (Information Commissioner, 2016). GDPR explicitly forbids unauthorised use of personal data and pentesters might be sanctioned for engaging in such activities.

What about the pentester, on a personal level? If they have to carry out an intensive investigation into some person's life in order to carry out a spear phishing or social engineering attack, both the pentester and the employee are potentially harmed. The pentester cannot subsequently un-know everything they have discovered and could become deeply uncomfortable about having to invade another person's privacy in this way in order to carry out the pentest. The employee's privacy is certainly being sacrificed for the company's benefit. While employers can require particular standards of behaviour at work, they do not have the right to pry into their employees' personal lives (Pincus & Trotter,1995; Richman, 2000). Moreover, such activities violate one of the core tenets of ethical practice: respect (Frankena, 1986).

The argument *for* spear phishing employees, or exploiting them through other aspects of social engineering, is that this mirrors what hackers might do to compromise the organisation. It could also be argued that assessing the extent of publicly-available personal information online may assist the affected employee to strategically reduce or restrict the size of their online footprint. Yet there is an undeniable "creepiness"

---

[1] https://www.darkreading.com/risk/how-lockheed-martin-phishes-its-own/d/d-id/1139629; http://theinstitute.ieee.org/technology-topics/cybersecurity/company-tests-how-employees-handle- social-engineering-attacks□
[2] http://www.govtech.com/security/Employee-Phishing-Expeditions-Among-States-Assessments- of-Cybersecurity-Awareness.html
[3] http://www.nj.com/healthfit/index.ssf/2016/06/in_security_test_hospital_phishes_its_own_employee.html

about an employer permitting this kind of investigation into their employees' personal lives (Rosenquist, 2015).

An open question is whether the new GDPR regulation permits this kind of action by employers. Spear phishing campaigns, in particular those conducted by pen testers, undeniably gather very personal data about employees that they have not provided for this purpose, which conflicts with the *raison d'être* of the new regulations.

However, the most compelling reason not to carry out spear phishing attacks on employees is revealed by recent research published by Caputo *et al.* (2014). They found no evidence that such efforts impacted subsequent link clicking behaviours, and therefore question the efficacy of the technique.

4   Developing a Privacy-Sensitive Employee Pen Test

Aim: Formulate a rigorous, comprehensive and dynamic pentesting process. This will be scientifically derived and refined rather than ad-hoc, the main feature of current testing regimens, as follows:

1. Carry out a literature review, investigating both research literature and publications from standards bodies and industry white papers. This will gauge the current "state of play" related to pentesting in the field.
2. (a) Construct an SME-specific pentesting framework that informs the investigation of employee-related vulnerabilities.
   (b) Suggest remediation actions that can be taken by organisations to address identified vulnerabilities.
3. Have the framework assessed by experts in the field, in order to refine and improve it.

4.1   Literature Review

The use of Social Engineering to exploit organisations has become more pervasive in recent times (Ashford, 2018; Costa, 2016; Weeks 2018; Smith, 2016). A human-centred penetration test can uncover vulnerabilities that make organisations open to social engineering attacks. Processes and frameworks that constitute human-centred penetration testing are discussed. We also consider whether these approaches are privacy sensitive and thus GDPR compliant.

The pretext to any penetration test is that it should be conducted in a legal and ethical manner. Prior to the test, consent must be given and signed off, a contract drawn up and appropriate people made aware that the test will take place (CSO, 2018). Any steps taken during the test must be lawful within the legal jurisdiction of the penetration test location (CSO, 2018; Ackroyd, 2014). In terms of ethical conduct, no one should come to any harm during a penetration test.

The Open Web Application Security Project (OWASP) is an open community which encourages organisations to create and work with trusted applications. OWASP recommend a number of Penetration Testing Methodologies. (OWASP, 2016) Two of the recommended include a human centred element:

(1) Penetration Testing Execution Standard (PTES) which includes Pre-engagement Interactions, Intelligence Gathering, Threat Modelling, Vulnerability Analysis, Exploitation, Post Exploitation and Reporting (PTES, 2012a)
(2) Penetration Testing Framework (PTF) is technically oriented with tool recommendations but also lists human centred approaches such a Vulnerability Analysis and Physical Security.(OWASP, 2016)

Although both of the above consider human aspects of pentesting, neither consider the privacy of the employees. For example, PTES lists, as part of its Technical Guidelines, a range of social networking sites to use for gathering information, some of which could contain private and sensitive information, e.g. gays.com (PTES, 2012b)

The Council for Registered Ethical Security Testers (CREST) (CREST, 2017) is an Accreditation Body for the information security industry and provide guidance in running Penetration Testing programmes. They recommend the following as good practice advice:

(1) Open Source Security Testing Methodology Manual (OSSTMM) includes a chapter on Human Security Testing
(2) National Institute of Standards and Technology (NIST) Special Publication 800-115 (SP800-115), includes a section on Social Engineering
(3) Information Systems Security Assessment Framework (ISSAF) includes a chapter on Social Engineering

Similar to the OWASP recommendations, none of the above consider approaches to help maintain the privacy of employees involved in a penetration test. Although (NIST) (SP800-115) and OSSTMM do mention that effects of penetration testing on employees should be considered. By not respecting privacy rights, there is the possibility that a penetration test may violate GDPR regulations.

Ackroyd (2014) and Dimkov *et al.,* (2010) addressed the issue of privacy and developed methodologies which attempted to make penetration testing easier on the employee. However their methodologies are oriented towards larger organisations and thus not appropriate for SMEs. In terms of the size of companies, none of the literature specifically considers a Human-centred approach to penetration testing for SMEs. However there is evidence that SMEs are indeed targeted by social engineering attacks (Smith, 2016). Thus, testing resilience to mitigate against these attacks would be beneficial, especially if privacy-respecting and GDPR compliant.

4.2 SME-Specific Human Pentesting Framework

We suggest a three-phase penetration testing framework to guide and inform ethical penetration testers carrying out human penetration tests: (1) Pentest Preparation, (2) Pentest execution, and (3) Remediation.

We asked five experienced penetration testers and security experts to comment on:|

(1) Whether the framework covers all the aspects of penetration testing.
(2) Whether it respects privacy.
(3) Whether it is feasible for SMEs to apply the suggested remediations.
(4) Whether they can suggest any refinements or improvements.

Based on their feedback, we refined and improved the framework, which we provide in the next Section.

5   Final Framework

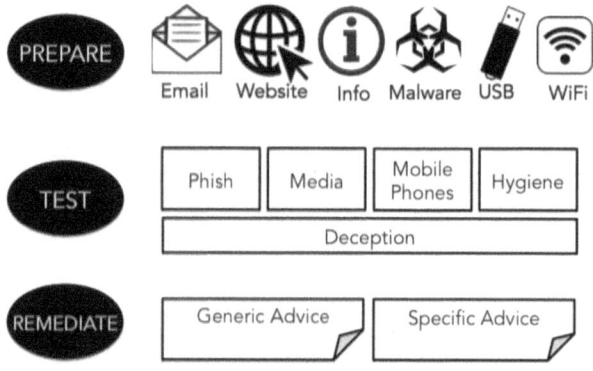

Figure 1: The **POINTER** Human Pentest Framework.
Pentester prepares materials, then tests human within workplace and offers remediation advice. No personal details will be recorded or included in reports.

Phase 1: Pentest preparation: (Ackroyd, 2014)

1) Speak to the CEO about setting up a "bait" website to be used in phishing pentesting. We will refer to this website as *BAIT* in the future discussion.
2) Tailor malware to be used in pentesting such that it reports only installations, but not the identity of the employee. We shall refer to this as *TITBIT* in the future discussion.
3) Set up an email address that looks similar to the CEO's: the *DOPPELGANGER*.
4) Ask the CEO to give all his employees a confidential mobile phone number, to be used only in emergencies. This will entail loaning a mobile phone to the

CEO with a new SIM card in it (this can be reused). This number will be referred to as *CEO-Mobile*.

5) Prepare **USB** sticks for distribution.
6) Set up a **rogue** WiFi.

Phase 2: Pentest execution: The pentest should cover the following areas (Kelm, 2014, Acquisti *et al*, 2017; Coventry *et al.*, 2014; Yevseyeva *et al.,* 2014; Denno, 2016, Ackroyd, 2014):

1) **PHISH:**
   a) ***PHISH with LINK***: The ***DOPPELGANGER*** sends a Phish message with an embedded link that redirects to the BAIT website put up by the pentester which appears to offers some very useful functionality appropriate to that particular company (as agreed by the CEO of the company)
      i) See if you can get people to create an account (they might use the same password they have used on other sites). Keep a tally of these
      ii) Execute a drive-by attack which essentially reports to the pentester that the an employee visited the website.
   b) ***PHISH with Malware or HTML ATTACHMENT***: The ***DOPPELGANGER*** sends a Phish message that purports to come from the CEO, with an attached file (TITBIT) with embedded executable functionality. The TITBIT file executable should inform the pentester that it has been opened, but not who opened it.
   c) ***PHISH with PDF ATTACHMENT***: The ***DOPPELGANGER*** sends an email that purports to come from the CEO, with a PDF file attached. The file itself is fine, but there is an embedded link that is suspect. If clicked, it will redirect the employee to the BAIT.
   d) ***WHALING***: The ***DOPPELGANGER*** sends an email that purports to come from the CEO, which asks the person to download a particular file and attend to it urgently. The link is similar to those generally used within the company. This could be Dropbox or Google Docs, for example. If clicked, this will redirect the employee to the **BAIT** website, which records the visit.
2) **MEDIA Drop (deception)**: Drop USB sticks with a folder called SECRET-IMAGES. The folder is full of files with extensions like ".png", "pdf" or ".jpg" but one or two (with enticing names) are actually exe files which will inform the pentester that they have been opened.
3) **Deception:**
   a) ***In Person***: Elicit the assistance of a fellow pentester who is not known to the company. They should arrive at the company with some kind of story, in order to persuade someone to "help" them by printing a CV from a USB stick. If an employee can be persuaded to plug in the USB stick, an executable will inform the pentester.
   b) ***Telephone Call***: Call and tell an employee a story about a very urgent need to contact the CEO, and try to elicit **CEO-Mobile**.
4) **Good Hygiene:**

a) ***Workplace***: Walk around the office space at the end of the day and see whether any computers have been left unlocked, whether mobile media have been left lying around.
   i) If anything is found, secure and return to owner.
   ii) If a computer is left unlocked, make a note of what functionality an attacker could have gained access to.
   iii) Check for confidential material in dustbins
   iv) Passwords: Check for WiFi and/or personal passwords publicly displayed in offices or hidden under keyboards. Check for written records of passwords. Check under keyboards and around desks for hidden post-it notes with passwords.
b) ***Backups***: Find out how backups are secured. Check whether these are encrypted.
c) ***Awareness***: Plug an inactive keylogger into a machine's USB (at the front of the machine) and see whether anyone spots it.

5) **Mobile Phones**: If people are permitted to read their work email on their phones, or use the company WiFi, check that employees:
   a) control access to the phone with a PIN/Password or Fingerprint (not Pattern).
   b) understand the need to limit permissions given to Apps installed on the phones.
   c) are in the habit of updating phones and apps to the latest version.
   d) use the company VPN if applicable.
   e) connect to the **rogue** WiFi hotspot you set up.

Phase 3: Remediation: Here we suggest two kinds of remediation:

5.1 Generic Advice

1) Identify a few approved password managers for the employee to choose from. Strongly recommend usage and provide installation support.
2) Recommend an organisation-approved VPN with multiple licences so all employees can use it on their mobile phones.
3) Ensure that technical measures are the first defence. Only where technical measures cannot detect attacks should the company rely on the users to detect anomalies. Examples are: group policies that prevent external storage devices from being access from computers, password protected screen savers and only admins can run executable files.
4) Institute a training programme so that staff know about hovering over a link to check the actual destination of links, which they should examine for authenticity. They should have the freedom to report links they are unsure about to their security staff, without risk of censure.
5) Lay down a clear policy for what to do should someone click on a link, or open a suspicious attachment.
6) If employees are permitted to read their work emails from their phones, or use the company network, ensure that minimum security standards have been implemented on the phone before access is permitted. Ask for a copy of their BYOD policy.

5.2 Specific Advice

1) Depending on the outcome of the pentest, deliver specific advice related to Phish resilience.
2) The approach should be to find out how to make compliance as easy as possible for employees. Punishments, shaming and excessive imposition of rules to control behaviour are counter-productive and ought not to be seen as the solution to any security weaknesses.
3) Depending on the identified vulnerabilities, recommend specific training to be delivered to employees.

6   Conclusion & Future Work

In this paper we report on the development of a penetration test that seeks to test employee resilience. We argue that such frameworks ought to be sensitive to ethical

issues, GDPR regulation and privacy preservation. We argue that the privacy of employees should be respected and preserved. We asked five security experts to comment and refined the framework based on their feedback. We are planning to give this framework to some student penetration testers to use so that we can gather feedback about how viable, helpful and effective it is in practice.

7   References

Ashford, W. 2018. More than one in 10 employees fall for social engineering attacks, Available from: https://www.computerweekly.com/news/252438572/More-than-one-in-10- employees-fall-for-social-engineering-attacks (Accessed 16 May 2018)

Acquisti, A., Adjerid, I., Balebako, R., Brandimarte, L., Cranor, L.F., Komanduri, S., Leon, P.G., Sadeh, N., Schaub, F., Sleeper, M. and Wang, Y. 2017. Nudges for privacy and security: Understanding and assisting users' choices online. ACM Computing Surveys (CSUR), 50(3), p.44.

Bacudio, A.G., Yuan, X., Chu, B.T.B. and Jones, M. 2011. An overview of penetration testing. International Journal of Network Security & Its Applications, 3(6), p.19.

Berger, H. and Jones, A. 2016, July. Cyber Security & Ethical Hacking For SMEs. In Proceedings of the 11th International Knowledge Management in Organizations Conference on the changing face of Knowledge Management Impacting Society (p. 12). ACM.

Caputo, D.D., Pfleeger, S.L., Freeman, J.D. and Johnson, M.E. 2014. Going spear phishing: Exploring embedded training and awareness. IEEE Security & Privacy, 12(1), pp.28-38.

Costa, C. 2016. Protect Yourself and Your Business from Social Engineering. Available from: https://www.sitepoint.com/protect-yourself-and-your-business-from-social-engineering/ (Accessed 16 May 2018)

Coventry, L., Briggs, P., Jeske, D and van Moorsel, A. 2014. Scene: A structured means for creating and evaluating behavioral nudges in a cyber security environment. In International Conference of Design, User Experience, and Usability. Springer, 229–239.

CREST. 2017. Penetration Testing - A Guide for Running an Effective Programme Available from: http://www.crest-approved.org/a-suppliers-guide-to-penetration-testing-services/index.html (Accessed 16 May 2018)

Denno, J. 2016. Attacking the Human - The Weakest Link in Cybersecurity. Masters Thesis. Utica College.

Evans, N.J. 2009. Information technology social engineering: an academic definition and study of social engineering-analyzing the human firewall. PhD Dissertation. Computer Engineering. Iowa State University.

Frankena, W.K. 1986. The ethics of respect for persons. Philosophical Topics, 14(2), pp.149-167. GOV.UK, 2018. Cyber Security Breaches Survey 2018, (Accessed 16 May 2018). Available from https://www.gov.uk/government/statistics/cyber-security-breaches-survey-2018.

Information Commissioner. 2016. ICO investigation reveals how charities have been exploiting supporters, (Accessed 16 May 2018). Available from https://ico.org.uk/about-the-ico/news-and-events/news-and-blogs/2016/12/ico-investigation-reveals-how-charities-have-been-exploiting-supporters/

Kelm, D. 2014. FoSA - Framework for Social Engineering Auditing, Masters Dissertation. Technische Universität, Darmstadt.

Kenner, M. 2017. Video surveillance at work breached employee privacy, ECHR rules. https://www.peoplemanagement.co.uk/news/articles/video-surveillance-breached-   privacy. Accessed July 2018.

Kumaraguru, P., Cranor, L.F. and Mather, L. 2009. Anti-phishing landing page: Turning a 404 into a teachable moment for end users. In Conference on Email and Anti-Spam (CEAS).

OWASP. 2016. Penetration Testing Methodologies, (Accessed 16 May 2018) Available from https://www.owasp.org/index.php/Penetration_testing_methodologies

Pickard-Whitehead, G. 2017 10 Phishing Examples in 2017 that Targeted Small Business. Aug 29. https://smallbiztrends.com/2017/08/phishing-examples-small-business.html (Accessed 16 May 2018)

Pincus, L.B. and Trotter, C. 1995. The disparity between public and private sector employee privacy protections: A call for legitimate privacy rights for private sector workers. American Business Law Journal, 33(1), pp.51-90.

PTES, 2012a. PTES Technical Guidelines, Available from http://www.pentest-standard.org/index.php/PTES_Technical_Guidelines (Accessed 4 June 2018)

PTES, 2012b PTES Technical Guidelines, Social Networking Websites, (Accessed 16 May 2018) http://www.pentest-standard.org/index.php/PTES_Technical_Guidelines#Social_Networking_ Websites (Accessed 4 June 2018)

Richman, A. 2000. Restoring the Balance: Employer Liability and Employee Privacy. Iowa Law Review, 86, p.1337.

Rosenquist, M. 2015. How Far Should a Company go to Test Employee's Resistance to Phishing. https://itpeernetwork.intel.com/how-far-should-a-company-go-to-test-employees-resistance-to-phishing/. August 13 (Accessed July 2018).

Saleem, J., Adebisi, B., Ande, R. and Hammoudeh, M. 2017, July. A state of the art survey-Impact of cyber attacks on SME's. In Proceedings of the International Conference on Future Networks and Distributed Systems (p. 52). ACM.

Smith, M. 2016. Social engineers reveal why the biggest threat to your business could be you. Aug 4. https://www.theguardian.com/small-business-network/2016/oct/04/social-engineers-reveal-biggest-threat-business (Accessed 16 May 2018)

Tang, A. (2014). A guide to penetration testing. Network Security, 2014(8), 8-11.

Team Graphus. (2017) Verizon Says Phishing Still Drives 90% of Cybersecurity Breaches. 2017. https://www.graphus.ai/verizon-says-phishing-still-drives-90-cybersecurity-breaches/ (Accessed 16 May 2018)

Tiller, J.S. 2004. The ethical hack: a framework for business value penetration testing. CRC Press.

TREND Micro. 2012. Spear-Phishing Is the Favored Targeted Attack Bait. November 28. https://www.trendmicro.com/vinfo/au/security/news/cybercrime-and-digital-threats/spear-phishing-is-the-favored-targeted-attack-bait (Accessed 16 May 2018)

Wlasuk, A. 2012. Small Business and Law Firms-Protecting the Security Interests of Clients. Vermont Bar Journal, 38, p.32.

Weeks, R. 2018. Five common social engineering attacks and small businesses. Available from: http://smallbusiness.co.uk/five-common-social-engineering-attacks-cybersecurity-training-2542739 (Accessed 16 May 2018)

Xynos, K., Sutherland, I., Read, H., Everitt, E. and Blyth, A.J. 2010. Penetration testing and vulnerability assessments: A professional approach. Proceedings of the 1st International

Cyber Resilience Conference, Edith Cowan University, Perth Western Australia, 23rd August 2010

Yevseyeva, I., Morisset, J., Turland, Coventry, L., Groß, T., Laing, C., and van Moorsel, A. 2014. Consumerisation of IT: Mitigating risky user actions and improving productivity with nudging. Procedia Technology 16 (2014), 508–517.

Yeo, J. 2013. Using penetration testing to enhance your company's security. Computer Fraud & Security, 2013(4), pp.17-20.

The Impact of Artificial Intelligence on the Human Aspects of Information and Cybersecurity

M. Malatji[1], A. Marnewick[1] and S. von Solms[2]

[1]Postgraduate School of Engineering Management, University of Johannesburg
[2]Department of Electrical and Electronic Engineering, University of Johannesburg
e-mail: masikem@gmail.com; amarnewick@uj.ac.za; svonsolms@uj.ac.za

Abstract

This paper presents the results of a literature survey on the impact of artificial intelligence on the human aspects of information and cybersecurity. Artificial intelligence and its two subfields, machine learning and deep learning, are briefly described though much emphasis is placed on the impact of their applications to the human aspects of information and cybersecurity. In addition, the paper presents arguments by those in favour of autonomous artificial intelligence designs that do not require human interventions as well as counter-arguments by those opposed to the idea for ethical and other reasons. The current and future security trends of the human-artificial intelligence integration are explored. The findings reveal that artificial intelligence is currently utilised only for augmenting human capacity in information and cybersecurity activities whereas the future trends are unknown. The study proposes the socio-technical systems approach for attaining the optimal security results through the human-artificial intelligence integration.

Keywords

Artificial intelligence, cybersecurity, human aspect, information security, machine learning, socio-technical system

1 Introduction

Information and cybersecurity incidents have grown rapidly both in scale and number (Fang *et al.*, 2018). Organisations are battling to keep pace with the proliferation of such incidents (U.S. Newswire, 2017). With 20 years of investigating and analysing cyber-incidents, Antuit (2018) consider the rapid expansion and sophistication of the recent cyber-attacks as unprecedented. There is also complete anticipation by security professionals that the cyber-threats will progressively become challenging and complex (Cisco, 2018). This has compelled many organisations to introduce somewhat unpredictable and chaotic processes (CyberSaint, 2017). What is information and cybersecurity though? Buczak and Guven (2016) consider it a set of technologies and processes responsible for protecting computer networks, associated software and data from unauthorised access, alteration, or destruction. Protection of these computer system networks has careened into a danger zone over the last decade (Greengard, 2016).

It is Buczak and Guven's (2016) position that each of the computer network security systems should have, at a minimum, an intrusion detection system (IDS), antivirus software, and firewalls. However, Greengard (2016) is adamant that firewalls have effectively become unreliable as application programming interfaces and cloud computing string together data across different enterprises. In the context of big data from the cloud cybersecurity has become a critical challenge and poses greater risk (Sabar *et al.*, 2018). This is exacerbated by a lack of human capacity to screen big volumes of data for proper threat analysis (Talwar and Koury, 2017). This prompted practitioners and researchers to look for new and better information and cybersecurity approaches (Greengard, 2016). Consequently, researchers have begun developing security solutions that employ artificial intelligence (AI). AI encompasses both machine learning and deep learning (Pumin, 2016). As the core AI subfield, machine learning is about effective simulation of human activities as applied to speech and pattern recognition, image processing, cybersecurity, and even decision-making (Greengard, 2016; Liu *et al.*, 2018). Essentially, AI is about machines that simulate intelligent human behaviour such as learning, thinking, and reasoning (Dragomir, 2017).

However, what are the current and future trends on the impact of AI to the human information and cybersecurity activities? To answer this question, the literature review study purpose has three objectives: (1) Examine the AI trends in information and cybersecurity; (2) Describe how the AI trends impact the human aspects of information and cybersecurity; and (3) Propose how the new 'people-technology' security integration could be achieved for optimal results. To examine the trends, a literature review protocol is proposed. The methods section describes the protocol in detail. The layout of this paper begins with the introduction section outlining the research purpose. Section 2 outlines the research approach and the execution of the approach is described in Section 3. Section 3 further reviews the AI trends in information and cybersecurity. The results of the literature survey are discussed in Section 4. The paper concludes with Section 5 where future research is also suggested. The adopted methodology to study the current and future trends on the impact of AI to the human information and cybersecurity activities is described in the next section.

2 Methodology

2.1 Literature Review Approach

The aim of the literature review process of this study is to (Silic and Back, 2014):

- Compile and classify articles according to themes devoted to AI trends in information and cybersecurity and their impact on human security aspects
- Analyse, understand, and show how the compiled literature addresses the research purpose stated in the introductory section
- Given the impact of AI on the human aspects of information and cybersecurity, propose how to accomplish the new AI-human integration for optimal results

In order to attain valid results for this type of research, a rigorous stand-alone literature review approach is followed.

According to Fink (2005), a stand-alone literature review approach must be systematic in following a methodological technique, explicit in explaining the procedures by which it was conducted, comprehensive in its scope of including all relevant material, and hence reproducible by others who would follow the same approach in reviewing the topic. A four-stage approach, each consisting of two steps, is adopted as summarised in Figure 1.

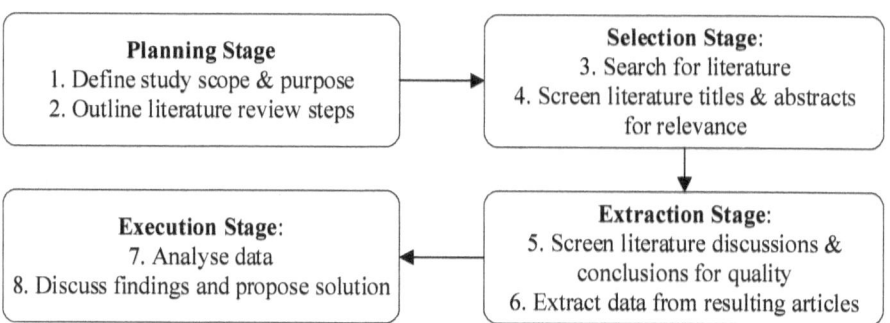

Figure 1: Systematic literature review process, derived from Okoli and Schabram (2010)

With reference to Figure 1, the four-stage systematic literature review protocol consists of the planning stage, selection stage, extraction stage, and execution (Okoli and Schabram, 2010). The planning stage is essentially Figure 1 as it outlines the literature review steps. The selection stage of the systematic literature review process is outlined in the next subsection.

2.2 Research Material Selection Scope

The study limited the review articles search to between January 2008 and May 2018 and a maximum number of 12 articles per journal. Levy and Ellis (2006) recommend that when repeated searches result in the same references, and with no new results from the same keywords, then the search is exhaustive. This is the search rule the researchers adopted. In addition, non-peer reviewed sources such as theses and dissertations, reports, conference papers, industry publications, and popular media were sought (Ridley, 2008). It is important to further augment the literature search in order to provide assurance that as many sources have been identified (Okoli and Schabram, 2010). According to Levy and Ellis (2006), this is achieved by further studying the reference sections of the relevant articles and performing both backward and forward searches. Backward search refers to references cited by the primary articles resulting from the researchers' keyword searches, and forward search relates to other publications citing articles compiled by the researchers. The following keywords were used to search for the literature and Table 1 shows the final results.

Database name	Initial search results	Excluded no. of articles	Total no. of articles reviewed
EBSCO – Academic Search complete	11	9	2
Access Engineering	541	541	0
Access Science	109	109	0
ACM Digital Library	409 773	409 773	0
Emerald	17	17	0
IEEE Xplore	390	385	5
JSTOR	87	87	0
OECD iLibrary	0	0	0
ProQuest Central	12 425	12 415	10
Sage Journals Online	58	57	1
ScienceDirect	259	257	2
SpringerLink	912	912	0
UJ Library Catalogue	5	5	0
Wiley Online Library	121	121	0
Google Scholar	19 800	19 792	8
Backward/forward search	0	0	3
TOTAL	444 508	444 476	**32**

Table 1: Total number of articles reviewed

The literature search conducted on May 18, 2018 was confined to 14 scholarly databases. Combined, these databases contain thousands of journals. In addition, the Google scholar search results of May 24, 2018 were included. The first top 20 Google scholar search results were screened. Only 8 were found to be relevant and of good quality. The screening of articles from the initial search results was based only on the titles and abstracts. Where the maximum of 12 relevant articles per database was not reached, the search results were augmented through backward and forward searches as recommended by Levy and Ellis (2006). Consequently, an additional 2 articles were identified through the EBSCO – Academic Search Complete database and 1 through ProQuest Central. At this stage, duplicates were also manually screened and eliminated. Table 1 was finalised with a total of 32 AI trends in information and cybersecurity articles. The systematic literature review relating to the AI trends in information and cybersecurity is described in the next section.

3   Related Work

With reference to the adopted literature review approach in Figure 1, the extraction stage is executed in this section. That is, the 32 articles in Table 2 are reviewed and the data as it relates to the research purpose are extracted and analysed.

3.1   AI Trends in Information and Cybersecurity

The main aim of information and cybersecurity is to minimise, or completely eradicate, the frequency of successful cyber-attacks (Yampolskiy and Spellchecker, 2015). It was previously mentioned that cyber-threats have become increasingly challenging to detect and respond to (Craig, 2018). This might be indicating that new information and cybersecurity measures are required (Dhananjay and Pandey, 2018). Dragomir (2017) has noticed that some of the new measures include the application of AI that is growing in adoption. The growth is attributed to perception by industry that AI has a quicker turnaround time to detection and reaction (Patil, 2016).

This is quite significant, especially, where traditional methods are too slow and insufficient to react (Wirkuttis and Klein, 2017). With its ability to recognise patterns of behaviour through massive datasets, AI could help detect a broad spectrum of cyber-threats and make intelligent decisions (Dilek *et al.*, 2015). The biggest threat from AI, however, is its potential for weaponisation (Carriço, 2018). This is because attackers will also leverage on AI's ability to learn from experiences and start developing AI-powered malware that traditional security systems will hardly be prepared for (Brundage *et al.*, 2018). Adding to this threat is the growing prevalence of polymorphous malware (malicious software with the ability to change its code) and zero-day attacks (type of attacks that strike and spread immediately), and viruses that can obfuscate for months or even years (Greengard, 2016).

With that in mind, the information and cybersecurity communities need to prepare for a future where AI-powered cyber-attacks will be autonomous (Hobbs, 2018). To prepare for this future, attention must also be paid to the security of AI applications themselves before they are deployed to other areas. Liu and Yu (2018) posit that as the usage of machine learning techniques gradually become widely accepted protecting its security at both the data learning and inference nodes becomes crucial. This is because a system may fail, either through design flaw or vulnerability exploitations on the nodes, to learn what the humans intended for it to and instead absorb malicious lessons (Yampolskiy and Spellchecker, 2015). Brundage *et al.* (2018) agree that AI systems are indeed susceptible to various security vulnerabilities distinct from traditional software's. Such vulnerabilities could also be exploited to automate cyber-attacks (Tadjdeh, 2018). If this happens, it could prove far-reaching and very dangerous for us all (Hobbs, 2018). Perhaps the danger comes from the fact that, if fully exploited, AI systems can attack targets much quicker than humans can (Brundage *et al.*, 2018). To this end, the literature has revealed that while AI-powered systems clearly surpass human performance in many ways, they are also vulnerable to attack in ways that humans never would (Brundage *et al.*, 2018). As described in the next subsection, human capabilities can significantly be augmented by AI when addressing organisational complexities (Jarrahi, 2018).

3.2 AI Trends Relating to Human Aspects of Security

Qualified personnel in information and cybersecurity are so scarce that organisations are turning to AI to fill the gaps (Fazzini, 2017). To shoulder the workload, it is expected that organisations will spend more on AI and machine learning to help improve security defences (Cisco, 2018). Although an ideal cyber-defense is to provide complete protection to users, we are still quite far from this scenario (Morel, 2011). In fact, Yampolskiy and Spellchecker (2015) argue that a 100% secure system does not exist because every security system eventually fails. Complete protection to users, therefore, is unlikely to ever be provided (Morel, 2016). In 2016 alone, the United States needed to fill 200 000 cybersecurity vacancies (Roberts, 2016). This shows that organisations wanting to deploy AI to bolster information and cybersecurity are not yet ready to remove the human from the entire process (Jack, 2016). Further, the application of AI to information and cybersecurity is not a tool in its own right; rather, AI still requires some level of human interaction for continuous improvement and, for example, to learn to understand new methods of attack and avoid false positive alarms (Maher, 2017).

False positive alarms can occur through the anomaly-based IDS technique where legitimate but previously unseen system behaviors are categorised as anomalies (Buczak and Guven, 2016). Practical examples of these include spear-phishing (when covertly malicious email is purported to be coming from a familiar source), application spoofing (when malware is masquerading as familiar and trusted software application), multimedia masquerading and other semantic social engineering attacks (Heartfield *et al.*, 2017). It would seem that no matter the levels of AI sophistication, humans will likely remain at the security controls and actively involved (Fazzini, 2017). It could be that humans still remain better positioned to render a more intuitive and holistic approach to decision making (Jarrahi, 2018). However, Pissanetzky (2016) holds a different view. According to the researcher, the Internet will ultimately be automated and secure without human intervention.

Whatever the future of AI holds, humans currently perform better cognitive functions of detecting, identifying and responding to cyber-attacks (Roberts, 2016). In a number of information and cybersecurity scenarios, Heartfield *et al.* (2017) observed that humans currently detect threats better than technical security checkpoints. However, the researchers qualify this assertion by stating that this is particularly the case, especially, when the threat is based on social engineering rather than exploitation of a specific technical flaw. Wirkuttis and Klein (2017) offer a different view. The researchers think that the current human and AI security capabilities are even. Moreover, they argue that since neither the human nor AI has individually proven total success in information and cybersecurity an organisational holistic view of the cyber-environment is therefore required in which AI is combined with human insight. Pissanetzky (2016) disagrees with the notion of integrating the human with AI applications to security. This researcher argues that human interventions should rather be reduced or completely eliminated as they introduce flaws and delays in response. In most cases, argue Rajbanshi *et al.* (2017), a delay in response time is usually caused by the sheer size and volume of cyber-incidents data, which is sometimes impossible for humans to analyse without automation.

Greengard's (2016) argument complements Pissanetzky's (2016) that the objective, quite simply, is to identify suspicious behaviour and patterns better, and build autonomous security frameworks that are more adaptable and resilient. Some experts take it further that the autonomy will inevitably be accomplished when the increasingly complex cybersecurity tasks are taken over by AI (Roberts, 2016). As matters currently stand though, cybersecurity techniques are desperately in need for change (Patil, 2016). Regardless of advances in AI and cybersecurity, Greengard (2016) is adamant that we will never be able to completely do away with the need for human interactions with machines. Landwehr (2008) is of the same view that even if we do succeed in developing what may seem like perfect AI security applications, attackers will continue to find creative ways to exploit social engineering approaches to trick users. As long as there are people, argues Greengard (2016), cybersecurity risks will never completely disappear. Whatever the case might be, the future of AI to the information and cybersecurity domain will depend on defining what humans and machines are each best suited at (Fazzini, 2017). Perhaps even the ethics of defining and delegating decision-making activities between humans and machines need to be looked at (Ramchurn *et al.*, 2012).

4   Results, Analysis, and Discussions

With reference to Figure 1, the final and execution stage of the systematic literature review is performed in this section and the findings are also presented.

4.1   AI Trends in Information and Cybersecurity

Generally, the intrusion detection system approach for identifying and responding to cyber-attacks utilises three techniques: signature-based, anomaly-based, and hybrid of the two. Most traditional information and cybersecurity solutions utilise the hybrid technique. The technique is usually adopted to increase the detection rates of known cyber-intrusions and reduce false positive alarm rates for unknown incidents (Buczak and Guven, 2016)). With increasing volumes of datasets resulting from the proliferation of the Internet of Things, cloud computing and edge devices, it has become difficult for traditional IDS methods to be effective. The literature reveals that with its ability to recognise patterns of behaviour through massive datasets AI could help detect a broad spectrum of cyber-threats and make intelligent decisions. Thus, it is safe to infer that AI has already surpassed the human intelligence when it comes to cyber-analytics of huge volumes of data. The literature further shows that AI systems are themselves also susceptible to various security vulnerabilities. Such vulnerabilities could be exploited to automate cyber-attacks. In this regard, the biggest threat from AI is its potential for autonomous weapons because attackers also have, access to and, the ability to leverage on AI advances. Society should therefore anticipate a possibility for a future replete with AI-powered weapons and malware that conventional IDS will be ill-prepared for. Put differently, the information and cybersecurity communities should prepare for a future where the impact of AI-powered cyber-attacks will be autonomous.

4.2   AI Impact to Human Aspects of Information and Cybersecurity

With organisations generating huge volumes of data on a daily basis, the literature revealed that it is impractical for any human to analyse such quantities of data. As a consequence, the application of AI has become increasingly more effective at analysing and identifying new data patterns and anomalies (Talwar and Koury, 2017). However, the application of AI to information and cybersecurity is currently used for bolstering security personnel. Although interest in deploying AI for human augmentation for cybersecurity purposes has also increased, it is still a long way off from making humans redundant. It is therefore generally accepted that organisations are not yet ready to remove the human from the entire security process. Furthermore, because the application of AI to cybersecurity is currently at an embryonic stage, it is argued that humans still perform cognitive functions better in terms of detecting, identifying and responding to new cyber-attacks. However, as time passes AI will learn enough from the data to start performing autonomous functions without human intervention; at least, this is what some researchers claim. This claim is at the heart of the argument by those who believe and those who do not believe that AI will, or should, completely replace human interaction. This question remains open for debate and further research.

4.3 Proposed Human-AI Security Symbiosis

The literature has shown that some are advocating for complete automation of AI and others not. It is therefore quite difficult to predict which way this may go. However, approaching AI as a panacea would be myopic because decades of research have shown that organisations are complex socio-technical systems (see Figure 2) and that any technological advances prove more powerful only if integrated into the social dimension of organisations (Sawyer and Jarrahi, 2014).

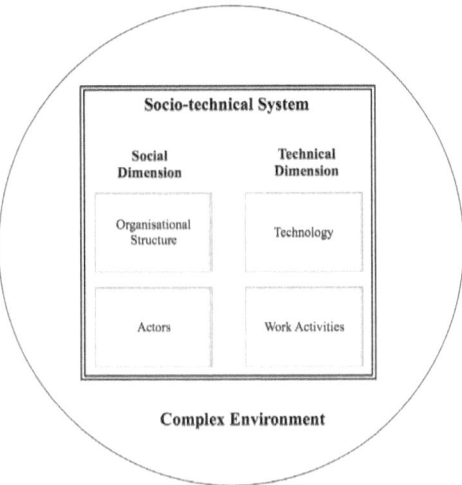

Figure 2: Socio-technical system, derived from Bostrom and Heinen (1977), Wu *et al.* (2015) and Oosthuizen and Pretorius (2016)

In this regard, the researchers propose the approach in Figure 3. This approach states that an optimal AI-human integration for information and cybersecurity can only be achieved if the social, technical, and environmental dimensions of an organisation are equally emphasised. The three dimensions are mutually interconnected.

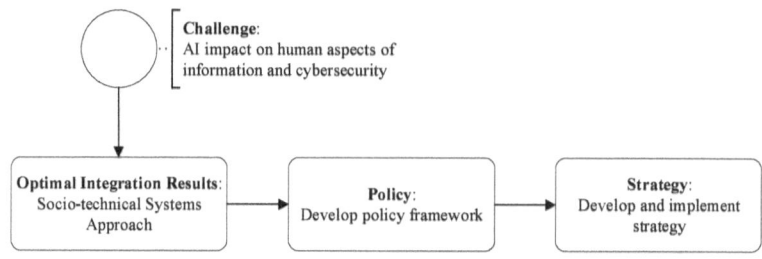

Figure 3: Socio-technical systems approach

5   Conclusion

With increasing volumes of data generated by systems, traditional intrusion detection systems have become less effective. Consequently, artificial intelligence applications have become widespread although currently for human augmentation. This is because humans are believed to currently perform cognitive functions much better than AI in terms of detecting, identifying and responding to new cyber-threats. There is a concern, however, that AI tools themselves may not be secure and attackers may produce AI-powered weapons soon. This is an area of research that requires further attention. The impact of AI to the human aspects of information and cybersecurity is therefore summarised in terms of the current and future scenarios. In the current scenario, the impact of AI is for bolstering human capacity. In the future scenario, however, the impact can go either way; that is, humans may become completely replaced by autonomous AI applications or humans and AI might mutually complement each other for optimal results. The researchers go with the latter where a socio-technical systems approach is recommended as a solution and requires further research in this regard. There is recognition of some limitations of the study and two are worth noting. On the one hand, there are various AI journals not screened. However, these journals are restricted in scope to contribute positively to our study as they focus mainly on the technical aspects of AI. On the other hand, a different combination of keywords would have yielded different but relevant search results. Researchers are therefore encouraged to explore this topic further.

6   References

Antuit (2018), "Artificial intelligence; Antuit launches cyfirma, a cybersecurity division delivering AI-driven threat intelligence", Journal of robotics & machine learning, pp. 7. ISSN 1944-1851.

Bostrom, R.P. and Heinen, J.S. (1977), "MIS problems and failures: A socio-technical perspective; part I: the causes", MIS Quarterly, Vol. 1 No. 3, pp. 17-32.

Brundage, M., Avin, S., Clark, J., Toner, H., Eckersley, P., Garfinkel, B., ... Filar, B. (2018), "The malicious use of artificial intelligence: Forecasting, prevention, and mitigation". ArXiv Preprint ArXiv:1802.07228.

Buczak, A.L. and Guven, E. (2016), "A survey of data mining and machine learning methods for cyber security intrusion detection", IEEE communications surveys & tutorials, Vol. 18 No. 2, pp. 1153-1176.

Carriço, G. (2018), "The EU and artificial intelligence: A human-centred perspective", European view, Vol. 17 No. 1, pp. 29-36.

Cisco (2018), "2018 annual cybersecurity report: Discover security insights, key findings, and the latest threat intelligence", available at: https://www.cisco.com/c/en/us/products/ security/security-reports.html?CCID=cc000160&DTID=esootr000875&OID=anrsc005983& _ga=2.257988170.1599669543.1526832714-2121005692.1526832714 (accessed 19 May 2018).

Craig, J. (2018), "Cybersecurity research – essential to a successful digital future", Engineering, Vol. 4, pp. 9-10.

CyberSaint (2017), "CyberSaint, Inc.; CyberSaint[Registered trade-mark] security releases breakthrough AI powered cybersecurity management platform", Journal of engineering, pp. 427. ISSN 1945-8711.

Dilek, S., Çakır, H. and Aydın, M. (2015), "Applications of artificial intelligence techniques to combating cyber crimes: A review", International journal of artificial intelligence and applications, Vol. 6 No. 1, pp. 21-39.

Dhananjay and Pandey, M. (2018), "Artificial intelligence in cybersecurity", Proceedings of the 7th national conference on emerging trends in information technology, New Delhi, India.

Dragomir, F. (2017), "Artificial intelligence techniques cybersecurity", Proceedings of the 12th international scientific conference strategies XXI, Bucharest, Romania, Vol. 3, pp. 147.

Fang, B., Ren, K. and Jia, Y. (2018), "The new frontiers of cybersecurity", Engineering, Vol. 4, pp. 1-2.

Fink, A. (2005). Conducting research literature reviews: From the internet to paper (2nd ed.). Thousand oaks, California: Sage publications.

Greengard, S. (2016), "Cybersecurity gets smart", Communication of the ACM, Vol. 59 No. 5, pp. 29-31.

Heartfield, R., Loukas, G. and Gan, D. (2017), "An eye for deception: A case study in utilizing the human-as-a-service-sensor paradigm to detect zero-day semantic social engineering attacks", IEEE computer society, pp. 371-378.

Hobbs, J. (2018), "AI enters the cyber attack realm", Signal, Vol. 72 No. 7, pp. 38-39.

Jack, D. (2016), "Will artificial intelligence revolutionize cybersecurity", The Christian science monitor. ISSN 08827729.

Jarrahi, M.H. (2018), "Artificial intelligence and the future of work: Human-AI symbiosis in organisational decision making", Business horizons, Vol. 61 No. 4, pp. 577-586.

Levy, Y. and Ellis, T.J. (2006), "A systems approach to conduct an effective literature review in support of information systems research", Informing science: International journal of an emerging transdiscipline, Vol. 9 No. 1, pp. 181-212.

Liu, Q. and Yu, S. (2018), "Survey on security threats and defensive techniques of machine learning: A data driven view", IEEE access, Vol. 6, pp. 12103-12117.

Maher, D. (2017), "Can artificial intelligence help in the war on cybercrime?", Computer fraud & security, pp. 7-9.

Morel, B. (2011), "Artificial intelligence and the future of cybersecurity", Proceedings of the 4th ACM workshop on security and artificial intelligence, Chicago, Illinois, United States, pp. 93-98.

Okoli, C. and Schabram, K. (2010), "A guide to conducting a systematic literature review of information systems research", SSRN electronic journal. 10. 10.2139/ssrn.1954824.

Oosthuizen, R. and Pretorius, L. (2016), "Assessing the impact of new technology on complex socio-technical systems", South african journal of industrial engineering, Vol. 27 No. 2, pp. 15-29.

Parry, K., Cohen, M., and Bhattacharya, S. (2016), "Rise of the machines: A critical consideration of automated leadership decision making in organizations", Group and organization management, Vol. 41 No. 5, pp. 571-594.

Patil, P. (2016), "Artificial intelligence in cyber security", International journal of research in computer applications and robots, Vol. 4 No. 5, pp. 1-5.

Pumin, Y. (2016), "When machines become men", Proceedings of the 3rd world internet congress, Wuzhen, China.

Pissanetzky, S. (2016), "On the future of information: Reunification, computability, adaptation, cybersecurity, semantics", IEEE access, Vol. 4, pp. 1117-1140.

Rajbanshi, A., Bhimrajka, S. and Raina, C.K (2017), "Artificial intelligence in cyber security", International journal of scientific research in computer science, engineering and information technology, Vol. 2 No. 3, pp. 2456-3307.

Ramchurn, S.D., Vytelingum, P., Rogers, A. and Jennings, N.R. (2012), "Putting the "smarts" into the smart grid: A grand challenge for artificial intelligence", Communications of the ACM, Vol. 55 No. 4, pp. 86-97.

Ridley, D. (2008). The literature review: A step-by-step guide for students. Sage publications Ltd.

Roberts, P.F. (2016), "Cybersecurity's artificial intelligence future", The Christian science monitor. ISSN 08827729.

Sawyer, S. and Jarrahi, M.H. (2014), "Sociotechnical approaches to the study of information systems. In A. Tucker and H. Topi (Eds.), Computing handbook, 3rd edition", Information systems and information technology, pp. 5.1—5.27. Boca Raton, FL: Chapman and Hall/CRC.

Sabar, N.R., Yi, X. and Song, A. (2018), "A bi-objective hyper-heuristic support vector machines for big data cyber-security", IEEE access, Vol. 6, pp. 10421-10431.

Silic, M and Back, A. (2014), "Information security: Critical review and future directions for research", Information management & computer security, Vol. 22 No. 3, pp. 279-308.

Tadjdeh, Y. (2018), "AI: A tool for good and bad", National defense, Vol. 102, pp. 774.

Talwar, R and Koury, A. (2017), "Artificial intelligence – the next frontier in IT security", Network security, pp. 14-17.

U.S Newswire (2017), "With global cyber attacks on the rise, Zenedge says artificial intelligence holds the answer", available at: https://search.proquest.com/docview/1922897220?accountid=13425 (accessed 19 May 2018).

Wirkuttis, N. and Klein, H. (2017), "Artificial intelligence in cybersecurity", Cyber, intelligence, and security, Vol. 1 No. 1, pp. 103-119.

Wu, P.P., Fookes, C., Pitchforth, J. and Mengersen, K. (2015), "A framework for model integration and holistic modelling of socio-technical systems", Decision support systems, Vol. 71, pp. 14-27.

Yampolskiy, R. and Spellchecker, M. (2016), "Artificial intelligence safety and cybersecurity: A timeline of AI failures", available at: Google scholar (accessed 29 May 2018).

Proceedings of the Twelfth International Symposium on
Human Aspects of Information Security & Assurance (HAISA 2018)

Warn if Secure or How to Deal with Security by Default in Software Development?

P.L. Gorski[1], L.L. Iacono[1], S. Wiefling[1] and S. Möller[2]

[1]TH Köln – University of Applied Sciences, Cologne, Germany
[2]Quality and Usability Lab, Technical University Berlin
e-mail: {peter.gorski, luigi.lo_iacono, stephan.wiefling}@th-koeln.de;
sebastian.moeller@tu-berlin.de

Abstract

Software development is a complex task. Merely focussing on functional requirements is not sufficient any more. Developers are responsible to take many non-functional requirements carefully into account. Security is amongst the most challenging, as getting it wrong will result in a large user-base being potentially at risk. A similar situation exists for administrators. Security defaults have been put into place here to encounter lacking security controls. As first attempts to establish security by default in software development are flourishing, the question on their usability for developers arises.

In this paper we study the effectiveness and efficiency of Content Security Policy (CSP) enforced as security default in a web framework. When deployed correctly, CSP is a valid protection mean in a defence-in-depth strategy against code injection attacks. In this paper we present a first qualitative laboratory study with 30 participants to discover how developers deal with CSP when deployed as security default. Our results emphasize that the deployment as security default has its benefits but requires careful consideration of a comprehensive information flow in order to improve and not weaken security. We provide first insights to inform research about aiding developers in the creation of secure web applications with usable security by default.

Keywords

Web Application Development, Web Frameworks, Content Security Policies, Warnings, Security by default, Usable Security

1   Introduction

Security by default has shown to be an effective measure in information systems administration. Especially non-security information workers do benefit from safeguards being in-place by default as this avoids vulnerabilities resulting from a lack of knowledge, comprehension or attention. Consequences that may result from an absence of security defaults are documented numerously. Examples span from publicly accessible Internet-connected personal devices (Tekeoglu and Tosun, 2015) and industrial machines (Bodenheim *et al.*, 2014) to database servers providing all kinds of data (Heyens *et al.*, 2015). With digital products and services respecting the security by default principle, these types of vulnerabilities are much more unlikely to appear. Still, the security defaults need to be carefully considered from a user-centred perspective. Otherwise the protection measures are perceived as a burden (National Cyber Security Centre, 2016). Random generated passwords used only once per device and printed on its respective case can be named as an example which is commonly applied on some class of Internet-connected products (e.g. wireless access points) (Lorente *et al.*, 2015).

As security by default proves to be beneficial in systems administration, the question arises whether it can also have a positive impact on software development. Even without a deep understanding about risks and attack models, domain specific security functionalities can be delivered by non-security specialists out of the box. In contrast, without security defaults, programmers must design and implement every protection feature by themselves.

Modern web frameworks support developers with implementing feature-rich and complex web applications in a structured and systematic manner. Due to many potential attack vectors and mandatory security requirements like authentication and authorization, input validation or secure communications, developing secure web applications is a challenging task (Lo Iacono and Gorski 2017). The "OWASP Top 10" (The OWASP Foundation, 2017) lists the ten most critical security risks in the context of web applications. Hence, web frameworks do include a range of security features with the intention to assist developers with applying respective countermeasures, often by enforcing suitable defaults. Many web frameworks take, e.g., the responsibility for implementing defences against Cross-Site Request Forgery (CSRF) (The OWASP Foundation 2017) attacks to avoid delegating this task to their users. One indication for this approach being effective is the vanishing of CSRF attacks from the latest "OWASP Top 10" list after being a permanent member for many years. In cases, in which the responsibility for implementing a security feature is neither clearly assigned nor communicated, the lack of sensible security defaults can lead to severe vulnerabilities. This has been shown by a qualitative usability study on how web developers deal with password storage (Naiakshina *et al.*, 2017). Since common web frameworks leave the developers alone with implementing a password database, many developers forget to hash and salt the passwords before storing them. This emphasizes that when developers get digital security wrong, this potentially impacts the security and privacy of a large user base.

In this work we focus on the Play Framework for Java and its design decision to enforce Content Security Policies (CSPs) (W3C, 2016) by default. CSPs are a mean against Cross-Site Scripting (XSS) (Vogt *et al.*, 2007) attacks which are part of the "OWASP Top 10" for many years and are ranked as number seven in the recent version. In a laboratory experiment we first evaluate the effect of integrating CSPs by default. Second, we compare how violations of CSPs are communicated to developers by the two browsers Chrome and Firefox which are using different design approaches for their CSP violation messages.

To be able to improve the usability of CSPs in software development frameworks, we want to give evidence to usability issues and quantify specific points of failures. This led us to the following research questions:

RQ1: How does the enforcement of CSP by default affect usability?

RQ2: Are state of the art implementations of CSP warnings an effective measure to support software developers with needed information?

2 Content Security Policies (CSPs)

CSPs (W3C, 2016) enable web application developers to declare if and what external artefacts can be loaded and included on a web page (Stamm *et al.*, 2010). The corresponding rules are sent within the HTTP response header "Content-Security-Policy" from the web server to the client. In case a HTTP response contains such a header, the web browser enforces the policies to the containing HTML page and its embedded sub-resources including e.g. images, fonts, styles and scripts. External sub-resources that are not complying with the specified rules will be rejected. Detected violations of CSP rules are communicated via red coloured messages with small warning icons in the browser's console. Example messages printed by Chrome and Firefox are depicted in Figure 1. CSP-instrumented browsers are available since 2015. Today, the latest versions of all major desktop and mobile browsers support CSP (Can I use, 2018). Thus, when deployed carefully, CSPs provide an effective mean to prevent content injection-based attacks like XSS (Stamm *et al.*, 2010; W3C, 2016) as a second line of defence behind measures like input validation or sanitisation.

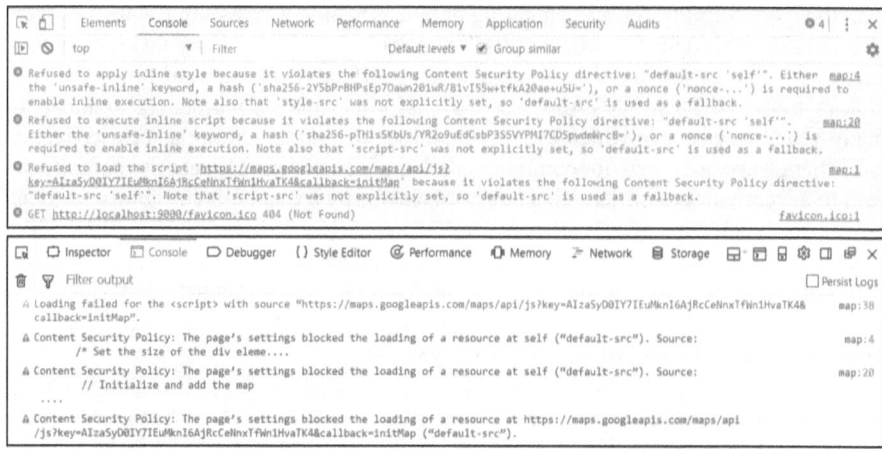

Figure 1: Example CSP violation messages displayed in Chrome (top) and Firefox (bottom). The messages were triggered by integrating Google Maps example code into an HTML template file in the context of a Play Framework based web application

CSP messages in browser consoles are no warnings in a narrow sense. Typically, warning messages try to communicate the risk of an insecure situation to the user giving crucial information which should help making an informed decision. Those are following and implementing the "Warn when unsafe" pattern proposed by (Garfinkel 2005). In contrast, CSP warnings display information about a CSP rule violation. Thus, this is a message of an enforced protection giving the information that a potential risk has been prevented, similar to messages of virus scanners or firewalls. Since CSP messages in a console are nevertheless designed in the shape of warnings or errors, we like to discuss if this rather follows by a "Warn when safe" pattern which has not yet been proposed in a software development context.

Web Framework	Programming Language	Content Security Policy Support	
Play Framework	Java / Scala	●/●	Available / included and enforced by default
Spring / Spring Boot	Java	●/○	Available (Spring Security Module) / neither included nor enforced by default
Ruby on Rails	Ruby	●/◐	Available (since Rails 5.2) / included but not enforced by default
Express.js	JavaScript	●/○	Available (helmet-csp middleware) / neither included nor enforced by default
Meteor	JavaScript	●/◐	Available (browser-policy package) / not included but enforced by default
Django	Python	●/◐	Available (Django-CSP middleware) / not included but enforced by default
Flask	Python	●/◐	Available (flask-csp extension) / not included but enforced by default
Laravel	PHP	●/◐	Available (laravel-csp middleware) / not included but enforced by default
Symfony	PHP	○/○	Not available / CSP header must be set manually
Gin	Go	●/◐	Available (e.g. Secure middleware) / not included but enforced by default
BeeGo	Go	○/○	Not available / CSP header must be set manually
ASP.NET	C#	●/◐	Available (e.g. NWebsec library) / not included but enforced by default

Table 1: List of popular web frameworks for the 2017 top programming languages Python, Java, C#, JavaScript, PHP and Go (Cass, 2017) and their available support for CSP

To integrate CSPs, software developers are required to configure their server-side web application to send a corresponding "Content-Security-Policy" HTTP header with each HTTP response. Several web frameworks ease this process and offer possibilities to activate CSPs in their configurations with little effort (cf. Table 1). However, in contrast to an easy integration of CSPs in web development frameworks, previous work showed that a secure deployment is difficult (cf. Section 3).

3   Related Work

As identified by large-scale analysis (Weissbacher *et al.*, 2014; Patil and Frederik 2016; Weichselbaum *et al.*, 2016; Calzavara *et al.*, 2018), misconfiguration of CSP is a key factor harming the effective implementation in deployed web applications. (Calzavara *et al.*, 2018) described five categories of typical misconfiguration: Typos and negligence, ill-formed policies, lack of reporting, harsh policies and vulnerable policies. In our study we could observe similar categories of vulnerable policies (cf. Section 5). In contrast to their methodology, only analysing already deployed policies, we present the first study to the best of our knowledge evaluating usability issues developers have when working with CSP enabled by default.

Warning messages in the console environment to support developers are hardly being explored. Only recently (Gorski *et al.*, 2018) found evidence for this type of warnings being effective in the context of API (Application Programming Interface) integrated security advice. Warnings were triggered by a Security API if insecure algorithms or parameters were used by developers for encryption or hashing and were displayed in the developers' programming console. In contrast to their work, we do not test an own or improved warning message design. In this work, we evaluate the current state of the art implementations of CSP console warnings in the Chrome and Firefox browsers in the situation of default CSP enforcement by the Play Framework.

Programmers have specific needs for information which cannot only be satisfied by warning messages. Using community driven Internet resources like Stack Overflow comes with the risk of adopting insecure code examples compared to official documentation web sites giving good security advice but showed to be less usable (Acar et al, 2016). (Acar et al, 2017b) evaluated 19 general online resources offering advice about secure programming. They described a very fragmented landscape in terms of topicality, content organization and covered topics, thus being limited supportive for specific and urgent information needs. However, we decided to allow participants of our study to use Internet search engines and any available online resource or CSP tooling to fulfil the programming task in the way they are used to and would typically use when not being in a usability study.

4   Methodology

We applied the following methodology to measure the effect of a whitelisting origin-only CSP enabled by default, only allowing sub-resources deriving from the same server as the embedding web page. We also wanted to compare possible effects on how CSP violations are communicated towards developers by the browsers Chrome and Firefox with their different design approaches for CSP violation messages.

4.1   Task Design

Participants were asked to integrate a map of the web mapping service Google Maps inside of a simple web application serving exactly one web page containing the map. The corresponding map should have a height of 400 pixels and a width of the browser window and should focus the Cologne Cathedral with a visible marker. The required geolocation coordinates were stated in the task. Also, a Google Maps API key was made available inside a text file.

We selected the official "Play Java Starter Example" (Play Framework, 2018b) for the latest Play version 2.6 to set up the study task. This template project was created especially for Play beginners. Thus, developers find well commented code and links to further documentation. This template was slightly extended by adding a "/map" resource path to the application by editing routes and adding a controller and a view with a prepared HTML scaffold for orientation at what position the map could be integrated. In the Control group CSP was deactivated by editing the application's configuration file as CSP is enabled by default within the Play project.

The participants had to write the code inside the IntelliJ IDEA IDE (Integrated development environment) (IntelliJ IDEA Web Site, 2018). The IDE IntelliJ IDEA Ultimate was chosen due to possession of the features syntax highlighting, auto-completion, on-the-fly compilation, assisted refactoring and debugging. In addition, the Model-View-Controller (MVC) (Krasner, 1988) project structure appeared to be easily accessible with this IDE. The task was considered as fulfilled if the Cologne Cathedral was displayed inside the corresponding browser (Chrome or Firefox) comparable to the screenshot depicted in Figure 2. We aborted the task if the participant's work on the solution had exceeded a duration of one hour.

Figure 2: Browser screenshot of the solved task showing the successful integration of a Google Maps via the Google Maps JavaScript API positioned to the Cologne Cathedral

The secondary task, which was not mentioned in the task description, was to handle the CSPs, which were enforced by the Play Framework. Listing 1 illustrates how a secure CSP for our study task looks like. All inline scripts and styles from the Google Maps documentation example (Google Maps, 2018) were placed into external server files to both prevent XSS attacks and enable flexibility on editing script code. The value "self" references to files which are placed on and delivered by the server and excludes inline scripts. Script, style, image and font sources were defined separately. Inline styles which are allowed to be loaded from Google Maps were defined as

Base64 encoded SHA256 hashes. The resulting CSP has to be placed inside the "application.conf" file of the Play project.

The messages logged in the console of Chrome and Firefox differ in terms of the provided information (cf. Figure 1). Thus, assuming that participants follow the hints given by the CSP violation messages inside the Chrome's JavaScript console, an expected possible solution might look similar to Listing 2. Chrome provides hints on how certain CSP conditions for a given violation could be corrected on each occurred CSP violation message (cf. Figure 1). For instance, for enabling inline execution it is required to add "unsafe-inline", a hash or a nonce to the policy. However, after whitelisting a given CSP violation in the Google Maps example, additional CSP violation messages appear inside the console since additional external resources (fonts, images, inline styles) are subsequently loaded by the CSP-enabled Google Maps scripts and style files. All CSP violation messages could be eliminated after five policy adjusting iterations with the result of Listing 2. According to security checks proposed by (Weichselbaum *et al.*, 2016) we assume that this is a secure solution. However, due to the presence of "localhost:9000" inside the CSP, the result might not work on a production server. Chrome did not give a hint to use the "self" value which references to the same origin (same scheme, host and port) as the web page.

```
contentSecurityPolicy = "
        default-src 'self';
        script-src 'self'
                https://maps.googleapis.com/;
        style-src 'self'
                https://fonts.googleapis.com/
                'sha256-UvsJ5gtL0c/whxmyVt4YoNv7YnPUd0tANZO1q3NshXE='
                'sha256-5KvpSTE2xdGq8rDdvgAPP3mCfTXBc1ohjt2UiAQt9k4='
                'sha256-VVOq+Ws/EiUxf2CU6tsqsHdOWqBgHSgwBPqCTjYD3U='
                'sha256-a2VR/Wq1VPr0+3GRY+1EmAQm7wjwwnDtPpcCPs2zTrw='
                'sha256-/4YlUlisxufO6wbKvYp4xV8Hkzxm85+1Tb31SjmAox0='
                'sha256-47DEQpj8HBSa+/TImW+5JCeuQeRkm5NMpJWZG3hSuFU=';
        img-src https://maps.gstatic.com/mapfiles/
                https://maps.googleapis.com/maps/;
        font-src https://fonts.gstatic.com/s/
        "
```

Listing 1: Sample solution of a Content Security Policy for our study task. Line breaks and indentations were inserted to improve readability.

```
contentSecurityPolicy = "
        default-src 'self';
        script-src http://localhost:9000/assets/javascripts/map.js
                https://maps.googleapis.com/;
        style-src https://fonts.googleapis.com/
                http://localhost:9000/assets/stylesheets/styles.css
                'sha256-UvsJ5gtL0c/whxmyVt4YoNv7YnPUd0tANZOlq3NshXE='
                'sha256-5KvpSTE2xdGq8rDdvgAPP3mCfTXBc1ohjt2UiAQt9k4='
                'sha256-VVOq+Ws/EiUxf2CU6tsqsHdOWqBgHSgwBPqCTjYD3U='
                'sha256-a2VR/Wq1VPr0+3GRY+lEmAQm7wjwwnDtPpcCPs2zTrw='
                'sha256-/4YlUlisxufO6wbKvYp4xV8Hkzxm85+1Tb31SjmAoxO='
                'sha256-47DEQpj8HBSa+/TImW+5JCeuQeRkm5NMpJWZG3hSuFU=';
        img-src https://maps.gstatic.com/mapfiles/
                https://maps.googleapis.com/maps/;
        font-src https://fonts.gstatic.com/s/
    "
```

Listing 2: Content Security Policy generated by following the advice provided with the CSP violation messages listed in the developer console of Google Chrome. Line breaks and indentations were inserted to improve readability.

Since Firefox only provides messages relating to the directive on which the policy violation has occurred and the blocked URL, we expect participants to copy the exact URL to the directive to remove this violation. However, many CSP messages follow after this procedure, since Google Maps reloads a high number of external resources (e.g. images). Since no additional hints are given to add the approximate path instead of the exact filename, we assume it is not possible to implement a CSP only with the information given by Firefox without consulting external resources.

4.2 Study Design

We conducted a between subjects laboratory experiment with three groups. A Control group was working on the task with disabled CSPs while using the Chrome browser. Another two groups differed by the used browser: Chrome or Firefox; both with CSP enabled. We chose these three conditions to (1) compare the times needed to fulfil the task with the Chrome browser and enabled or disabled CSPs. (2) We wanted to evaluate whether there is an effect triggered by the differently designed CSP violation messages in Chrome and Firefox. The presence or non-presence of CSPs was not communicated to the participants.

Due to the highest market share among web browsers (W3Schools, 2018), Chrome was chosen for the Control group. We assumed a second Control group with Firefox as not being necessary since the solution procedures for the given task are almost identical to Chrome.

Test persons were advised to use the official Google Maps JavaScript API documentation (Google Maps, 2018) as a starting point, but they were free to use all available Internet resources. The participants were asked to think aloud during the programming task. Audio and video were recorded with the recording software OBS Studio (Open Broadcaster Software, 2018). The video included the screen content. In addition, a small-sized video of the participant taken by the display webcam was placed in the bottom right corner. During the study observation, we used a self-developed audio and video stream annotation system to manually document actions and key events associated with automatically generated real time stamps. After the experiment, it was possible to add the corresponding video file into the software and jump on klick to the according time in the recording for review, analysis and coding.

In a semi-structured exit interview, we obtained additional data. The questions comprised self-assessments of functionality and security regarding the developed web application as well as basic questions about previous experiences with operating systems, Play Framework, IntelliJ IDEA, CSPs and (secure) software development.

4.3 Experiment Procedure

Participants were assigned by round robin to the three experiment conditions. After welcoming the participant and offering water and candy bars, a consent form was explained and signed by all participants of the study. Our institution does not have a formal IRB process for computer science studies, but we took care that our study complied with the European General Data Protection Regulation (The European Union, 2016). In the next step, all participants were briefed for Play's MVC paradigm in accordance with a briefing protocol. The Play development environment comprised of the integrated development environment (IDE) IntelliJ IDEA. The corresponding browser development tools of Firefox or Chrome were explained as well. Following the briefing, participants were handed a task sheet explaining and illustrating the primary programming task. After clearing general questions, the examiner started the recording and streaming by pressing a key combination on the keyboard, asked the participant to start and left the laboratory. The examiner followed the experiment by observing all participant's actions via screen, video and audio transmission in a separate room next door, logging relevant actions with the developed audio and video stream annotation system.

The experiment was conducted inside a usability laboratory of our institute. The room used for the experiments was specifically designed to create a pleasant atmosphere for the participants. It was furnished comparable to a living and working room in order to avoid appearing as a "sterile experiment room".

After task completion, the participants answered the questions of the semi-structured exit interview. Then the participants were informed about CSPs, the reason of choosing the Play Framework and the purposes of the secondary task. Participants were asked not to talk about these contents while the study was conducted.

We iteratively tested the study design and experiment procedure in a pilot study with three participants prior to the experiments. After analysing the results, the hardware and software setting of the underlying observation infrastructure as well as the exit survey and the task design were revised.

4.4 Recruitment

We invited 43 bachelor and master students of our faculty via email knowing that they have previous experience with web development, Java, JavaScript and the Play Framework. In the invitation email we asked them to participate in a study about web programming. We wrote that this study includes a small programming task in the premises of our university, which will last about one hour. We did not mention a security context or the Play Framework. Five candidates rejected and eight did not answer to the invitation, even after sending a reminder. The remaining 30 candidates voluntarily participated in the study within a period of three weeks in May 2018. We could not compensate them for their participation but offered water and candy bars for their physical wellbeing.

5   Analysis

In the following sections we present the results of our data analysis. First, we characterise our participants before analysing task solutions. We compare the Control condition with the Chrome condition to evaluate the effect of enabled or disabled CSPs on time needed to fulfil the task. It is evaluated whether we could observe an effect caused by different CSP violation message design approaches implemented in Chrome and Firefox. Furthermore, the functionality and security of task solutions are analysed.

5.1   Participants

The study took place in 2018 and was completed with 30 participants, ten in each condition. Their age was between 19 and 31 years (Mean 25.2, SD 3.1). Only one of the participants was female, all others were male. 19 were bachelor students (Mean semester 8.0, SD 2.2) and 11 were master students (Mean semester 2.2, SD 1.2).

Except of one person in the Control group, all had previously developed at least one web application in a university course. Their mean experience with software development in total was 4.1 years (SD: 2.3), 4.8 years (SD: 1.9) with the programming language Java and 2.4 years (SD: 1.4) with JavaScript. The lower value for the total experience in comparison to Java experience can be explained by the students not counting their first semesters of learning programming (typically with Java) to their experience with developing software applications. This was revealed during the interviews. 73% (22/30) had already been paid for programming, which indicates a certain level of professionalism in software development.

One third (10/30) never considered any security measure during software development. The others mentioned the application of scattered security functionalities in the interview including e.g. secure connections via TLS, input validation against Cross-Site-Scripting, authentication, authorization, session cookies and security tokens. Thus, the general experience with security in web development in this sample can be described as limited.

The participants were experienced with the offered development environment. Thus, during the experiments we did not encounter any problems triggered by our setup. Only two participants in the Chrome condition were not familiar with the Windows operating system and four had not used the Play Framework before (Control: 3; Chrome: 1). However, the latter four were able to finish the task comparably fast. 16 were familiar with the IntelliJ IDEA IDE, evenly distributed on the conditions

(Control: 5; Chrome: 5; Firefox: 6). Every participant reported having used browser developer tools before.

5.2 Task Solutions

Figure 3 illustrates the distributions of total time needed by participants to solve the task in all three conditions. First, we compare the Control condition with the Chrome condition. In both of the groups with participants that used the Chrome browser, the independent variable was the default CSP behaviour of Play. The mean time in the Control group was 16 minutes (median = 9.9) in comparison to a mean time of 56.6 minutes (median = 60) in the Chrome group with CSPs enabled by default. The samples in the Chrome group are not normally distributed as seven of ten experiments in this group were aborted after a maximum task duration of one hour. Thus, the upper quartile is also the median (60 minutes). There is no time overlap between both conditions (Mann-Whitney U test; U=0; p<0.001). Thus, we can reject the null hypothesis; participants trying to solve the task in the Chrome group being confronted with CSPs needed significantly more time than participants in the Control condition with seven of ten participants exhausting the maximum study time of 60 minutes. There is also a clear visual tendency that participants in the Firefox condition with enabled CSP by default needed more time to solve the task than participants in the Control condition with Chrome and disabled CSP (cf. Figure 3).

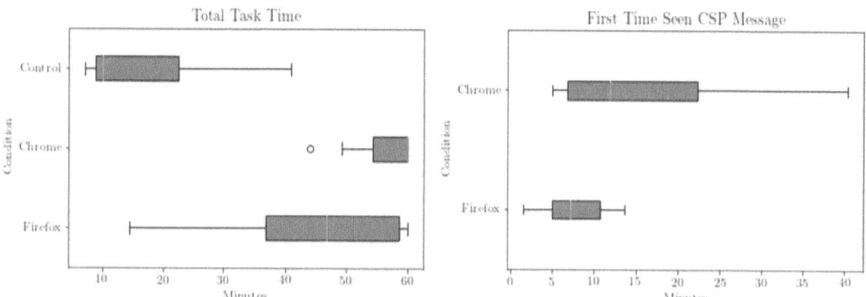

Figure 3: Comparison of total times to solve the task in all three study conditions (left) and of first time seen a CSP Message (right)

Second, we compare the processing time between the Chrome and the Firefox group, both conditions with enabled CSP by default (Mann-Whitney U test; U=24.5; p=0.022). The participants using the Firefox browser finished the experiment in a mean time of 43.8 minutes (median = 46.9). Thus, there is a statistical tendency of participants finishing the task faster in the Firefox condition (p < 0.05). In this group, three experiments needed the complete time frame of 60 minutes. This means in total we terminated 50% of all 20 experiments which included CSP by default after one hour. In each condition with CSP enabled by default, three participants had used CSPs before. However, none of them configured the policy securely. Three of these six participants did not solve the task in the given time frame of one hour.

5.3 Functionality and Security

To be able to assess whether a task solution was solved functional and secure, we coded the developed sources at the end of an experiment. The solution was rated as functional if the map was shown in the browser as demanded by the task description (cf. Section 4.1 and Figure 2). For the evaluation of security, we only focused on the CSP and followed the checks proposed by (Weichselbaum *et al.*, 2016). The solution was rated as insecure if the keyword "unsafe-inline" was used without either nonce-source or hash-source; an object-source was not explicitly nor implicitly set by the fallback default-source; or a wildcard was used in a whitelist. In addition, approaches which had switched off the CSP were coded as insecure. The coding results were compiled independently by two authors and were solved by discussion on mismatch. The security of non-functional solutions was not rated.

All solutions in the Control condition were functional in comparison to nine in the Firefox group and in contrast to only four in the Chrome group. The seven participants with non-functional solutions did not see any map in the browser (cf. Figure 2) during the experiment. Only one did not open the browser console and thus, did not see a CSP message. Three test persons saw and read the messages but were not able to find out how to proceed with the given information. The last three of the non-functional group tried to configure a CSP but were not able to find a policy that would have allowed to show the Google map.

In the semi-structured exit interview, participants were asked to rate their agreement to the statements "I think I solved this task correctly" and "I think I solved this task securely" on the following five-point Likert scale: strongly agree (5); agree (4); neutral (3); disagree (2); strongly disagree (1). The objective results for functionality are also represented in the subjective ratings with mean values of 4.8 (SD 0.4) in the Control, 4.3 (SD 0.9) in the Firefox and 2.8 (SD 1.3) in the Chrome condition.

None of the 20 participants in the Chrome and Firefox group developed a secure solution. Table 2 lists the reasons for insecure task coding, which appeared in our experiments.

	Chrome Condition	Firefox Condition
Not functional	6	1
"unsafe-inline"	1 "script-src", 2 "script-src" and "style-src"	2 "script-src", 1 "script-src" and "style-src"
Wildcard	-	1 "default-src *"
CSP = null	1	3
all security header filters disabled	-	1
all default filters disabled	-	1

Table 2: Non-functional results and reasons for insecure task coding

It is striking that six test persons in the Chrome condition produced non-functional results. In the Firefox group it is remarkable that six participants just allowed all external sources to be included on the web site by disabling CSP completely or setting a default wildcard. The two test persons who disabled Play filters got the information from the official Play documentation web site, other two copied and pasted insecure code snippets from Stack Overflow posts. The remaining two unsuccessfully tried to configure a CSP but ended up with disabling the mechanism. These seven test persons who switched off CSP rated their solution's security as low with a mean rating of 2.6 of 5 (SD: 0.9; median: 3.0). In the interview they explained "I set CSP to null (laughing) to bypass the error. Afterwards I didn't configure it in more detail", "I had no choice" or "I disabled CSP to make it work". The six participants who found a working CSP configuration using the directive "unsafe-inline" rated their application to be secure with a mean rating of 3.6 of 5 (SD: 0.7, median: 4.0). In fact, the application of "unsafe-inline" makes a CSP insecure.

In the following, we analyse if observations in both groups are related to the different CSP violation messages of Chrome and Firefox (cf. Section 2). Participants in the Chrome condition saw the CSP message in the browser console in mean after 17 minutes (median = 11.9) in comparison to a mean time of 7.5 minutes (median = 7.2) in the Firefox group (cf. Figure 3). The participants in the Firefox condition found the messages significantly ($p < 0.05$) earlier in the experiment than in the Chrome condition (Mann-Whitney U test; U=23.0; p=0.0396). However, as GUI-elements of the developer tools in Chrome and Firefox are almost identical to use and as we had briefed every participant about these tools (cf. Section 4.3), we assume that the significant difference is a result of software development being a high creative task, typically not following one specific behaviour pattern. Another reason for the significant difference between the Chrome and the Firefox group could be found in specific test persons' individual characteristics which we did not measure. We were not able to find a significant difference in the total development experience between the two groups.

The first three reactions of each participant to the CSP violation messages in the browser's console were diverse. They range from (a) initially ignoring it over (b) editing code on spec, (c) searching and checking project files to (d) reading in Play and Google Maps documentations and using a search engine. However, we could not find a statistical significant difference for subsequent actions indicating further information needs. The difference between the Chrome and the Firefox group in passed time before Google Search was used after seeing the CSP message was not significant (Firefox mean: 3.1 minutes, SD: 2.1; Chrome mean 3.6 minutes, SD: 2.9). Neither for entering CSP related key words like e.g. "default-src", "unsafe inline" or "content security policy" into Google Search or into the search function of Play's documentation the first time after having seen the CSP message (Firefox mean: 7.6 minutes, SD: 9.8; Chrome mean 12.1 minutes, SD: 16.0).

6 Discussion

The study results reveal several issues of Play's design decision to enable CSP by default following the fail-safe defaults principle (Saltzer and Schroeder, 1975). It furthermore shows, however, that also the general web development environment contributes to the discovered issues as not all resides inside the frameworks sphere of influence, including e.g. CSP messages in browsers, IDE support and information given by service providers. Those will be discussed in the following sections. We give explicit answers to RQ1 in Section 6.1 and to RQ2 in Section 6.2.

6.1 CSP by Default

It came as a surprise and was an unexpected situation for all participants in the Chrome and Firefox condition when the map did not show up after integrating the code snippet provided in the Google Maps API documentation: "I'm not allowed to call the Google Maps API because of any security settings. This usually works." There is a design shift from "developers have to switch on security" to "developers have to directly manage security". Our results show a negative effect on functionality and security: 35% (7/20) of our participants in the Chrome and Firefox group with CSP by default were not able to achieve a functional solution and none of the 20 participants developed a secure solution.

The current design of the default origin-only enforcing CSP in Play resulted in developers being uncertain about the functionality of their code. This uncertainty had been further amplified by a lack of information about what was happening. Consequently, errors were assumed to be in the own source codes and caused the revision of various project files for functional or logical mistakes. The common trial-and-error strategy failed as the security by default mechanism blocked the trials and left the developer with no additional hints on the cause of the non-functioning application. This leads to confusing an in-place security mechanism with flawed code. The observed program behaviour is regarded as a mistake sourced in the own implementations. To ensure that this is not the case or to finally get some insights on the problem cause, participants even used third party runtime environments like "JSFiddle" (JSFiddle, 2018) or created local HTML files outside the Play project to test their code. Two participants disabled all security headers (cf. Table) to identify a cause of the problem. Thus, the CSP integration design can lead to completely disabled security headers affecting also other security defaults or settings.

This emphasizes that informative feedback is crucial for developers to support them in narrowing down the real cause of a problem. Warning messages in the browser console are one pillar in this respect. Our study showed, however, that an effective information flow requires additional feedback at many more locations and layers within the development environment and during the development process respectively. As the developers do make extensive use of documentation, the enhancements of documentation with security-related aspects is one such missing piece. Thus, also service providers have an information obligation (Gorski *et al.*, 2016) to add missing CSP-related information to their documentation (cf. Section 6.3). Web frameworks do have a special mode of operation while developing a web application. When this mode is enabled, the framework provides detailed error messages in respect to compile or runtime errors. This could be enhanced with feedback on the current state and context of the application. Along these lines, such a framework provided feedback could link to additional resources such as CSP generators (cf. Section 6.4).

6.2   CSP Violation Message Design

The design of CSP violation messages does influence the information flow too, as the situation hardly changed after participants had seen the CSP violation message. They had difficulties to understand the given indications in the browser console: "Honestly, I have no idea why the map isn't displayed. The messages do not really explain that. It can't be so difficult." As proved by (Gorski *et al.,* 2018) in the context of Security APIs, warning messages displayed in development consoles can be an effective measure to improve software security. But, in general, warning messages have to be designed with usability in mind to be beneficial for users (Bauer *et al.* 2013). CSP warnings presented by Chrome and Firefox could not help any of our participants to configure a functional and secure policy as information to four main questions were missing or unclear: What is triggering the message and what is the reason? How to configure CSPs and where to set them?

6.2.1   What is triggering the message and what is the reason?

CSP messages in Chrome and Firefox are designed in red colour to gather attention. Indeed, they were perceived by 19/20 of our participants when they opened the JavaScript console of the browser. They were mainly interpreted as errors ("Always the same error message, I've no idea what I can do with it", "An error is displayed"). In fact, these messages give information about an enforced CSP which had been violated. Thus, this is a message of a working security mechanism in a safe situation which is perceived as an error. This safe situation had been changed to a more unsafe situation by 13/20 participants by disabling CSP and even further reaching other security means.

Adding a correct policy entry could result in many more messages showing up at the next test run. The amount of warnings displayed in our study was critical. Participants were confronted with many messages at once, with a maximum number of 105 triggered by loading many small images building the map. Participants had to iteratively edit the CSP to configure scripts, styles, fonts and images and control the effect to the messages displayed in the console. This required iterative process was a hurdle. When test persons just deactivated CSP, all messages disappeared.

Participants who switched off CSP completely actually knew that it was lowering security but disabled the security mechanism to be able to solve the given task (cf. Section 5.3). Thus, knowing that there is a more secure implementation could lead to responsible reaction in production, maybe delegating the task to other developers or investing more time in learning how to manage CSPs. This might also indicate that the relevance of CSP to the application's security was assessed high. Thus, the effect of the default enforcement of CSP on the relevance perception of the developers is an interesting topic for future work.

6.2.2   How to configure CSPs and where to set them?

In comparison to Firefox, Chrome includes the information that it is required to add "unsafe-inline", a hash or a nonce to the policy to enable inline execution. However, no recommendation for the offered three directive options is given. Only one participant in the Chrome condition tried to add the given hash value to the policy. No one tried to add a nonce. Except by the name there is no indication that the use of the "unsafe-inline" directive will result in an insecure CSP configuration. The rather high security ratings of participants which used the "unsafe-inline" directive seems to reflect a demand of more and better information. Further studies could evaluate whether showing a specific console warning could help to give advice how to improve a CSP when the "unsafe-inline" directive is applied.

It was also a problem for test persons to find out where the CSP should be configured, manifested in numerous comments on the warnings like "What is "default-src" and where do I have to set this?" or "I have to google "default-src", because I have no idea what this is". Participants tried to edit or change CSP at various places of the framework, not only in the recommended application configuration file but also e.g. in controller files, filter files or in meta tags inside of view files.

Settings in the "application.conf" file will override default settings loaded from different files (Play Framework, 2018a). Thus, commented configuration lines in the "application.conf" file do not mean to disable a default configuration. They rather match the defaults and are just commented for documentation purposes in starter Play projects. This did not match our participants' expectations how a configuration file works. Rather a list of enabled features was expected which can be disabled by commenting them out.

6.3   Information Resources

The information given by the browser CSP messages was not enough. During the study 18/20 tried to get further information about CSP by using Google Search or the search function in the Play documentation. Participants searched for CSP information also directly on the Google Maps documentation web site (Google Maps, 2018). As the CSP for our task should whitelist this Google service only, the idea of getting a ready to use CSP directly from the service provider is plausible. However, a ready to use policy is not given by the official documentation (Google Maps, 2018; West and Medley, 2018) as explicitly demanded by one test person: "Oh man, just give an example!". In case of the deployed Google Maps service, this would perfectly fit in the already given "Tips and troubleshooting" section, which was also read by participants. At least there should be explained how to gain a secure configuration for typical use cases. It is promising future work to evaluate if specific service related information about CSP configuration and ready to use examples can support web application developers building more secure software and whether this approach can improve transparency of dependencies to external resources.

6.4   Tool Support

During the experiments none of the participants searched for a CSP generator or related tools. After every change to a code or style block, a new hash value has to be generated, e.g a base64 encoded SHA-265, in order to update the CSP. An IDE integration could help developers with this process by offering the possibility to add or replace a hash to the CSP configuration file automatically or calling this support for a specific inline style or script block. Also, the "nonce" directive could be directly supported by the framework. It is promising future work to evaluate tool support for CSP deployment. This could be tools inside the IDE or also external support.

7 Limitation

The presented results are bound to several study specific factors which are discussed in the following section. First, the recruited group is not representative for the heterogenous group of software developers as the sample of participants came only from Germany. We chose a convenience sample of students, like (Acar, 2017a; Naiakshina, 2017) who also conducted studies with students, but only invited candidates with experience in web development (cf. Section 5.1).

Second, the study was designed to evaluate the effect of enforcing CSP by default in a framework for web application development in the first place. The time needed by participants to open the JavaScript console in a browser and see a CSP violation message varied considerably between both groups (cf. Section 5.2). Thereby, the time participants were dealing with these warnings also varied. Thus, making conclusions about the effect of different warning messages is only possible to a limited extend by our results. Conducting a follow up study with an adjusted study design only focusing on warning design effects will be future work.

Our study design also limited the time frame to one hour, as the participants offered their time on a voluntary basis. It is unknown if more time to work on the task would have changed the functionality or security in experiments which we had to terminate (seven in the Chrome and three in the Firefox condition). However, in these cases, participants seemed to be slightly annoyed and unmotivated to continue. That was shown in comments like "That is terrible" or "I have no clue what causes this error". Thus, we assume demanding for more time would not have been appropriate for this specific study task.

Our task did not include handling security relevant data. Thus, in our laboratory experiment a real risk was missing. This can be different in real world settings, potentially resulting in developers having a different motivation to configure CSP. Seven participants decided to disable the CSP mechanism. However, unawareness and lack of appropriate documentation were a major issue, which will occur in realistic settings likewise.

8 Conclusion

Just to follow the "security by default" principle is not enough in the context of software development. If these are not integrated with usability in mind they are likely to get in the developers' way. The current designs of CSP violation messages, documentation and IDE support are individually and in combination neither effective nor efficient nor do they lead to a satisfying result for users. The results of this study show that developers who are inexperienced with CSP will currently not be able to intuitively or quickly build a secure policy. CSP was misconfigured, was bypassed or it prevented participants to successfully implement the given study task. Thus, we conclude a correct configuration of CSPs to be a time-consuming and complex task and the decision to enable this security measure by default in the Play Framework should be carefully improved. However, our study unveiled a multi-layered issue likewise related to providers of frameworks, IDEs, browsers and services.

Software developers do not only have to be well informed or warned on insecure cases but also of secure cases in which security measures intervene by default unrecognizable in the background. Thus, we propose, in addition to the "Warn when unsafe" pattern (Garfinkel 2005), a "Warn if secure" or "Warn at intervention" for CSP application by default to transparently inform developers about this security measure and prevent the negative effects we observed in this study.

Future work should focus on the complex interplay of warning message design, the quality and availability of information resources and tools to support developers with the deployment of CSPs and other security defaults in a usable way. This empowers programmers to write more secure web applications, resulting in less vulnerable software putting end-users at risk.

9 Acknowledgments

The authors would like to thank all participants of this study for their voluntary participation. This work has been funded by the German Federal Ministry of Education and Research within the funding program "Forschung an Fachhochschulen"(contract no. 13FH016IX6).

10 References

Acar, Y., Backes, M., Fahl, S., Kim, D., Mazurek, M. L. and Stransky, C. "You get where you're looking for: The impact of information sources on code security." The 2016 IEEE Symposium on Security and Privacy. May 2016.

Acar, Y., Stransky, C., Wermke, D., Mazurek, M. L. and Fahl, S. (2017a). "Security Developer Studies with GitHub Users: Exploring a Convenience Sample", Thirteenth Symposium on Usable Privacy and Security (SOUPS 2017), Santa Clara, CA, U.S.A., pp. 81-95, USENIX Association.

Acar, Y., Stransky, C., Wermke, D., Weir, C., Mazurek, M. L. and Fahl, S. (2017b) "Developers need support, too: A survey of security advice for software developers.", Proceedings of SecDev 2017: IEEE Secure Development Conference, September 2017.

Bauer, L., Bravo-Lillo, C., Cranor, L. & Fragkaki, E. (2013) "Warning Design Guidelines." Technical, Report CMU-CyLab-13-002

Bodenheim, R., Butts, J., Dunlap, S., Mullins, B. (2014). "Evaluation of the ability of the Shodan search engine to identify Internet-facing industrial control devices". International Journal of Critical Infrastructure Protection 7, pp. 114–123.

Calzavara, S., Rabitti, A. and Bugliesi, M. (2018). "Semantics-Based Analysis of Content Security Policy Deployment", ACM Trans. Web, Volume 12, Number 2, January 2018, DOI: https://doi.org/10.1145/3149408

Can I use (2018), "Can I use Content Security Policy Level 2", https://caniuse.com/ #feat=contentsecuritypolicy2 (Accessed 14 May 2018)

Cass, S. (2017), "The 2017 Top Programming Languages", IEEE Spectrum Web Site https://spectrum.ieee.org/computing/software/the-2017-top-programming-languages (Accessed 15 May 2018)

The European Union (2016), "Regulation (EU) 2016/679 of the European Parliament and of the council of 27 April 2016 on the protection of natural persons with regard to the processing of personal data and on the free movement of such data, and repealing Directive 95/46/EC (General Data Protection Regulation)", Official Journal of the European Union, https://publications.europa.eu/en/publication-detail/-/publication/3e485e15-11bd-11e6-ba9a-01aa75ed71a1 (Accessed 18 July 2018)

Garfinkel, S. L. (2005), "Design principles and patterns for computer systems that are simultaneously secure and usable", PhD thesis, Massachusetts Institute of Technology.

Google Maps (2018). "JavaScript API – Overview". https://developers.google.com/maps/documentation/javascript/adding-a-google-map (Accessed 15 June 2018)

Gorski, P. L. and Lo Iacono, L. "Towards the Usability Evaluation of Security APIs", Tenth International Symposium on Human Aspects of Information Security & Assurance (HAISA 2016), Frankfurt, Germany, July 19-21, pp. 252-265.

Gorski, P. L., Lo Iacono, L., Wermke, D., Stransky, C., Möller, S., Acar, Y. and Fahl, S. (2018), "Developers Deserve Security Warnings, Too - On the Effect of Integrated Security Advice on

Cryptographic API Misuse", Fourteenth Symposium on Usable Privacy and Security (SOUPS 2018), Baltimore, MD, USA, USENIX Association.

Heyens, J., Greshake, K., Petryka, E. (2015). "MongoDB Databases at Risk". https://uds.cispa.saarland/wp-content/uploads/2015/02/MongoDB_documentation.pdf (Accessed 15 June 2018)

Intelli JIDEA Web Site (2018), https://www.jetbrains.com/idea/ (Accessed 12 June 2018)

JSFiddle (2018), https://jsfiddle.net/ (Accessed 15 June 2018)

Krasner, G. E. and Pope, S. T. (1988). "A cookbook for using the model-view controller user interface paradigm in Smalltalk-80", Journal of Object Oriented Programming, Volume 1, Issue 3, August/September 1988, pp26-49, SIGS Publications.

Lo Iacono, L. and Gorski P. L. (2017), "I Do and I Understand. Not Yet True for Security APIs. So Sad", 2nd European Workshop on Usable Security (EuroUSEC), Paris, France, 2017.

Lorente, E.N., Meijer, C., Verdult, R. (2015). "Scrutinizing WPA2 Password Generating Algorithms in Wireless Routers", 9th USENIX Workshop on Offensive Technologies (WOOT), Washington, D.C., USA , 2015.

Naiakshina, A., Danilova, A., Tiefenau, C., Herzog, M., Dechand, S. and Smith, M. 2017. "Why Do Developers Get Password Storage Wrong?: A Qualitative Usability Study". Proceedings of the 2017 ACM SIGSAC Conference on Computer and Communications Security (CCS '17). ACM, New York, NY, USA, 311-328. DOI: https://doi.org/10.1145/3133956.3134082

National Cyber Security Centre (2016). "NCSC password infographic". https://www.ncsc.gov.uk/file/1472/download?token=XKMKqHJX (Accessed 15 June 2018)

Open Broadcaster Software (2018), "OBS Studio", https://obsproject.com/. (Accessed 17 May 2018)

The OWASP Foundation (2017), "OWASP Top 10 – 2017, The Ten Most Critical Web Application Security Risks", https://www.owasp.org/index.php/Category:OWASP_Top_Ten_Project. (Accessed 15 May 2018)

Play Framework (2018a), "Documentation – Configuration file syntax and features", https://www.playframework.com/documentation/2.6.x/ConfigFile. (Accessed 15 May 2018)

Play Framework (2018b), "Downloads – Play Starter Projects", https://www.playframework.com/download#starters. (Accessed 15 May 2018)

Saltzer, J. H., and Schroeder, M. D. (1975). "The protection of information in computersystems". Proceedings of the IEEE, 63.9, S. 1278–1308.

Stamm, S., Sterne, B., Markham, G. (2010). "Reining in the web with content security policy", Proceedings of the 19th International Conference on World Wide Web, ACM, pp. 921–930.

Tekeoglu, A., Tosun, A. S. (2015). "Investigating security and privacy of a cloud-based wireless IP camera: NetCam", 24th International Conference on Computer Communication and Networks (ICCCN), IEEE, Las Vegas, NV, USA, pp. 1–6.

Vogt, P., Nentwich, F., Jovanovic, N., Kirda, E., Kruegel, C., Vigna, G. (2007). "Cross Site Scripting Prevention with Dynamic Data Tainting and Static Analysis". 14th Network and Distributed System Security Symposium (NDSS), San Diego, CA, USA, 2007.

W3C (2016), "Content Security Policy Level 3", W3C Working Draft, 13 September 2016. https://www.w3.org/TR/CSP/. (Accessed 13 May 2018)

W3Schools (2018). "Browser Statistics - The Most Popular Browsers", https://www.w3schools.com/browsers/default.asp. (Accessed 18 May 2018)

Weichselbaum, L., Spagnuolo, M., Lekies, S. and Janc, A. (2016), „CSP Is Dead, Long Live CSP! On the Insecurity of Whitelists and the Future of Content Security Policy", Proceedings of the 2016 ACM SIGSAC Conference on Computer and Communications Security (CCS '16), New York, NY, USA, pp. 1376-1387, DOI: https://doi.org/10.1145/2976749.2978363

Weissbacher, M., Lauinger T., Robertson W. (2014), "Why Is CSP Failing? Trends and Challenges in CSP Adoption", Proceedings of Research in Attacks, Intrusions and Defenses. RAID 2014. Lecture Notes in Computer Science, vol 8688, pp 212-233, Springer, Cham, DOI: https://doi.org/10.1007/978-3-319-11379-1_11

West, M. and Medley, J. (2018), "Web Fundamentals – Content Security Policy", https://developers.google.com/web/fundamentals/security/csp/ (Accessed 18 May 2018)

Analysis of Published Public Sector Information Security Incidents and Breaches to Establish the Proportions of Human Error

M. Evans, Y. He, I. Yevseyeva and H. Janicke

Cyber Security Centre, De Montfort University, England
e-mail: mark.evans4@my365.dmu.ac.uk; ying.he@dmu.ac.uk; iryna@dmu.ac.uk;
heljanic@dmu.ac.uk

Abstract

The information security field experiences a continuous stream of information security incidents and breaches, which are publicised by the media, public bodies and regulators. Despite the need for information security practices being recognised and in existence for some time the underlying general information security affecting tasks and causes of these incidents and breaches are not consistently understood, particularly with regard to human error. This paper analyses recent published incidents and breaches to establish the proportions of human error, and where possible subsequently utilises the HEART human reliability analysis technique, which is established within the safety field. This analysis provides an understanding of the proportions of incidents and breaches that relate to human error as well as the common types of tasks that result in these incidents and breaches through adoption of methods applied within the safety field.

Keywords

Information security, incidents, breaches, human error, HEART, GISAT

1   Introduction

The ICO data security incident trends (Information Commissioner's Office, 2017) shows that a number of UK sectors have experienced significant increases in reported information security incidents in Q4 2017. In some sectors such as the health sector this is primarily due to incidents that relate to people and human error. Despite this the information security community does not have a thorough understanding of what constitutes a human error and often resorts to general basic awareness or training on information security following an incident rather than dealing with the causal factors (Mahfuth et al., 2017). Current practices fall short of identifying the actual root cause of human error related information security incidents even though people are recognized as being the weakest link in information security controls (Furnell et al., 2018; Halevi et al., 2017; Mahfuth et al., 2017; Metalidou et al., 2014; Parsons et al., 2017). There are also no established human error information security frameworks in practice to enable not only effective resolution of human error related information security incidents but also the prevention of these events.

The aim and motivation for this research is to analyse and establish the volumes and causes of information security incidents and breaches, published by the Information Commissioner's Office (ICO) and the UK National Health Service (NHS), that relate to human error. Where sufficient data has been published, incidents are mapped to the established Human Error Assessment and Reduction Technique (HEART) human reliability analysis method, which is widely utilised within the safety field, to understand the types and context of tasks which are associated with the published incidents and breaches.

This research provides original contribution to knowledge through the analysis of recent public sector information security incidents and breaches in order to understand the proportions that relate to human error as well as the common generic task types (GTT), as defined within the HEART (Williams, 1992) technique, and general information security affecting tasks (GISAT) (Evans et al., 2018) that lead to these events. The research also supports the applicability of the HEART human reliability analysis technique within the information security field.

The remainder of paper is structured as follows. Section 2 presents related research into the human factor of information security. Section 3 provides an overview of the method applied for the research into published information security incidents and breaches and section 4 presents the results of the research. Section 5 delivers the key findings and section 6 concludes the research and outlines future work.

2   Related Work

There have been many research articles published on the topic of information security but proportionally very few articles dedicated to the human factor and specifically human error. In our previous research (Evans et al., 2016) we emphasised this gap in current research and also emphasised the need for empirical research into human error effects on information security assurance to understand the underlying causes of human error. Human error is defined as non-deliberate, unintentional or accidental cause of poor information security (Werlinger et al., 2009). Amongst published articles human error is identified as being associated with a large proportion of information security incidents or breaches (Komatsu et al., 2013; Stewart and Jürjens, 2017) and the most critical factor in the management of information security (Stewart and Jürjens, 2017). Literature has consistently presented that effective information security management must essentially embrace the human factor in addition to technology (Asai and Hakizabera, 2010; Frangopoulos et al., 2014; Stewart and Jürjens, 2017; Werlinger et al., 2009) and that the security of IT systems and platforms have been undermined by human failings (Lacey, 2010).

Human error quantification has varied in published literature. Frangopoulos et al (Komatsu et al., 2013) presented that 42 percent of security incidents resulted from human error whereas Stewart (Stewart and Jürjens, 2017) stated 65 percent were due to some forms of human error. Alavi et al (Alavi et al., 2016) presented research, which found that 64 percent of security incidents were directly related to human error. Whereas Asai and Hakizabera (Asai and Hakizabera, 2010) stated in their research that 80 percent of information security breaches are caused by human error. The information security field should study methods used within the safety field (Lacey, 2010) where it was found that 90 percent of accidents were caused by human failure. It was also presented that new interventions are required to change human behaviour (Lacey, 2010) and that few information security practitioners have an understanding of proven methodologies for changing human behaviour. It was also stated that factors such as stress, lack of training or supervision, and bad system or process design are the underlying causes of breaches (Lacey, 2010) and also that information security management remains relatively weak in conducting root cause analysis of minor incidents.

3   Method

The method employed by this research was to understand the proportions of human error related incidents from published public sector incidents and personal data breaches by the UK Information Commissioner's Office (ICO) and the UK National Health Service (NHS). As there is greater incident detail published for the NHS personal data breaches we were able to use a set of GISATs to map the breaches to, in order to provide a richer level of understanding regarding the specific tasks that were being performed when the incident occurred. Once the GISATs were established we were subsequently able to map to the HEART GTTs.

HEART was initially published in 1985 and used by numerous organisations and sectors as a mechanism to address the issue of human reliability (Williams, 1992). HEART has been widely used in industry, primarily the nuclear industry (Chandler et al., 2006; Lyons et al., 2004). A detailed HEART user manual (Williams, 1992) was written in 1992 for Nuclear Electric plc, now EDF Energy. The HEART method comprises of a set of 9 GTTs as shown in table 1 with associated nominal human unreliability and upper bounds and also 38 error producing conditions (EPC) and their accompanying strength values. The GTTs are a core component of the HEART technique which looks to match the task under consideration with a predefined list of task descriptions.

A	Totally unfamiliar task, performed at speed with no real idea of the likely consequences of actions taken.
B	Shift or restore system to a new or original state at a single attempt without supervision or procedures.
C	Complex task requiring a high level of understanding and skill.
D	Fairly simple task performed rapidly or given insufficient or inadequate attention.
E	Routine, highly-practiced, rapid task involving relatively low level of skill.
F	Restore or shift a system to original or new state following procedures, with some checking.
G	Completely familiar, well designed, highly practiced routine task occurring several times per hour, performed to highest possible standards by highly motivated, highly trained and experienced persons, totally aware of implications of failure, with time to correct potential error, but without the benefit of significant job aids.
H	Respond correctly to system command even when there is an assisting or automated supervisory system providing accurate interpretation of system state.
M	Miscellaneous task for which no description can be found.

Table 1 – HEART GTTs (Williams, 1992)

The Q4 2017 incident trends published by the ICO (Information Commissioner's Office, 2017) were analysed to ascertain a greater degree of understanding of the proportions of human error related information security incidents. In addition to analysis of the ICO data, security trend analysis was also performed on the published NHS serious incidents requiring investigation (SIRI) level 2 incidents relating to Q3 2017 (Department of Health, 2017). Further analysis of the incidents was conducted by mapping each of the 124 human error related SIRI level 2 incidents to a set of General Information Security Affecting Tasks (GISAT), which subsequently enabled the mapping to the HEART GTTs. The GISATs were developed during our wider research and empirical feasibility study into 12 months of reported information security incidents within public and private sector organisations.

The primary focus of this research was public sector incidents and breaches but also undertook analysis of combined data for all sectors, including private sector, to enable a holistic set of results. In order to enable the analysis to be performed and establish which incidents were likely, possibly or unlikely related to human error, we developed the mapping below based upon analysis of the published incidents.

Category	Human Error Likelihood	Rationale
Data left in insecure location	Likely	The data would likely be left by a person unintentionally
Data posted/faxed to incorrect recipient	Likely	The data would likely be posted or faxed to the wrong recipient unintentionally
Data sent by email to incorrect recipient	Likely	The data would likely be emailed to the wrong recipient unintentionally
Failure to redact data	Likely	The data would likely be redacted unintentionally
Failure to use bcc when sending email	Likely	The failure to use bcc would likely be unintentional
Insecure disposal of hardware	Possibly	The insecure disposal of hardware could be technical, procedural or possibly human error
Insecure disposal of paperwork	Possibly	The insecure disposal of paperwork could be technical, procedural or possibly human error
Loss/theft of only copy of encrypted data	Possibly	The category covers both loss of equipment ,which is likely to be unintentional human error, but also mainly theft of equipment which is unlikely to be human error
Loss/theft of paperwork	Likely	The category covers both mainly loss of paperwork which is likely to be unintentional human error but also infrequent theft of paperwork which is unlikely to be human error
Loss/theft of unencrypted device	Possibly	The category covers both loss of equipment, which is likely to be unintentional human error, but also mainly theft of equipment which is unlikely to be human error
Other principle 7 failure	Possibly	This is a broad category and incidents could possibly be as a result of unintentional human error
Verbal disclosure	Likely	The data would likely be disclosed by a person unintentionally
Cyber incidents	Unlikely	The cyber incident category tends to relate to malicious or intentional acts so is unlikely to be human error

Table 2 – Mapping of ICO data security incident categories to human error likelihood

4   Results

The results of the analysis of the published public sector (Central and Local Government and Health) personal data breaches and NHS SIRI level 2 incidents are presented in the tables and figures below.

The analysis of published personal data breaches by the ICO for all sectors can be shown in table 3 and figure 1. It was established that 64% of the incidents were likely to be as a result of human error and that a further 27% could possibly be as a result of human error. Therefore, combining both categories provides a view that 91% of all personal data breaches reported to the ICO could have been as a result of human error.

All Sectors		
Human Error Likelihood	Count	Percentage
Likely	521	63.92
Possibly	220	26.99
Unlikely	74	9.07

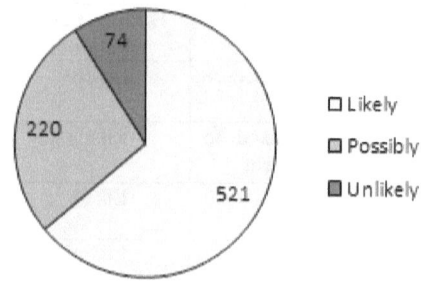

Table 3 – Human error likelihood of ICO data security incident trends for all sectors

Figure 1 – Likelihood of human error ICO data security incident trends for all sectors

The analysis was also performed on specific central government, local government and health sectors. The analysis found that incidents were likely to relate to human error for these three sectors between 70% and 82%. However, taking into account the possible human errors the percentages increased significantly. This accumulation found that data security incidents relating to human error was possibly 96% for central government and 98% for both local government and health sectors.

Central Government Sector		
Human Error Likelihood	Count	Percentage
Likely	20	80
Possibly	4	16
Unlikely	1	4

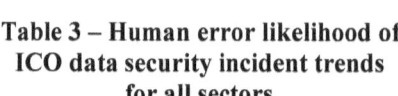

Table 4 – Human error likelihood of ICO data security incident trends for central government

Figure 2 – Likelihood of human error ICO data security incident trends for central government

Local Government Sector		
Human Error Likelihood	Count	Percentage
Likely	76	81.72
Possibly	15	16.12
Unlikely	2	2.15

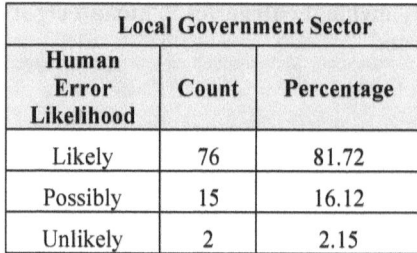
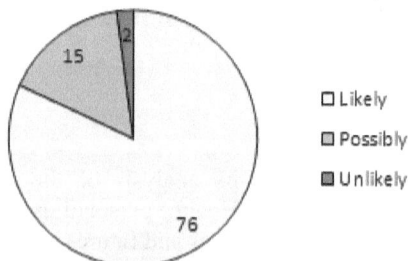

Table 5 – Human error likelihood of ICO data security incident trends for local government

Figure 3 – Likelihood of human error ICO data security incident trends for local government

Health Sector		
Human Error Likelihood	Count	Percentage
Likely	199	69.09
Possibly	84	29.16
Unlikely	5	1.73

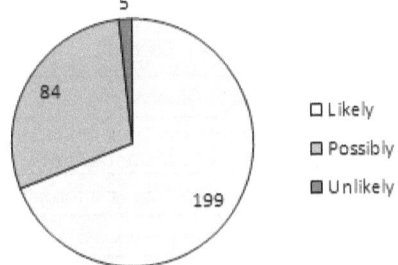

Table 6 – Human error likelihood of ICO data security incident trends for health

Figure 4 – Likelihood of human error ICO data security incident trends for health

Each of the 148 reported NHS SIRI incidents and associated details were analysed and it was identified that 124 (84%) of the most serious NHS personal data security incidents pertained to human error.

SIRI Level 2 Incidents		
Human Error	Count	Percentage
Yes	124	83.8
No	24	16.2

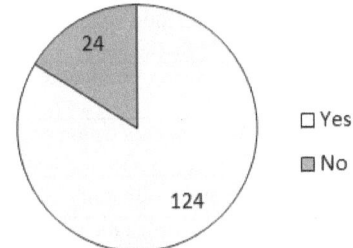

Table 7 – NHS SIRI level 2 incidents

Figure 5 – Proportion of human error for NHS SIRI 2 incidents

This analysis of the Q3 2017 NHS SIRI level 2 incidents found that 42 (34%) were posting an item or information, 31 (25%) were sending an email, and 22 (18%) were safeguarding information or equipment. We were able to manually map each incident to the list of GISATs using the rich details published for each incident by the NHS. The details of this granular analysis and mapping to GISATs can be seen in table 8 and figure 6.

General Information Security Affecting Tasks (GISAT)	Count	Percentage of human error incidents	HEART GTT
GISAT1- Sending an email	31	25.00	G
GISAT2 - Entering, updating or deleting data within a system, file or document	5	4.03	D
GISAT3 - Posting an item or information	42	33.87	E
GISAT4 - Configuring a system	1	0.81	C
GISAT5 - Administering a system	0	0.00	D
GISAT6 - Scanning a document	1	0.81	E
GISAT7 - Printing a document	1	0.81	D
GISAT8 - Providing information verbally	2	1.61	D
GISAT9 - Delivering information or equipment	2	1.61	E
GISAT10 - Filing or sorting information	3	2.42	E
GISAT11 - Reading or checking an email, file, document or item	0	0.00	G
GISAT12 - Safeguarding information or equipment	22	17.74	E
GISAT13 – Destroying information or equipment	6	4.84	D
GISAT14 – Accessing a location or environment	0	0.00	D
GISAT15 - Faxing information	2	1.61	D
GISAT16 - Sharing or handing over information or equipment in person	6	4.84	G

Table 8 - Mapping of NHS SIRI 2 incidents to GISATs and association with HEART GTTs

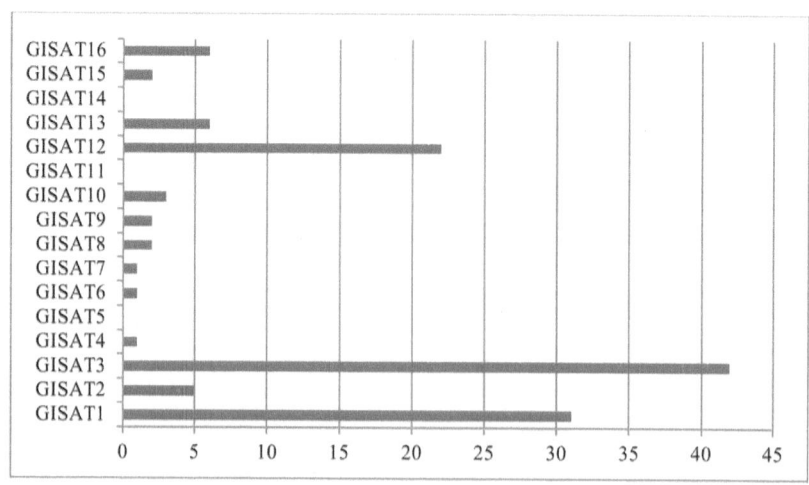

Figure 6 - Mapping of NHS SIRI 2 incidents to GISATs

Once the NHS SIRI level 2 incidents had been mapped to the GISATs it was possible to create a conceptual mapping to the HEART GTTs. The mapping can be seen in table 8. In addition the volumes of each selected GTTs that have been mapped to the Q3 2017 SIRI level 2 incidents can be seen below. It was established that none of the published incidents were able to be mapped to GTTs A, B, F, H or M.

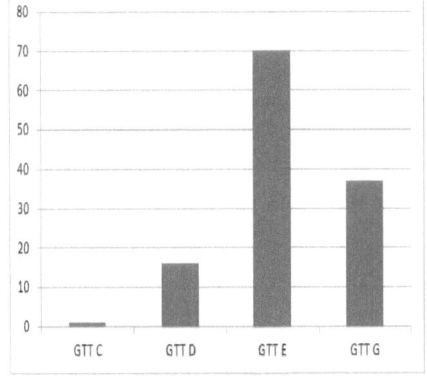

GTT	Count	Percentage
C	1	0.8
D	16	12.9
E	70	56.45
G	37	29.83

Table 9 – HEART GTT mapping to NHS SIRI level 2 incidents

Figure 7 – HEART GTT mapping to NHS SIRI level 2 incidents

5 Discussion

Following analysis of the published data it was identified that 64% of reported incidents across all sectors were likely to be as a result of human error, which aligns to the research published by (Alavi et al., 2016; Stewart and Jürjens, 2017). In addition a further 27% could also possibly be as a result of human error. Therefore, the analysis found that 91% of data security incidents reported to the ICO could possibly have been as a result of human error suggesting actual rates of human error related information security incidents is higher than currently understood by the information security community. These high volumes of possible human error information security incidents align to the proportions of human failure that led to accidents in the safety field (Lacey, 2010). This supports the view that the established root cause methods utilised within the safety field would demonstrate a higher proportion of human error behind current information security incident and breach events than currently recognised.

Each of the 148 reported NHS SIRI level 2 incidents and associated details were analysed and it was identified that 124 (84%) of the most serious NHS personal data security incidents pertained to human error which again aligns to published research (Asai and Hakizabera, 2010).

Following analysis of the published NHS SIRI level 2 incidents it was identified that the most common general information security affecting task was postage of information followed by the use of email showing that focus should be applied to external sharing and communication of information. The analysis of the same incidents against the HEART GTTs found that the most common generic task type associated with information security incidents is a routine, highly-practiced, rapid task involving relatively low level of skill.

6 Conclusions and Future Work

In conclusion, it has been identified that the actual volumes of personal data breaches and information security incidents are greater than currently understood by the information security community. Therefore, in order to reduce the volumes of breaches and incidents the information security field should understand applied human reliability analysis techniques applied within the safety field. The application, and adaptation, of methods of working applied within the safety field will enable the underlying root causes of human error to be understood and acted upon, which will reduce future volumes of information security incidents and breaches. In addition, organisations should focus on routine operational tasks performed by employees that involve the external sharing or communication of confidential or personal data.

We will be continuing our research into the feasibility of human reliability analysis within the information security field including publishing associated 12 months feasibility studies, which have been undertaken within public and private sector organisations. In addition, HEART will be adapted to produce an Information Security

Core Human Error Causes (IS-CHEC) product, which will be developed as a key element of the ongoing empirical action research.

7   References

Alavi R, Islam S, Mouratidis H. An information security risk-driven investment model for analysing human factors. Inf Comput Secur 2016;24:205–27. doi:10.1108/ICS-01-2016-0006.

Asai T, Hakizabera AU. Human-related problems of information security in East African cross-cultural environments. Inf Manag Comput Secur 2010;18:328–38. doi:10.1108/09685221011095245.

Chandler T, Chang J, Mosleb A, J. M, Boring R, Gertman D. Human Reliability Analysis Methods Selection Guidance for NASA. Natl Aeronaut Sp Adm 2006:175.

Department of Health. IG Publications. 2017.

Evans M, Maglaras L, He Y, Janicke H. HEART-IS: A Novel Technique fro Evaluating Human Error-Related Information Security Incidents. Computers & Security, 2018;Submitted.

Evans M, Maglaras LA, He Y, Janicke H. Human behaviour as an aspect of cybersecurity assurance. Secur Commun Networks 2016;9:4667–79. doi:10.1002/sec.1657.

Frangopoulos ED, Eloff MM, Venter LM. Human Aspects of Information Assurance: A Questionnaire-based Quantitative Approach to Assessment 2014.

Furnell S, Khern-am-nuai W, Esmael R, Yang W, Li N. Enhancing security behaviour by supporting the user. Comput Secur 2018;75:1–9. doi:10.1016/j.cose.2018.01.016.

Halevi T, Memon N, Lewis J, Kumaraguru P, Arora S, Dagar N, et al. Cultural and psychological factors in cyber-security. Proc 18th Int Conf Inf Integr Web-Based Appl Serv 2017;13:43–56.

Information Commissioner's Office. Data security incident trends. 2017.

Komatsu A, Takagi D, Takemura T. Human aspects of information security. Inf Manag Comput Secur 2013;21:5–15. doi:10.1108/09685221311314383.

Lacey D. Understanding and transforming organizational security culture. Inf Manag Comput Secur 2010;18:4–13. doi:10.1108/09685221011035223.

Lyons M, Adams S, Woloshynowych M, Vincent C. Human reliability analysis in healthcare : A review of techniques. Int J Risk Saf Med 2004;16:223–37.

Mahfuth A, Yussof S, Baker AA, Ali N. A systematic literature review: Information security culture. 2017 Int. Conf. Res. Innov. Inf. Syst., IEEE; 2017, p. 1–6. doi:10.1109/ICRIIS.2017.8002442.

Metalidou E, Marinagi C, Trivellas P, Eberhagen N, Skourlas C. The Human Factor of Information Security: Unintentional Damage Perspective. Procedia - Soc Behav Sci 2014;147:424–8. doi:10.1016/J.SBSPRO.2014.07.133.

Parsons K, Calic D, Pattinson M, Butavicius M, McCormac A, Zwaans T. The Human Aspects of Information Security Questionnaire (HAIS-Q): Two further validation studies. Comput Secur 2017;66:40–51. doi:10.1016/j.cose.2017.01.004.

Stewart H, Jürjens J. Information security management and the human aspect in organizations. Inf Comput Secur 2017;25:494–534. doi:10.1108/ICS-07-2016-0054.

Werlinger R, Hawkey K, Beznosov K. An integrated view of human, organizational, and technological challenges of IT security management. Inf Manag Comput Secur 2009;17:4–19. doi:10.1108/09685220910944722.

Williams JC. A User Manual for the HEART Human Reliability Assessment Method 1992.

Defining and Modelling the Online Fraud Process

J. Kävrestad and M. Nohlberg

School of Informatics, University of Skövde, Skövde, Sweden
e-mail: joakim@kavrestad@his.se; marcus.nohlberg@his.se

Abstract

As we have become more and more active online so has online criminals. Looking at one type of Internet crimes, online frauds, it is apparent that any-one can be targeted by a fraudster online. It has also been shown that online frauds keep increasing from year to year. It has even been estimated that one third of the adult population in America encounters online fraudsters, annually. In this paper we aimed to increase the knowledge about online frauds. We did this by producing a model that describes the process and aspects of an online fraud as well as a proposed definition of the term "online fraud". In this paper, we present the model and definition that we created and demonstrate their usefulness. The usefulness is demonstrated in our validation step, where we applied the definition to known online fraud schemes. We also conducted an interview in which the model was said to be useful in order to explain how an online fraud scheme was carried out, during a criminal prosecution. As such, that demonstrates that our model can be used to increase the understanding of online frauds.

Keywords

Online fraud, Definition, Model.

1   Introduction

With the technical development, most people has come to be present online in one way or another. You could even argue that a separate shadow-community has been established online. Looking at how the Internet has evolved it is now common to socialize, shop, pay bills and more on the Internet. However, as society have become more and more active online there has subsequently been a rise in criminal online activity that, in different ways, tries to exploit Internet users for malicious intents. One such activity that is constantly increasing is online frauds. During the last couple of years, several online fraud schemes received a lot of attention in media and they serve to show that lots of criminals are continuously trying to defraud as many Internet users as possible. Some of these fraudulent schemes includes the Microsoft phone scam (TechAdvisor, 2016), Internet romance frauds (Marimow & Hedgpeth, 2016) and Facebook frauds (ActionFraud, 2016).

Even if online fraudsters is not a new phenomenon, the number of online frauds continue to rise. In Sweden, The Swedish National Council for Crime Prevention (BRÅ) stated, in 2017, that frauds in general had doubled in the past ten years. BRÅ also shows that over 50% of the frauds are computer related (BRÅ, 2018). In 2013, IC3 (Internet Crime Compliant Center) reported that online frauds were increasing in America as well (IC3, 2013). Further, it is evident that a large number of internet users are targeted by online fraudsters, as one example, Pratt, Holtfreter and Reisig estimates that one third of the American adult population experience victimization – annually (Pratt, Holtfreter, & Reisig, 2010).

As of today, Swedish legislation does not have a comprehensive definition of what online fraud is. There are only two computer related crimes defined in Swedish law: computer intrusion and computer fraud. However, computer fraud in this context only covers crimes against databases and automatic data management (Polisen, 2018). Looking outside of Sweden there are several definitions available. In 2009 Alnajim discussed that Internet could be a method to carry out frauds (Alnajim, 2009). A more comprehensive definition was given by The Australian Federal Police in 2014 (AFP, 2018):

" The term 'online fraud' refers to any type of fraud scheme that uses email, web sites, chat rooms or message boards to present fraudulent solicitations to prospective victims, to conduct fraudulent transactions or to transmit the proceeds of fraud to financial institutions or to others connected with the scheme. "

This definition lists the possible arenas were frauds can be committed. A potential drawback of that could be that it excludes frauds that are taking place in other arenas, such as social networks. A common denominator over in the discussed literature seems to be that online fraud is a fraud were the Internet is used. However, no one seems to discuss what "using the Internet" actually means. In this paper we propose a definition of online fraud and a descriptive model that explains the process and other aspects involved in an online fraud. To cover practical as well as legal aspects we make use of action based research where we include investigators from the Swedish police in the research process and validate our results with a representative from the Swedish court system.

With this approach we aim to reach conclusions that can provide a better understanding of online frauds in a global context as well as being practically applicable in the justice system, in Sweden as well as globally.

1.1 Research goals

This paper explores how the term "online fraud" can be defined and explains the aspects of an online fraud process. However, even if online fraud is a term used all over the world, as a crime it is to some extend defined in legislation. As such, the intent of this paper is to provide insight into what characterizes online frauds that can be implemented in any local jurisdiction rather than a fit-all legal definition. This paper aims to reach the following research goals:

Goal 1: Create a definition of online fraud.

Goal 2: Create a descriptive model that explains the process and aspects involved in an online fraud.

1.2 Outline

The rest of this paper is structured as follows. Section 2 describes the method used in this study. Section 3 presents the outcome of the study and Section 4 presents a discussion on the results presented and possible directions for future research.

2 Methodology

The research aim was addressed using an action based approach with qualitative interviews. As described by SBU, an action-based approach allows the participants to take an active part in the research (SBU, 2014). In this case investigators from the Swedish police was involved in the study as interview subjects and a series on semi-structured interviews was held with them. The interviews was transcribes and analysed using thematic coding as described by Robson (2011). The study began by constructing a definition and a model of online fraud based on the sources presented in the introduction. That was used as input for the first round of interviews. The model and definition was then updated and new interviews was held and the process was iterated until all participants were satisfied.

Lincoln and Guba (1985) describes four criteria's for quality in research; Credibility, Transferability, Dependability and Conformability. The main tasks conducted in this study to ensure credible results involved taking care to document the research process in order to make the study easy to replicate and understand. Also, Lincoln and Guba suggest using triangulation to increase the probability of producing reliable results. Triangulation was using in two ways in this study. First, separate interviews were held with different respondents, different investigators from different departments of the Swedish police. Second, after all interviews where completed, a final interview was held with a person from a different professional background than the other subjects. The respondent in the final interview was a judge from a Swedish court. Finally the definition was further validated by using lists of online fraud schemes presented by IC3 (2018) and ActionFraud (2018) to ensure that the definition covered all the listed fraud schemes The research process is visualized in Figure 1.

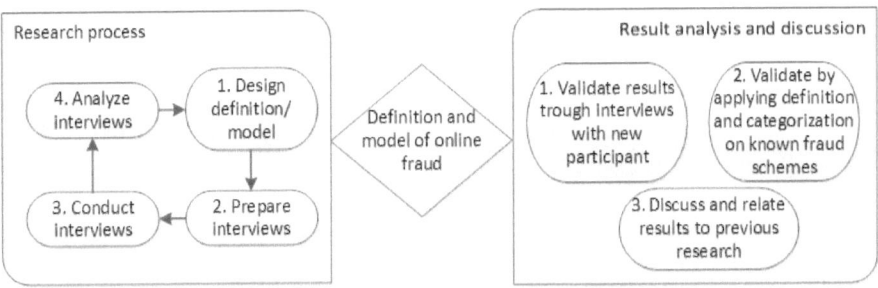

Figure 1: Research process overview (Authors own)

3   Results

This section presents the results of the study. Since an iterative method was used, the results from each step in the research process will be presented. The final sub-section will present the final definition and model of online fraud.

3.1   Preparation

Using the background literature, presented in the introduction section, a proposed definition and model was created before the first round of interviews. First, Swedish law states that a fraud is when someone tricks someone else into doing something that person would not normally do. That implies that a fraud must have the following entities:

- A fraudster that commits the fraud
- A victim that is defrauded

In criminology means, opportunity and motive is often discussed as the aspects of a crime (Sarnecki, 2009). It seems reasonable to include those aspects in the definition of online fraud and in this step it is done as follows:

- Means: The tools needed/used to commit the fraud
- Opportunity: The ability of the fraudster to get access to an attack vector
- Motive: The reason why the fraudster commits the fraud

The previous discussion on current definitions of online fraud indicates that a common denominator in earlier definitions is the fact that online fraud is fraud that uses the Internet as the means for the crime. This would indicate that an online fraud is a fraud where some computerized tools are used in order to commit fraud. With this conclusion the following suggested definition was created:

"Online fraud is a fraud where computerized tools are used as the means needed to commit the crime."

Given that definition, the online fraud process was modelled as shown in Figure 2.

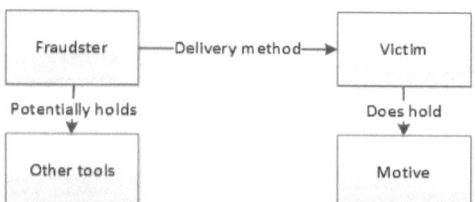

Figure 2: Prototype model that was presented to participants (Authors own)

The model reflects the fraudster and victim as entities. Further, the fraudster can hold tools used for the fraud and the victim must hold something that the fraudster wants to get. Finally the fraudster and victim must be connected through a delivery method.

3.2 Interview round 1

During the first interview round, interviews with two persons was held. One of the participants worked as an investigator of financial crimes with the Police department in Örebro and the other was a former investigator who now worked with coordinating online fraud investigations within the Swedish police. These and all other interviews in the study was conducted and transcribed in Swedish. Citations from the interviews are translated to English. Citations and summaries presented in this paper was reviewed by the participants to reduce the risk of any information being changed or misinterpreted in the translation. The participants were handed the model and definition from the previous step before the interviews, they served as a starting point for the interviews. The interviews in this step then served to provide answers to the following questions:

- What should decide if a crime is to be classified as online fraud or not?
- What characterizes online fraud?
- What should control how to classify online frauds?

The participants expressed that there is currently no common definition of online fraud but a main factor is that the frauds are carried out over the Internet in some way. A key point that was expressed is that just using digital tools in some way is not enough for a fraud to be classified as an online fraud. It should rather be classified depending on the how the fraud is delivered to the victim, or as one participant expressed it:

"...it is that Internet has been used in some way, either that the contact has been taken through the Internet or that the whole transaction has been carried out over the Internet."

A lot was said about fraud as a crime that clearly showed that a key factor is that for something to be classified as a fraud it must include that a fraudster persuades a victim into giving up something of value. Thus, a fraud brings monetary loss for the victim and equal monetary gain for the fraudster.

Based on the input from the interviews it is evident that a definition of online fraud must include that a fraud must be delivered over the Internet in order to be called an online fraud. However, it is also evident that there are several delivery methods that are used to commit online frauds. Consider the process of using an automated dialler to call peoples analogue phones and defraud them. That scheme begins in a digital manner but end up being analogue. On the other hand, Microsoft frauds as described by TechAdvisor (2016) begins with an analogue call and ends up being an online fraud when the user is persuaded into installing software on his computer. Considering the input from the interviews and the distinct differences in the different fraud schemes the definition was updated as follows:

Online fraud is a fraud where computerized tools are used for full or partial delivery of the fraud.

The word fraud was intentionally left undefined in this definition. This is to make the definition of online fraud depend on the legal definition of fraud, thus making it work in a global context and if the law is changed. Given the new definition, the model was redesigned to reflect that the delivery of an online fraud can be separated into several steps. The model produced in this step is presented in Figure 3.

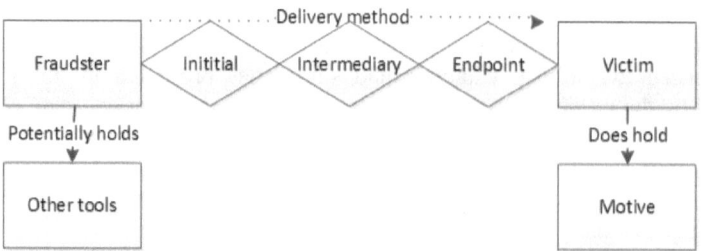

Figure 3: Model after first interview round (Authors own)

3.3   Interview round 2

This interview round used the model and definition from the previous round as input and served to answer the following questions:

- What are the strengths and weaknesses about the model and definition?
- What changes should be made to the model end definition?

Given the information from the second interview round the definition is fine and does not need further updates. It was pointed out that it is preferable to make the definition depend on the legal definition of fraud.

For the model it was pointed out that the model should reflect that a fraud is about a fraudster affecting the victim into giving something up. The victim giving something up rather than the perpetrator just taking it is what differs fraud from theft. Also, the keyword "motive" was not seen as clear and was suggested to be changed to a word that reflects that the motive is to get something of value. Based on the response the following changes was made to the model, resulting in the model shown in Figure 4.

- The word motive was changed to "Article of value/money"
- An arrow indicating that the fraudster wants the valuable was added
- Arrows showing that the Fraudster deceives the Victim into giving up the valuable was added.

In the resulting model (Shown in Figure 4) the boxes represent the entities that are present in any fraud; a fraudster, a victim and some article of value or money. The tilted boxes visualize the different steps in the delivery of a fraud. The dotted line shows relationships; in this case the presence of a delivery method and that the fraudster wants the article of value. Finally the dashed lines indicates the actions that needs to take place, namely that the fraudster is persuading the victim of giving him or her the article of value.

After this round the participants from the police was pleased with the definition and model. Thus, no more interviews were held. Instead, the model and definition was validated as presented in the next sub-section.

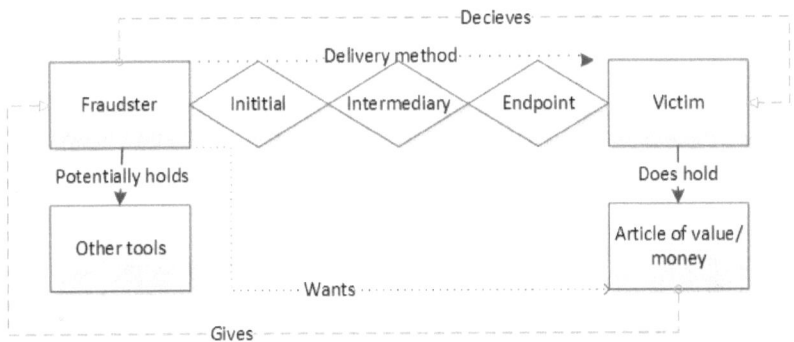

Figure 4: Final model of the process of online fraud (Authors own)

3.4   Validation

The results of this study was validated by conducting an interview with a judge from a Swedish court and by practical implementation of the definition by matching it to actions commonly referred to as online fraud schemes. The interview served to answer the following three questions:

- Q1: What is online fraud?
- Q2: What are your thought about the definition and its model?
- Q3: In what ways do you think that the definition and model can be used?

The information gathered from this interview provided the following answers to the three questions:

- Q1: The participant concluded that a fraud is a crime were a fraudster is deceiving a victim into giving him something of value.
- Q2: The interview showed that the participant thought that the model matched the definition and that the definition covered all aspects of online fraud.
- Q3: The participant said that she thought that the model could be used to explain to jurors how a specific online fraud crime was actually executed.

To summarize, this interview generated information about the model and definition that matches the information gathered in the previous steps and validated the statement that a fraud is a crime were the fraudster is deceiving a victim into giving him something of value. Further, this participant said that the model could be used as a tool to explain to jurors how a certain crime was committed – thus indicating a practical use of the model.

To further validate the correctness of the definition it was tested in real world scenarios by matching is against lists of online fraud schemes presented by IC3 (2018) and ActionFraud (2018).In total, the two sites listed 35 different schemes as online fraud schemes.

Most of the schemes used in this validation was concluded to be online frauds according to the definition. However some schemes was not considered online frauds according to the definition that we propose. This was due to the fact that they did not meet the legal criteria's to be considers fraud in Swedish legislation due to one of the following requirements for an act to be consider fraud under Swedish law (SFS1962:700, 2018):

- A fraud must involve monetary gain or include gaining something of monetary value for the fraudster and equal loss for the victim
- A fraud must involve that the victim is deceived into giving up something of value to the fraudster

This leads to that acts such as identity theft and computer intrusions cannot count as online frauds within Swedish legislation since they do not count as frauds. And given the definition that we propose, *Online fraud is a fraud where computerized tools are used for full or partial delivery of the fraud,* an act has to be a fraud to be an online fraud. However, the acts that was not considered online frauds because of this reason would have been matched by the definition of online fraud if they were considered frauds, legally.

Further, some acts were considered *possible* matches for the definition and because the description of the acts gave room for several different way of carrying them out. In these cases, the way that they was to be carried out would determine if they match the definition or not. The possible matches where the following:

- Credit card fraud: If the attacker steals the credit card it should not be considered fraud, however if the fraudster deceives the victim into giving up his credit card details it would count as online fraud.
- Nigerian letter: if sent over e-mail Nigerian letters are online frauds, however when sent over physical mail they are not.
- Phishing: phishing e-mail aimed at gaining personal information or injection malicious software into the victims computers are not online frauds. However, if phishing is used to obtain money it is considered online fraud.
- Account takeover: If an account is compromised by hacking, it is not a fraud. However if the victim is deceived into giving up the log in information to his bank account that is fraudulent.

This practical implementation of the definition shows that the definitions excludes actions that are not considered frauds by law and frauds that are not carried out online.

Also, it does include schemes that are defined as frauds and were a part of the delivery method is digital. This indicates that the definition does work in reality.

4 Conclusions

In this paper we use an action-based approach implemented by using iterative semi-structured interviews with investigators from the Swedish police to develop a definition of online fraud. We then used triangulation as suggested by Lincoln and Guba (1985) to validate our results. The validation process included an interview with a person with a different perspective and background, namely a judge from a local court. We also tested the practical use of the definition by matching it against known online frauds schemes. The outcome of this process was the following definition of online fraud:

"Online fraud is a fraud where computerized tools are used for full or partial delivery of the fraud"

This definition meets the key criteria's that for an act to count as an online fraud it has to, first and foremost, be considered a fraud. Second, what decides if the fraud is online or offline should be determined by the way that it is communicated with the victim. During the study it became evident that a fraud may be partially delivered in an online fashion and should then still be considered an online fraud, this is also covered by the definition that we propose. To further clarify the concept of online fraud we also developed a model of online fraud. The model is intended to provide an overview of the components and events that are present in an online fraud scheme. The final model is presented in Figure 4.

5 Discussion

The aim of this study was to increase the knowledge about online fraud by developing a definition and model that described the aspects of online fraud. As described in the background literature there are currently different understanding of what constitutes an online fraud and this can make it tedious to study the area. Further, as stated by the judge in the validation interview, our results can be used to explain to jurors what happened in a specific fraud case. It's easy to make the argument that it is crucial for a working justice system that jurors and laypersons understand how a crime was committed in full. Thus, as our work can contribute to a better understanding of online fraud, it also contributes to the justice system.

It should be mentioned that this study was conducted in the context of the Swedish legal system. We have taken great care to make the results generalizable in that context by implementing our results in the real world scenario and conducting interviews with a person from a different branch of the legal system than the interview participants. It is our strong belief that, since our definition is based on the legal definition of fraud, it is also applicable globally. There is, however, a need for further research in order to make that claim. As for the model, aspects of it does depend on the Swedish legal definition of frauds, namely that a fraud must include the fraudster getting something of monetary value. As such, it may be hard to use without modification in some other countries. However, the model still gives insight into the online fraud process that would be globally useful.

It should also be noted that while this study is focused at online frauds it does provide insight into online crime in a more general meaning. What is interesting, on that topic, is that several criminal activities online are not conducted by computer professionals. Rather, it appears as if traditional criminals are to a large extent making use of the Internet to commit traditional crimes in a more convenient, online manner.

6   References

ActionFraud. (2016). Alert: Watch out for Facebook Marketplace fraud. Retrieved from https://www.actionfraud.police.uk/news/alert-watch-out-for-facebook-marketplace-fraud-dec16

ActionFraud.   (2018).   Online   Fraud.   Retrieved   from https://www.actionfraud.police.uk/node/298

AFP. (2018). Online fraud and scams Retrieved from https://www.afp.gov.au/what-we-do/crime-types/cyber-crime/online-fraud-and-scams

Alnajim, A. M. (2009). *Fighting Internet Fraud: Anti-Phishing Effectiveness for Phishing Websites Dectection.* Durham University,

BRÅ. (2018). Bedrägerier och ekobrott. Retrieved from https://www.bra.se/brott-och-statistik/statistik-utifran-brottstyper/bedragerier-och-ekobrott.html

IC3. (2013). *2012 Internet Crime Report.* Retrieved from Fairmont, WV

IC3. (2018). Internet Crime Schemes. Retrieved from https://www.ic3.gov/crimeschemes.aspx

Lincoln, Y. S., & Guba, E. G. (1985). *Naturalistic inquiry* (Vol. 75): Sage.

Marimow, A. E., & Hedgpeth, D. (2016). Md. man convicted of fraud in 'Internet romance scheme'. *The Washington Post.* Retrieved from https://www.washingtonpost.com/local/public-safety/he-wooed-them-and-fleeced-them-maryland-man-convicted-of-running-online-romance-fraud-scheme/2016/05/05/24112c5e-12be-11e6-93ae-50921721165d_story.html?utm_term=.bb6fb203a73a

Polisen. (2018). It-relaterade brott - utsatt Retrieved from https://polisen.se/utsatt-for-brott/olika-typer-av-brott/it-relaterade-brott/

Pratt, T. C., Holtfreter, K., & Reisig, M. D. (2010). Routine Online Activity and Internet Fraud Targeting: Extending the Generality of Routine Activity Theory. *Journal of Research in Crime and Delinquency, 47*(3), 267-296. doi:10.1177/0022427810365903

Robson, C. (2011). Real world research: A resource for users of social research methods in applied settings 3rd edition. In: West Sussex: John Wiley & Sons.

Sarnecki, J. (2009). *Introduktion till kriminologi*: Studentlitteratur.

SBU. (2014). Utvärdering av metoder i hälso-och sjukvården: En handbok. *Stockholm: SBU–Statens beredning för medicinsk utvärdering.*

SFS1962:700. (2018). *Brottsbalk*: Sveriges Riksdag.

TechAdvisor. (2016). Microsoft phone call scam: don't be a victim. Retrieved from https://www.techadvisor.co.uk/how-to/security/microsoft-phone-scam-dont-be-victim-tech-support-call-3378798/

Human Factors in a
Computable Cybersecurity Risk Model

S. Williams[1] and D.A. Marriott[2]

[1]Defence Science and Technology Laboratory, United Kingdom
[2]Defence Science and Technology, Edinburgh, South Australia
e-mail: swilliams2@dstl.gov.uk, damian.marriott@dst.defence.gov.au

Abstract

Computable risk models are used for risk management in organisations to assess possible cybersecurity threats to the system and consider appropriate response options. These models might include humans, but usually do not contain information about how human factors have a role in information security. We describe the necessary aspects to consider when designing a framework for including human factors in a risk model, based on the example of a spear-phishing attack. Some key elements of this framework were implemented as a proof of concept using Chimera, a computable cybersecurity risk model.

Keywords

Human factors, spear-phishing, computable risk model, semantics, cybersecurity

1   Introduction

It is well understood that human factors (HF) have an important role in the information security and risk management of socio-technical systems (Schultz, 2005), although cybersecurity risk models often group humans as homologous objects in the system. This study has considered the question of how do we include (these) HF in computable risk models to ensure that appropriate security controls are used effectively to reduce cybersecurity risk and to minimise utility risk, which is disruption to the user's duties and the broader business operations. For the purposes of this study the National Institute of Standards and Technology (NIST) risk management terminology has been used where risks are a function of likelihood and impact of a threat occurring (NIST, 2012).

Previous work has considered how to dynamically calculate and balance security risk with utility risk (Billard, 2015). This study is cognisant of both security and utility risks, and is interested in how HF can affect the cybersecurity risks to a socio-technical system by affecting the likelihood and impact of threats (Aleroud et al., 2017). Similarly, security controls can be adapted for HF to ensure that all users of the system are better protected against cybersecurity threats. We aimed to integrate key aspects of the body of literature around HF in cybersecurity into a model and to demonstrate how HF can add value to a computable tool.

This paper will outline the concept and challenges faced with this task, introduce the concept of a cyber hazard and then show a proof of concept implementation of key elements in a semantic risk management tool. The implementation used to test this approach is based on Chimera, a semantic modelling and inference tool which itself is based on earlier risk management tools and methods (Chakravarthy et al., 2015).

2   Framework and challenges developing a computable model with HF

Our proposed HF risk model is a semantic ontology, which models a set of concepts and the semantic associations among them. The model includes static HF such as job role and relevant training undertaken, as well as dynamic factors (email load, for example), to improve tailoring of security controls for a system user or situation. The model tailors controls to individual needs so system users are more responsive to them, and utility threats only occur when necessary. Utility threats are threats that could disrupt the user's duties and broader business operations; these should be considered and balanced against often competing security-driven controls. A semantic ontology allows a flexible approach to the way that information is added to the model, depending on the amount of detail available in the data (i.e. the level of abstraction). New humans who interact with components already in the cyber risk model can be added in easily.

HF related to a user may influence how they respond to a cybersecurity threat. For example certain job roles involve frequent email use to initiate business relationships, so humans in these roles might be more responsive to spear-phishing emails posing as new potential clients. Our model has been developed based on the targeted phishing example as there was relevant literature available to support a good understanding of the HF involved in this threat (Sheng et al., 2010, Vishwanath et al., 2011, Pattinson et al., 2012). These include individual factors (for example visibility, suggestibility, responsiveness, culture, technical knowledge or authority), workplace-specific factors (such as workload, job role, confidence in IT security, morale, information and trust in procedures), or threat-specific factors (in the spear-phishing use case this would be email content, sender familiarity or credibility and use of persuasion tools) (Ovelgönne et al., 2017). Some factors, including workload, affect the likelihood of being exposed to a risk; whereas others, such as cybersecurity training or job role, will limit the impact of a particular threat once exposed.

We developed a framework by reviewing published literature on HF involvement in spear-phishing, then applying the measurable and relevant factors, described above, into our risk model with the appropriate level of detail.

2.1   Defining the effect size

There is a wide range of HF potentially relevant to a cybersecurity threat, which must be captured in the model. The weightings of each of the HF vary between system users, and are dynamic to situational changes. Only HF with a correlation to risk (from empirical data) are included in the model, and these are matched to a security control. Both factors which greatly influence threat likelihood or impact, and those with smaller effects, must be included in the computable HF model. Since the computable

HF model uses correlational data, it will not model a human's motivation or the underlying reasons for association of HF with susceptibility to specific cybersecurity threats. The effect size is based on empirical data, so confidence of these correlations should be communicated clearly.

HF are associated with either the whole organisation, applied to a group who work in the same organisational unit, all users of a piece of equipment, or to individual humans. The interactions between HF for different scopes must be considered for the model. However it is not possible, for many HF, to measure the effect size of each factor and compute how different combinations affect a system user's susceptibility to cybersecurity threats.

2.2 Human factor dynamic profiles

Including additional human instances and HF in the model will ensure that the organisation's diversity is captured, but it increases the model complexity. This could be managed by considering how some HF are often seen together, for example those related to a certain job role. Clustering system users into profiles, based on their HF, makes it simpler to estimate susceptibility and match controls.

A dynamic profile could be used to incorporate dynamic HF at run-time, and adapt controls to a human and the current situation. The dynamic aspect comes in by adding information about the environment, time of day or current workload. The dynamic profile is used to set a threshold for action, either to protect against general cyber risks or block a specific vulnerability to a threat. This is proportional; the threshold can change for different contexts. These profiles could be designed based on experimental data with weightings assigned based on statistical models such as linear regression, Principle Component Analysis (PCA) or clustering on real-world data sets. It is important that privacy is respected when used in an organisation, so that data which is included is limited to that which has prior consent to be collected and used in the model.

The use of dynamic profiles in our model will provide a better outcome for an organisation with a diverse workforce, by reducing users' susceptibility to cybersecurity threats through tailored controls. This simultaneously has the effect of reducing utility risks by virtue of reducing the application of blanket controls (which generally inhibit utility such as through reductions in efficiency) where the risk assessment, taking into account the HF profile, concludes they are not warranted.

2.3 Pairing with controls

Different security controls can be implemented depending on the dynamic HF profile of users involved and the environment. Controls are split into people-based and technology-based actions which are linked to design-time (modelled at a different time to the risk exposure) and run-time (at a time concurrent with the risk exposure) actions respectively. People-based controls promote enduring behaviour changes by increasing security knowledge (e.g. training relevant to identifying spear-phishing emails). Technology-based controls reduce immediate exposure to cybersecurity risks by limiting threats (e.g. increasing the sensitivity of the junk filter on incoming emails). Both types of control are deployed taking into account HF.

At present in the model, a threat is considered fully mitigated following deployment of an appropriate control; although in the future it would be better to quantify the effectiveness of a control. The model must compare the impact of combinations of controls on risk, and the impact of applying a control to a human compared to application across the entire organisation. A user's HF profile will affect how well they respond to a particular control. Further, utility risks, cost and security workarounds should be considered when choosing controls in the model.

Risk may change following a change in the dynamic HF profile, or based on feedback from a control (e.g. feedback from an online training game). Table 1 shows examples of how the default control action for a cyber hazard (see next section) can be tailored to individual needs based on their HF profile.

Cyber hazard	Default action	Adaptation to HF model
Untrustworthy attachment	Obstructive security warning for all system users	Nudging techniques (Voyer, 2015): a passive, or less obstructive, reminder for those trained
External URL	Allow click through to the hyperlink	Replace hyperlink with text for those less security aware; remove altogether for those who have failed an online security training game
Email from a known suspicious source	Move email to junk folder	Delay user interaction with the suspicious email until the next morning
Email (undetected spear-phishing)	No analysis of the email content	Flag use of Cialdini's persuasion factors for susceptible HF profiles (Cialdini, 2007)

Table 1: Control actions and adaptation to situation

2.4 Cyber hazards

In dynamic risk modelling, we differentiate between cyber hazards and cyber threats whereby a realised hazard is a circumstance or event that increases the likelihood or potential impact of a risk occurrence, but does not in itself constitute a risk occurrence. Conversely, a realised threat produces an adverse impact, i.e. risk occurrence. We do not believe this distinction between cyber hazard and threat has been made previously. Cyber hazards can indicate (and give advance warning of) a potential cyber threat. Here, hazards are steps towards or precursors of a risk occurrence and signal opportunities to apply extra caution. This application of extra caution can be regulated by HF.

Where there are hazards detected at run-time, we may only want this information to be acted upon in certain situations, for example with users that have not had cybersecurity training and are not in a technical role. The controls for hazards are less critical than for risks due to the nature of hazards being precursors to (but not actual) risk occurrences. Therefore they are open to controls which are persuasive actions, such as nudging, rather than absolute actions, such as blocking. The selection of such persuasive controls can more readily take into account HF, which has the potential to reduce security risks by HF-tailored pre-emptive controls whilst also reducing utility risks by being less absolute or even absent where users have sufficient cybersecurity awareness.

2.5 Spear-phishing example

Spear-phishing emails are a problem because actions resultant from them can lead to disruption, loss of trust and financial consequences, and these cyber threats are getting increasingly sophisticated and difficult to identify (Hong, 2012). We modelled a spear-phishing attack in the risk model framework and included HF where they fit the model requirements of being measurable and quantifiable. The attack is divided into stages which have technical control point failures and cyber hazards identified (see Figure 1). Individual and situational HF can affect a system user's susceptibility to phishing, and the persuasive measures in a phishing email may be more effective on some users depending on their HF.

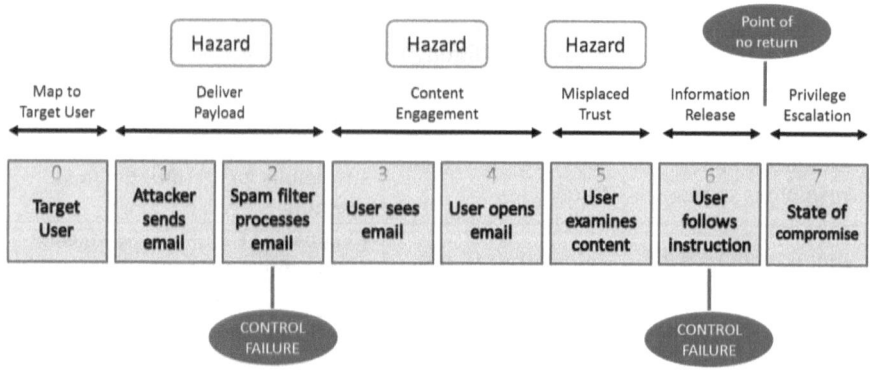

Figure 1: The stages of a spear-phishing attack

People are usually selected to receive spear-phishing emails based on being known to have access to something of interest to the attacker. Target attributes (Stage 0) can be described by visibility (online and offline), responsiveness and culture (individual, workplace, and even national) (Rocha Flores et al., 2015, Vroom and Von Solms, 2004, Butavicius et al., 2017).

After arriving into the user's inbox, different HF weightings shape whether a spear-phishing email is actually read (Stages 3-4). Some important HF include cultural factors, workload, technical knowledge, job role and confidence in IT security. The initial email properties relevant are subject, credibility, expectation and sender familiarity or authenticity, which could be computed in our risk model.

When considering email content (Stage 5), a user's responsiveness and suggestibility contribute to their perception of the motivation of the sender (Williams et al., 2017). Use of persuasion factors will change susceptibility, depending on HF such as workplace morale, emotional plea, reciprocity, social influence, urgency, credibility, training, and job role (Cialdini, 2007).

The impact of trusting a spear-phishing email, and acting on its instructions is determined by the information released (or other action such as deleting or encrypting data; Stages 6-7). HF related to the trait of compliance may influence this. It is at this stage, when information is released or other unauthorised actions are carried out on the system, that a threat is realised and there is a risk occurrence. Before that, there are a number of hazards present, e.g. when the email is processed and spooled ready for the user (Stage 2), when the email is seen and opened by the user (Stages 3-4), and when the email content is examined by the user (Stage 5). Controls may be deployed, informed by HF, at the hazard and threat stages (e.g. see Table 1).

3   Proof of concept implementation using Chimera

The Chimera tool from the UK's Defence Science & Technology Laboratory (Dstl) builds upon existing risk management tools and methods (Chakravarthy et al., 2015), security standards (e.g. RFC 4949), and uses semantic modelling and inference for automated threat determination and mitigation strategies for Information & Communications Technology (ICT) systems. Chimera takes a system design, composed of assets and their relationships, and identifies threats to the assets and suggests mitigation strategies from expert knowledge encoded in the semantic model. Here we show how Chimera can be adapted to include HF in its design-time risk management approach using a simple use case. TopBraid Composer™ (TopQuadrant™, 2018) was used to model the ontology; screen grabs below are taken directly from the tool to demonstrate SPIN rules (see Figures 3-5).

The assets and their relationships of interest in the use case are depicted in Figure 2, comprising organisations (MOD, DSTL), humans (DSTLStaff_1, DSTLStaff_2, CyberSpecialist_1, UKMilitary_1), logical and physical assets (ApacheServer_T3, IntensePC_1, TerminalService_1, PythonFlaskWebServer_S1, Snorby_1), and the relationships between them. Organisations control humans that in turn control assets. For illustrative purposes the screen grab from Chimera in Figure 2 has been manually overlaid with HF properties that have been asserted or inferred by SPIN rules as described in the following.

In order to demonstrate the implementation of HF at an organisational level, and then at an individual level, we consider cybersecurity training. The organisations and humans in the model may have a Boolean property, *hasTraining*. In our fictitious scenario, we have one organisation (MOD) which has the *hasTraining* property set to *true*, whereas for the other (DSTL) it is set to *false*. This indicates that MOD have a good cybersecurity training regime in place. These settings would be determined and set perhaps on an annual basis, i.e. essentially statically or in design time. One human (CyberSpecialist_1) has the *hasTraining* property set to *true* directly, and this would be set when the training was completed and perhaps reset if the training proficiency lapses. We have a SPIN rule in place to add at run time the *hasTraining* property from an organisation to humans it controls unless that property is set directly on a human (see Figure 3). The result of the rule for *hasTraining* on our model is that DSTLStaff 1&2 gain their organisational setting of *false*, CyberSpecialist_1 retains its existing setting of *true*, and UKMilitary_1 gains its organisational setting of *true*. That is, the more general setting is adopted in the absence of the more specific.

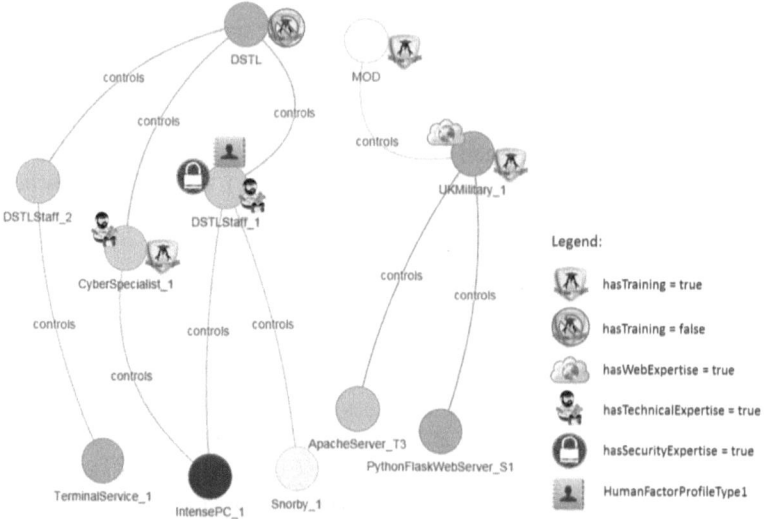

Figure 2: Chimera representation of objects and their relationships, overlaid with HF properties

```
spin:body  ▽
    CONSTRUCT {
        ?h chimera-generic:hasTraining ?ot .
    }
    WHERE {
        ?human (rdfs:subClassOf)* chimera-generic:Human .
        ?h a ?human .
        ?org (rdfs:subClassOf)* chimera-generic:Organisation .
        ?o a ?org .
        ?o chimera-generic:controls ?h .
        OPTIONAL {
            ?h chimera-generic:hasTraining ?ht .
        } .
        OPTIONAL {
            ?o chimera-generic:hasTraining ?ot .
        } .
        FILTER (!bound(?ht)) .
    }
```

Figure 3: *hasTraining* SPIN rule

spin:body ▽

```
CONSTRUCT {
    ?h chimera-generic:hasWebExpertise true .
}
WHERE {
    ?human (rdfs:subClassOf)* chimera-generic:Human .
    ?h a ?human .
    ?aserv (rdfs:subClassOf)* chimera-IATB:ApacheServer .
    ?a a ?aserv .
    ?h chimera-generic:controls ?a .
}
```

Figure 4: *hasWebExpertise* SPIN rule

The relationships between humans and assets in the model connect system users to logical and physical assets. We use the control relationships to indicate job roles from which we infer HF. For instance, there is a rule (see Figure 4) that sets the *hasWebExpertise* property to *true* for anyone who controls an Apache server (UKMilitary_1). Similarly for anyone who controls an IntensePC we set *hasTechnicalExpertise* (DSTL_Staff_1, CyberSpecialist_1), and for anyone who controls Snort or Snorby we set *hasSecurityExpertise* (DSTL_Staff_1).

A more refined model might aim to capture this kind of expertise information for individuals, however, in the absence of that data we argue that the approach above is an improvement over not taking into account these HF when considering risk analysis.

The SPIN rule in Figure 5 assigns humans to a particular HF profile if they have technical expertise and at least either security or web expertise.

spin:body ▽

```
CONSTRUCT {
    ?h a chimera-IATB:HumanFactorProfileType1 .
}
WHERE {
    ?human (rdfs:subClassOf)* chimera-generic:Human .
    ?h a ?human .
    ?h chimera-generic:hasTechnicalExpertise true .
    OPTIONAL {
        ?h chimera-generic:hasSecurityExpertise ?se .
    } .
    OPTIONAL {
        ?h chimera-generic:hasWebExpertise ?we .
    } .
    FILTER ((?se = true) || (?we = true)) .
}
```

Figure 5: Human Factor Profile SPIN rule

4   Conclusions and future work

We present the framework and an implementation for including key human factor elements in an ontology-based risk model at design time.

Others have used data-driven approaches to look at how susceptibility to cyber-attack is related to features of human behaviour, including job role (Ovelgönne et al., 2017). We are using a similar approach to tailor security controls to the user based on their

HF, to improve response to the controls and reduce utility risk. We describe the benefit of including even a small number of HF in the model to acknowledge the diversity of system users in an organisation. The HF weightings and control pairings in our model must be validated, possibly from published experimental data sets.

We have also covered concepts which are necessary for implementation in a run-time model and introduced the concept of a cyber hazard. Future work will include HF in run-time risk management using this tool. The algorithm (e.g. SPIN rules) can learn and add knowledge from previous scenarios, because a new data point is added for each change to a HF variable. There is no action until the defined threshold is reached, when an appropriate control is chosen. Our model could be used to capture the complexity of cybersecurity risk management in socio-technical systems, and current application of this model will be limited by data regulations and by information that is available about humans in the organisation.

5   Acknowledgements

We thank Sam R. & Andrew F. of the NCSC and A. Chakravarthy (Dstl) for useful discussions and help generating Figure 1.

The contents include material subject to Crown Copyright © 2018 Dstl and Commonwealth of Australia.

6   References

Aleroud, A. and Zhou, L. (2017). "Phishing environments, techniques, and countermeasures: A survey", Computers & Security, 68, pp. 160-196.

Billard, A. (2015), "Security and Utility Risk Evaluation (SURE) Framework for Dynamic Cyber Systems", DSTO-TR-3080, Defence Science and Technology, Australia.

Butavicius, M.A., Parsons, K., Pattinson, M.R., McCormac, A., Calic, D. and Lillie, M. (2017), "Understanding susceptibility to phishing emails: Assessing the impact of individual differences and culture", Proceedings of the 11th International Symposium on Human Aspects of Information Security and Assurance, pp. 12-23.

Chakravarthy, A., Chen, X., Nasser, B. and Surridge, M. (2015), "Trustworthy systems design using semantic risk modelling", 1st International Conference on Cyber Security for Sustainable Society, pp. 49-81

Cialdini, R.B. (2007), "Influence: The psychology of persuasion", New York: Collins, pp. 173-174.

Hong, J. (2012), "The state of phishing attacks", Communications of the ACM, 55(1), pp. 74-81.

NIST (2012), "Guide for conducting risk assessments", NIST SP800-30Rev1, National Institute of Standards and Technology, U.S.

Ovelgönne, M., Dumitras, T., Prakash, B.A., Subrahmanian, V.S. and Wang, B. (2017), "Understanding the Relationship between Human Behavior and Susceptibility to Cyber Attacks: A Data-Driven Approach", ACM Transactions on Intelligent Systems and Technology (TIST), 8(4), p.51.

Pattinson, M., Jerram, C., Parsons, K., McCormac, A. and Butavicius, M. (2012), "Why do some people manage phishing e-mails better than others?", Information Management & Computer Security, 20(1), pp. 18-28.

Rocha Flores, W., Holm, H., Nohlberg, M. and Ekstedt, M. (2015), "Investigating personal determinants of phishing and the effect of national culture", Information & Computer Security, 23(2), pp. 178-199.

Schultz, E. (2005), "The human factor in security", Computers & Security, 24, pp. 425-426.

Sheng, S., Holbrook, M., Kumaraguru, P., Cranor, L. F. and Downs, J. (2010), "Who falls for phish?: a demographic analysis of phishing susceptibility and effectiveness of interventions", Proceedings of the SIGCHI Conference on Human Factors in Computing Systems, ACM, pp. 373-382.

TopQuadrant™ (2018), TopBraid Composer™, https://www.topquadrant.com/tools/modeling-topbraid-composer-standard-edition/. (Accessed 24 May 2018)

Vishwanath, A., Herath, T., Chen, R., Wang, J. and Rao, H. R. (2011), "Why do people get phished? Testing individual differences in phishing vulnerability within an integrated, information processing model", Decision Support Systems, 51(3), pp. 576-586.

Voyer, B.G. (2015), "'Nudging' behaviours in healthcare: Insights from behavioural economics", British Journal of Healthcare Management, 21(3), pp. 130-135.

Vroom, C. and Von Solms, R. (2004), "Towards information security behavioural compliance", Computers & Security, 23(3), pp. 191-198.

Williams, E.J., Beardmore, A. and Joinson, A.N. (2017), "Individual differences in susceptibility to online influence: A theoretical review", Computers in Human Behavior, 72, pp.412-421.

Self-disclosing on Facebook can be Risky: Examining the Role of Trust and Social Capital

D.Calic[1], M.Brushe[2], K.Parsons[1] and C.Brittain[2]

[1]Defence Science and Technology Group, Edinburgh, South Australia
[2]School of Psychology, University of Adelaide, South Australia
e-mail: {dragana.calic; kathryn.parsons}@dst.defence.gov.au; {mary.brushe;
christopher.brittain}@student.adelaide.edu.au

Abstract

Social media has become core to our daily interactions, enabled by people's willingness to share feelings, opinions, and even the most mundane details of their lives. These self-disclosure practices raise many questions about why people disclose in such a public manner, despite the potential risks. The present study examined self-disclosure on Facebook and considered two factors that may encourage people to share more information: trust and social capital. Self-disclosure, trust and social capital have not been previously studied in combination. Trust was considered in terms of an individual's trust in Facebook, and general trust, as a personality disposition. Two types of social capital, namely, bridging and bonding, were measured. Data collection involved an online survey completed by 263 Australian Facebook users. The results showed that general trust was not related to self-disclosure on Facebook. However, trust in Facebook, as well as bridging and bonding social capital all correlated with self-disclosure on Facebook. Regression analysis revealed that bridging social capital was the only independent variable that significantly predicted self-disclosure on Facebook. This is alarming because bridging social capital could be linked to more security risks, as people are focused on the benefits of broadening their online networks, rather than the potential risks of sharing personal information with a large number of people. Findings from this research offer important insights about why people may be inclined to share information on social media, and could be useful in the communication of social media risks.

Keywords

Self-disclosure; Trust; Social capital; Facebook.

1 Introduction

Social media has an important role in today's increasingly interconnected world. Recent reports have indicated that 79% of Australians are on social media (Sensis, 2017). Social media use is premised on people sharing their personal and sensitive information, and even the most mundane details about their lives. This has motivated a plethora of research to explore why people self-disclose in such a public manner. This research is important because it enables us to better understand how people engage online, what may influence their online communication and interactions, and how these practices can lead to cybersecurity risks.

The present study focuses on self-disclosure on Facebook and considers two factors that may explain why people share information: trust and social capital. Trust is considered in terms of an individual's level of trust towards Facebook, and also general trust as a personality characteristic. Social capital is considered in terms of an individual's perceptions of their networks and resources that they may have access to as a result of their Facebook use and connections.

Self-disclosure on social media is most commonly studied in terms of the positive benefits that it may provide to the individual user (e.g., Ellison *et al.*, 2007, Maksl *et al.*, 2013, Skoric *et al.*, 2016). However, in this study, in this study we are interested in how self-disclosure can lead to cybersecurity and privacy risks. This information can be used to educate and train people about the potential risks associated with sharing personal and sensitive information on social media.

2 Background

Facebook is currently the most popular social media platform in Australia. Of 17 million monthly active Australian social media users, 12 million use Facebook daily (Cowling, 2018). The immense popularity of Facebook means that it has been the focus of the majority of social media research (Stoycheff *et al.*, 2017).

Although a number of studies have considered self-disclosure, trust and social capital, no study to date has considered these three constructs in combination. For example, decades of research in face-to-face settings have established that trust is a key factor in building social capital (Putnam, 2000). More recently, trust has been linked to individuals' willingness to self-disclose online (Chang *et al.*, 2014, Taddei *et al.*, 2013). Social capital has been conceptualised as a benefit of Facebook use (Ellison *et al.*, 2007, Liu *et al.*, 2016), and self-disclosure is, for the most part, an essential function of using Facebook. This research explores a potential relationship between trust in the social media platform (i.e., the extent to which people perceive Facebook as a trusted social media platform), trust as a personality characteristic (i.e., the extent to which some people are just more trusting), self-disclosure, and social capital. Throughout the following sections, we define the three constructs, and provide a brief overview of relevant research.

2.1   Main constructs: Self-disclosure, trust and social capital

Self-disclosure refers to the process by which an individual voluntarily discloses personal information to others (Cozby, 1973). Given that the most common motivation for using Facebook is the desire to maintain close contact with family and friends (Abramova *et al.*, 2017, Joinson, 2008, Skoric *et al.*, 2016), the majority of social media users will disclose personal information to strengthen these relationships (Maksl *et al.*, 2013, Skoric *et al.*, 2016). Online self-disclosure has been associated with improved well-being, opportunities to maintain relationships with absent friends, as well as ways to establish new friendships and find support (e.g., Abramova *et al.*, 2017, Ellison *et al.*, 2007, Taddei *et al.*, 2013). However, self-disclosure may lead to negative outcomes, such as exposure to inappropriate content, scams, and privacy issues (e.g.,

Abramova *et al.*, 2017, Brittain *et al.*, 2017, Christofides *et al.*, 2012, De Zwart *et al.*, 2012, Parsons *et al.*, 2016).

For the purposes of this research, ***trust*** is considered in two distinct ways: general trust as a personality disposition, and the extent to which an individual trusts a particular product or service. Trust as a personality disposition is a general propensity or willingness to trust others (Mayer *et al.*, 1995). Trust has been broadly defined as "willingness to be vulnerable, based on positive expectations about the actions of others" (Bos *et al.*, 2002, Mayer *et al.*, 1995). Trust in a product or service implies that consumers believe that the product or service providers can keep their promises and act in responsible ways (Devos *et al.*, 2002). This study considers an individual's trust in Facebook as a product or service.

It is generally agreed that the development of ***social capital*** is one of the key benefits of social media use (Burke *et al.*, 2011, Ellison *et al.*, 2007), and may be key to understanding why people share information on social media, in spite of the risks. Putnam (2000) conceptualised two distinct forms of social capital: bridging and bonding social capital. Bridging social capital refers to the capacity to access resources, through a wide variety of social relationships and networks. It is derived from socially weak ties that connect individuals to people of different lifestyles and backgrounds (Granovetter, 1973).

On a social media platform like Facebook, bridging social capital can be found within Facebook friends who are co-workers or classmates. These individuals can provide useful information, link people to new ideas, perspectives and opportunities. From a security perspective, people with greater bridging social capital are likely to be exposed to more cybersecurity risks, as they are likely to be more focused on the immediate benefits of creating links rather than the potential future risks of sharing their personal information with a larger number of people. Connecting with a large number of weak ties can expose individuals to increased risk of cybercrime and identity theft, which can translate into real world threats such as theft, stalking and damage to reputation (Brittain *et al.*, 2017, Ramsey *et al.*, 2010). Bonding social capital involves more sustained support from individuals who share strong, intimate ties and reciprocal relationships, such as family and close friends.

2.2 Previous research: Self-disclosure, trust and social capital

Online self-disclosure has been shown to be related to both general trust (Frye *et al.*, 2010, Parsons *et al.*, 2016, Tait *et al.*, 2015), and trust in online providers (Chang *et al.*, 2014, Taddei *et al.*, 2013). Tait *et al.* (2015) found that trust and extraversion predicted self-disclosure, and revealed that participants who reported a greater propensity to trust were more likely to disclose information about their home location, family, and place of birth. Comparably, Chang *et al.* (2014) found that trust in Facebook predicted self-disclosure of basic information (e.g., gender, current city), and sensitive information (e.g., email, profile picture, birthdate), but no relationship was found for highly sensitive information (e.g., phone numbers, religious views, address).

Previous research on the relationship between self-disclosure and social capital has been inconsistent. For example, Liu et al. (2014) found that self-disclosure was significantly and directly related to bridging social capital but was not associated with bonding social capital. Conversely, Maksl et al. (2013) found that perceptions of bridging and bonding social capital on Facebook predicted overall comfort levels with sharing personal information. More recently, Liu et al. (2016) conducted a meta-analysis examining over 50 studies which explored the relationships between how people use social media, and bridging and bonding social capital. While they found that using social media contributes to development of both bridging and bonding social capital, it was more strongly associated with bridging social capital than with bonding social capital.

2.3   The present study

The primary aim of this study was to investigate self-disclosure on Facebook and how it relates to people's trust in Facebook as a platform, their general trust as a personality disposition, and perceptions of their social capital. Specific research questions and hypotheses were:

Hypothesis 1a: Respondents who have higher levels of trust in Facebook will be more likely to self-disclose on Facebook compared to those who have a lower level of trust in Facebook.

Hypothesis 1b: Individuals who are more trusting in general will be more likely to self-disclose on Facebook compared to those who have a lower level of general trust.

Research Question 1: What is the relationship between self-disclosure and bridging and bonding social capital?

Research Question 2: To what extent can trust and social capital explain why people self-disclose?

3   Method

Data collection involved an online survey, administered through the web-based platform Qualtrics. Participants were recruited through an undergraduate psychology student pool who gained course credit for participation, and also by advertising on researchers' Facebook pages. The survey included a set of demographic questions and validated psychometric instruments to measure the constructs of interest.

3.1   Participants

To take part in the study, participants had to be over the age of 18, have an active Facebook account and be fluent English speakers. The survey was completed by 263 participants (96 (36.5%) male, 163 (62.0%) female, and 4 (1.5%) did not specify their gender). The sample was well represented in terms of age and education levels. Although 40% of the sample was aged between 20 and 24, other age categories were well represented (i.e., 15% were under 20 years of age, 18% were 25-29, 14% were

30-39, 8% were 40-49, and 5% were in the 50 years and over category). In terms of education level, the sample was also well distributed across the different categories. The majority of participants had either completed an undergraduate (i.e., 32%) degree or were undertaking an undergraduate degree (i.e., 30%). Four percent had not completed high school, and 13% had completed a postgraduate university degree.

3.2 Measures

3.2.1 Self-disclosure

The self-disclosure measure was based on Parsons *et al.* (2016) and Brittain *et al.* (2017), and combined a measure of *self-disclosure behaviour* (i.e., information that people share) with a measure of *privacy behaviours* (i.e., a behavioural checklist of what individuals specifically do to protect their privacy on Facebook). This combined measure had a Cronbach's alpha of .81. Specifically, these factors were measured in the following way:

- *Self-disclosure behaviour* was measured using two subscales from Seidman's Self-Presentation Scale (Seidman, 2013). The Belongingness Behaviours-Communication subscale (Cronbach's α = .76) consists of two items asking participants to indicate their frequency of posting and commenting on other's content (e.g., status, timeline). The Self-Presentational Behaviours subscale (Cronbach's α = .85) consists of six items, and asks participants to indicate how frequently they post particular content about their life and events (e.g., photos, profile information, status). Both subscales were measured on a 7-point Likert scale (from 1 = never to 7 = all of the time).

- To measure *privacy behaviours* participants were presented with a checklist to capture what types of specific information (e.g., work place, phone number, date of birth, email, address) they disclosed and to whom (i.e., Don't Know, Only Me, Friends, Friends of Friends or Everyone) (Cronbach's α = .85).

3.2.2 Trust

Trust in Facebook is a four item measure developed by Chang *et al.* (2014). It focuses on understanding the extent to which users believe that Facebook is a trustworthy platform which will protect their privacy. The measure uses a 7-point Likert scale (1 = strongly disagree to 7 = strongly agree), and the Cronbach's alpha in the current study was .93.

Generalised Trust Scale assesses trust as a personality disposition in regards to an individual's trust in both generalised others (Generalised Trust) and romantic partners (Partner Trust) (Couch *et al.*, 1996). For this study, we assessed Generalised Trust, measured on 20 items using a 7-point Likert scale (1 = strongly disagree to 7 = strongly agree). The Cronbach's alpha was .81.

3.2.3   Social capital

Social Capital Scale (Ellison *et al.*, 2014), adapted from Williams (2006), has two sub-constructs: bridging and bonding social capital. *Bridging social capital* sub-scale has nine items and measures the degree to which people perceive they can access diverse ideas and a broader community through their social network. *Bonding social capital* sub-scale measures the degree to which an individual can receive meaningful support and help from their close social network. Each scale consists of nine items measured on a 7-point Likert scale (1 = strongly disagree to 7 = strongly agree). Cronbach's alphas were .87 and .84 for bridging and bonding social capital, respectively.

4   Results

Preliminary testing was conducted to inspect the data in preparation for analysis. Inspection of the distribution indicated that the data was only slightly positively skewed, with no major violations to the assumptions of normality.

Pearson's two-tailed correlation was performed to explore the relationship between the constructs. The results of the analysis and the main descriptive statistics are displayed in Table 1.

Constructs	M (SD)	1	2	3	4	5
1. Self-Disclosure	45.30 (10.22)	-	.162**	-.002	.362**	.192**
2. Trust in Facebook	14.07 (5.27)		-	.214**	.301**	.164**
3. General Trust	96.86 (11.94)			-	.006	.214**
4. Bridging Social Capital	42.69 (9.26)				-	.300**
5. Bonding Social Capital	43.52 (9.64)					-

$** p < .001$

Table 1: Pearson's two-tailed correlations matrix for Self-disclosure on Facebook, General trust, and Social capital ($N = 263$)

4.1   Self-disclosure and trust

There was a small, significant positive correlation ($r = .162$, $p < .001$) between self-disclosure and trust in Facebook. This means that, in support of hypothesis 1a, individuals who reported higher levels of trust in Facebook may be more likely to self-disclose compared to those with lower levels of trust in Facebook. However, no significant relationship was found between individuals who were more trusting in general and their self-disclosure on Facebook ($r = -.002$, $p > .05$). Therefore, hypothesis 1b was not supported.

4.2 Self-disclosure and social capital

There was a significant positive correlation between *bridging* social capital and self-disclosure ($r = .36$, $p < .001$). This indicates that the more individuals perceive they can access diverse ideas and a broader community through their Facebook network, the more likely they are to self-disclose. Similarly, there was a small significant positive correlation with *bonding* social capital ($r = .19$, $p < .001$), suggesting that the more individuals perceived they can receive meaningful support from their social network, the more likely they may be to self-disclose. These results address Research Question 1.

4.3 Self-disclosure, trust and social capital

As shown in Table 2, a multiple regression analysis was conducted to investigate the extent to which trust in Facebook and social capital can explain why people self-disclose on Facebook (addressing Research Question 2). Given that general trust did not correlate with self-disclosure, it was not included in regression analysis (refer to Table 1). Bridging social capital, bonding social capital, and trust in Facebook explained approximately 13% of the variance in self-disclosure on Facebook. The analysis also revealed that *bridging social capital* was the only variable that significantly predicted self-disclosure.

Variable	*β(standardised)*	*t*	*p*
$F_{(3,259)} = 14.18$, adjusted $R^2 = .131**$			
Trust in Facebook	.052	.85	.396
Bridging Social Capital	.320	5.11**	<.001
Bonding Social Capital	.088	1.44	.150

** $p < .001$

Table 2 Summary of the multiple regression analysis predicting Self-Disclosure: Trust in Facebook, Bridging and Bonding Social Capital (N = 263)

5   Discussion

This study explored why people share on Facebook. It considered two factors that may explain people's self-disclose practices: trust and social capital. Unlike a lot of previous research, which has most commonly focussed on the potential benefits of self-disclosure on social media (e.g., Ellison *et al.*, 2007, Maksl *et al.*, 2013, Skoric *et al.*, 2016), in this study, we explored the findings in terms of potential cybersecurity and privacy risks.

We found that trust in Facebook was related to self-disclosure on Facebook (Hypothesis 1a), indicating that people who reported higher levels of trust in Facebook may be more likely to self-disclose on Facebook compared to those with lower levels of trust in Facebook. This is in line with previous research which also found that users who believed that Facebook is a trustworthy platform were more likely to share their information on Facebook (Chang *et al.*, 2014, Mesch, 2012). This may be attributed to platforms such as Facebook focusing on creating a sense of trust by, for example, enabling users to modify and "control" their privacy settings, and thus encouraging them to share even more information. Efforts to reduce security threats should focus on increasing awareness of this, to ensure people recognise the potential risks of sharing personal and sensitive information, regardless of their security settings. However, it is important to note that the present study was conducted prior to the Cambridge Analytica data breach scandal, and the number of people who trust Facebook to protect their privacy has dropped significantly since the scandal (Kanter, 2018). It is therefore important to replicate our research to assess how this potential drop in trust will influence the relationship with self-disclosure on Facebook, and other social media platforms.

We also investigated if people who are more trusting in general would be more likely to self-disclose on Facebook (Hypothesis 1b). This hypothesis was not supported, and this is in line with previous research (Frye *et al.*, 2010, Mesch, 2012). However, our finding is inconsistent with research by Joinson *et al.* (2010) and Tait *et al.* (2015). A likely explanation for this inconsistency could be attributed to the use of different self-disclosure and trust measures. For example, Tait *et al.* (2015) measured self-disclosure using four items from the International Personality Item Pool (IPIP), and may not have sufficiently captured the complexity of the construct.

Although Maksl *et al.* (2013) found that perceptions of bridging and bonding social capital predicted comfort levels with sharing personal information, our results are consistent with the findings of, who found only bridging social capital to be associated with self-disclosure on social media. This finding is also in line with a recent meta-analysis, which revealed that using social media was more strongly associated with bridging social capital than with bonding social capital (Liu *et al.*, 2016).

From a cybersecurity and privacy perspective, this is an interesting and potentially alarming finding. Bridging social capital is likely to be linked to more cybersecurity risks, as people are more focused on the immediate benefits of creating links and broadening their networks, rather than the potential future risks of sharing their personal information with a larger number of people. This is in line with previous research (Brittain *et al.*, 2017, Christofides *et al.*, 2012, De Zwart *et al.*, 2012).

5.1 Limitations and future directions

In this study, trust and social capital explained approximately 13% of the variance in self-disclosure. Although this contribution was statistically significant, it highlights the importance of examining additional variables in future studies that may help to explain why people share on social media. It is only by understanding the reasons for self-disclosure that we can hope to educate and train people about the potential risks.

It is also important to note that, although a reasonably large sample size was obtained, and although the participants were not sourced solely from undergraduate student population, the results may not be generalisable to the entire Australian population. A further limitation of this study is that it relied on self-report, and as a result, responses may have been subjected to the social desirability bias. This study attempted to overcome this by including a behavioural measure of self-disclosure. Nevertheless, a more objective assessment of individuals' self-disclosure that could be used in future research would be to analyse participants' social media accounts.

6 Conclusion

As social media continues to permeate people's daily lives, more research needs to explore if and how people engage online, what may influence their online communication and interactions, and how these practices can lead to cybersecurity risks. The current study builds upon past work to examine the relationship between self-disclosure, trust and social capital on Facebook. By having a better understanding of why people share personal and sensitive information on social media, we will be better able to educate people about the potential risks associated with self-disclosure on social media.

We found that general trust was not related to self-disclosure on Facebook; however, trust in Facebook was. Both bridging and bonding social capital were related to self-disclosure on Facebook. However, bridging social capital was the only independent variable that significantly predicted self-disclosure on Facebook. This highlights the importance of education efforts focusing on the potential risks associated with connecting to a large number of users. While this practice has the benefit of increasing bridging social capital, it also increases the number and severity of cybersecurity risks that individuals are exposed to.

7 References

Abramova, O., Wagner, A., Krasnova, H. and Buxmann, P. (2017), "Understanding Self-Disclosure on Social Networking Sites-A Literature Review", Twenty-third Americas Conference on Information Systems, Boston.

Bos, N., Olson, J., Gergle, D., Olson, G. and Wright, Z. (2002), "Effects of four computer-mediated communications channels on trust development", ACM Conference on Human Factors and Computing Systems, CHI Letters, ACM.

Brittain, C., Parsons, K., Calic, D. and Brushe, M. (2017), "'Anti'-social media: Narcissism and self-control as predictors of Facebook self-disclosure", Australasian Conference on Information Systems (ACIS), Hobart, Australia.

Burke, M., Kraut, R. and Marlow, C. (2011), "Social capital on Facebook: Differentiating uses and users", Proceedings of the SIGCHI Conference on Human Factors in Computing Systems, Vancouver, BC, Canada, New York: ACM Press.

Chang, C.-W. and Heo, J. (2014), "Visiting theories that predict college students' self-disclosure on Facebook", *Computers in Human Behavior,* Vol. 30, pp 79-86.

Christofides, E., Muise, A. and Desmarais, S. (2012), "Risky disclosures on Facebook: The effect of having a bad experience on online behavior", *Journal of Adolescent Research,* Vol. 27, No. 6, pp 714-731.

Couch, L. L., Adams, J. M. and Jones, W. H. (1996), "The assessment of trust orientation", *Journal of Personality Assessment,* Vol. 67, pp 305-323.

Cowling, D. (2018), Social Media Statistics Australia – January 2018. SocialMediaNews.

Cozby, P. C. (1973), "Self-disclosure: a literature review", *Psychological Bulletin,* Vol. 79, No. 2, pp 73-91.

De Zwart, M., Henderson, M., Lindsay, D. and Phillips, M. (2012), "Legal risks of social media", *Legaldate,* Vol. 24, No. 1, pp 8-9.

Devos, T., Spini, D. and Schwartz, S. H. (2002), "Conflicts among human values and trust in institutions", *British Journal of Social Psychology,* Vol. 41, No. 4, pp 481-494.

Ellison, N. B., Gray, R., Lampe, C. and Fiore, A. T. (2014), "Social capital and resource requests on Facebook", *New Media & Society,* Vol. 16, No. 7, pp 1104-1121.

Ellison, N. B., Steinfield, C. and Lampe, C. (2007), "The benefits of Facebook "friends:" Social capital and college students' use of online social network sites", *Journal of Computer-Mediated Communication,* Vol. 12, No. 4, pp 1143-1168.

Frye, N. E. and Dornisch, M. M. (2010), "When is trust not enough? The role of perceived privacy of communication tools in comfort with self-disclosure", *Computers in Human Behavior,* Vol. 26, No. 5, pp 1120-1127.

Granovetter, M. S. (1973), "The strength of weak ties", *American journal of sociology,* Vol. 78, No. 6, pp 1360-1380.

Joinson, A. N. (2008), "Looking at, looking up or keeping up with people? Motives and use of Facebook", Proceedings of the SIGCHI conference on Human Factors in Computing Systems, New York, ACM.

Joinson, A. N., Reips, U.-D., Buchanan, T. and Schofield, C. B. P. (2010), "Privacy, Trust, and Self-Disclosure Online", *Human-Computer Interaction,* Vol. 25, pp 1-24.

Kanter, J. (2018), Trust in Facebook has spectacularly nosedived after its enormous data breach. Business Insider Australia.

Liu, D., Ainsworth, S. E. and Baumeister, R. F. (2016), "A Meta-Analysis of Social Networking Online and Social Capital", *Review of General Psychology,* Vol. 20, No. 4, pp 369–391.

Liu, D. and Brown, B. B. (2014), "Self-disclosure on social networking sites, positive feedback, and social capital among Chinese college students", *Computers in Human Behavior,* Vol. 38, pp 213-219.

Maksl, A. and Young, R. (2013), "Affording to exchange: Social capital and online information sharing", *Cyberpsychology, Behavior, and Social Networking,* Vol. 16, No. 8, pp 588-592.

Mayer, R. C., Davis, J. H. and Schoorman, F. D. (1995), "An integrative model of organizational trust", *Academy of management review,* Vol. 20, No. 3, pp 709-734.

Mesch, G. S. (2012), "Is online trust and trust in social institutions associated with online disclosure of identifiable information online?", *Computers in Human Behavior,* Vol. 28, No. 4, pp 1471-1477.

Parsons, K., Calic, D. and Barca, C. (2016), "Self-Disclosure on Facebook: Comparing two Research Organisations", Australian Conference of Information Systems (ACIS), Wollongong, Australia.

Putnam, R. D. (2000), *Bowling Alone*. New York, Simon & Schuster.

Ramsey, G. and Venkatesan, S. (2010), "Cybercrime strategy for social networking and other online platforms", *Licensing Journal,* Vol. 30, No. 7, pp 23-27.

Seidman, G. (2013), "Self-presentation and belonging on Facebook: How personality influences social media use and motivations", *Computers in Human Behavior,* Vol. 54, pp 402-407.

Sensis (2017), Sensis Social Media Report 2017, Sensis.

Skoric, M. M., Zhu, Q., Goh, D. and Pang, N. (2016), "Social media and citizen engagement: A meta-analytic review", *New Media & Society,* Vol. 18, No. 9, pp 1817-1839.

Stoycheff, E., Liu, J., Wibowo, K. A. and Nanni, D. P. (2017), "What have we learned about social media by studying Facebook? A decade in review", *New Media & Society,* Vol. 19, No. 6, pp 968-980.

Taddei, S. and Contena, B. (2013), "Privacy, trust and control: Which relationships with online self-disclosure?", *Computers in Human Behavior,* Vol. 29, pp 821-826.

Tait, S. and Jeske, D. (2015), "Hello stranger! Trust and self-disclosure effects on online information sharing", *International Journal of Cyber Behavior, Psychology and Learning,* Vol. 5, No. 1, pp 42-55.

Williams, D. (2006), "On and Off the 'Net: Scales for Social Capital in an Online Era", *Journal of Computer-Mediated Communication,* Vol. 11, pp 593-628.

Investigating the Knowledge-Behaviour Gap in Mitigating Personal Information Compromise

J. Scott and J. Ophoff

Dept. of Information Systems, University of Cape Town, Cape Town, South Africa
e-mail: SCTJAS002@myuct.ac.za; jacques.ophoff@uct.ac.za

Abstract

In response to information threats users instinctively increase security measures, such as firewalls and anti-virus software. However, users do not give enough attention to their behaviour, more specifically, their security behavioural practices. This paper proposes that the knowledge-behaviour gap affects a user's security behavioural practices and this, in effect, threatens personal information security. The knowledge-behaviour gap assesses why users do not put their information security and privacy knowledge into practice. The Information-Motivation-Behavioural Skills Model is used to highlight the different factors which affect the knowledge-behaviour gap, with empirical data collected using an online survey. Despite the wide conformity of opinions within literature, a key finding of this research is that users' awareness of information security threats has an insignificant effect on their self-reported preventive behaviour. The significance of this finding is that users require a deeper technical understanding of information security threats to engage in effective preventive behaviour.

Keywords

Information Security; Personal Information Compromise; Behavioural Skills; Motivation; Preventive Behaviour; Knowledge-Behaviour Gap; Information-Motivation-Behavioural (IMB) Skills Model

1   Introduction

There are numerous online threats to users' personal information. In recent years, privacy breaches have also risen at an unprecedented rate; each year approximately 700 privacy breaches are publicly reported in the United States (Fortier & Burkell, 2015). In response to these attacks users instinctively add security measures, but the effectiveness of these measures depends on self-efficacy to ensure that they are not bypassed. The ability to configure and use security measures correctly is often overlooked but is a vital factor in mitigating personal information risks.

It has been shown that knowledge is a predictor of security behaviour (Parsons et al., 2014). The wider the gap between users' information security and privacy knowledge, and their behaviour, the more likely they are to fall victim to personal information attacks, such as identity theft (Crossler & Belanger, 2017). Crossler and Belanger also suggest that a knowledge-belief gap affects how users engage in security and privacy behaviours, thus affecting the broader knowledge-behaviour gap. The primary research question to be addressed in this study is: *How does the knowledge-behaviour gap affect user behaviour associated with the mitigation of personal information* compromise? This study uses the Information-Motivation-Behavioural (IMB) Skills Model as a theoretical framework to examine the knowledge-belief gap.

The remainder of this paper is structured as follows. First a review of relevant literature leads to the development of our research hypotheses. Next the research methodology is briefly explained. Data analysis and a discussion of the results follow. Lastly a summary and ideas for future work are given.

2   Background

Users have distinct levels of knowledge of security and privacy threats. In addition, "what an individual thinks he can do may be different from what the individual's actual knowledge is" (Crossler & Belanger, 2017, p. 4075). This describes the essence of the knowledge-belief gap. To protect oneself against personal information threats, users should want to protect themselves as well as have the necessary skills to do so.

If users do not have the knowledge to protect their personal information, they put themselves at a greater risk of identity and information theft. Moreover, even if users believe to have high competency in the use of technology, they still need actual knowledge to take the necessary steps to engage in a preventive behaviour. Therefore, the greater the disparity between users' actual and perceived knowledge, the more likely they are to put their personal information at risk. This is because their actual skills do not align with what they require to protect their information (Crossler & Belanger, 2017). Simply listing what to do and what not to do regarding security and privacy behaviour has a limited impact on security measures; both perceived and actual behaviour must be considered to implement effective security measures (Rhee et al., 2009).

2.1   Knowledge and Beliefs

When one assesses the 'knowledge' aspect of the knowledge-belief gap, a user's information/awareness of potential security threats and their consequences are considered. This is defined as, "both behaviour-related information and 'myths/heuristics that permit automatic or cognitively effortless behaviour-related decision-making" (Chang et al., 2014, p. 173). Considering the IMB model's link between information and motivation it can be argued that if users possess more information about security threats they should be more motivated to engage in preventive behaviour. This is because the user will be more aware of the severity of information attacks (Crossler & Belanger, 2017). When one assesses the 'belief' aspect of the knowledge-belief gap, a user's perceived confidence at performing a behaviour (self-efficacy), is assessed. Perceived behavioural skills, along with actual skills, are necessary to enact a preventive behaviour (Crossler & Belanger, 2017).

Security of devices such as mobiles and personal computers have become essential as users use these assets in their daily operations. As people are sharing more information on these mobile devices, threats to personal information are multiplying. Often, this is due to users not understanding the consequences of sharing this information (Steijn &

Vedder, 2015). Users might be aware that securing their mobile devices is important, but in many cases, they do not know how to implement this security effectively leaving their devices vulnerable to threats (Miller, 2017).

Privacy breaches can be understood as disclosure of information without consent, and this disclosure can be both intentional and unintentional. Privacy issues have become a major consequence of the 'information age', as users are faced with a trade-off between better service delivery, and the privacy that they need to sacrifice to obtain the improvement in service (Norberg et al., 2007). This sacrifice relates greatly to the users' level of information/awareness in relation to information privacy (Macada & Luciano, 2010).

2.2   Motivation

As security and privacy measures often involve costs (e.g. decreased usability) it may be necessary to motivate users to perform desired actions. These approaches will be specific to users and their personal objectives. Motivation can be organized into two paradigms; intrinsic and extrinsic (Yoo et al., 2012). Intrinsic motivation refers to behaviour which cannot be linked to external outcomes, suggesting that engagement in certain activities is done to provide satisfaction or fulfilment and that the user is inherently interested in the task. Extrinsic motivation is driven by external rewards or performing the activity to avoid negative consequences. Many users are extrinsically motivated to engage in security practices, as they try to avoid personal information threats (Yoo et al., 2012). In these cases, the negative consequences of attacks on personal information motivate users to exercise a preventive behaviour (Wall & Lowry, 2013).

2.3   Self-Efficacy and Behavioural Skills

Self-efficacy is a performance-based measure of perceived capability and is defined as "people's judgments of their capabilities to organize and execute courses of action required to attain designated performances" (Choi et al., 2013, p. 10). Self-efficacy has been a major focal point in evaluating perceived skills and relates to the beliefs that users have about those skills. Research that has been conducted on security and privacy has found that self-efficacy plays a leading role in the regulation and motivation of preventive behaviour, as users' perception of their technical skills affects their level of engagement with technology (Crossler & Belanger, 2017). It leads to positive emotions and cognitions as users feel more confident with their ability to protect their information (Schunk, 1995). This confidence creates the motivation to comply with security policies, as users believe that they have a better understanding of the security risks that they face (Wall & Lowry, 2013).

Users have perceptions of their security and privacy skills that have been impacted by past experiences and assessments. Self-efficacy beliefs determine how much time users will devote to setbacks, or how long they will persevere to overcome these setbacks (Bandura et al., 2003). The greater users' perception of their skills and knowledge, the more likely they are to engage in a preventive behaviour and thus reduce the knowledge-behaviour gap. This is because the user becomes more aware of the negative consequences associated with potential security threats.

2.4   Information-Motivation-Behavioural Skills Model

The IMB model has been a significant tool in explaining health-related behaviour but has not been widely used to investigate security preventive behaviour (Crossler & Belanger, 2017). Its usage is applicable in the information security and privacy area, as it is also being used to investigate the nature of users' choices to engage in a behaviour. As shown in Figure 1, the model's constructs include *information*, *motivation*, and *behavioural skills*, which are required to engage in *preventive behaviour* (Chang et al., 2014). Using the model, we theorise that preventive behaviour encompasses users' information/awareness of information security threats, their motivation to engage in a security practice, and both the actual and perceived behavioural skills that they possess. To the extent that users are well informed, motivated to act, and possess the requisite behavioural skills, it is probable that they will experience positive security outcomes (Fisher et al., 2003).

According to the IMB model, information is a prerequisite for enacting certain behaviour. This includes information about security threats, behaviour-related information about effective preventive measures, and policies or informal rules to aid in decision-making. In the case of information security and privacy, this would be all the preventive information regarding how to protect oneself online, the types of security threats, and the effects of these threats. Users who are mindful of information security and privacy have a more positive view on engaging in security mechanisms, and this attitude generally leads to compliance intentions (Crossler & Belanger, 2017).

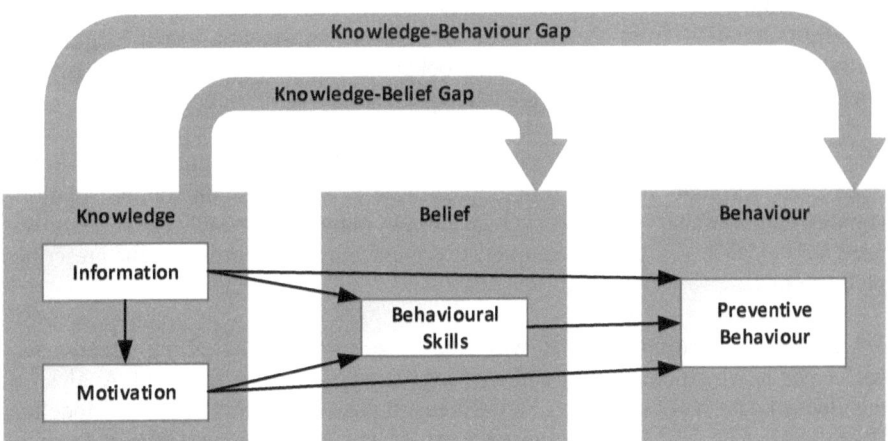

Figure 1: IMB Model Constructs and Knowledge Gaps

Motivation refers to how driven users are to adopt information security and privacy behaviour, and how likely it is for them to continue this behaviour for a prolonged period. Finally, users require specific behavioural skills to increase the likelihood of them engaging in security and privacy behaviour. From this the following hypotheses are derived:

> H1: Information (knowledge) about security and privacy threats will have a positive effect on self-reported preventive behaviour.

> H2: Motivation to perform security- and privacy-related practices will have a positive effect on self-reported preventive behaviour.

> H3: Behavioural skills (self-efficacy) will have a positive effect on self-reported preventive behaviour.

> H4: Information about security and privacy threats will have a positive effect on motivation.

> H5: Information about security and privacy threats will have a positive effect on behavioural skills.

> H6: Motivation to perform security- and privacy-related practices will have a positive effect on behavioural skills.

3 Methodology

The study adopted a positivist research philosophy, using a quantitative method to collect data. A survey strategy using a questionnaire was used to collect data about participants in a systematic manner. Questions for each of the IMB constructs were adopted from previous studies: behavioural skills (self-efficacy) from Rhee et al. (2009); motivation from Belanger et al. (2017); information (knowledge) from Bulgurcu et al. (2010); and preventive behaviour from Dupuis et al. (2016). All questions used a 7-point Likert scale (strongly disagree to strongly agree).

The survey was created and managed in Qualtrics (http://qualtrics.com/) and distributed through Prolific (https://prolific.ac/) which is an online platform connecting researchers and participants. Simple random (probability) sampling was used. Participants were paid to complete the questionnaire, according to the prescribed platform rates.

To ensure the resulting dataset was free of errors a data-cleaning process was performed in which incomplete and unengaged responses were removed. Analysis of the cleaned data was done using Partial Least Square Structural Equation Modelling (PLS-SEM). PLS-SEM is "an ordinary least squares (OLS) regression-based method which uses available data to estimate the path relationships in the model" (Hair et al., 2013, p. 14). The approach is suitable for validating predictive models. The SmartPLS 3 (https://www.smartpls.com/) software was used for analysis.

4   Data Analysis and Discussion

A total of 267 questionnaire responses were received. 18 responses were removed during the data-cleaning process. The final dataset consisted of 249 valid responses which was split 42% (n=105) male, 57% (n=143) female, and one preferring not to answer. The age distribution was positively skewed with most respondents being between the ages of 26 and 35 years old (n=102), followed by respondents between the ages of 36-45 years old (n=51). A single question regarding the respondent's knowledge of computers and IT was asked using a 7-point scale, with 34% self-reporting that their IT knowledge was Above Average, followed by Average (24%), and Good (19%). Only two respondents had a self-perception that their IT knowledge was Poor. The reported mean was 4.76, indicating that generally respondents perceived their IT knowledge to be average. The assumption is therefore that respondents have a basic understanding of information security threats.

4.1   Analysis of the Measurement Model

The IMB model used in this study consists of both reflective and formative constructs. Information, Motivation, and Behavioural Skills are reflective constructs, whereas Self-Reported Preventive Behaviour is a formative construct. "Reflective measurement models are assessed on their internal consistency reliability and validity. The criteria for reflective measurement models cannot be universally applied to formative measurement models" (Hair et al., 2014, p. 98). Therefore, different evaluation techniques were used to assess the results of these constructs.

As recommended, reflective indicators which had an outer loading of less than 0.40 were removed (Hair et al., 2014). Regarding internal consistency reliability all constructs were above the recommended composite reliability threshold (0.70). Regarding convergent validity the average variance extracted (AVE) for variables were above the recommended threshold (0.50). Finally, discriminant validity was measured using the heterotrait-monotrait (HTMT) ratio of correlations, which showed that all variables were below the 0.90 threshold. All model evaluation criteria were met, providing support for the measures' reliability and validity.

Formative measurement constructs were assessed using three steps: establishing construct validity through factor analysis, examining any collinearity issues, and significance of path coefficients. In this process two measurement items were removed, after which tests showed satisfactory results.

4.2   Analysis of the Structural Model

The structural model was tested to estimate the path coefficients, which calculates the strength of the relationships between variables. The coefficients of determination (R^2) values were estimated to determine the variance explained by the independent variables. The analysis shows that 55.9% of the variation in Behavioural Skills can be explained by the variation in Information and Motivation. Similarly, 21.1% of the variation in Motivation can be explained by the variation in Information. Finally,

64.7% of the variation in Self-Reported Preventive Behaviour can be explained by the variation in Information, Motivation, and Behavioural Skills. Compared to previous studies in information security with similar variables, the values show a medium to high effect size.

Bootstrapping with 5,000 samples (recommended by Hair et al., 2014) was used to test the significance of the structural paths (hypotheses). The bootstrapping results show that, except for H1, all hypotheses are supported. The PLS path modelling estimation, including path coefficients and p-values, is shown in Figure 2. The results of hypothesis testing are summarised in Table 1.

4.3 Discussion

4.3.1 Information

Despite the conformity of opinions within literature that a user's knowledge about information security threats improves their preventive behaviour, findings show that information has an insignificant effect on self-reported preventive behaviour (H1). The composite reliability values indicate that the construct has high internal consistency, so one can assume that the indicators effectively measured users' knowledge. Our findings contradict the assumption that if a user possesses more information regarding threats, the more likely they are to take preventive measures.

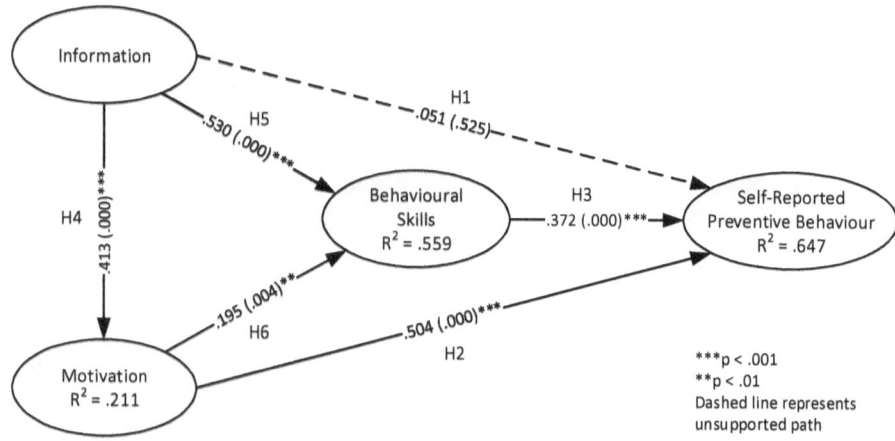

Figure 2: Structural Model Analysis

Hypothesis	Path Coefficient	T Value	P Value	Supported?
H1	.051	.914	p = .525	Not supported
H2	.504	5.000	p < .001	Supported
H3	.372	3.043	p < .001	Supported
H4	.413	6.263	p < .001	Supported
H5	.530	8.661	p < .001	Supported
H6	.195	2.905	p < .01	Supported

Table 1: Overview of Findings

Macada and Luciano (2010) reported that the sacrifices users make regarding their personal information could be related to a lack of general knowledge about IT. Thus, even if users are aware of threats, they require a deeper technical understanding of how to protect their information to prevent personal information compromise.

The relationship between information and behavioural skills (H5) was highly significant. These results are supported by Stajkovic and Luthans (1998), as it was reported that if a user's knowledge of security threats is above average they have a stronger form of self-conviction about their ability to safeguard their resources and personal information.

The relationship between information and motivation (H4) generated a statistically significant result and can be reinforced by Crossler and Belanger (2017) in that the more information users possesses about security threats, the more motivated they will be to engage in a preventive behaviour. This is because the user will have a greater awareness of the consequences of potential security threats.

4.3.2   Motivation

This research sought to test whether motivation drives users to exercise a preventive behaviour; the negative consequences of personal information attacks initiate preventive behaviour. The questionnaire attempted to determine if the key reason for exercising a preventive behaviour was to avoid negative consequence such as viruses. Motivation showed a significant relationship with the self-reported preventive behaviour construct (H2), showing in this survey that users tend to engage in a preventive behaviour to avoid negative consequences such as viruses.

For H6 it had to be determined how motivation and behavioural skills (self-efficacy) were related. It has been reported in literature that self-efficacy is a predictor of security and privacy-related intention (e.g. Bulgurcu et al., 2010). This hypothesis proved to be significant and provide further evidence for this. Schunk (1995) reported that if people perceive that they are performing tasks more successfully, or if they are becoming more competent whilst performing tasks, their motivation increases.

4.3.3   Behavioural Skills

To engage in a preventive behaviour a user must possess specific behavioural skills. These skills include both actual and perceived skills (Crossler & Belanger, 2017). The significant result for H3 reiterates that behavioural skills plays a leading role in the regulation and motivation of users' security behaviour, as perception of technical skills affects their level of engagement with technology.

5   Conclusion

Threats to personal information will always be present if users are engaging with IT. Our research question addressed the proposed gap between knowledge and behaviour, investigating how this affects self-reported preventive behaviour aimed against personal information compromise. We proposed a theoretical perspective based on the IMB model. Although information was shown to have an insignificant effect on preventive behaviour (H1 was not supported), if users mobilise the motivation and behavioural skills required to effectively engage in a preventive behaviour, they are likely to diminish the knowledge-behaviour gap (H2-H6 was supported). Our results show that the IMB model can be used to investigate information security factors which contribute to these gaps, and how these factors link to a users' preventive behaviour.

Since the research was purely quantitative future research could contribute more depth of understanding through a qualitative methodology, asking what specific preventive behaviour measures users feel they need to improve. A qualitative approach would also work well for the information and motivation constructs to determine specific factors which drive users to engage in a preventive behaviour and their exact level of knowledge of security and privacy threats.

6 Acknowledgement

This work is based on the research supported wholly / in part by the National Research Foundation of South Africa (Grant Numbers 114838).

7 References

Bandura, A., Caprara, G. V., Barbaranelli, C., Gerbino, M., & Pastorelli, C. (2003). Role of Affective Self-Regulatory Efficacy in Diverse Spheres of Psychosocial Functioning. Child Development, 74, 769-782.

Belanger, F., Collignon, S., Enget, K., & Negangard, E. (2017). Determinants of early conformance with information security policies. Information & Management, 54(7), 887–901.

Bulgurcu, B., Cavusoglu, H., & Benbasat, I. (2010). Information Security Policy Compliance: An Empirical Study of Rationality-Based Beliefs and Information Security Awareness. MIS Quarterly, 34, 523-548.

Chang, S., Choi, S., Kim, S.-A., & Song, M. (2014). Intervention Strategies Based on Information-Motivation-Behavioral Skills Model for Health Behavior Change: A Systematic Review. Asian Nursing Research, 8, 172-181.

Choi, M., Levy, Y., & Anat, H. (2013). The Role of User Computer Self-Efficacy, Cybersecurity Countermeasures Awareness, and Cybersecurity Skills Influence on Computer Misuse. Pre-ICIS Workshop on Information Security and Privacy (SIGSEC) (pp. 1-19). New York: WISP 2012 Proceedings.

Crossler, R., & Belanger, F. (2017). The Mobile Privacy-Security Knowledge Gap Model: Understanding Behaviors. Proceedings of the 50th Hawaii International Conference on System Sciences (pp. 4071-4080). Hawaii: Hawaii International Conference on System Sciences.

Dupuis, M., Crossler, R., & Popovsky, B. E. (2016). Measuring the Human Factor in Information Security and Privacy. (pp. 3676-3685). Hawaii: 49th Hawaii International Conference on System Sciences.

Fisher, W., Fisher, J., & Harman, J. (2003). The Information–Motivation–Behavioral Skills Model: A General Social Psychological Approach to Understanding and Promoting Health Behavior. In W. Fisher, J. Fisher, & J. Harman, Social Psychological Foundations of Health and Illness (pp. 82-102). London: Blackwell Publishing Ltd.

Fortier, A., & Burkell, J. (2015). Hidden Online Surveillance: What Librarians Should Know to Protect Their Own Privacy and That of Their Patrons. Information and Technology Libraries, 34, 59-72.

Hair, J., Ringle, C., & Sarstedt, M. (2013). Editorial-partial least squares structural equation modeling: Rigorous applications, better results and higher acceptance. Long Range Planning, 46(1-2), 1-12.

Hair, J., Hult, T., Ringle, C., & Sarstedt, M. (2014). A Primer on Partial Least Squares Structural Equation Modeling (PLS-SEM). California: SAGE Publications.

Macada, A., & Luciano, E. (2010). The influence of human factors on vulnerability to information security breaches. Proceedings of the Sixteenth Americas Conference on Information Systems (pp. 1-9). Lima: Americas Conference on Information Systems.

Miller, K. (2017). What We Talk about When We Talk about "Reasonable Cybersecurity": A Proactive and Adaptive Approach. The Computer & Internet Lawyer, 34, 1-8.

Norberg, P., Horne, D., & Horne, D. (2007). The Privacy Paradox: Personal Information Disclosure Intentions versus Behaviors. The Journal of Consumer Affairs, 41, 100-126.

Parsons, K., McCormac, A., Butavicius, M., Pattinson, M., & Jerram, C. (2014). Determining employee awareness using the Human Aspects of Information Security Questionnaire (HAIS-Q). Computers & Security, 42, 165–176.

Rhee, H., Kim, C., & Ryu, Y. (2009). Self-efficacy in information security: Its influence on end users' information security practice behavior. Computers & Security, 28, 816-826.

Schunk, D. (1995). Self-Efficacy, Motivation, and Performance. Journal of Applied Sport Psychology, 7, 112-137.

Stajkovic, A., & Luthans, F. (1998). Social cognitive theory and self-efficacy: going beyond traditional motivational and behavioral approaches. Organisational Dynamics, 26, 62-74.

Steijn, W., & Vedder, A. (2015). Privacy concerns, dead or misunderstood? The perceptions of privacy amongst the young and old. The International Journal of Government & Democracy in the Information Age, 20, 299-311.

Wall, J., & Lowry, P. (2013). Control-Related Motivations and Information Security Policy Compliance: The Role of Autonomy and Efficacy. Journal of Information Privacy & Security, 9, 52-79.

Yoo, S., Han, S., & Huang, W. (2012). The roles of intrinsic motivators and extrinsic motivators in promoting e-learning in the workplace: A case from South Korea. Computers in Human Behavior, 28, 942-950.

The BYOD Information Security Challenge for CIOs

A. Musarurwa and S. Flowerday

Department of Information Systems, Rhodes University, South Africa
e-mail: amusarurwa@hotmail.com; s.flowerday@ru.ac.za

Abstract

This paper highlights the way in which Chief Information Officers (CIOs) can mitigate the challenges that are posed by the Bring Your Own Device (BYOD) phenomenon. In terms of this phenomenon, employees inadvertently become unintended administrators as they have control of the devices they use. Previously, information security management was the preserve of the CIO and the Information Technology (IT) department, where trained IT employees managed all devices. Consequently, the advent of BYOD has shifted much of the responsibility from the IT personnel to the organisation's employees. This paper presents an employee behavioural management approach that CIOs may adopt to mitigate the BYOD information security challenges. This paper addresses the impact of BYOD, on the CIO's functional, transformational and strategic roles. Subsequently, an employee behavioural intention model is recommended as a way of mitigating these challenges. This BYOD Information Security Behavioural model, which was evaluated through an expert review process with CIOs in the Zimbabwe banking sector, encompasses six constructs: attitude, knowledge, habit, environment, governance and training.

Keywords

Bring Your Own Device (BYOD); General Data Protection Regulation (GDPR); Information Security Culture; Information Security Management

1 Introduction

Throughout the evolution of organisational information security management, the information technology (IT) administrator has always been the reference point for all IT issues and solutions (Jamf, 2017). The management of IT equipment and systems has been directed by an organisational policy framework owned by the Chief Information Officer (CIO). However, the advent of mobile devices has resulted in smartphones, phablets, tablets and many other mobile devices penetrating the organisational IT boundaries. As Ullman (2011) points out, the consumerisation of information technology has changed information security management in organisations, particularly as a result of the introduction of enterprise mobility through the bring your own device (BYOD) phenomenon. In this paper, BYOD is viewed as a phenomenon or new business practice by management which gives employees the privilege of using their own individual mobile devices to carry out work-related tasks (Alagbe, 2016).

In 2012, Gartner predicted that from 2018 the primary focus of endpoint breaches would shift to smartphones and tablets. In this evolution, Bongiorno, Rizzo, and Vaia (2018) highlighted that most organisations underestimate the risk faced in the BYOD practice since they focus more on the devices being used than on the enterprise's entire mobility landscape, which includes their employees. A study conducted by PwC (2015) concluded that the BYOD practice has taught organisations numerous lessons across various industries, including retail, transportation, manufacturing, healthcare, and banking. Sathyan, Anoop, Narayan and Vallathai (2016) argue that enterprise mobility has been adopted by organisations to enhance their marketing channels, improve productivity in the office, boost customer satisfaction, as well as offer shopping experiences or process sales through the mobile devices. A customer survey on cybersecurity and enterprise mobility reported on by Zetlin (2017) found that half of the respondents used their personal devices for work, but they did not take basic security precautions, a fact made more worrying from a risk management perspective because 27% of those users reported having had their devices lost or stolen. All these exposures and challenges are posing serious information security challenges for CIOs.

This paper begins by introducing the BYOD unintended administrator and giving a purview of the challenges he/she poses. The paper then proceeds to explore the information security challenges faced by CIOs in a BYOD environment. The paper classifies the unintended administrator challenges into three key organisational roles for CIOs, namely, the functional role, the transformational role and the strategic role. The paper also briefly explores the impact of the General Data Protection Regulation (GDPR) on the CIO and BYOD information security. A recommendation on how to address these information security challenges is put forward in the form of an information security behavioural approach. The paper also discusses a survey conducted in the Zimbabwean banking sector and concludes with a recommendation for a BYOD information security behavioural (BISB) model which shows how CIOs can develop information security behaviour with regard to BYOD. The next section explores the BYOD unintended administrator in detail, presenting a case on how this has affected the CIOs.

2 The BYOD Unintended Administrator

Bongiorno et al. (2018) point out that the growth in mobile device usage has seen employees demanding to use their mobile devices on which to run critical business applications. The employees who own these devices carry critical applications used by the organisation and have thus become the unintended administrators of the organisation's information. The unintended administrator is not necessarily trained or aware of the information security risks and challenges that are associated with the BYOD phenomenon. This inadvertently shifts the management of the organisational information security from the information technology (IT) administrator to the unintended administrator. This shift leaves the organisation at risk of data and information security breaches which can permeate the organisation through the behaviour of these unintended administrators. Kaneshige (2016) contends that the uptake of BYOD is now pervasive and mission critical, leaving CIOs with the dilemma as to how to control the unintended administrator without simultaneously inconveniencing the business. Whilst the CIO and his team do not have direct control over the mobile devices being used in the BYOD practice, it remains the CIO's responsibility to make sure that the information contained in the devices as well as their operation do not compromise the organisation's information security policies and standards.

3   Research methodology

The research approach followed in this paper was in the form of a literature review of the BYOD security challenges and an expert review where the experts were bank CIOs. The challenges that the CIOs face where identified and classified under the three CIO roles, namely, the functional, the transformational and the strategic roles. Accordingly, a questionnaire was created to identify the type of challenges that the CIOs face in these three roles. The questionnaire was then distributed to 18 CIOs in the Zimbabwean banking industry via Survey Monkey. From the 18 CIOs, a total of 18 complete responses were obtained. The results obtained are presented later in this paper.

4   CIO challenges in BYOD

Information security is the greatest challenge in the BYOD practice across all industries (Bauer & Bernroider, 2017). Costa, Merlo, Verderame, & Armando, (2015) point out that if the employees, who are viewed as unintended administrators in this paper, do not keep the device they use in the BYOD practice up to date with security software patches, that device becomes the most vulnerable point of the organisation's network. Studies conducted by Vorakulpipat, Sirapaisan, Rattanalerdnusorn, and Savangsuk (2017) have shown that most organisations are lagging behind in setting up comprehensive BYOD policies. They argue that the CIO's role is to ensure that the unintended administrator's productivity grows and the organisation remains competitive. Bongiorno et al. (2018) maintain that the CIO's role is increasingly becoming less functional, but more transformational and strategic. To achieve this portfolio shift, the CIO is faced with the task of harnessing the challenges that the unintended administrator brings and converting them into competitive benefits for the business. The CIO is also faced with the task of breaking down boundaries. A publication by the CIO.com (2018) states that "[t]he key to CIO success in modern-day business is to break boundaries. Boundaries between systems and data. Boundaries between business and IT. Boundaries between the status quo and new mandates for agility and transformation. Employees want their mobile devices to run the critical applications" (p. 2).

The following section considers the challenges that the CIO faces as a result of the influence of the unintended administrator. These challenges are classified under the three CIO roles. In the 2017 state of the CIO report, Muse (2017) shows that between 2010 and 2017 the CIO's roles moved from being 34% functional to being only 20% functional. At the transformational level, the CIO role was cited as having grown from 45% to about 50% and, on the strategic front, the role had grown from 21% to 31% in the same period. Table 1 below shows the year by year distribution of the CIO roles between the years 2010 and year 2017.

CIO roles	2010	2011	2012	2013	2014	2015	2016	2017
Functional (%)	34	43	23	19	19	22	27	20
Transformational (%)	45	46	23	56	47	52	45	50
Strategic (%)	21	11	25	25	34	27	27	31

Table 1: CIO roles between 2010 and 2017 (Muse, 2017)

Table 1 shows that there is a general shift in CIO roles from functional to more transformational and strategic roles. To delineate this impact, the next section explores these roles in more detail.

5 Impact of the GDPR on the CIOs role

The GDPR came into effect on the 25th of May 2018 replacing the existing data protection framework under the EU Data Protection Directive (Kingsley, 2018). This regulation emphasises transparency, security and accountability by data controllers at the same time strengthening the rights of the data owner over their data contained by organisations. The rights of the data owner under the GDPR include among other things, subject access, to have inaccuracies corrected, to have information erased, to object to direct marketing, to restrict the processing of their information, including automated decision-making as well as data portability (Data Protection Commissioner, 2018).

In this paper the CIOs main challenge is ensure the security of the data that is on the organisation's device. The rights that the user get through the GDPR put the CIO under a precarious position as some users may resists the CIOs control under the guise of the regulation. On a portable device, the organisational data co-exists with the user's data which therefore demands that the CIO must have a sophisticated means by which to meet both the organisational data security standards and the data owners' rights. The next section attends to the BYOD impact on the CIO's role profile.

6 Impact on the functional role of the CIO

The functional role of the CIO is basically the management of the business-as-usual tasks which form the day-to-day management of the IT functions. This includes establishing both stability and relevance for enterprise IT. Functional IT duties are not going away, but they are being minimised to some degree as a result of automation (HP, 2017). The functional roles include user support, security management and many other operations conducted daily. The BYOD practice has influenced the functional roles in the following areas:

i. Most employees involved in the BYOD phenomenon do not have permission from their organisation. Driven by their preferences, employees have begun bringing their "shadow" devices of preference to the workplace, resulting in the rise of "Shadow IT". Trend Micro (2012) points out that, "[a]s consumerization proves to be irreversible, and threatens to become an IT nightmare by increasing security risk, data loss and financial exposure, it's clear that a lack of strategy could prove devastating. The best approach to effectively manage a consumerised workforce is to embrace consumerisation in order to unlock its benefits and reap its full business potential" (p. 1).

ii. Security and compliance costs are the direct responsibility of the CIO. In the BYOD practice, the CIO does not have total control of the mobile device, however the expectation remains that the organisation must be compliant with the information security and regulatory standards. Bagchi (2013) remarked that in the banking industry, compliance with regulation and the maintenance of a high standard of information security are primary requirements. If a bank embraces the BYOD policy, the CIO finds him/herself "caught between a rock and a hard place" as there is need for the organisation to leverage on the digital changes while at the same time retaining the integrity from a security perspective.

From a functional role perspective, the CIO is faced with some requirements that compromise the standard security rules. For example, there is a requirement to ensure that the operational standards are upheld while at the same time satisfying the business needs. The next section attends to the impact of the BYOD on the transformational role of the CIO.

7   Impact on the transformational role of the CIO

Today, CIOs are spending more time on transformational actions such as bringing in line IT initiatives with business goals and cultivating the IT and business partnership. Research on the 16th State of the CIO conducted by Muse (2017) found that CIOs are actively involved in driving customer acquisition and retention, leading and directing product innovation and collaborating on customer initiatives which transform the businesses. Managing the BYOD policy emerges as one such transformational role with which the CIO is tasked. In this transformational role, CIOs are faced with a range of challenges which are as a result of the existence of the unintended administrator. These include, but are not limited to, the following:

i. Embracing the cloud services for business agility. The unintended administrators make use of some cloud services which may be insecure for the organisation's documents. Examples of such include Dropbox, Google drive, One drive, iCloud and many others. In as much as these tools provide convenience and agility, they also expose organisational information to data loss and information theft (Bongiorno et al., 2018).

ii. Designing digital innovation is also one of the key roles that face the CIO. Bongiorno et al. (2018) contend that moving apps and workloads to the cloud, ensuring that legacy software can synchronise to off-premises apps, and keeping networks and systems secure remain the core functional tasks of the

CIO role. In this digital scramble, Muse (2017) also remarks that the boards of directors, chief executive officers and business colleagues are turning the CIO's role into a lead digital transformation driver to win customers and drive revenue growth.

In the transformational role, the CIO is faced with the challenge of ensuring that the business has the ability to offer the new services without compromising on the organisational policy standards. However, the unintended administrator accesses cloud computing services that may expose the organisation's security standards.

8 Impact of the strategic role of the CIO

CIOs are also focusing on strategic endeavours such as motivating business innovation and identifying strategic opportunities for competitive differentiation. Emerging technologies, such as artificial intelligence and the internet of things (IoT), generate headlines and the CIO is expected to drive the business strategic focus through them. The unintended administrator has compelled CIOs to drive strategic initiatives with a view to the security impact on the organisation at large. Stackpole (2017) purports that CIOs have, over the years, become the centre of digital innovation in organisations. This realisation entails an organisational requirement that the CIO remains competitive in the digital scramble, without putting the organisation at risk. Thus, the CIO needs to be vigilant and aware of the following strategic aspects:

i.   CIOs are required to be the digital revolution drivers who improve the productivity of the employees without compromising the information for the organisation. The fact that the BYOD unintended administrator has disrupted the organisational strategic plans marks another "Achilles heel" for the CIO in trying to catch up. Wiech (2015) warns that the mobile devices have redefined the way banking is conducted, at the same time demanding a shift in information security management of the devices that interface with the banking systems.

ii.   The unintended administrator at times acquires new mobile devices that are more sophisticated. In addition, they use devices from multiple vendors which makes it difficult for the CIO to keep track of the upgrades and maintenance. To drive the organisation's strategy, the CIO should be able to keep abreast of new innovations that satisfy the organisational strategic aspirations. Nevertheless, the unintended administrator is always ahead while the CIO follows.

The adoption of BYOD practice is blurring the line between work and personal life such that the information security boundary that is supposed to exist between work and personal life is now invisible. The challenges that are experienced by the CIO at the functional, transformational and strategic levels are all visibly influenced by the unintended administrator. To that effect, this paper recommends that the solution lies in addressing the administrator. In as much as the technical solutions exist for BYOD practice, Blizzard (2015) contends that technical solutions alone are not enough. There is need to attend to the unintended administrators' behavioural patterns in their usage of the BYOD. The next section explores information security management and how CIOs can mitigate the challenges that emerge as a result of the existence of the unintended administrator.

9   A taxonomy for information security management in the BYOD

Singh and Phil's (2012) definition, which expresses information security as the standards for guarding data and information from illegal access, is used in this paper. Brien et al. (2013), believe that an "organisational culture that is information security aware will minimize risks to information assets and specifically reduce the risk of employee misbehaviour and harmful interaction with information assets" (p. 2). Whilst allowing the BYOD practice holds many advantages and benefits for organisations, if not properly managed it will have disastrous consequences for organizations. In BYOD practice, the employee is the administrator and thus no endpoint security management policies can be enforced by the organisation's IT.

Olalere, Abdullah, Mahmod, and Abdullah (2015) argue that the biggest BYOD challenge is that organisational data are being delivered and managed by devices that are not managed by IT departments. They believe that these have security implications pertaining to data leakage, data theft and regulatory compliance, especially in the case of the banking industry. The GDPR sets out the responsibilities that organisations have in ensuring the privacy and protection of personal data, and also provides data subjects with certain rights, assigns powers to regulators to ask for demonstrations of accountability and even imposes fines in cases where organisations are not complying with GDPR requirements.

Inspired by inconsistencies in the current research on BYOD information security, Downer and Bhattacharya (2016) introduced a new taxonomy for classifying BYOD security challenges. This taxonomy divides BYOD information security challenges into two dimensions:

i.   **Dimension 1:** Security challenges are categorised according to the areas of the organisation they affect most, such as the hardware or the software security as well as human resources.

ii.   **Dimension 2:** In this dimension, challenges are classified by primary concern, key common characteristics and inferred relationships. For instance, equipment challenges are classified into deployment challenges and technical challenges. Deployment challenges are experienced prior to implementation while technical challenges are experienced during the entire BYOD lifecycle. The human resource challenge may be divided into policy and regulation challenges.

This paper expands on the human resource challenge, which has an impact on the organisational policies and regulations. In order to understand BYOD information security, all dimensions should be analysed in their respective stages. Several attempts to address BYOD information security have concentrated on one of the two dimensions stated above. Figure 1 shows the proposed categories for BYOD security challenges.

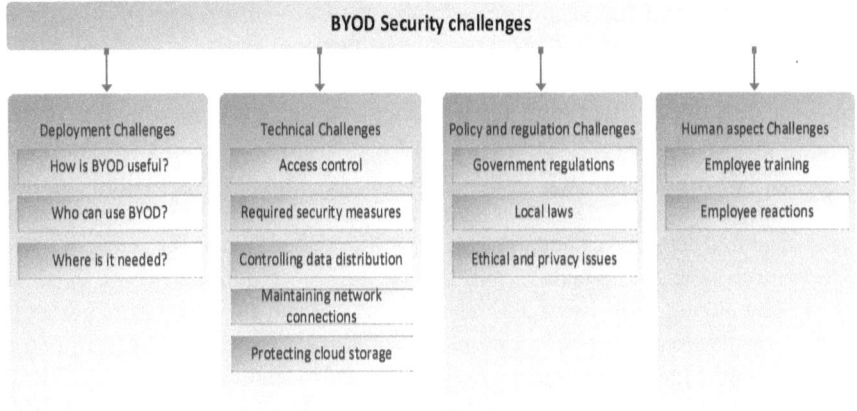

Figure 1. Taxonomies for BYOD Security Challenges (Downer & Bhattacharya, 2016)

Whilst the approach cited in Figure 1 addresses all the facets of BYOD practice, this paper proposes that there is a need to concentrate more on the challenges related to human aspects. Employee behaviour is something that needs attention as it determines how employees will implement all the other sections. This paper also proposes that measures to address human aspect challenges will not be sufficient unless they have been developed into a culture. Whilst training is important, a change in employee behaviour is crucial if BYOD security challenges are to be combatted. Provided behaviour is intentional, its occurrence may be predicted thus guiding the actions that ensue (Bada, Sasse, & Nurse, 2015). It may therefore be concluded that information security behaviour is probably the additional component of the model. Thus, information security regarding BYOD can be strengthened by exploring the two dimensions proposed by Downer and Bhattacharya (2016). In the technical dimension, existing security measures relating to BYOD practice are discussed in the following section.

10   How CIOs can mitigate the BYOD challenges

An organisation is driven by its culture and the unintended administrator forms part of this culture. Accordingly, in addressing BYOD challenges the first thing CIOs need to address is to make sure employees understand the organisation's regulations and policies. Secondly, this paper recommends that the organisational information security culture should be influenced in such a way that it supports a behavioural intention to heed the risks associated with BYOD. Thirdly, this paper recommends an operational component, namely, the implementation of a BISB model.

i. Understanding regulations: The European Union introduced the General Data Protection Regulation (GDPR)(EU) 2016/679, which is a regulation on data protection and privacy for all individuals within the European Union; it also addresses the exporting of personal data outside the EU (Overstraeten, Cumbley, & Pauly, 2016). Essentially, the EU GDPR is a set of rules on the way companies should process subjects' personal data.

ii. Understanding the organisational culture: Organisational culture (OC) is a widely documented topic the definitions of which are published in various contexts and industries. In the banking industry, OC is viewed as the shared beliefs and values that develop within the banking organisation. These beliefs and values guide the behaviour of its members in order to maintain suitable patterns in social systems to achieve coordinated behaviour aimed at survival in the dynamic environment. Another definition by Lundy and Cowling (1996) views OC as the way things are done in a particular organisation. This definition provides a casual but practical description of culture without necessarily providing an understanding of it.

iii. Building a BYOD information security culture: IT as a business enabler for organisations has become ubiquitous in today's workplace (Singh & Phil, 2012). The outcome of interactions between IT and OC can result in the acceptance and effective use of IT or user resistance, total rejection or even sabotage (Mehri & Yeganeh, 2015). Accordingly, when there is a misfit between IT and OC, three options exist:
   - ➢ reject the IT so as to seek one that is more compatible with the culture
   - ➢ redesign the technology before implementing it
   - ➢ proceed to adopt new IT options and face the challenges as they present themselves.

From the discussion it is clear that IT is a change agent for culture. The rate and direction of such change is basically driven by the rate of participation within the organisation. Another cardinal aspect of the impact of IT on culture is information security (Kuusisto & Ilvonen, 2003). It is therefore in the interests of every CIO to ensure that the organisation builds a culture with the behavioural intention to promote information security. The next section focuses on the constructs which were identified as central to building a BYOD information security culture.

11 Implementing a BYOD Information Security Behavioural (BISB) model

The operational way that the CIO can mitigate the challenges of the unintended administrator is through the implementation of a model that promotes the ultimate objective of securing the device. In developing this paper, a literature review was conducted on a commercial bank in Zimbabwe followed by a survey among CIOs in the banking industry in Zimbabwe as well. The results of the survey were subjected to statistical tests culminating in the identification of various individual and organisational traits. Ultimately, a set of six constructs was identified as follows:

1. **Attitude.** A study conducted by Allam, Flowerday and Flowerday (2014) suggests that attitude is dictated by what people think. In this paper, attitude refers to what employees think about BYOD information security; this includes the technology they use and the organisational policy framework.
2. **Knowledge.** Separate studies define knowledge as what people know (Allam et al., 2014; Kruger & Kearney, 2006; Safa, Von Solms, & Furnell, 2016). In this context, knowledge can be defined as what employees know about BYOD information security in a bank in Zimbabwe.
3. **Habit.** Social theorists have agreed that people generally act habitually in the world, not reflectively (Hopf, 2010). Vance, Siponen, and Pahnila (2012) define habit as a routinised form of past behaviour, while Pahnila, Siponen, and Mahmood (2007) view habit as unconscious or automatic behaviour.
4. **Environment.** Organisational traits include the microenvironment, which was identified as being one of the key role players in the formulation of employee behavioural intention (Thomson, 2012). According to Farooq and Amin (2017), an appropriate environment is associated with a better information security culture.
5. **Governance.** Organisational governance is another key component identified as having an impact on information security behaviour. Information security management theorists assert that employee behaviour needs to be directed and censored to ensure that it is amenable to organisational information security standards (Dillon, Stahl, & Vossen, 2015; Rastogi & Solms, 2012; Vroom & Von Solms, 2004).
6. **Training.** Training on the information security plan for the organisation is another key component identified in the literature review as a pillar on which an information security culture is built. Because employees come from different backgrounds, many of them lack basic awareness of the consequences of breaching information security guidelines (Al-shehri, 2012).

12 Behavioural intention

Many studies focus directly on the individual as the locus of behaviour. According to Tharp (2009), that complex whole which includes knowledge, belief, arts, morals, law, custom, and any other capabilities and habits acquired by man as a member of society forms the behavioural intention which can be summed up as a culture. The literature review conducted for this paper uncovered links between culture and information security behavioural intention. This behavioural intention thus translates into the security culture exhibited by employees in the organisation.

Figure 2 illustrates the combination of individual and organisational traits culminating in a BYOD information security behavioural (BISB) model. These constructs were explored individually and found to contribute to the behavioural intention of employees.

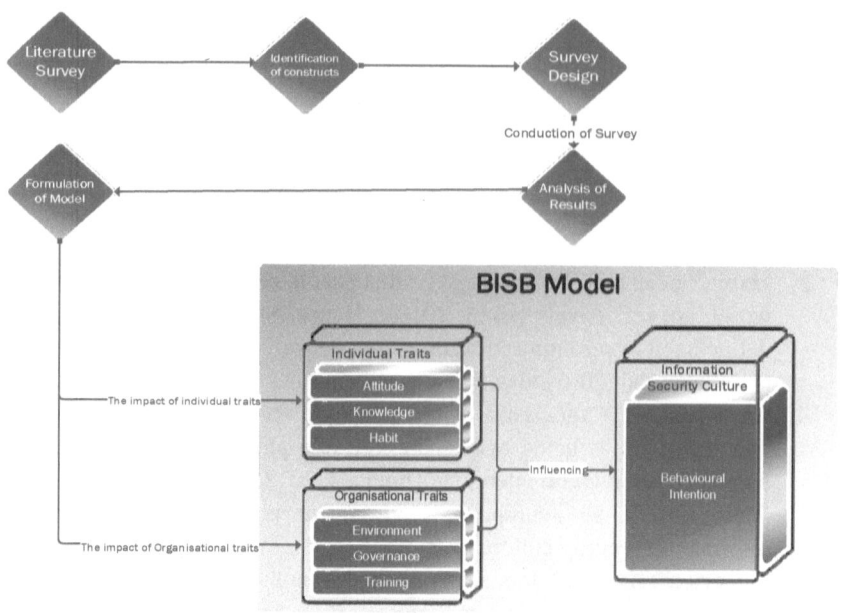

Figure 2: The BYOD Information Security Behavioural Model (BISB)

As Figure 2 shows the research process followed culminating into, individual and organisational traits which were combined to form the BISB model. The next section gives a high-level analysis of the findings from the survey conducted on CIOs in the Zimbabwe banking sector.

In this survey, a set of questions were distributed to 18 CIOs. The questions were designed to obtain an understanding of the spectrum of challenges that CIOs face in their functional, transformational and strategic roles. The next section presents the qualitative analysis of the findings.

13   Analysis and Findings

From the findings presented above it is clear that the CIO is definitely in need of a model or framework that ensures that the information security and data security standards for their organisations are not compromised. The promulgation of the GDPR shifted the pendulum of data control towards the data owner. To this end, implementing and enforcing information security standards that support adherence to a high information security mitigation becomes difficult for the CIO. This paper premised the BYOD challenges on three CIOs roles profiles which are the functional role, the strategic role as well as the transformational role. The findings of the survey revealed all three role components. From a functional role perspective, BYOD has shifted from the management of devices distributed by the IT department to a position where every employee who owns a device participates in the BYOD. Accordingly, IT functions have become more complex and dependent on the goodwill of the unintended administrator. From a transformational perspective, BYOD has acted as a vehicle for transformation, as it enables the CIO to roll out the products and services that the organisation consumes. For instance, in a bank where customer relationship managers want to open bank accounts on the move, they can make use of a mobile device to capture and scan documents instantly. From a strategic perspective, BYOD has become an enabler of strategy implementation. Ultimately, the biggest challenge remains information security. The paper proposes an Information security behavioural model along six traits of attitude, knowledge habit, environment governance and training. These traits were deemed to be instrumental in influencing the employee's behavioural intention towards the BYOD information security.

Table 2 shows results of a survey conducted in the Zimbabwe financial services sector along a five-point likert scale showed that about 70% of the CIOs agreed that the BISB model can be applied to mitigate the information security challenges faced by the CIOs on the BYOD.

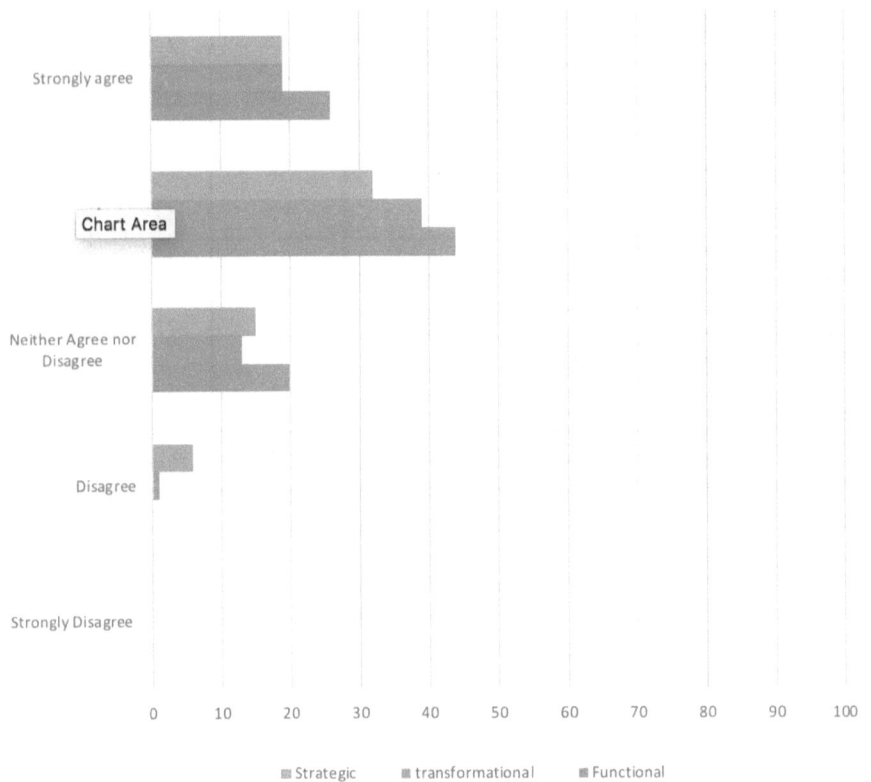

Figure 3: Analysis and Findings

Figure 3 shows a high-level presentation of the survey results. As the figure shows, the CIOs generally agreed that BYOD does affect their functional, transformational and strategic roles. The majority of CIOs felt that most of the challenges experienced were in relation to the CIO's functional role. Table 1 below shows the responses per question regarding each role profile.

Functional	Completely Disagree	Disagree	Neither Agree Nor Disagree	Agree	Completely Agree
With regulations like the GDPR and PCDISS, which aim for complete protection of consumer data and adherence to strict standards. In a BYOD enviromnent,these standards can be upheld.	0	0	4	11	3
Bring Your Own Device (BYOD) is a rapidly growing trend with benefits to the organisation but it introduces risk to the organisation. The risks out weigh the benefits.	0	0	5	12	1
BYOD unneccessarily increases the organization's management effort, both for maintaining an accurate inventory of the devices, keeping operating systems' software up-to-date and supporting the increasing number of device types.	0	0	7	6	5
In BYOD users should not be allowed to install their own personal applications on their devices but they should install only whitelisted applications by the organisation	0	0	4	4	10
The notion of the 'unintended administrator' inherent in BYOD poses a challenge to the success of BYOD. CIOs should put policies in place to ensure the user devices are compliant to the organisational policies. Do you agree?	0	0	0	11	7
Transformational	Completely Disagree	Disagree	Neither Agree Nor Disagree	Agree	Completely Agree
Making the necessary organizational changes to adopt BYOD may require a shift away from centralized systems towards more open enterprise systems and this change can present challenges to enterprises in particular over security, control, technology and policy to the traditional IT model within organisations. Do you agree?	0	1	3	8	6
Organisational culture can be a barrier to implementing BYOD policies. To successfully implement BYOD, CIOs must have buy in from employees and other stakeholders to successfully transform their organisations. Do you agree?	0	0	1	10	7
There is a risk that BYOD policies can infringe on the privacy of employees in the name on corporate data protection, what strategies can CIOs implement in order to curb against infringing on user's private information	0	0	5	11	2
BYOD represents a fairly new way of doing things in organisations.Management of its implemenation is of paramount importance if it is to be a success	0	0	4	10	4
Strategic	Completely Disagree	Disagree	Neither Agree Nor Disagree	Agree	Completely Agree
The strategic importance of BYOD cannot be ignored but the threats it poses to enterprise security cannot be ignored as well. The strategic importance of BYOD outweighs the associated risks	0	0	2	10	6
BYOD requires CIOs to make modifications to the current IT infrastructure so that it's BYOD compliant. CIOs do not need to identify which applications their employees are using to interact with corporate data.	0	0	4	7	7
In BYOD, understanding the sensitivity of your data and setting appropriate security measures will help to ensure that your intellectual property is not compromised. For example, in a Banking environment, customer information is of paramount importance. In this vein, BYOD cannot be successfully implemented in all environments including banks?	0	6	3	9	0
BYOD is seen as a benefit for employees that increases employee loyalty. Do you agree?	0	0	6	6	6

Table 2: CIO Survey Responses

Table 2 show the questions which were used to conduct the survey. The results were then presented in Figure 2. From the spread of the results the analysis positively confirms that the CIO's role will be made easier if there is an operational model around the BYOD.

The findings from the literature review conducted as well as the analysis of the CIO role suggest that the CIO indeed require a people driven approach towards mitigating the BYOD information security challenges as across the CIOs role profile cited in this paper as follows:

- Functional role: On a functional role perspective, the CIO requires the right attitude from the devices users in order for him to be able to mitigate the BYOD information security risks. Knowledge is also needed to create the requisite environment to create the correct habits among the employees from an organisational governance framework that allows training.
- Strategic role: The strategic role also requires the rightful attitude from the employees coupled with the appropriate habits that promote information security. These will be in an environment that offers the correct training on knowledge around the information security risks and information security governance.
- Transformational role: For every organisation to transform, there is need for the correct habits towards information security, which are also coupled with the knowledge, governance and the training to satisfy the organisation's strategic aspirations

From the summary above the findings indeed point to the fact that building an information security aware behavioural intention is an important solution that the CIO can embrace. This paper therefore proposes that CIOs should adopt the BISB model.

14   Conclusion and Future Work

This paper focused on the impact of the BYOD on the three CIO roles. It may accordingly be noted that if effective security behaviour is practised over time, an information security culture may result, as advocated by the BISB. As this model recommends, when an organisation builds an information security culture for the unintended administrator, the three individual traits and three organisational traits should be considered. Whilst the CIO's role is evolving gradually towards transforming the organisation through strategic digital offerings, the unintended administrator remains the primary challenge in their fulfilment of the new role. This paper also noted that there are technical solutions that can be used in BYOD practice but recommends that the real solutions in addressing the unintended administrator is through the BISB model.Future work will include additional tests on the CIO roles. Attention will also be given to the regulatory and policy impact of the BYOD. Furthermore, since the introduction of the GDPR by the European Union on 25 May 2018 marked a new era in data protection laws globally, the impact of the GDPR on BYOD and the CIO roles will be a point of focus.

15 References

Al-shehri, Y. (2012). Information Security Awareness and Culture. British Journal of Arts and Social Sciences, 6(1), 61–69.

Alagbe, A. (2016). The Security Implication of BYOD : Mobile Devices in the Workplace. University of Strathclyde, Glasgow.

Allam, S., Flowerday, S. V., & Flowerday, E. (2014). Smartphone information security awareness: A victim of operational pressures. Computers and Security, 42, 55–65.

Bada, M., Sasse, A., & Nurse, J. R. C. (2015). Cyber security awareness campaigns: Why do they fail to change behaviour? Proceedings of the International Conference on Cyber Security for Sustainable Society. London.

Bauer, S., & Bernroider, E. W. N. (2017). From Information Security Awareness to Reasoned Compliant Action : Analyzing Information Security Policy Compliance in a Large Banking Organization, (October 2016). http://doi.org/10.1145/3130515.3130519

Beth Stackpole. (2017). CIOs adjust to their new reality | CIO. Retrieved February 3, 2018, from https://www.cio.com/article/3162718/cio-role/state-of-the-cio-2017-the-new-reality.html

Blizzard, S. (2015). Coming full circle: Are there benefits to BYOD? Computer Fraud and Security, 2015(2), 18–20. http://doi.org/10.1016/S1361-3723(15)30010-5

Bongiorno, G., Rizzo, D., & Vaia, G. (2018). CIOs and the Digital Transformation: A new Leadership role (1st ed.). Milan, Italy: Springer International Publishing.

Brien, J. O., Islam, S., Bao, S., Weng, F., Xiong, W., & Ma, A. (2013). Information security culture: Literature Review. Minerva. Melbourne.

CIO.com. (2018). The modern CIO's role is more challenging than ever. Retrieved February 3, 2018, from https://hybridit.cio.com/transformation

Costa, G., Merlo, A., Verderame, L., & Armando, A. (2015). Automatic security verification of mobile app configurations. Future Generation Computer Systems. http://doi.org/10.1016/j.future.2016.06.014

Crawshaw, J., Budhwar, P., & Davis, A. (2017). Human Resource Management : Strategic and International Perspectives. (Jonathan Crawshaw, P. S. Budhwar, & A. Davies, Eds.)Sage Publications Ltd. London, United Kingdom: Sage Publications Ltd.

Data Protection Commissioner. (2018). The GDPR and You, 11. Retrieved from https://www.dataprotection.ie/docs/30-11-2016-GDPR-and-You-Preparing-for-2018/1604.htm

Dillon, S., Stahl, F., & Vossen, G. (2015). BYOD and Governance of the Personal Cloud. International Journal of Cloud Applications and Computing , 5(2), 23–35.

Downer, K., & Bhattacharya, M. (2016). BYOD security: A new business challenge. In 2015 IEEE International Conference on Smart City, SmartCity 2015, Held Jointly with 8th IEEE International Conference on Social Computing and Networking, SocialCom 2015, 5th IEEE International Conference on Sustainable Computing and Communic (pp. 1128–1133). New York, USA: IEEE.

Farooq, O., & Amin, A. (2017). National culture, information environment, and sensitivity of investment to stock prices: Evidence from emerging markets. Research in International Business and Finance, 39 (3), 41–46.

Gartner. (2012). Enterprise Mobility : Trends, Challenges and Solutions Gartner at a Glance. Las Vegas.

Hopf, T. (2010). The logic of habit in International Relations. European Journal of International Relations, 16(4), 539–561.

HP. (2017). The Strategic CIO' s Playbook Table of Contents.

Jamf. (2017). Conditional Access : Going Beyond Perimeter-Based Security The Modern Workplace and the Next Generation of Security.

Kingsley. (2018). An introduction to the General Data Protection Regulation.

Kruger, H. A., & Kearney, W. D. (2006). A prototype for assessing information security awareness. Computers and Security, 25(4), 289–296. http://doi.org/10.1016/j.cose.2006.02.008

Kuusisto, T., & Ilvonen, I. (2003). Information Security Culture in Small and Medium Size Enterprises. Frontiers of E-Business Research, 431–439.

Mehri, B., & Yeganeh, E. (2015). The impact of national and organizational culture on information technology (I) Abstract : Karaj.

Minda Zetlin. (2017). State of the CIO 2017: Priorities that can't wait | The Enterprisers Project. Retrieved February 3, 2018, from https://enterprisersproject.com/article/2017/4/state-cio-2017-priorities-cant-wait

Muse, D. (2017). State of the CIO: 2017. Idg, 1–12. Retrieved from http://core0.staticworld.net/assets/2017/02/20/state_of_the_cio_exec-summary_2017.pdf

Olalere, M., Abdullah, M. T., Mahmod, R., & Abdullah, A. (2015). A Review of Bring Your Own Device on Security Issues. SAGE Open, 5(2), 11.

Overstraeten, T. Van, Cumbley, R., & Pauly, D. (2016). The General Data Protection Regulation: A Survival Guide.

Pahnila, S., Siponen, M., & Mahmood, A. (2007). Employees' behavior towards IS security policy compliance. In Proceedings of the Annual Hawaii International Conference on System Sciences (pp. 1–10). Honolulu, Hawaii.

PwC. (2015). Bring Your Own Device (BYOD) and customer Data Protection- Are you ready? Contracting Business. London.

Rastogi, R., & Von Solms, R. (2012). Information Security Service Culture – Information Security for End-users. Journal of Universal Computer Science, 18(12), 1628–1642.

Sathyan, J., Anoop, Narayan, N., & Vallathai, S. K. (2016). A Comprehensive Guide to Enterprise Mobility. (CRC Press, Ed.)Infosys press (An Auerbac). Boca Raton: CRC Press.

Singh, M. N., & Phil, M. (2012). B . Y . O . D. Genie Is Out Of the Bottle – " Devil Or Angel ." Journal of Business Management & Social Sciences Research, 1(3), 1–12.

Sohini Bagchi. (2013). Public Banks still skeptical of BYOD. Retrieved January 18, 2018, from http://www.cxotoday.com/story/banking-sector-in-india-still-wary-of-byod/

Sohrabi Safa, N., Von Solms, R., & Furnell, S. (2016). Information security policy compliance model in organizations. Computers and Security, 56, 1–13. http://doi.org/10.1016/j.cose.2015.10.006

Symantec. (2012). 2012 Norton Cybercrime Report. Norton Cybercrime Report. Massachusetts.

Tharp, B. M. (2009). Defining " Culture " and "Organizational Culture": From Anthropology to the Office. Interpretation a Journal of Bible and Theology, 1–5.

Thomson, G. (2012). BYOD: Enabling the chaos. Network Security, 2012(2), 5–8. http://doi.org/10.1016/S1353-4858(12)70013-2

Tom Kaneshige. (2016). CIO Challenge with BYOD: Don't Fall Down the Rabbit Hole | CIO. Retrieved February 1, 2018, from https://www.cio.com/article/2395938/byod/cio-challenge-with-byod--don-t-fall-down-the-rabbit-hole.html

Trend Micro. (2012). Consumerization Survey Report The Consumerization of IT, 1–8.

Ullman, E. (2011). BYOD and Security. Tech & Learning (Vol. 31).

Vance, A., Siponen, M., & Pahnila, S. (2012). Motivating IS security compliance: Insights from Habit and Protection Motivation Theory. Information and Management, 49(3–4), 190–198. http://doi.org/10.1016/j.im.2012.04.002

Vorakulpipat, C., Sirapaisan, S., Rattanalerdnusorn, E., & Savangsuk, V. (2017). A policy-based framework for preserving confidentiality in BYOD environments: A review of information security perspectives. Security and Communication Networks, 2017. http://doi.org/10.1155/2017/2057260

Vroom, C., & Von Solms, R. (2004). Towards information security behavioural compliance. Computers and Security, 23(3), 191–198.

Wiech, D. (2015). Banks and others accounting for BYOD. Retrieved July 30, 2016, from http://www.it-director.com/content/banks-and-others-accounting-for-byod/

Rationalising Decision Making about Risk:
A Normative Approach

A. M'manga[1], S. Faily[1], J. McAlaney[1] C. Williams[2]

[1]Bournemouth University, Poole, United Kingdom
[2]Defence Science and Technology Laboratory, Porton Down, United Kingdom
e-mail: {ammanga, sfaily, jmcalaney}@bournemouth.ac.uk;
cwilliams@mail.dstl.gov.uk

Abstract

Techniques for determining and applying security decisions typically follow risk-based analytical approaches where alternative options are put forward and weighed in accordance to risk severity metrics based on goals and context. The reasoning or validity behind decision making can, however, prove difficult to determine in conditions characterised by uncertainty stemming from environments with insufficient or incoherent information. This paper approaches the problem by proposing a conceptual model that provides security decision making traceability through auditing decision makers' rationalisation of risk. Additionally, the model highlights the role metacognition plays in identifying and understanding information affordances used for decision making.

Keywords

Normative decision-making, Context-awareness, Uncertainty, Risk-perception, Security

1 Introduction

Security analysts regularly face the challenge of justifying decisions made under risk and uncertain conditions. While uncertainty stems from various sources such as dynamic conditions and information limitations, complications in decision making also arise because risk stems from multiple factors, rather than a single root cause (Hoffman et al., 2017). Analysts aim at identifying the best possible option, given the limited information; few decisions are actually made with absolute certainty (Huber, 2014) reflecting the difference between optimising in rational decision making, and satisficing in bounded rationality (Simon, 1972) driven, naturalistic decision making. When decision making under risk and uncertainty fails, the post-incident privilege of hindsight available to others fails to portray the complexity of decision making in action. Similarly, value is lost when decision making knowledge gained remains tacit and cannot be communicated. To address these problems, the research aimed at formulating a systematic approach for providing traceability to the rationale behind security decision making during risk and uncertainty.

2   Related work

Decision making research has typically followed the normative or descriptive approach. Normative approaches model how decisions should be made; descriptive approaches understand how decisions are actually made. The normative approach's usefulness may be seen in its ability in providing theoretical adequacy for rational choice, whereas the descriptive approach's usefulness may be seen through empirical validity by uncovering insight in decision making (Bell et al., 1988). An alternative view is the categorisation of decision making research, based on the study environment. This may be the lab-based approach where studies are conducted in controlled environments and data collection is determined by predefined tests, or the naturalistic approach where studies are conducted in real settings and data collection is based on the observation of actual events (Klein, 2008). The differences in approaches do not imply that one is better than the other, but that each is suitable based on research objectives.

Descriptive research on expert decision making during risk and uncertainty focusses on context-specific decision making. This has been led by Klein's (1999) research on naturalistic decision making, where they identified that during uncertainty, experienced firefighters use situational familiarity to make quick decisions as opposed to weighing all available options. In the same line, Wong presents a research series on how criminal intelligence analysts think (Wong, 2014: Wong and Kodagoda, 2015; Gerber et al., 2016). Among the various strategies identified, they suggest that during the absence of clear facts, a leap of faith occurs between intuition and insight that allows the decision makers to reach a preliminary comprehension of a situation. Hibshi et al., (2014) explores techniques taken by security experts as they transition through levels of situation awareness to identify security requirements. They identify that experts seem to skip some stages of situation awareness and this may be attributed to situation familiarity based on experience.

What is common in the above literature is the realisation that experts take leaps in decision making. While these findings are insightful, they do little in providing traceability to the rationale behind decision making and this is where normative approaches are beneficial through the provision of blueprints upon which sensemaking may be traced and communicated. Early work by Rasmussen (1974) on the Decision ladder template has played a key role in identifying the generic categories of activity in decision making, and similarly, Boyd (1996) and Endsley (1995) played key roles in formalising the awareness steps leading to decision making. Unfortunately, normative approaches are usually too high-level and generalised, rendering them incapable of providing low-level context-specific information.

3   Model Design

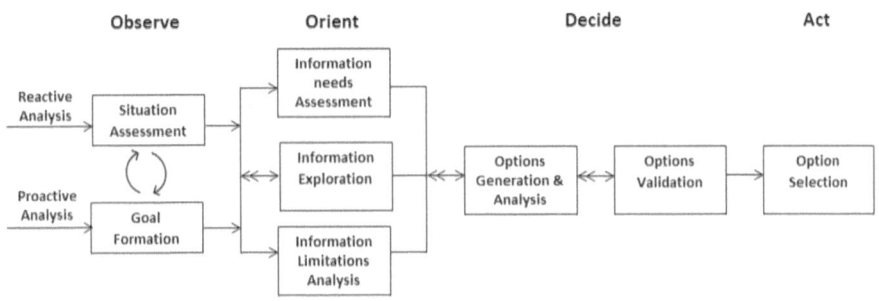

Figure 1: Risk Rationalisation Flow

We propose a normative model that provides traceability to security analysts' rationalisation of risk under uncertain conditions. The normative model builds on lessons learned from two studies with cyber security analysts and was formalised systematically using OODA (Boyd, 1996). The first study (M'manga et al., 2017) was conducted with 10 analysts from three different organisations with the aim of investigating factors influencing analysts' interpretation of risk during proactive risk analysis (vulnerability assessment and goal conflicts). Findings included risk interpretation influencers and risk analysis workflows. Building on the first, the second study (M'manga et al., 2018) was conducted with 30 analysts from 11 different sectors, it aimed at investigating risk rationalisation steps taken during reactive risk analysis (incidence response).

The normative model consists of eight steps to risk rationalisation and contains two complementary elements; the flow and actions collectively referred to as the risk rationalisation process (RRP). The first element is a risk rationalisation flow (RRF) highlighting cognitive sequences and iterations during risk rationalisation. Illustrated in Figure 1, RRF indicates two alternative starting points; the Reactive risk analysis beginning with *Situation assessment* and continues to *Goal formation,* or the Proactive risk analysis that takes the inverse approach of beginning with *Goal formation* and continues to *Situation assessment.* The difference is based on the understanding that incidents precede response strategy in reactive analysis; therefore situation assessment begins before goals are formed, while the inverse is true for proactive analysis. The second phase of RRF consists of the three cognitive actives; *Information needs assessment, Information exploration and Information limitations analysis.* The adjacent illustration indicates that the steps may overlap and occur in various orders. *Options generation and analysis*, *Option validation*, and *Option selection* form the final three steps and they occur in sequence. Risk rationalisation is an iterative process and this is illustrated in RRF by the double back arrows at each point of possible iteration.

The second element of the normative model consists of the risk rationalisation actions (Figure 2). The actions address the lack of low-level detail in normative models by providing context-oriented meta-cognitive questions at each rationalisation step.

Metacognition is defined as awareness or analysis of one's own thinking processes, and this may further be explained as the knowledge of knowledge (what one knows about cognition), or the regulation of knowledge (how one uses that knowledge to regulate cognition) (Schraw and Moshman, 1995). For instance, to understand the rationale behind the characterisation of a situation, the question "how may a situation be understood?" is presented. The risk rationalisation actions take this a step further by defining sub-procedures clarifying the questions which could, in this case, be through *data correlation*, explained as the putting together of disparate data sets to derive meaning. By using the steps, meta-cognitive questions and sub-procedures, our normative approach aims at understanding the rationale behind decision making irrespective of the decision maker's expertise. We detail the eight RRP steps below.

3.1 Situation assessment

Situation assessment corresponds to OODA's Observe. During this step, the aim is to understand how the decision maker identifies factors aiding in situation understanding and not the actual analysis of the situation. The meta-cognitive question "how may the situational be understood?" is presented and expanded into four possible sub-procedures;

- Knowledge of a situation: Recognition through situation familiarity and the knowledge of normal.
- Knowledge of evidence: Recognising information affordances in an environment to achieve greater awareness.
- Situational time-line: Recognising whether a situation is static or evolving, current or elapsed.
- Data Correlation: Recognising available or required data correlation needs to achieve greater awareness.

3.2 Goal formation

Goal formation is the second step corresponding to OODA's Observe. The objective is to understand the strategies used to establish decision goals, identify tensions that may restrict goals from coming to fruition, and the determination of the relevance scope within which a decision is made. The relevance scope acts as a minimum level for the continued pursuit of a goal. For example, analysts we interviewed in M'manga et al., (2017) expressed that the inner workings of some of the proprietary security products they used were unknown to them. However, based on the product's benefit, they found uncovering the potential risk unnecessary.

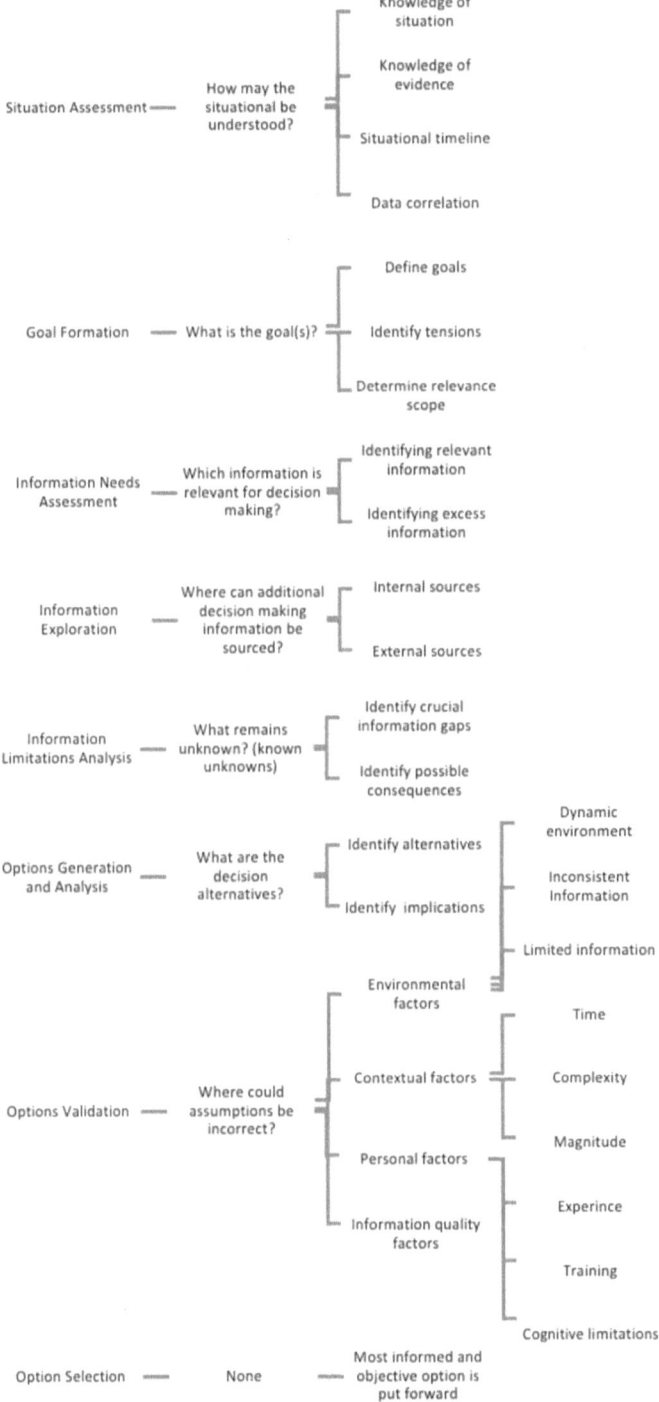

Figure 2: Risk Rationalisation Actions

3.3   Information needs assessment

Information needs assessment is one of three steps corresponding to OODA's Orient. The objective is to understand how the decision maker identifies information relevant to decision making and excess information for filtering. The decision maker's assessment is based on information credibility determined by factors identified during *Situation assessment* and the relevance scope identified during *Goal formation.* Typical examples are the procedures taken to identify false positives.

3.4   Information exploration

During Information exploration, it is recognised that decisions are determined by information availability and when information is unavailable, possible alternatives are explored. The focus is therefore placed on understanding the strategies for identifying the alternative sources of information. To the decision maker, the exploration of additional information sources is subject to time availability. Information sources may be subject matter experts within an analysts' environment (e.g. legal officer, public relations manager), or external expertise such as Computer Emergency Response Teams (CERTs).

3.5   Information limitations analysis

Information limitations analysis is driven by the question, what remains unknown? This is presented with the aim of understanding how the decision maker identifies critical information gaps and the conclusion drawn from the knowledge. Information gaps refer to the known-unknowns critical for informed decision making. For example, it would greatly aid an analyst to acknowledge that an attack vector has been identified although the motive remains unknown. Knowledge of the motive could hint at the possibility of a follow-up attacks leading to better preparedness (Rashid et al., 2016).

3.6   Options generation and analysis

Options generation and analysis is the first of two steps corresponding to OODA's Decide. Based on the cumulative understanding from the previous steps, the decision maker identifies possible options for decision formulation and their implications. For example, an analyst's response to a data breach could be to refrain from disclosing the breach, even though data protection regulations advise otherwise. The aim of the step is to identify and understand the reasoning behind options considered by the decision maker. At this point, poor understanding may inadvertently lead to meta-risk; risk resulting from risk response (e.g. increased threat exposure).

3.7   Options validation

Options validation focusses on uncertainty by verifying if there were elements of uncertainty hindering the decision making process and how it was managed. To simplify the understanding and expression of uncertainty, the meta-cognitive question posed is; where could assumptions be incorrect? Validating one's own actions is by no means an easy task. Failure at the stage introduces a second form of meta-risk, which is the risk of risk understanding due to uncertainty. We categorise the elements of uncertainty into four groups:

- *Environmental factors*: dynamic environments, inconsistent or limited information from the environment.
- *Contextual factors*: time limitations, situation complexity or magnitude.
- *Personal factors*: experience, training and cognitive limitations.
- *Information factors*: accurate, current, relevant specific, understandable, comprehensive, unbiased and comparable (Wang et al., 2005).

3.8 Option selection

Option Selection corresponds to OODA's Act. As a final step, the most informed and objective option is put forward as the basis for a decision. The option should not come as a surprise where the rationale is traceable.

4 Model validation

The model was validated using cognitive walkthroughs (Rieman et al., 1995) with three security analysts (P1 -3). The three validated the model's logic flow, and not its ability to support risk rationalisation. P1 and P2 worked as part of a cyber security team monitoring events within their organisation and possessed 1-3 years' professional experience in security. P3 worked as part of a counter-terrorism and intelligence unit and possessed over 24 years of relevant experience. Each participant was provided with a copy of RRP and given a brief tutorial on its use. Participants were then presented with a scenario about a hypothetical data breach that incorporated tensions related to possible decisions and uncertainty due to insufficient information. The scenario required the analysts to decide whether to make a breach on a university's network known to affected parties in advance, after remediation, or not at all, and taking into account that some of the breached data was already on the Internet. The participants were asked to compare the model with decisions they would make in the scenario. In addition, P3 run a second validation scenario, based on his experience in counter-terrorism. Each walkthrough took approximately 40 minutes, and the participants presented their critiques of the model's logic. Opinions were divided on whether *Option validation* was an independent step or a part of *Option generation and analysis*. We concluded that it remains an independent step to cater for understanding inexperienced decision makers lacking the ability to generate and validate decision alternatives consecutively.

5   Conclusion and future work

This paper presented a normative model for rationalising analysts' decision making about risk and uncertainty. The propose of the model is not to propose a new approach to decision making, but rather to propose a systematic approach capable of communicating and providing traceability to the rationale behind security decision making during risk and uncertainty. To address this we considered the shortfalls presented in descriptive approaches which usually provide no explanation for expert judgement and the shortfalls in normative approaches which are usually too high level to derive contextual meaning. The benefit and use of the model are in several folds. Firstly the model is designed as a series of steps, meta-cognitive questions and sub-procedures that may be used as a blueprint by stakeholders unfamiliar with risk analysis procedures in security such as the different approaches to proactive and reactive analysis. Second, the model may be used in training analysts be identifying gaps in their reasoning when compared to model steps. And third, the model may be used as a basis for eliciting design requirements that would facilitate decision making about risk through the identification of critical areas of risk rationalisation.

The model places emphasis on validation and the consideration of uncertainty by highlighting the iterative nature of decision flows, presenting an options validation step, and the consideration of meta-risk in various forms. We believe that the model will complement existing decision making and awareness approaches lacking a focus on risk and uncertainty. For future work, we are investigating techniques to elicit design requirements for risk-based decision making, based on data collected using RRP.

6   References

Bell, D. E., Raiffa, H., and Tversky, A. (1988), *Decision making: Descriptive, normative, and prescriptive interactions,* Cambridge University Press.

Boyd, J. R. (1996), The essence of winning and losing. *Unpublished lecture notes,* Vol. 12, No. 23, pp123–125.

Endsley, M. R. (1995), Toward a theory of situation awareness in dynamic systems. *Human Factors: The Journal of the Human Factors and Ergonomics Society,* Vol. 37, No. 1, pp32–64.

Gerber, M., Wong, B. L. W., and Kodagoda, N. (2016), How Analysts Think: Intuition, Leap of Faith and Insight. *Proceedings of the Human Factors and Ergonomics Society Annual Meeting,* Vol. 60, No. 1, pp173–177.

Hibshi, H., Breaux, T., Riaz, M., and Williams, L. (2014), Towards a framework to measure security expertise in requirements analysis. *In: Evolving Security and Privacy Requirements Engineering (ESPRE), 2014 IEEE 1st Workshop,* pp146-155._

Hoffman, R. R., Mueller, S. T., and Klein, G. (2017), Explaining Explanation, Part 2: Empirical Foundations. *IEEE Intelligent Systems,* Vol. 32, No. 4, pp78–86.

Huber, O. (2014), Complex problem solving as multistage decision making. *In: Complex problem solving: The European perspective,* pp151–173.

Klein, G. (1999), *Sources of power: How people make decisions*. MIT press.

Klein, G. (2008), Naturalistic decision making. *Human Factors: The Journal of the Human Factors and Ergonomics Society*, Vol. 50, No. 3, pp456–460.

M'manga, A., Faily, S., McAlaney, J., and Williams, C. (2017), Folk Risk Analysis: Factors Influencing Security Analysts' Interpretation of Risk. *In: 3rd Workshop on Security Information Workers 12-14 July 2017 Santa Clara, USA. Usenix Association.*

M'manga, A., Faily, S., McAlaney, J., Williams, C., Kadobayashi, Y., and Miyamoto, D. (2018), Eliciting Persona Characteristics for Risk Based Decision Making. *In: Proceedings of the 32nd International BCS Human Computer Interaction Conference.* BCS.

Rashid, A., Naqvi, S. A. A., Ramdhany, R., Edwards, M., Chitchyan, R., and Babar, M. A. (2016), Discovering 'unknown known' security requirements. *In: 38th International Conference on Software Engineering.* ACM Press, pp 866–876.

Rasmussen, J. (1974), *The human data processor as a system component. Bits and pieces of a model.* Roskilde, Denmark: Danish Atomic Energy Commission. No. Risø-M-1722.

Rieman, J., Franzke, M., and Redmiles, D. (1995), Usability evaluation with the cognitive walkthrough. *In: Conference companion on Human factors in computing systems.* ACM, pp387–388.

Schraw, G. and Moshman, D. (1995), Metacognitive theories. *Educational Psychology Review*, Vol. 7, No. 4, pp351–371.

Simon, H. A. (1972), Theories of bounded rationality. *Decision and organization*, Vol.1, No. 1, pp161–176.

Wang, Y. R., Pierce, E. M., Madnik, S. E., Fisher, C. W., and Zwass, V. (2005), *Information quality*. Armonk, N.Y. ; London, England: M.E. Sharpe.

Wong, B. L. W., 2014. How Analysts Think (?): Early Observations. *In:* IEEE, pp296–299.

Wong, B. L. W. and Kodagoda, N. (2015), How Analysts Think: Inference Making Strategies. *Proceedings of the Human Factors and Ergonomics Society Annual Meeting*, Vol. 59, No. 1, pp269–273.

Easing the Burden of Security Self-Assessments

C. Schmitz[1], A. Sekulla[2], S. Pape[1], V. Pipek[2] and K. Rannenberg[1]

[1] Goethe University Frankfurt, Chair of Mobile Business & Multilateral Security,
Germany
[2] University of Siegen, Institute of Information Systems, Germany
e-mail: {christopher.schmitz; sebastian.pape; kai.rannenberg}@m-chair.de;
{andre.sekulla; volkmar.pipek}@uni-siegen.de

Abstract

A web-based platform was developed to support the inter-organisational collaboration between small and medium-sized energy providers. Since critical infrastructures are subject to new security regulations in Germany, the platform particularly serves for the exchange of experience and for mutual support in information security. The focus of this work is the security self-assessment component. In order to ease the burden of going through a long questionnaire we have implemented small, motivating modules that are spread across the platform. The data entered is used for an individual risk assessment but also for a fine granular inter-organisational security benchmarking which builds a common added value for the entire community on the platform and strengthens the community building process. We implemented a prototype of the platform and evaluated the it in a focus group.

Keywords

Security Management, Security Self-Assessment, Collaborative Knowledge Management

1 Introduction

Gathering information for risk and security self-assessments can be a cumbersome task. In general, the security managers need to answer an often long collection of questions built on established standards (e.g. Swanson 2001, ISO/IEC 27019, IEC 62443). For instance, the NIST security self-assessment contains more than 200 questions (Swanson 2001). Self-assessments offer advantages over external security audits: they are less expensive, they can be implemented in local organisational routines, and they allow more control on critical information about an organisations' IT infrastructure. But they are also challenging: the actors' bias towards the inner-organisational discourses may leave blind spots. Furthermore, analyses, as well as decisions for counter-measures, require a continuous improvement of competencies with regard to existing as well as future IT infrastructures and the related threats. These challenges are particularly relevant for small and medium-sized enterprises (SMEs) that provide infrastructural services, and which often do not have the capacities to run a full-fledged information security department and rely on external expertise (Dax et al. 2017).

In many areas, individuals and organisations with a local lack of expertise turn to support communities on the internet. These communities are not only valuable in offering their members concrete support to solve a specific problem, they also offer an interaction space to collaboratively consolidate and improve the general knowledge on the issues at stake, and offer additional problem solving strategies (e.g. by means of recommender systems, cf. Ackerman et al. 2013). This approach cannot immediately be transferred to areas with specific vulnerabilities, e.g. information security in power grid infrastructures. Framing conditions like the high sensitivity of the infrastructure-related information, legal or regulatory requirements, and the complexity of dependencies between grid technologies, IT systems supporting their management, and possible threats require a more cautious approach to unlock the helpful dynamics of community processes.

We have developed a platform for security managers supporting small and medium-sized energy providers. The central tool of this platform is a self-assessment component to support security managers to manage the recent legal requirements to monitor and improve the information security of their infrastructures. In our approach, users can model the existing information security measures of their infrastructure (in terms of security controls following ISO/IEC 27001) using security maturity levels, which can then be compared and published in an anonymised way to the results from other participating organisations. The platform then provides information (in a Q&A section) on improving with regard to specific controls, as well as a controlled community section in which strategies of improvement can be discussed with other information security managers. We built small modules which are shown in other parts of the platform. Those modules allow the users to answer the questions or update the maturity levels along the way when interacting with other parts of the platform. By making use of motivational elements and showing questions one by one in other parts of the platform, we aim to ease the burden of going through a lengthy list of questions. This is especially the case when respondents update the answers entered and need to decide if the current answer is still valid. Lessons from other platforms showed, that structured processes of information consolidation and improvement through users help the perceived value of the information provided dramatically.

The remainder of this paper is organised as follows: Section 2 discusses related work, Section 3 gives an overview of our platform, and Section 4 discusses the connection of self-assessment with user motivation and community building. Section 5 reports about a brief evaluation. Section 6 concludes and outlines future research.

2   Related Work

With the World Wide Web as a breakthrough technology, building knowledge communities became an actual practice in professional contexts (e.g. Lesser et al. 2000). Although these community platforms intended an open, flexible support for problem-solving processes, the delicacy of the social and business-related processes behind the "innocent" knowledge exchange very soon became apparent: Articulating a problem was often considered as uncovering a personal or organisational deficit, solutions that were offered came with unclear quality assurances, and the work of narrowing down a problem as well as developing a solution that would fit all local needs went far beyond simple "Q&A" patterns (Pipek and Won, 2003).

For platforms hosting knowledge communities, several strategies were developed to ease these problems. The idea of "FAQ" (Frequently asked questions) developed to relieve experts from answering the same basic questions over and over. It was combined with processes to keep them up to date (e.g. the "Answer Garden" system, Ackerman and McDonald 1996). Pipek and Won (2003) suggested to focus more on connecting users looking for a problem solution with experts who could help them, less on making knowledge explicit and store it online. For particularly sensitive issues, the anonymity of the person asking for help as well as of persons answering is guaranteed (e.g. patientslikeme.com).

Self-assessment as another technique to counter negative effects of "deficit disclosure", and even allows a continuous monitoring and improvement, has become a heavily discussed approach in learning communities (e.g. Castle and McGuire, 2010). To some extent, self-assessment approaches also help in organisational learning (e.g. in the general improvement of IT infrastructures, e.g. Curley 2004, in approaches of quality management, e.g. Saunders and Mann 2005, and – with regard to information security – e.g. Swanson 2001). But this was never done in combination with online support for knowledge communities. There exist the so-called "Information Sharing Analysis Centres" (ISACs). ISACs are organisations that gather and analyse security-related information from their members and provide them with analysis results and reports. In contrast to them our approach addresses the individual organisation and provides them with individual risk analysis and benchmarking scores. Furthermore, our platform enables a direct knowledge sharing.

3   The SIDATE Platform

Especially SMEs often struggle to achieve an adequate security level, although some of them are obliged to get certified against the ISO/IEC 27001. This holds for instance for energy providers and other critical infrastructures in Germany. A natural solution to support them is to stimulate collaboration. For this, we have built an inter-organisational collaboration platform for energy providers. It enables energy providers to assess their security level and to improve their security also by inter-organisational discussions. We systematically elicited the requirements in several workshops (Dax et al. 2016). The platform consists of four main components aiming to support knowledge sharing between the organisations:

- **Security measures catalogue:** The security measures component is a catalogue of security measures which is maintained by security experts. Users can comment on the measures, suggest new measures and rate them according to their costs, efficacy and usability.
- **Questions and answers:** The Q&A component should support and structure inter-organisational discussions. Registered users can ask security-related questions and can finally mark answers as correct. All users can rate questions and answers and can either sort them by rating or creation date. In order to have a

more structured inter-organisational communication threads can be filtered according to tags or security controls.

- **Document sharing:** In the document sharing component the participating organisations can share relevant documents in a structured way, e.g. best practices or official documents specifying the binding legal requirements.
- **Security self-assessment:** The security self-assessment component constitutes the core component of the platform. Using this component, organisations can assess their security risk level in order to better understand their exposure to relevant security risks. Moreover, they can compare their security status (on different abstraction level) with that of similar organisations.

In the following, we focus on the self-assessment component which constitutes the central element of the platform. It consists of the three sections data input, benchmarking and risk assessment that are complemented by three superordinate modules being spread across the platform. We describe them below:

3.1 Data Input Section

The first step of the risk assessment process is to gather the required information. The necessary user data is entered in the data input section (see Fig. 1). The organisations model the security measures of their infrastructure by assessing the maturity levels of the implemented security controls (in terms of controls following the ISO/IEC 27001). Here, the widely known ISO/IEC 27019 security controls (which are more specific security controls for the energy utility industry) are used as questionnaire items. Since they equally address technical and organisational aspects of information security they represent a wide range of security measures that can be implemented in an organisation. The items are structured in the same categories and sub-categories the security managers already know from the original standard. The users are furthermore supported by the feature to show either all controls, only those controls that are not assessed yet or only those controls that have already been assessed which makes sense in order to check in a user-friendly way whether all controls are still up to date.

3.2 Benchmarking Section

The benchmarking section (see Fig. 2) enables organisations to compare their security status with similar organisations. Their maturity levels are juxtaposed (in an anonymised way) with that of other organisations.

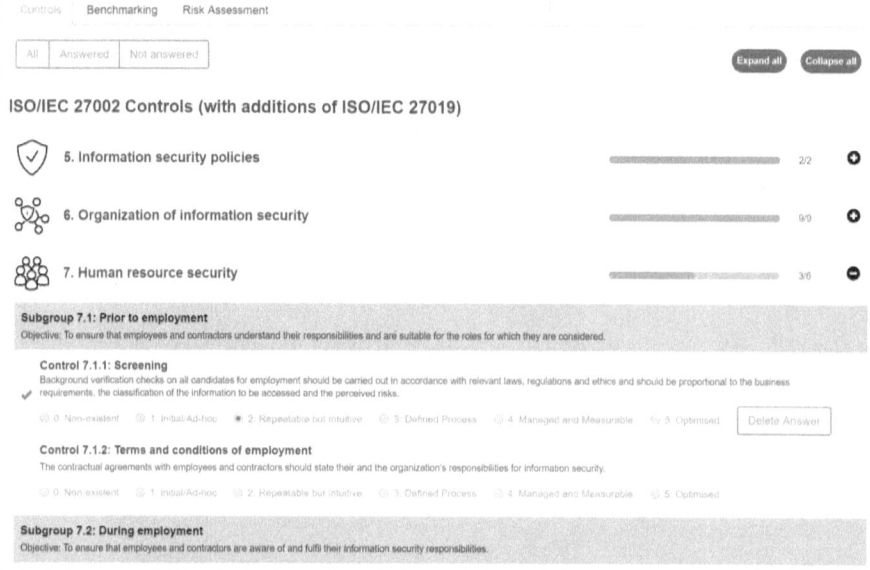

Figure 1: Data Input Section

For each control, the organisation's maturity level is shown along with the average maturity level by the other organisations. For a more in-depth analysis, the distribution of maturity levels per control is also presented as well as a relative benchmarking score which indicates how well the organisation performs compared to the others. In this section, one can also re-assess the maturity levels. The benchmark is shown on different abstraction levels: on a control level and on the aggregated levels of the control groups and sub-groups of the ISO/IEC 27019. The groups and sub-groups are presented in the same structure as in the original standards, like in the data input section.

3.3 Risk Assessment Section

In the risk assessment section a scenario-based risk analysis is conducted to calculate the organisation's security risk score as well as the risk for a collection of relevant attack scenarios. This supports the security managers in identifying the most critical risks they are exposed to. Describing the risk assessment framework and the other data sources would go beyond the scope of this work.

3.4 Superordinate Modules

Additionally, we have implemented three superordinate modules directly supporting the self-assessment component. The modules are displayed in other components of the platform aiming to connect the different parts of the platform in order to stimulate the users to frequently assess respectively to re-assess security controls.

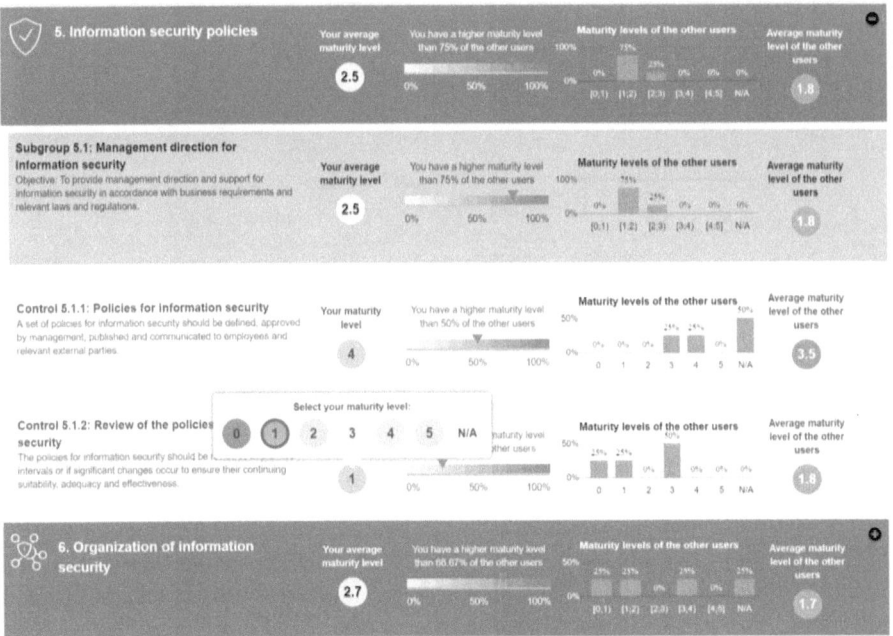

Figure 2: Benchmarking Section

Figures 3 and 4 show their graphical use interfaces. By requesting to keep the data complete and up-to-date we try to keep the entire data on a representative level.

1.) A control that has already been evaluated may have an obsolete maturity level and should be updated to obtain a more representative status. Therefore, the first module (see Fig. 3) requests the user to update resp. to re-assess a security control at regular intervals. This is also important from the perspective of information security management systems, since they require constant and iterative handling of information security measures.

2.) In case of missing maturity levels the second module requests the user to evaluate the security controls that have not been evaluated yet. In particular, the aim is to ensure that the data is complete. The more controls have been evaluated, the better the outcomes of the risk assessment and the better they can be compared with other results. The presented controls are further prioritized with regard to their information value for the risk assessment, e.g. to enable a new attack scenario in the risk assessment. The module also indicates such information.

3.) The third module, shown in Figure 4, is positioned in the security measures catalogue. While a user is viewing such a measure in detail, he or she gets asked to evaluate the respective security control for the self-assessment component. Again, this should improve the data completeness and up-to-dateness.

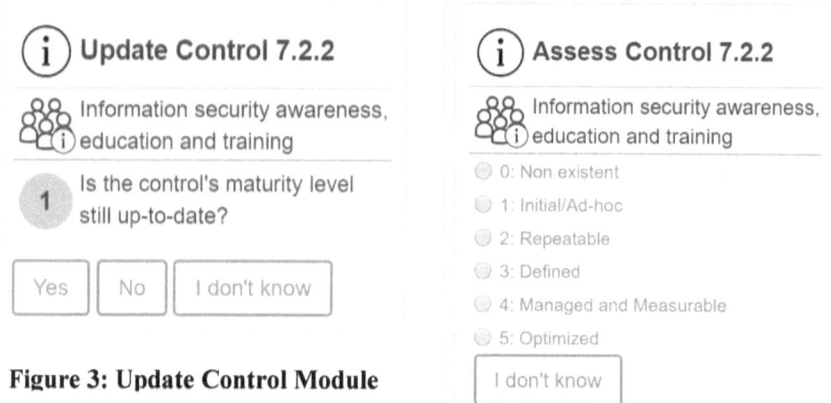

Figure 3: Update Control Module

Figure 4: Assess Control Module

4 Usability Aspects

To improve interaction and activity in the SIDATE platform, the interaction between users need to be carefully planned. Looking at the individual user, a good usability and interesting collaboration anchors need to be provided. But it is also important to have the further development of the associated community in mind.

4.1 Motivating Updates and Additional Input

One way to increase activity on the online platform is to keep the entry barriers as low as possible (Girgensohn and Lee, 2002). The self-assessment tool serves as a guided entry to model the maturity level of an organisation's IT security. Later changes can be easily made as soon as a user is logged in on the platform without the questionnaire. He can easily add further data and information to his information security status without having to navigate directly into the associated self-assessment module in order to additionally reach the subordinate category in such a way that he can evaluate the corresponding control.

Section 3 described the self-assessment component in more detail. The component does not include any community functions itself. Since this component may contain sensitive data, functions for exchange and interaction between users could be counterproductive. They could lead to falsified data or no input of the requested data being carried out. The modules presented below are primarily intended to ensure that the dataset entered is complete and up-to-date. This enables the self-assessment and the benchmarking to work properly on these data and make meaningful comparisons. Only after the own data has been entered, the other users' ratings become visible as a direct comparison. This should again increase the motivation to enter complete data.

The asses control module (Fig. 4) indicates that when the corresponding control is evaluated, a new attack scenario is activated within the risk analysis of the self-assessment module. This should increase the motivation to enter complete ratings and unlock a kind of success because "individuals are more likely to gain self-based achievement rather than enjoyment in the process of sharing knowledge" (Yang and Lai, 2010). Hence, while users are viewing such a measure in detail they get asked to evaluate the respective security control for the self-assessment module and the benchmarking process. Again, this should improve the up-to-dateness and data completeness and is implemented through the related control module.

4.2 Supporting the Community Building Process

The activity of the users of a platform is an important aspect of the community building process. Beside the user activity, another goal of an online platform for cooperation is the creation of added value for all parties involved. Girgensohn and Lee (2002) describe the so-called socio-technical-capital as "a resource produced as a side effect of technology-mediated social interaction". Resnick (2001) notes that it can be accumulated and made available to create value for people. It should influence the users among themselves in such a way that they interact more with each other. To encourage users to participate further, it is recommended to "repeat social interaction" (Kollock, 1996) which is implemented in particular with the help of additional modules directly related to the presented self-assessment module. It is intended to encourage users to constantly interact with the platform. The self-assessment itself has no functions for direct interaction between the users but the small modules have indirect effects on further interactions on the entire platform, as they allow for an anonymous comparison with the results others have provided.

If there is a need for an improvement in their own information security landscape, users can start to enter and participate in online discussions that are specific to the controls where deficits may be rooted in. It is not necessary to disclose that there are deficits in a user's own organisation but the discussions can aim for a general optimization with regard to that control. It remains (formally) open whether a participant is looking for or providing expertise – this positioning is left to the discourse itself. The aim is to awake the interest to exchange ideas with other users of the platform in order to learn from their experiences and to profit from the resulting social-technical-capital. Thus, with the help of the self-assessment module and the associated superordinate modules, a community building process is initiated that increases the activity of all interaction methods integrated on the platform.

5 Evaluating the Platform in a Focus Group

To evaluate the platform, we have conducted a workshop with ten experts from eight small or medium-sized energy providers. Due to the legal requirements, the majority of the organisations were certified against ISO/IEC 27001 so they successfully went through all the necessary processes. Therefore, most of the participants had good security know-how. One of them was a trainer for ISO/IEC 27001 security auditors.

We have presented the most relevant platform features in a live demo. The attendees could always interrupt the presentation and ask questions to make sure they understood everything. Afterwards, the experts were invited to discuss the platform in a moderated discussion. We asked them for general feedback and for suggestions for improvement based on their own experiences. We also stimulated discussions among the experts and moderated it in the way to work out the most relevant aspects.

The participants emphasised the simple structure and the user-friendly design of the platform. Their comments and the way they discussed the platform and its functions also clearly demonstrated they understood the purpose of the different functions and how to use them. Apart from those usability aspects, many of the comments were addressing the ISO/IEC 27001 certification. There was consensus among the experts that the platform was helpful for an internal pre-audit before the official ISO/IEC 27001 audit starts. They argued for instance that the organisations have to conduct a risk analysis prior to the official audit anyway, and such a self-assessment would be very helpful for SMEs who often struggle to identify and assess the risks they are exposed to. The experts also agreed that the approach to go through the ISO/IEC 27019 controls makes a lot of sense because this is what the auditor finally checks.

The users' positive evaluations on both the platform's usability and its general ideas have a positive effect on the users' activity and it strengthens the community building process which helps the entire community. To further improve the platform the experts suggested integrating a recommender feature that derives optimal security measures and recommends a list of actions to the security team. According to the benchmarking component, it would be useful to have a benchmarking with companies already certified against ISO/IEC 27001.

6   Conclusion and Future Work

Security self-assessment frameworks support security managers to assess their organisation's security level. Applying those frameworks can be a cumbersome task since many of them are based on long questionnaires. Apart from that, additional information and inter-organisational discussions, e.g. with regard to the selection of security measures, can often be helpful especially for SMEs who often do not have the capacities to run a full-fledged security department. In order to address these issues, a web-based collaboration platform for security management was developed, supporting energy providers. The security self-assessment component constitutes the central feature of the platform. It helps security managers to identify relevant attack scenarios and allows them to benchmark their security status with that of similar organisations. Complementarily, small modules were implemented that are spread across the platform. They allow the users to complete or update the data needed for the self-assessment along the way when interacting with other parts of the platform. By making use of motivational elements and showing questions one by one in other parts of the platform, we aim to ease the burden of security self-assessments (e.g. going through a long questionnaire).

Furthermore, we have implemented a prototype of the platform and have evaluated it in a focus group, concentrating on usability aspects but also on the conceptual ideas of the platform. The next steps are to address the experts' feedback and to work on a recommender function for security measures based on the results of the security risk analysis. Another open task is to analyse how to design the inter-organisational sharing of recommended measures in a privacy preserving way.

7 Acknowledgement

This research was supported by the German Federal Ministry of Education and Research (grant numbers: 16KIS0239K, 16KIS0240). We thank Leon Alexander Herrmann and David Bug for their contribution to the prototype implementation.

8 References

Ackermann, M. S., McDonald, D. W. (1996), „Answer Garden 2: Merging Organizational Memory with Collaborative Help", *CSCW'96*, ACM Press, pp97-105.

Castle, S. R. and McGuire, C. (2010), "An analysis of student self-assessment of online, blended, and face-to-face learning environments: Implications for sustainable education delivery", *International Education Studies*, Vol. 3, No. 3, p36.

Curley, M. G. (2004), Managing information technology for business value: practical strategies for IT and business managers (IT best practices series), Intel press.

Dax, J., Ivan, A., Ley, B., Pape, S., Pipek, V., Rannenberg, K., Schmitz, C. and Sekulla, A. (2017): "IT Security Status of German Energy Providers", Technical Report, Cornell University, arXiv.

Dax, J., Ley, B., Pape, S., Schmitz, C., Pipek, V. and Rannenberg, K. (2016): Elicitation of Requirements for an inter-organizational Platform to Support Security Management Decisions, *10th Int. Symposium on Human Aspects of Information Security & Assurance*, HAISA 2016, Frankfurt, Germany, Proceedings.

Girgensohn, A., Lee, A. (2002), "Making Web Sites Be Places for Social Interaction", *CSCW'02*, New Orleans, Louisiana, USA.

Kollock, P. (1996), "Design Principles for Online Communities", *Harvard Conference on the Internet and Society*, Cambridge, MA.

Lesser, E. L., Fontaine, M. A. and Slusher, J. A. (eds.) (2000), *Knowledge and Communities*. Butterworth-Heinemann, Oxford, UK.

Pipek, V. and Won, M. (2002), "Communication-oriented Computesr Support for Knowledge Management", *Informatik/Informatique - Magazine of the Swiss Informatics Societies*, Vol. 1, pp39-43.

Resnick, P. (2001), "Beyond Bowling Together: SocioTechnical Capital", *J.M. Carrol (ed.), Human-Computer Interaction in the New Millennium, Addison-Wesley*, pp647-672.

Saunders, M. and Mann, R. (2005), "Self-assessment in a multi-organisational network", *IJQRM*, Vol. 22, Issue 6, pp554-571.

Swanson, M. (2001), "Security Self-Assessment Guide for Information Technology Systems", *NIST Special Publication 800-26*.

Yang, H.-L. and Lai, C.-Y. (2010), "Motivations of Wikipedia content contributors", *Computers in Human Behavior*, Vol. 26, Issue 6, pp1377-1383.

Author Index

www.ingramcontent.com/pod-product-compliance
Lightning Source LLC
Chambersburg PA
CBHW020732180526
45163CB00001B/206